The Texture of the Lexicon

The Texture of the Lexicon

*Relational Morphology and
the Parallel Architecture*

RAY JACKENDOFF AND JENNY AUDRING

OXFORD

UNIVERSITY PRESS

OXFORD
UNIVERSITY PRESS

Great Clarendon Street, Oxford, OX2 6DP,
United Kingdom

Oxford University Press is a department of the University of Oxford.
It furthers the University's objective of excellence in research, scholarship,
and education by publishing worldwide. Oxford is a registered trade mark of
Oxford University Press in the UK and in certain other countries

Published in the United States of America by Oxford University Press
198 Madison Avenue, New York, NY 10016, United States of America

British Library Cataloguing in Publication Data

Data available

Library of Congress Control Number: 2019940874

ISBN 978–0–19–882790–0

Printed and bound by
CPI Group (UK) Ltd, Croydon, CR0 4YY

Contents

PART I THE THEORY

PART II USING AND REFINING THE TOOLS

PART III BEYOND MORPHOLOGICAL THEORY

Acknowledgments

How did this book come about? You might say it's Geert Booij's fault. In 2010, he had a visiting appointment at Harvard. Having nothing better to do, he started coming to Ray's research seminar across town at Tufts, where, among other things, he introduced the group to his new framework of Construction Morphology. On the strength of that connection, Ray was invited to speak at Geert's retirement symposium in Leiden in 2012, for which it so happened that Jenny, as a former student of Geert's, was one of the organizers. On the strength of *that* connection, Jenny invited Ray to contribute a chapter to *The Oxford Handbook of Morphological Theory*, which she and Francesca Masini were then beginning to compile. However, she deemed Ray's initial effort seriously unacceptable: too much syntax and not enough morphology! He asked her for advice, and we started talking about how to do it right. And we never stopped. Ray's visit to the Max Planck Institute in Nijmegen in 2014 afforded an opportunity to really dig in, and by the end of the stay, it dawned on us that we might have not just a handbook chapter on our hands, but an actual book. And here it is. Throughout the long process of fleshing out all the details, Geert has been a constant source of inspiration, advice, and encouragement. We thank him deeply.

A second major thanks goes to the Max Planck Institute for Psycholinguistics in Nijmegen, and especially to Peter Hagoort, its Director, for giving Ray the opportunity to visit for a month in the springs of 2014, 2015, and 2016. This is when we really developed the gory details of the theory, fighting out the details of the formalization and what each piece of it meant. The MPI also gave us the chance to present pieces of the work in progress to a sophisticated and engaged audience, and this milieu probably had a lot to do with the sizable helping of psycholinguistics that emerges throughout the book.

We must thank as well Jay Keyser, with whom, over the years, Ray has had the joy of discussing innumerable aspects of just about anything, including, in the past few years, lots of morphology. We are grateful for his engagement, wisdom, and common sense in so many aspects of this project, not to mention in all sorts of other fascinating things. Peter Culicover too has been a constant and eager sounding board; we have benefited immensely from his perspective, ingenuity, and energy.

Many other people have played a role in helping us think through and sharpen our ideas, among them the late Sylvain Bromberger, Lila Gleitman, Bob Ladd, Claartje Levelt, Pim Levelt, Antje Meyer, Harry van der Hulst, Maryanne Wolf, and Pienie Zwitserlood. Ray got to try out many half-baked ideas in the Tufts research seminar, whose members included at various times Naomi Caselli, Neil Cohn, Rabia Ergin, Ari Goldberg, Katya Pertsova, Anita Peti-Stantić, Anastasia Smirnova, Rob Truswell, Eva Wittenberg, the late Martin Paczynski, and the late Irit Meir. In addition, Inbal Arnon, Geert Booij, Esther Breuer, Peter Culicover, Ev Fedorenko, Nikos Koutsoukos, Anita

Peti-Stantić, Anastasia Smirnova, Andrew Spencer, Harry van der Hulst, Heike Wiese, and Eva Wittenberg read substantial chunks of our manuscript and offered important advice. Many thanks to them all.

We have also benefited from the opportunity to present parts of the framework to audiences in Leiden (LUCL), Nijmegen (Max Planck Institute), Utrecht (Syntax-Interface Colloquium), and Amsterdam (ACLC); at MIT, Harvard (Language & Cognition Group), the University of Massachusetts (3rd American International Morphology Meeting), Yale, University of Pennsylvania, University of California San Diego, and Ohio State University; as well as in Budapest (16th International Morphology Meeting), Dubrovnik (RCAB 2017), Düsseldorf, Guildford (Surrey Morphology Group), Haifa (10th Mediterranean Morphology Meeting), Leuven (Morphology Days), Humboldt University, Lyon (AnaMorphoSys), Münster (Workshop Mentale Repräsentation grammatischen Wissens), Olomouc, Oslo, Paris (Colloque de Syntaxe et Sémantique; 10th International Construction Grammar Conference), Potsdam (9th International Morphological Processing Conference), Trier and Zürich (SLE 2017).

We must not forget to thank a host of cafés in which we spent many intense hours hashing out our ideas, particularly The Fuzz in Nijmegen, Anne & Max in Utrecht, The Eye in Amsterdam, and, in The Hague, Madeleine, Lot, and our all-time favorite, Zuid.

Among other sources of support, we need to thank Ed Merrin, who donated Ray's chair at Tufts and who has subsequently become a dear friend; Teresa Salvato, who has made the Center for Cognitive Studies at Tufts such an enjoyable place to work; Ted Gibson and Ev Fedorenko, in whose lab at MIT Ray has found a post-retirement home; and the Robert J. Glushko and Pamela Samuelson Foundation, for support of Ray's research. Jenny used part of her Veni grant (#275-70-036) to work on the book, for which she is grateful to The Netherlands Organisation for Scientific Research. Julia Steer, our editor at OUP, has been a steady and warm source of encouragement, enthusiasm, and forbearance throughout the long slow process of constructing the book, and Vicki Sunter, Guy Jackson, and Lucy Hollingworth made the production process go remarkably smoothly.

Given the scope of the questions we have posed for ourselves here, it has proven impossible (at least for us) to read and assimilate everything that has been published in the relevant disciplines, each of which has a literature whose rate of expansion rivals that of the universe. Accordingly, we apologize in advance to all authors whose work we have failed to cite adequately.

The wugs in Chapters 3 and 4 appear by the kind permission of Jean Berko Gleason. Parts of earlier versions of Chapters 1, 2, 7, and 8 have appeared in the following publications:

Ray Jackendoff and Jenny Audring (2016). 'Morphological schemas: Theoretical and psycholinguistic issues', *The Mental Lexicon* 11, 467–93. doi: 10.1075/ml.11.3.06.jac
Peter Culicover, Ray Jackendoff, and Jenny Audring (2017). 'Multiword constructions in the grammar', *Topics in Cognitive Science*, 9, 552–68. doi: 10.1111/tops.12255

Ray Jackendoff and Jenny Audring (2018). 'Morphology and memory: Toward an integrated theory', *Topics in Cognitive Science*, special issue in honor of Lila Gleitman, doi: 10.1111/tops.12334

Ray Jackendoff and Jenny Audring (2019). 'Relational Morphology in the Parallel Architecture', in J. Audring and F. Masini (eds.), *The Oxford Handbook of Morphological Theory*. Oxford: Oxford University Press, 390–408.

Finally, this book could not have been written without the patience and loving support of our respective partners, Hildy and Maurice. We thank them with deep love and gratitude.

Abbreviations and symbols

1	1st person
2	2nd person
3	3rd person
aff	derivational affix
C	consonant
C$_0$	zero or more consonants
C$_1$	one or more consonants
Coda	syllabic coda
CxG	Construction Grammar
CxM	Construction Morphology
DAT	dative case
DEF	definite
DM	Distributed Morphology
FEM	feminine gender
HPSG	Head-Driven Phrase Structure Grammar
IMP	imperative
INDEF	indefinite
INF	infinitive
IP	Intonational Phrase
LFG	Lexical Functional Grammar
LTM	long-term memory
MASC	masculine gender
MGG	Mainstream Generative Grammar
NEUT	neuter gender
NOM	nominative case
Nuc	syllabic nucleus
OT	Optimality Theory
PA	Parallel Architecture
PAST	past tense (morphosyntactic)
PAST	past time (semantic)
PL	plural (morphosyntactic)
PLUR	plural (semantic)
POSS	possessive
PRES	present tense (morphosyntactic)
PRES	present time (semantic)
PRESPT	present participle
Prt	particle
PTCP	past participle
RM	Relational Morphology
S	strong syllable
SG	singular

SI	Structural Intersection
SPE	*Sound Pattern of English* (Chomsky and Halle 1968)
VOT	voice onset time
W	weak syllable
WM	working memory
ρ	rhyme (portion of syllable)
σ	syllable
σ́	stressed syllable
ω	phonological word
±alv	alveolar
±asp	aspirated
±cont	continuant
±son	sonorant
±vel	velar
...	phonological variable
* *	two phonological strings are the same except for material between stars
*	Kleene star: unlimited repetition
< >	optional material (semantic, morphosyntactic, phonological) between brackets
< >	orthographic material between brackets (in section 8.4)

PART I
THE THEORY

1

Situating Morphology

1.1 What's this book about?

This book began life with the aim of recasting morphology in the spirit of the Parallel Architecture (Jackendoff 1997, 2002). But the enterprise turned out not to be so straightforward. Larger challenges continually intruded: the interplay between grammar and lexicon, the balance between regularity and idiosyncrasy, and the psychological plausibility of the theory's basic constructs. In confronting these issues, the inquiry grew well beyond exploring the form and content of morphologically complex words. Surprising consequences emerged for the organization of the lexicon, consequences which called for a major reconceptualization of linguistic theory. It therefore became necessary to ask not only how morphology fits into linguistic theory, but *what kind of linguistic theory morphology can fit into*. Thus the book has ended up interweaving themes at three levels: morphology, the structure of the lexicon, and the place of the language capacity in the human mind. The ensemble of these three leads us to an approach that we will call *Relational Morphology* (*RM*).

What is this reconceptualization of linguistic theory, and what is it about morphology that leads us there? We sketch it here, as a preview of what is to come.

Since the generative revolution in the 1950s, diverse frameworks for linguistic theory, focusing on syntax, have emphasized the ability of speakers to understand and create an unlimited number of expressions they have never heard before—von Humboldt's "infinite use of finite means" (von Humboldt 1836/1999: 91).[1] This emphasis continues up to the present. For instance, Berwick and Chomsky (2016: 2) speak of the "...Basic Property of language: that a language is a finite computational system yielding an infinity of expressions." From this perspective, the grammar of a language must above all characterize the productive patterns. Those aspects of language that are not productive are typically consigned to the lexicon, which is often thought of as little more than a ragbag of idiosyncrasies. Knowledge of language therefore comes to be factored into a regular, productive grammar and an idiosyncratic, unruly lexicon.

In fact, though, the lexicon is not as unruly as all that. It is full of patterns—perhaps not fully productive patterns, but patterns nonetheless. Consider, for instance, the suffix *-(t)ion*. Given that it appears in thousands of words, it is tempting to propose a word

---

[1] A fine point: Weydt (1972) observes that von Humboldt was talking not about an infinity of *sentences*, but about an infinity of expressible *thoughts*. Some thoughts might of course require less than or more than one sentence for their expression. Nevertheless, the slogan has been understood in the lore as concerning the productivity of syntax in particular, and it is in this sense that we invoke it here.

The Texture of the Lexicon. First edition. Ray Jackendoff and Jenny Audring © Ray Jackendoff and Jenny Audring 2020.
First published in 2020 by Oxford University Press. DOI: 10.1093/oso/9780198827900.001.0001

formation rule that derives *confusion* from *confuse, explosion* from *explode*, and so on. However, such a rule has to be prevented from deriving the nonwords **refusion* and **exposion* from the verbs *refuse* and *expose*. Moreover, it can't derive words like *commotion* and *contraption*, because there are no words **commote* and **contrap* to derive them from. Yet they are surely instances of the *-(t)ion* suffix. Hence a speaker has to learn which *-(t)ion* nominals actually exist, and has to store them in the lexicon— whether or not they are based on existing verbs.

This problem is ubiquitous in morphology. Patterns of this sort cannot be captured by productive rules; they require principles that some theories have called **lexical redundancy rules** or **lexical rules** and that we will call **schemas**. On the face of it, then, it looks as though linguistic theory must countenance two sorts of principles: generative rules in the grammar for productive patterns, and schemas in the lexicon for limited or nonproductive patterns.

But now consider idiomatic expressions like *shake hands, call the shots*, and *raining cats and dogs*. Because of their semantic idiosyncrasy, these expressions have to be listed in the lexicon. Still, at the same time, they contain the perfectly regular plural suffix *-s*. The plural forms should therefore be derived by the productive plural rule, and should not be listed in the lexicon, which is supposedly reserved for idiosyncratic information. We therefore face an apparent paradox: in these expressions, the plural form must both be listed in the lexicon and generated by the grammar.

We resolve the paradox by proposing that the plural pattern can be used in two distinct ways. First, it can be used **generatively** to create new items like *wugs* or *coelacanths*, which are not listed in the lexicon. Second, it can be used **relationally** to express generalizations among lexically listed collocations such as *shake hands* and *call the shots*. In principle, all productive rules allow these two possibilities. For instance, the syntactic structure of the English transitive VP is used generatively to create novel VPs such as *smash the tomatoes* and *forget the banana*. But stored items such as *raining cats and dogs* and *shake hands* are also perfectly formed transitive verb phrases. This is surely not a coincidence. We therefore propose that the rule for the English VP, like the rule for the plural, can be used both generatively and relationally. It is the latter use that captures the generalization among stored expressions with VP structure.

The distinction between productive rules and lexical redundancy rules then comes down to this: Productive rules can be used both generatively, to create novel forms, and relationally, to express limited generalizations inside the lexicon. Lexical redundancy rules, in contrast, can be used only relationally. But now an intriguing change of perspective presents itself, which we call the **Relational Hypothesis**: *All* rules/schemas can be used *relationally*, while only a *subset* of them can be used *generatively* as well. In other words, we depart from the view in which the productive rules are where the action is, and in which lexical redundancy rules are sort of an afterthought. We arrive instead at a view in which the grammar is grounded in the relations among lexical items, and in which *generativity* is the add-on, albeit a very important one. This represents a radical shift in focus for linguistic theory: the rich network of relations inside the lexicon is at least as important as the generation of novel forms—and the theory must take responsibility for nonproductive patterns just as much as for productive ones.

In the course of our exposition of Relational Morphology, a number of important positions emerge on traditional boundaries within linguistic theory:

- The boundary between lexicon and grammar is eliminated.
- The boundary between core and peripheral phenomena (Chomsky 1981) is eliminated.
- The distinction between productive and nonproductive patterns is permeable. As implied by the Relational Hypothesis, the two are no longer the responsibility of distinct parts of the grammar.
- The boundary between morphology and syntax is maintained, but in a way that respects their similarities and their interaction.
- The boundary between competence (the theory of linguistic representations) and performance (the theory of how linguistic representations are put to use in comprehension and production) is maintained, but in such a way that the competence theory can be directly embedded in the performance theory.
- The boundary between language and the rest of the mind is maintained, but in a fashion that situates language vis-à-vis other cognitive domains.

Many aspects of our approach have been in the literature and "in the air" for a long time. Hence some of the constructs that we propose and defend here look like relatively minor tweaks on existing theoretical mechanisms. What we think is relatively original is our synthesis of these ideas into a coherent whole. No single one of the tweaks is especially significant on its own. But when put all together, a lot of pieces fall nicely into place and produce a clear and flexible picture that connects with all sorts of issues in language and cognition, a picture that we think can be considered a new paradigm.

Part I of the book (Chapters 1–3) is devoted to working out the line of reasoning we have just sketched, developing a view of the lexicon and the place of morphology in it. Part II (Chapters 4–6) puts the theory to the test *qua* morphological theory, showing how it accounts for a broad variety of traditional concerns in morphology. Part III (Chapters 7–9) explores how Relational Morphology can connect with issues of language processing and language acquisition, and how the tools of Relational Morphology might be extended to a range of linguistic phenomena outside morphology. Finally, observing that RM's conception of the lexicon amounts to a theory of linguistic memory, we speculate as to how many of its features can be found in other cognitive domains.

1.2 The Parallel Architecture

To set the stage for Relational Morphology, we outline the *Parallel Architecture* (PA: Jackendoff 1997, 2002), on which RM is based. The central goal of this framework is to integrate all the components of language such that they fit together naturally, and such that language as a whole fits into the rest of the mind. Two components of this framework have been developed in detail: *Conceptual Semantics* (Jackendoff 1983, 1990) and *Simpler Syntax* (Culicover and Jackendoff 2005). The present work extends its scope to morphology. We draw freely on the closely related frameworks of Construction Grammar (CxG: Fillmore, Kay, and O'Connor 1988; Goldberg 1995, 2006; Croft 2001; Hoffmann and Trousdale 2013) and especially Construction Morphology (CxM: Booij 2010, 2018a).

Like many other theories of language, the Parallel Architecture takes language to be a mental phenomenon. Indeed, if anything, we are more explicitly mentalistic than Mainstream Generative Grammar (MGG: Chomsky 1965, 1981, 1995), in that we construe Chomsky's (1986) term "knowledge of language" very literally: knowledge must somehow be ensconced in the brain. In this spirit, we frame the basic questions of linguistic theory as follows:

- What linguistic elements does a speaker store in memory, and in what form?
- How are these elements combined online to create novel utterances?
- How are these elements acquired?

Our commitment to mentalism also leads us to insist on a strong connection between linguistic theory ("competence") and accounts of language acquisition and language processing ("performance"). Thus we appeal freely to psycholinguistic considerations, especially in Chapter 7. Furthermore, when possible, we wish to make connections between language and other mental capacities. This issue too crops up here and there in our story, most explicitly toward the end of Chapter 8.

Beyond its mentalism, the basic premise of the Parallel Architecture as laid out in Jackendoff (2002) is that linguistic structure is determined by (at least) three formal systems: phonology, syntax, and semantics. Each of them is built from its own characteristic primitives and principles of combination. In phonology, the basic constructs include syllable and foot structure, prosodic word structure, a metrical grid, an intonation contour, and, where appropriate, a tone tier (Liberman and Prince 1977; Goldsmith 1979; Selkirk 1984). Syntax is built from lexical categories such as N, V, and A, their phrasal projections NP, VP, AP, etc., functional categories such as Det and Aux, plus principles of agreement, long-distance dependencies, and so on. Similarly, in any substantive theory of meaning,[2] semantic structure is built out of primitives such as (conceptualized) objects, events, times, and places, rather than the NPs and VPs of syntax. We factor in morphology in a few moments.

Versions of this general idea of independent components include Stratificational Grammar (Lamb 1966), Lexical-Functional Grammar (LFG: Bresnan 1982, 2001), Autolexical Syntax (Sadock 1991), Role and Reference Grammar (Van Valin and

---

[2] In addition to Conceptual Semantics, the semantic component of the PA (Jackendoff 1983, 1990, 2002), such theories range from formal semantics (Heim and Kratzer 1998), to Cognitive Grammar (Lakoff 1987; Langacker 1987; Talmy 2000) and approaches from artificial intelligence (Schank 1973; Minsky 1975).

LaPolla 1997), and others. Along with these other theories, the PA contrasts sharply with Mainstream Generative Grammar, which assumes without argument that the only "generative engine" in the grammar—the only source of combinatoriality—is syntax, and that phonology and semantics are derived from it.[3]

Just having three kinds of structure is not enough, of course. The structures need to be linked to each other, in order that language can map sound to meaning and vice versa. The PA encodes these relationships in terms of what we will call *interface links*, which connect pieces of structure in one level to pieces in another. As will be seen throughout this study, the interface links are as important a part of the grammar as the structures they link.

Figure 1.1 sketches the basic layout of the PA. A well-formed sentence has well-formed structures in each of the three domains, plus well-formed links among the structures. The double-headed arrows denote interfaces. Importantly, they represent *correspondences* or *correlations* between levels, not *derivations* from one level to another.[4] Syntactic structures play a role in mapping between phonology and meaning; but certain aspects of the mapping, for instance aspects of information structure, can be mapped directly between phonology and conceptual structure, bypassing syntax, as indicated by the dashed arrow in Figure 1.1.

In turn, each of the components in Figure 1.1 can be divided into distinct subcomponents, also linked by interfaces. Within phonology, there are independent tiers for segmental structure, tone, metrical structure, and prosodic contours, tied together by interfaces. Similarly, semantics can be seen as containing separate tiers of propositional structure (who did what to whom) and information structure (topic, focus, common ground, discourse-old vs. discourse-new information, etc.). Within syntax, the f-structure of LFG (Bresnan 2001) and the Grammatical Function tier of Simpler Syntax (Culicover and Jackendoff 2005) can likewise be treated as independent tiers.

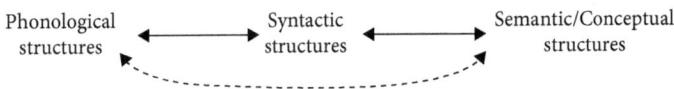

Phonological structures ⟷ Syntactic structures ⟷ Semantic/Conceptual structures

Figure 1.1 The Parallel Architecture

---

[3] Chomsky explicitly states this as an assumption several times in *Aspects* (Chomsky 1965: 16, 17, 75, 198), but to our knowledge he has never defended it or even questioned it since, at least on empirical grounds.

Marantz (2005) and Phillips and Lau (2004) attack the PA on the grounds that, in invoking three "generative engines" instead of one, the PA is not sufficiently constrained. We find this critique misguided. Every theory of language requires an account not only of syntactic well-formedness but also of phonological and semantic well-formedness, that is, some counterpart of the PA's phonological and semantic "generative engines." And indeed, Culicover and Jackendoff (2005) show that the PA's syntax is *highly* constrained, in that it has no movement, no cycles or phases, and a minimal number of null elements. Furthermore, its empirical coverage includes a wide range of phenomena that have never been treated in traditional generative grammar or its direct descendant, the Minimalist Program. See also Jackendoff (2010, 2011, 2015).

[4] It is essential to this conception to recognize that there is no such thing as an interface *level*, a notion often invoked in the literature. This is a category mistake. An interface has to be an interface *between* two (or more) distinct levels of representation. It cannot be characterized in terms of only one of the levels involved. When talking about syntax, it may be convenient to call something, say, the "conceptual-intentional interface," as in Chomsky (1995), but this has to be understood as an abbreviation for that level of syntax over which the syntax-conceptual structure interface is defined. See Jackendoff (1997: Chapter 2) for more discussion.

Thus the large-scale architecture in Figure 1.1 is mirrored in the finer-scale architecture of its individual components. It is of course an empirical issue to determine exactly what tiers are necessary, what each of them accounts for, and how each one interfaces with the others.

Stating the relations among components in terms of interfaces rather than derivations has an important advantage: it allows us to situate the language faculty naturally in an overall view of the mind. Consider what it takes to be able to talk about what we see: our linguistic representations must somehow be linked to a visually-based representation of how objects look, how they are oriented, and how they move in space. Such *spatial representations* cannot be derived from language or vice versa. Rather, they have to be connected to language by a system of linking principles (Jackendoff 1987, 1996; Landau and Jackendoff 1993). Similarly, phonological structures must ultimately map into motor instructions to the vocal tract and *be* mapped from auditory input. These mappings too are independent of syntax, and are best treated as a set of interface principles (see Chapter 6).

This situation finds parallels in the rest of the mind. Figure 1.2 suggests some of the connections among perceptual and cognitive faculties. The visually based representations of shape and spatial layout that correlate with language must also be correlated with representations derived through hapsis (the sense of touch) and through proprioception (the senses of body posture and orientation). Similarly, when reaching for an object, action is often visually guided, through principled correspondences between visual perception and the formulation of action. There is no way that any of these representations can be *derived* from the others. Rather they must be related by principles that establish equivalences or correspondences between them— interfaces in our sense.

Thus in the Parallel Architecture, the internal components of language are connected to each other in the same way as language is connected with the rest of the mind, and in the same way as other faculties of mind are connected to each other—a sort of integration impossible to achieve in a classical generative framework.[5]

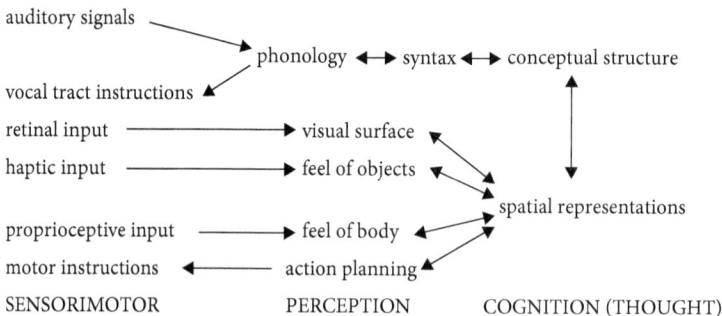

Figure 1.2 The Parallel Architecture embedded in the rest of the mind

[5] Even internal to language, the assumption of syntactic primacy is problematic. Culicover and Jackendoff (2005, especially Chapters 2 and 3) show how much of the complexity of MGG syntactic structure stems from the assumption that all semantic complexity is to be derived from syntax. They further show that a Parallel Architecture approach leads to syntactic structures that are not only simpler but also empirically more adequate.

Because the PA is in a sense modular, it offers the possibility of adding further representational systems and further links between them. For instance, in place of vocal phonology, sign language has a phonology of structured gesture, with interfaces to vision and the motor system. Orthography has its own internal principles that define the alphabet and spelling conventions such as the use of upper and lower case. It also obviously requires an interface to the visual system, so that the reader can see what writing looks like, as well as an interface to phonology and/or morphology that stipulates how spelling correlates with pronunciation. The PA also encourages us to seek a natural approach to further aspects of language use, such as multilingualism and register, as well as to diverse manifestations of language such as narrative, conversation, and song. We briefly take up some of these topics in Chapter 8.

1.3 The Parallel Architecture's lexicon

A standard assumption, inherited from traditional grammar and the structuralists (Aronoff 1994 traces it all the way back to the seventeenth century), is that the lexicon is where words live, and it is the home of arbitrariness and idiosyncrasy in language. It is strictly distinguished from the grammar, which consists of a collection of productive, general rules that capture all linguistically significant regularities. Since the rules are responsible for building the unlimited variety of utterances, the lexicon has tended to take a back seat. As suggested in section 2.6, we wish to reverse this emphasis, and to explore the texture of the lexicon from the perspective of the Parallel Architecture. We begin by asking: What is a "lexical item"?

We first observe that Figure 1.1 has no "lexical component." This is not an omission. As in (practically) every theory, a word, the stereotypical lexical item, is a linkage of a piece of phonology, a piece of meaning, and a collection of (morpho)syntactic features such as category, grammatical number, gender, and so on. Thus words partake of all three components of the Parallel Architecture (we get to morphology in the next section). Example (1) is a more or less common-practice notation.[6]

(1)
$$\begin{bmatrix} \text{Semantics:} & \text{[PIG]} \\ \text{Syntax:} & \text{N} \\ \text{Phonology:} & \text{/pɪg/} \end{bmatrix}$$

---

[6] It is possible that the syntactic level of *pig* also includes the morphosyntactic feature SINGULAR. For ease of exposition, we omit it for the moment; we address the issue in section 2.6.

As is customary, we use the notation PIG informally to stand for the meaning of *pig*, whatever that might be. We notate internal semantic structure only when it is relevant to syntactic and morphological combinatoriality. Nevertheless, we are committed to a rich semantics that is coterminous with human concepts. We differ from treatments of lexical semantics such as Lieber (2019), who characterizes "lexical conceptual structure" as the part of meaning relevant to syntax. She thinks of it as a "semantic skeleton," separate from the "semantic body," which is "a less formal part that contains those encyclopedic elements of meaning that are of no syntactic relevance." One of the major arguments of Jackendoff (1983, 1990) (see also Jackendoff 2002: Sections 9.6, 9.7) is that such a division cannot be made systematically. Rather, the aspects of meaning that are relevant to syntax, such as animacy and argument structure, are otherwise thoroughly integrated into the system of meaning, and are not a separate level or a separate kind of structure.

The notation we adopt here replaces the large square brackets in (1) with a coindexing notation that associates the three pieces of structure.

(2)   Semantics: PIG_1
       Syntax: N_1
       Phonology: $/pɪg/_1$

Coindex 1, shared by the three structures, marks **interface links** between the three components—an explicit association between them in long-term memory. Thereby the word constitutes a small part of the interface. Knowing the word requires knowing not just the contents of the three levels but also the fact that they are linked. In other words, there is no separate "lexical interface": words are part of the more general interfaces between the three levels.

Thinking in terms of processing, a word serves as a small "bridge" running between phonology, syntax, and meaning. In language comprehension, if you encounter /pɪg/ in phonology, the interface links entitle you to posit a corresponding N in syntax and PIG in semantics. In production, the bridge is used in the other direction: if you want to express the concept PIG, you can do so with a corresponding N in syntax and /pɪg/ in phonology.

In a syntactic phrase, each word has a representative in each component, linked by coindices. (3b) shows the structure of *the pig*, composed from the structure of *pig* in (2) and *the* in (3a).

(3)   Semantics: a. DEF_2 b. $[PIG_1; DEF_2]_3$
       Syntax: Det_2 $[_{NP} Det_2 N_1]_3$
       Phonology: $/ðə/_2$ $/ðə_2 \, pɪg_1 /_3$

The links coindexed 1 and 2 in (3b) come from the lexical items *pig* and *the* respectively. In effect, each word is spread across the three levels.[7] The link coindexed 3 encodes the fact that the entire phrase forms a unit with linked semantic, syntactic, and phonological structures.

Each level of representation is responsible just for its own structure. For instance, in (3b) the syntax per se "knows" only that there is a determiner followed by a noun, together forming a noun phrase; it does not distinguish *the pig* from, say, the syntactically identical *this cat*. Phonology and semantics play no role in syntax except to the extent that they are associated via interface links.

A word's subcategorization is easily incorporated into this format. Consider a transitive verb like *devour*. Instead of assigning to its lexical entry a subcategorization feature like the traditional (4a), or a feature that triggers the marking of case on the object, the entry can be stated in the form (4b)—a piece of linguistic structure containing variables.

---

[7] This characterization invites comparison with Distributed Morphology (DM: Halle and Marantz 1993; Harley 2014; Siddiqi 2019), which similarly separates the structure of words into syntactic features, Vocabulary (phonology), and Encyclopedia (semantics). However, DM's derivational formalism is incompatible with the PA.

(4)   a.   [+ __ NP]

    b.   Semantics: [DEVOUR (Agent: X, Patient: Y_y)]$_5$

         Syntax: $[_{VP} V_4 NP_y]_5$

         Phonology: /dəvawr$_4$…$_y$/$_5$

The syntax of (4b) is a transitive VP. Its verb is linked by coindex 4 to the phonology /dəvawr/. Its object is linked by a *variable coindex y* to a phonological variable, denoted by the ellipsis: the verb doesn't care how its object is pronounced. However, if the direct object NP is absent, the VP is ill-formed. Turning to the semantic side, coindex *y* also links the direct object to the Patient argument of the semantic function DEVOUR (X,Y). Finally, coindex 5 connects the entire structure of all three levels. This is exactly what a subcategorization feature is supposed to say.[8]

Both *pig* and *devour* are stereotypical lexical items: words with content in all three components, together making up a Saussurean sign. However, there are also many types of nonstereotypical lexical items. We briefly mention some of them.

A first case is words that lack one or more of the levels. For instance, *hello, gosh,* and *oops* arguably have no syntactic category: they can serve as full utterances, and they combine only paratactically. Hence they establish a direct phonology-to-semantics linkage, bypassing syntax, as suggested by the dashed connection in Figure 1.1.

Another class of words, such as epenthetic *it,* complementizer *that,* do-support *do,* and the *of* in *picture of Bill* are meaningless and serve only as "grammatical glue." These words specify only a link between phonology and syntax, and hence are not Saussurean signs.

Here the PA diverges from the versions of Construction Grammar (e.g. Goldberg 1996; Croft 2001; Boas and Sag 2012) that stipulate that every lexical item is a linking of form (phonology and syntax) and function (semantics). The PA allows for lexical items that link just phonology and syntax, with no semantic effects (Jackendoff 2013). This difference between the theories comes up repeatedly in morphological and phonological patterns such as allomorphy, inflectional classes, and final devoicing (Chapters 5–6), as well as in extensions of the PA to orthography and generative metrics (Chapter 8).

Next, consider idioms such as *chew the fat* ('converse idly'). They have regular internal syntactic structure, in this case $[_{VP} V [_{NP} Det N]]$, yet because of their non-compositional meaning, they have to be stored in memory. Sometimes it is advocated that idioms are stored in a special "place" in the grammar, perhaps an "idiom list." However, the fact that they have internal syntactic structure is sufficient to distinguish them from words; and apart from this difference, idioms and words are in exactly the same format. Hence idioms too can be considered lexical items; no special "place" is necessary. (We return to idioms in section 2.6.)

---

[8] Two further points on the notation in (4b) bear mention. First, The Agent argument X is linked to subject position by independent principles and therefore does not need a coindex in the lexical entry (Jackendoff 1990). Second, it might have been expected that the semantic function DEVOUR would be coindexed with the verb in syntax and the pronunciation /dəvawr/ in phonology, yet it is not. Section 4.13 explains this notational choice, which we maintain throughout our exposition.

In addition to idioms, which have idiosyncratic meanings, speakers know hundreds of multi-word collocations that mean just about what they should, but that, in the face of alternatives, are known to be "the right way to say it." Some examples: *black and white* (cf. *#white and black*), *here and there* (*#there and here*), *absolutely ridiculous* (*#absolutely funny*), *make a change* (*#do a change*), *mow the lawn/?grass*, (*cut the grass/#lawn*). These too must be listed, despite their internal syntactic structure (Di Sciullo and Williams 1987; Jackendoff 1997; Christiansen and Arnon 2017; Culicover, Jackendoff, and Audring 2017). Thus they should be regarded as yet another variety of lexical item.

Once we admit the possibility of folding grammatical structure into the lexicon, we can also recast ordinary phrase structure rules as stored pieces of structure that have only a syntactic level. For instance, the procedural rule (5a) for the English transitive VP can be restated as the declarative template (5b), with two variables to be instantiated. Such pieces of syntactic structure are the basic units of Tree-Adjoining Grammar (Joshi 1987); Janet Fodor (1998) calls them "treelets," and the usage-based tradition (e.g. Pine and Lieven 1997) calls them "slot-and-frame patterns.".

(5)   a.   *Procedural formulation:*
           $VP \rightarrow V - NP$ ('Expand a VP as V followed by NP')
      b.   *Declarative formulation:*
           Syntax: $[_{VP} V - NP]$ ('A VP can consist of a V followed by NP')

Within the Parallel Architecture, (5b) can be treated as just another sort of lexical item. Just as lexical items such as *hello* and epenthetic *it* lack the full complement of levels, so does (5b). Just as idioms are lexical items with internal syntactic structure, so is (5b); it is unusual only in that syntactic structure is *all* it has. Finally, just as a lexical entry such as *devour* (4b) contains variables, so does (5b); it is unusual only in that it consists *entirely* of variables. In particular, it is another lexical item that is not a Saussurean sign.

This construal of phrase structure rules presents a possibility not available in the standard conception: some syntactic structures might be intrinsically linked to characteristic meanings and therefore be more word-like. Such a possibility has been the motivating force behind Construction Grammar, back to its founding documents (e.g. Fillmore, Kay, and O'Connor 1988). An example is the demonstration by Gleitman et al. (1996) that symmetrical predicates such as *similar* behave asymmetrically in the configuration *X is similar to Y*, not because they are inherently asymmetrical, but because subject position imposes a figural perspective on X, against which Y is the standard of comparison. That is, the asymmetry arises from semantic structure that is linked directly with syntactic structure, not with particular words (see also Landau and Gleitman 2015 and section 8.2.3). This sort of generalization is difficult to capture in a traditional architecture, in which syntactic structures per se can carry no meaning.

The examples enumerated in this section lead us to consider the possibility of treating all rules of grammar as lexical items. We can think of the lexicon as a multidimensional space, with words like *pig* in one corner and phrase structure rules like (5b) in the opposite corner, and with many sorts of items in between. All can be considered lexical items. (For elaboration of this point, see Zwicky 1989; Goldberg 1996, 2006;

Croft 2001, 2003; Jackendoff 2002, 2011, 2015. Construction Grammarians sometimes call this heterogeneous collection the "constructicon.")

To be sure, the distinction between lexicon and grammar is so deeply ingrained
that it may be difficult to conceive of abandoning it. However, we have already begun
to see some advantages in doing so. First, instead of having two components of grammar with entirely different formats, we have only one. The traditional distinction
between words and rules surfaces instead as the absence or presence of variables in
lexical items. Second, this formalization allows for meaningful constructions: pieces
of syntax that, just like words, are associated directly with meaning, a possibility
denied in MGG but amply supported by evidence from Construction Grammar.

1.4 Morphological structure and morphological schemas

We now begin to extend this approach to morphology, starting with a morphologically structured word like *piggish*. (6a) repeats the structure of *pig*; (6b) shows *piggish*
(semantics very approximate).

(6)   Semantics: a. PIG_1 b. $[LIKE (PIG_1); SLOPPY, GREEDY]_6$
       Morphosyntax: N_1 $[_A N_1 aff_7]_6$
       Phonology: $/pig/_1$ $/pig_1 if_7/_6$

Let's see what all this coindexation means. Coindex 6 in (6b) notates interface links
between the meaning, the morphosyntax, and the phonology of the whole word *piggish*, in the same way that coindex 1 in (6a) connects the three levels of *pig*. Coindex 7
notates the contribution of the suffix: morphosyntactically it is an affix, linked to the
pronunciation /ɪʃ/.[9] Coindex 1 is the interesting one. Within the entry of *piggish*, it
functions as an interface link that connects the three components of the base. But in
addition, by virtue of being the same as the coindex of *pig* in (6a), it also marks what
we will call a **relational link** between corresponding components of the two words.
The presence of the relational link is what gives *piggish* its internal morphological
structure. More generally, it is by virtue of relational links to other lexical items that
an item can be morphologically decomposed.[10]

To be a bit more explicit about the status of the coindices: they are to be understood
as marking the ends of association lines between pieces of structure in the lexicon. We
could instead use association lines to notate *pig*, *piggish*, and their connection, as in
Figure 1.3. The solid lines denote interface links, which connect different levels within
the same word; the dashed lines denote relational links, which connect the same levels
of different words.[11]

---

[9] Again, see section 4.13 for why coindex 7 does not appear also on LIKE.
[10] However, as stressed by Anderson (1992), *piggish* may be "atomic" from the point of view of phrasal syntax,
which treats *piggish* just like any morphologically simple adjective such as *fat*.
[11] A version of our relational links appears in the Network Model of Bybee (1995, 2010). However, the links in
Bybee's network are explicit only in phonological connections, and the network does not contain schemas (which
we introduce in a moment).

Semantics: PIG   [[LIKE (PIG)]; SLOPPY]

Morphosyntax: N   [$_A$ N   aff]

Phonology: /pɪg/   /pɪg ɪʃ/

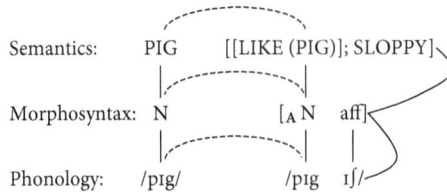

Figure 1.3 Interface and relational links as association lines

Visually appealing though this notation might be, it rapidly degenerates into spaghetti when one tries to do anything at all elaborate. We therefore retain the coindexing notation, despite its less iconic character.[12]

In the case of *piggish*, the relation between the three levels of structure is one-to-one: for each part in phonology, there are corresponding parts in morphosyntax and/or semantics, and vice versa (aside from the feature SLOPPY). But this isn't always the case. Consider the plural of *sheep*, namely *sheep*, notated in (7b).

(7)   Semantics: a. SHEEP$_8$ b. PLUR [(SHEEP$_8$)]$_9$
      Morphosyntax: N$_8$ [$_N$ N$_8$ PL]$_9$
      Phonology: /ʃip/$_8$ /ʃip/$_{8,9}$

In this example, coindex 9 marks the interface link between the three levels of the word. Coindex 8 marks the interface link between the meaning SHEEP and the morphosyntactic Noun in both singular and plural *sheep*. Coindex 8 also marks a relational link between singular and plural *sheep*. So far this is parallel to *pig* and *piggish* in (6).

The interest, however, lies in the morphosyntactic plural. It is necessary in order to control determiner and verb agreement (*those sheep are...* vs. *that sheep is...*). However, morphosyntactic plural is not linked to phonology. Rather, the plural is pronounced the same as its base; this is marked by the dual coindexation 8,9 in the phonology. Thus there is no need for a phonological "zero morpheme"; so-called zero morphology is simply a piece of morphosyntax unlinked to any dedicated piece of phonology. We discuss a host of noncanonical cases like this in Chapters 4–6.

Next, we wish to express the parallelism among all the *-ish* words—*piggish*, *childish*, *foolish*, *thuggish*, and so on. In order to do this, we introduce a schema for the *-ish* suffix. (8) gives the structure of two more *-ish* words, and (9) is the schema.

(8)   a. Semantics: [LIKE (CHILD$_{10}$); SILLY, IMMATURE]$_{11}$
         Morphosyntax: [$_A$ N$_{10}$ aff$_7$]$_{11}$
         Phonology: /tʃaɪld$_{10}$ ɪʃ$_7$ /$_{11}$

      b. Semantics: [LIKE (FOOL$_{12}$)]$_{13}$
         Morphosyntax: [$_A$ N$_{12}$ aff$_7$]$_{13}$
         Phonology: /fuːl$_{12}$ ɪʃ$_7$ /$_{13}$

---

[12] In principle, the coindexing notation could be more explicit if it kept the coindices for interface and relational links distinct, parallel to the association lines in Figure 1.3. However, as we show in section 4.13, this leads to severe notational congestion. In the interest of readability, we adopt the less precise notation.

(9)   Semantics: $[\text{LIKE}\ (\text{X}_x)]_y$
      Morphosyntax: $[_A\ \text{N}_x\ \text{aff}_7\ ]_y$
      Phonology: $/\ldots_x\ \text{ɪʃ}_7\ /_y$

Informally, (9) says that an adjective ending in *-ish* can mean 'like X', where the meaning 'X' is expressed by a noun whose phonology precedes *-ish*. The notation in (9) is interpreted as follows:

- The morphosyntax and phonology of the affix in (9) are linked by coindex 7. This coindex also appears in all the instances of the schema in (6b) and (8a,b). Hence it also marks a relational link that identifies *-ish* as the affix that they all share.
- (9) contains variables in semantics (X), syntax (N), and phonology (…). These are linked together by the **variable coindex x**. This coindex can mark a relational link with any word that has the same pattern of structure. For example, *x* in (9) forms a relational link with coindex 1 in *piggish*, with coindex 10 in *childish*, and with coindex 12 in *foolish*.
- The three levels of the schema as a whole are linked by the variable coindex *y*. This too can mark a relational link to anything with the same pattern of structure. For instance, *y* in (9) marks a relational link with coindex 2 in *piggish*, coindex 11 in *childish*, and coindex 13 in *foolish*.
- SLOPPY, GREEDY, SILLY, and IMMATURE are not connected with anything in the schema; these are the idiosyncratic parts of the word meanings.

Hence we might say that coindex 7 in (9) denotes the *same* structure in the schema and its instances, while *x* and *y* denote structure that is *equivalent* or *parallel* among the schema and its instances.

This being the lexicon, there are also many sorts of partial resemblances among words ending in *-ish*. *Bookish* and *feverish* share coindex 7 on phonology and morphosyntax, but they do not mean 'like a book' or 'like a fever'. Adjectives such as *oldish* and *warmish* have as their base an adjective rather than a noun, and they mean something like 'X to some degree'; this calls for another schema that happens to coincide in its phonology. *Squeamish, lavish, and brackish* are adjectives, and they have the right phonology and word class to be identified as having the suffix *-ish*. But their bases are not words of present-day English; they are examples of an important configuration to which we return repeatedly: morphologically complex words with a nonlexical base. Finally, words such as *radish, rubbish, furnish*, and *vanish* also end in *-ish*, but they are not even adjectives, so their resemblance to words with the *-ish* suffix is purely phonological. Each of these cases is "exceptional" in its own way, and the deviations can be expressed in terms of the presence or absence of particular relational links to schema (9).

(9) encodes a traditional "word formation rule" in terms of a declarative schema—a description of a possible structure in English. As suggested above, it can be informally paraphrased as (10a). This general characterization is shared by other constraint- and schema-based frameworks such as LFG, HPSG, Cognitive Grammar, Construction

Grammar, and Construction Morphology. In contrast, the rules of MGG are proced-ures like (10b); they have an "input" and "output," and they apply in sequence to per-form derivations.[13]

(10)   a. *Declarative formulation:*
        "An adjective ending in *-ish* can mean 'like X', where the meaning 'X' is
        expressed by a noun whose phonology precedes *-ish*."
      b. *Procedural formulation:*
        "Take a noun that means 'X' as input, and add *-ish* to its phonology,
        outputting an adjective that means 'like X.'"

At first glance, these two formulations might look like notational variants, and one might wonder why it matters which of them one chooses. Why should one give up rules in favor of schemas? Chapter 2 takes this question up in detail. However, an important differ-ence can already be mentioned here. Unlike the word formation rule informally stated in (10b), schema (9) is in the same format as the words in (2), (4b), (6), (7), and (8): it consists of linked pieces of semantic, morphosyntactic, and phonological structure. Hence, unlike a traditional word formation rule, it can be considered a lexical item. The crucial differ-ence between (9) and its instances is that it contains variables, so it cannot be used in an utterance without instantiating its variables. This is what makes it a bound form.

This formulation finds a strong parallel with subcategorization of *devour* in the previous section. The suffix *-ish* needs an N in exactly the way that *devour* needs an NP (as has been observed by Selkirk 1982, Kiparsky 1982, Sadock 1991, and Lieber 1992, among others). To emphasize the similarity, we might want to think of *-ish* as a "morphologically bound form" and *devour* as a "syntactically bound form." This outcome illustrates further our position that rules of grammar are actually part of the lexicon. The fact that the schema format serves for both represents a nice step in unifying morphology with syntax, and it provides further motivation for treating morphological schemas as lexical items.

1.5 Morphology in the Parallel Architecture

What's the place of morphology in linguistic theory? Common practice—including introductory texts—sandwiches morphology rather uncomfortably between phon-ology and syntax. Is that where it should be? Could it instead be reduced to some sort of syntax, or to some sort of phonology? Or is it an independent module of language, with its very own principles?

---

[13] Our use of the terms "declarative" and "procedural" comes out of the computational tradition, and it differs somewhat from their use in the literature on memory. By "declarative," we have in mind the sort of mental repre-sentation in terms of which words are encoded—not just their meanings, which might be assigned to "semantic memory," but also their syntactic and phonological properties. By "procedural," we have in mind the sort of mental representation that encodes instructions for the active building of combinatorial structure. This may per-haps fall under the "procedural memory" of cognitive psychology and neuroscience.

Phrasal phonology ⟷ Phrasal syntax ⟷ Phrasal semantics

↕ ↕ ↕

Word phonology ⟷ Morphosyntax ⟷ Lexical semantics

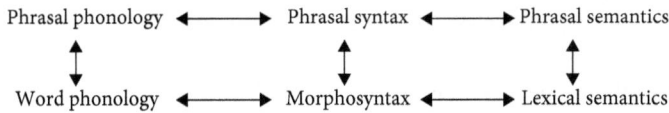

Figure 1.4 Morphology in the Parallel Architecture

On the basis of the tiny sample of morphology laid out in the last section, we can already begin to see how morphology fits into the Parallel Architecture. The internal structure of the words discussed in the previous section includes semantic, (morpho-) syntactic, and phonological material—just like the structure of phrases. This parallelism suggests that the components of grammar form a 3×2 matrix, as sketched in Figure 1.4. In this arrangement, the horizontal interfaces are correspondences between representations built from distinct sets of primitives—phonological, syntactic, and semantic. At the same time, phonology, syntax, and semantics each have a phrasal subcomponent and a word-level subcomponent, connected by the vertical interfaces. (This sort of arrangement has been proposed as long ago as Bach 1983, and more recently by Ackema and Neeleman 2004 and van der Hulst 2006.)

Let us walk through the components of Figure 1.4 that are relevant to morphology: morphosyntax and its interfaces to phrasal syntax, word phonology, and lexical semantics.

First of all, morphosyntax is conceived of as an independent formal system that licenses the structure of complex words. Its primitives include syntactic category, morphosyntactic features such as tense, person, number, gender, and case, morphological features such as inflectional class, and word-internal constituents such as roots, stems, and affixes.

Next, consider the vertical interface between morphosyntax and phrasal syntax. Both components make reference to the X^0 ("lexical") categories N, V, and A, and both are sensitive to inflectional features, though in quite different ways. The two components intersect at the level of maximal X^0s—the largest morphological units and the smallest phrasal ones.

However, the two components differ in what other categories they have access to. Phrasal syntax builds maximal X^0s into larger categories like NP, VP, and S, but, aside from inflectional features, it is for the most part ignorant of the internal structure of words, that is, syntax is (mostly) morphology-free (Zwicky 1996; Corbett and Baerman 2006).[14] Reciprocally, morphosyntax typically has no access to phrasal categories (an observation codified by Botha 1981 as the No Phrase

---

[14] However, Booij (2010: Chapter 8), Booij and Audring (2018a), Bruening (2018), and Siddiqi (2019) document a number of cases in which phrasal syntax is sensitive to derivational morphology. Bruening and Siddiqi take from this that morphology should be completely assimilated into phrasal syntax, a conclusion with which we do not concur.

Constraint)—although phrasal intrusions do occur in compounding and occasionally in derivation.[15]

Turning to other aspects of Figure 1.4, phonology, like syntax, has a dual nature. Word phonology concerns the phonological shape of words, including such matters as phonotactics, word stress, and vowel harmony. Phrasal phonology concerns phenomena such as sandhi, phrasal stress, and intonation contours. The two intersect at the level of the phonological word.

The phonological phenomena of greatest interest to morphological theory, of course, are the interface principles that link word phonology to morphosyntactic structure. Morphosyntactic constituents stereotypically map one-to-one onto discrete phonological strings. For instance, the word *piggish* is typically analyzed as made up of two morphemes, a noun pronounced /pɪg/ and an affix pronounced /ɪʃ/. However, languages are full of deviations from the stereotype, as seen for example in plural *sheep* above. In fact, practically all the difficulties with morphology—and all the fun and danger—lie in noncanonical correspondences, in which the phonological form of complex words does not split cleanly into identifiable morphosyntactic constituents: zero morphology (including conversion), syncretism, stem allomorphy (including umlaut and ablaut), portmanteau forms, multiple exponence, truncation, infixation, circumfixation, and reduplication, among others. Even *piggish* potentially presents a problem, in that the /g/ syllabifies with the suffix, rather than with the stem, where it most naturally belongs. The ubiquity of these phenomena has led to widespread skepticism toward the morpheme as a viable construct of morphological theory (e.g. Mohanan 1986; Anderson 1992; Blevins 2016; Lieber 2019). Chapters 4–6 show how Relational Morphology describes a range of such noncanonical mappings.

On the semantic side of Figure 1.4, similar considerations obtain. "Lexical semantics" specifies the repertoire of meanings of words, idioms, and schemas, i.e. the range of "lexical conceptual structures," in the sense of Jackendoff (1983, 1990). "Phrasal semantics" encompasses the composition of word meanings into larger chunks of meaning, and includes matters such as argument structure, focus, and scope of quantification, which involve the relations of multiple semantic constituents. (There is probably more interpenetration between lexical and phrasal semantics than in the other two domains—an issue we needn't address here.)

---

[15] Examples of phrasal intrusions include the underlined parts of (i). (The stress pattern in (i.a,b,c) is consistent with compounding.)

(i)   a. smoked pork shoulder boiled dinner; health and welfare fund; "I have a dream" speech
      b. do-it-yourselfer; stick-to-itiveness
      c. I...am now in wake-up-at-4-am mode.   [Peter Culicover, email 20 Nov 2018]
      d. *French*: trompe l'oeil; boite-sans-soif   [Di Sciullo and Williams 1987]
      e. matter-of-factness; matter-of-factly   [Di Sciullo and Williams 1987]

Matter-of-factly, for instance, apparently has a word-internal phrasal constituent, as in (ii), violating the canonical relation of morphology and syntax.

(ii)   [$_{Adv}$ [$_{NP}$ *matter of fact*] [$_{aff}$ *ly*]]

See Meibauer (2007) and Trips (2016) for some discussion, and Shimamura (1986), Wiese (1996b), Dressler (2006), Bauer, Lieber, and Plag (2013: Chapter 22), and Booij and Audring (2017) for a wide range of similar cases.

What might be called "morphosemantics" is the interface mapping between morphosyntactic structure and word meaning. Morphological patterns can be used to express a heterogeneous collection of semantic functions—matters like plurality, time, aspect, modality, possession, evidentiality, causation, and endearment, but also on occasion semantic factors farther afield, which we will not attempt to enumerate (see Talmy 2000 and Bauer 2002). More generally, the range of possible semantic connections between elements of a compound is far less constrained than the range available in phrasal syntax (Jackendoff 2010), and this is true as well in derivational morphology, as argued for instance by Bach (2002).

The morphosyntax-semantics interface is also responsible for the effects of morphological combination on argument structure. For example, a derived event nominal such as *abandonment* preserves the argument structure of the corresponding verb *abandon*: alongside *the army abandoned the fortress*, with Agent and Patient arguments, we have *the army's abandonment of the fortress*, with parallel arguments in parallel positions. However, other relationships between the derived item and its base are also possible. An agentive *-er* nominal like *baker* refers to the Agent argument of *bake*—a baker is someone who bakes things. And a result nominal with *-tion* like *inscription* denotes the Patient (or Theme) argument of *inscribe*— an inscription is something that someone has inscribed. (We discuss some of these cases in Chapter 4.)

Overall, then, the scope of morphology can be seen as encompassing morphosyntax plus its interfaces to phrasal syntax, word phonology, and lexical semantics. Of course, in order to understand an interface, one must understand both ends of what the interface connects. Hence the other components of the grammar cannot be neglected.

1.6 Further comparisons between morphosyntax and phrasal syntax

We now look a bit further into the long-standing question of how closely related morphosyntax is to phrasal syntax. (See Anderson 2004 for further discussion.)

Early generative grammar conceived of morphological complexity as being transformationally derived from syntax. For instance, Lees (1960) derived *the writer of the book* from *he writes books*. Baker (1988) and Distributed Morphology (Halle and Marantz 1993; Marantz 1997; Embick and Noyer 2007; Harley 2014; Siddiqi 2019) have similarly championed deriving morphological structure from phrasal syntax, though with different machinery from Lees.

In contrast, approaches such as Aronoff (1976, 1994), Sadock (1991), Spencer (2013), Blevins (2016), Stump (2016), and Gisborne (2019) treat morphology as its own component, not beholden to syntax. An influential version of this view, originating with Chomsky's (1970) Lexicalist Hypothesis, is that words are built "in the lexicon," prior to lexical insertion, while phrases are built of complete words "in the syntax." This position was strongly encouraged by Wasow's (1977) influential paper distinguishing adjectival (lexical) passives from verbal (syntactic) passives. The separation of lexical (or morphological) rules and syntactic rules is a central feature of Lexical Phonology (Kiparsky 1982; Mohanan 1986), of HPSG (Pollard and Sag 1994) and of LFG (where it is called "Lexical Integrity": Bresnan and Mchombo 1995; Bresnan 2001; Asudeh and Toivonen 2014), as well as many independent morphological theories, such as Aronoff (1976), Botha (1981) (the "No Phrase Constraint"), Di Sciullo and Williams (1987), Anderson (1992), Hale and Keyser (2002), Spencer (2005, 2013), and Trips (2016).

For Relational Morphology, morphosyntax is neither "before" nor "after" phrasal syntax. Nor are morphology and syntax in different "places," such that one "happens in the lexicon" and the other "happens in the grammar." Rather, as argued in sections 1.3 and 1.4, "the grammar" is *part* of the lexicon. The architecture in Figure 1.4 suggests that morphosyntax is distinct from phrasal syntax but related to it. While phrasal syntax deals with how words are combined to form phrases, morphosyntax deals with the structure *inside* words. It is then an empirical question what morphosyntax looks like and how much it shares with phrasal syntax.

As a hint that this is the right approach, we first mention a few differences between phrase and word grammar that demonstrate their distinctness. (See also Mohanan 1996 and Williams 2007.) First, phrasal syntax includes syntactic phrases such as NP and VP; morphosyntax (for the most part—see note 15) does not. On the other hand, morphosyntax has affixes, and phrasal syntax does not. (Particles and clitics hover somewhere between the two; we will not try to sort them out here.)

Two very important features of phrasal syntax are absent from morphosyntax (see also DiSciullo and Williams 1987):

- Phrasal syntax allows for "displacement," including long-distance dependencies such as wh-constructions. Morphosyntax does not.
- Phrasal syntax often countenances free variation in word and/or phrase order. Morphosyntax does not countenance free variation in affix order (or at least it is *very* rare —see Chapter 4, note 12).

Some things are found in morphosyntax but not phrasal syntax, for instance:

- Morphology may show inflectional class distinctions, whereby the same morphosyntactic property is expressed by different phonology. Phrasal syntax has no direct counterpart.[16]
- Morphosyntax allows noun incorporation, in which the incorporated noun has the same thematic role as a phrasal argument. (11) is an example from Baker (1988: 76–7), citing Woodbury 1975:

---

[16] Close analogs might be verb classes in Romance and Germanic that choose auxiliary *have* vs. *be*, or verb classes in French that choose *à* vs. *de* before an infinitival complement. These cases involve relatively arbitrary classes that realize syntactic functions in different fashion. (We are grateful to Andrew Spencer for these examples.)

(11)   Onondaga, Iroquoian:

    a.   (*Phrasal argument*)

        Waʔ- ha   -hninu-ʔ   neʔ o -yvʔkw -aʔ

        PAST- 3MASC/3NEUT -buy   -ASP the PRE-tobacco -SUF

        'He bought the tobacco.'

    b.   (*Incorporated argument*)

        Waʔ- ha   -yvʔkw - ahni:nu -ʔ

        PAST-3MASC/3NEUT- tobacco- buy   -ASP

        'He bought tobacco.' (= 'He tobacco-bought')

Unlike phrasal syntax, but typical of morphological patterns, the incorporated noun (usually) cannot bear determiners or other modifiers.[17]

- Morphosyntax includes the possibility of templatic morphology, in which a word form specifies a sequence of affix slots, and each slot can be occupied by an affix appropriate to it. There need be no evidence in this sequence for constituent structure. Phrasal syntax has nothing of the sort (although clitic sequences in Romance and Slavic are possible exceptions, if they count as syntax). (12) is a Navajo example drawn from Spencer (1991: 209). (Roman numerals are affix slots; The *ł* in slot IX is absent from the full form, evidently for phonological reasons.)

(12)   Navajo:

    náánáoshtééł

    nááná- Ø -o   -sh -ł -tééł

    I   IV VII VIII IX   X

    SEMEL-ITERATIVE + DO + OPT + 1SG + CL + STEM

    'that I might bring him again'   [semel-iterative = 'repeated once']

Differences such as these are hard to account for in a theory in which morphology is "syntax all the way down."

Other phenomena display a strong continuity between phrasal and morphological grammar. These are at odds with the position that morphology is "in the lexicon," a separate "place" from "the grammar," or that morphology is a completely *sui generis* module.

- English multi-morphemic prepositions such as those in (13a) look like compounds: the noun in the middle is bare and does not admit modification. Those in (13b), though, have a determiner preceding the noun, which alternates with possessives, such as (13c); these look phrasal.

---

[17] The literature on noun incorporation is conflicted as to whether it arises in syntax (e.g. Sadock 1980; Baker 1988) or through lexical word-formation rules (e.g. Mithun 1986; Rosen 1989; Anderson 2004); see Massam (2017) for a recent survey. In the present approach, the morphological and semantic properties of noun incorporation are defined in morphological terms, while the relation of incorporated nouns to phrasal arguments is likely treated in terms of "sister schemas" of the sort to be developed in sections 4.8 and 8.2.

(13) a. in place of, on top of, in front of, in line with, in lieu of, instead of, in spite of,
          in cahoots with, by dint of, in synch with, by virtue of, in consideration of
      b. in the place of, for the sake of, in the midst of
      c. in your place, for Bill's sake, in their midst

Given the phonological and semantic similarity of these patterns (and the fact that some nouns such as *place* occur in both), it would seem a peculiar accident if the former class were built "in the lexicon" and the latter "in the syntax" by unrelated principles. In the PA account, they are string-identical aside from the presence of a determiner, but they have different syntactic structure: e.g. (14a) vs. (14b).

(14) a. $[_{PP} [_{P} \text{ in place of }] \text{ NP}]$ (compound)
      b. $[_{PP} \text{ in } [_{NP} \text{ the place } [_{PP} \text{ of NP}]]]$ (phrasal idiom)

Another such case involves place names, e.g. *Biscayne Bay* (compound noun) vs. *the Bay of Biscay* (NP); we discuss these in section 2.6 (especially note 13) and section 8.1.3.

- Horn (1993, to appear) and Ghomeshi et al. (2004) discuss an English construction, variously called **Cloning** or **Contrastive Focus Reduplication**, which focuses the denotation of the reduplicated element to either a more generic or a more specialized range:

(15) I'll make the tuna salad, and you make the salad-salad.
      Political reality, important as it is, comes in a distinct second to reality-reality.
                         (Bill McKibben, *The Nation*, December 19/26, 2016: 15)

The reduplication can involve a word stripped of its inflection (16a) or a string larger than a word (16b). Hence the construction straddles morphological and phrasal grammar.

(16) a. We're not one of those couple-couples.
      b. Are you, um, living-together-living together?

So here we have a single productive rule that apparently does not care whether it is phrasal or morphological. Lidz (2001) reports a similar case in Kannada.

- Some cells of inflectional paradigms can be filled by either a complex word or a phrase. For instance, the comparative in English is expressed either periphrastically, i.e. through a syntactic modifier (e.g. *more incredible*), or through a morphological affix (*fatter*), depending on the phonology of the base. Other examples appear in Ackerman and Webelhuth (1999), Haspelmath (2011), and Booij and Audring (2017) (for more on periphrasis, see Chumakina and Corbett 2013).

In each of these cases, it strikes us as counterproductive to insist that one variant is "built in the syntax" while the other is "built in the lexicon," using different sorts of principles. Here, the variants are semantically nearly identical patterns, except that one happens to be phrasal and the other morphological. The architecture in Figure 1.4 allows a construction to slip easily between phrasal and morphological—or to partake of both, taking on characteristics appropriate to the inside of words or to combinations of words, as the case may be.

1.7 Conclusions

This chapter has sketched the outlines of a morphological theory based on the Parallel Architecture. The rest of the book is devoted to fleshing it out. However, even at this preliminary stage, we can already envision at least six major points that break from tradition in their view of the language faculty.

First, of course, is that, instead of localizing the generativity of language in the syntax alone, the Parallel Architecture parcels it out among separate but linked components.

Second, there is no independent "lexical interface" or "lexical layer." As shown in section 1.3, a lexical item is part of the interface between semantics, syntax, and phonology. Lexical items usually have pieces of structure in all three components, connected by interface links. But there are also items that are missing one or even two of the three components.

Third, sections 1.3 and 1.4 have broken down the distinction between words and rules. Procedural or generative rules have been replaced with schemas, which, like words, are declarative pieces of semantic, syntactic, and/or phonological structure, connected by interface links. A lexical item is more word-like to the extent that its content is fully filled out. It is more schema-like to the extent that it contains variables that must be instantiated in order for the schema to be used in an utterance. At the extreme end of this continuum are items made up entirely of variables, such as the VP schema. Chapter 2 develops this point, demonstrating the advantages of schemas over traditional rules.

Fourth, as discussed in section 1.4, the relations between words (e.g. *pig* and *piggish*) are explicitly encoded as relational links, rather than by deriving one from the other. Relational links also encode the relation between a word and a pattern of which it is an instance (e.g. *piggish* and the *-ish* schema).

Fifth, as discussed in section 1.5, there is no morphological component per se. The work traditionally attributed to morphology is divided among morphosyntax—the syntax of words—and its interfaces to phrasal syntax, word phonology, and lexical semantics.

Sixth, as discussed in section 1.6, we have broken down the strong division between phrasal syntax "in the grammar" and morphosyntax "in the lexicon." For one thing, there is no independent "grammatical component"; principles of phrasal syntax are now in the lexicon. But in addition, many phenomena have both phrasal and morphological realizations. At the same time, preserving the distinction between phrasal syntax and morphosyntax allows us to acknowledge their differences.

Putting these all together, we arrive at a view of knowledge of language quite distant from the traditional dichotomy between grammar and lexicon. Not only does the lexicon contain all the words, rules, and constructions of the language; it has to be richly textured in order to capture all the relations among lexical items that are standardly accounted for through morphological rules. We thus find ourselves in a radically new landscape, which from a traditional point of view may feel quite alien. We urge the reader to bear with us: we think the payoff of this conceptual realignment is worth the effort.

2

The functions of schemas

2.1 The tradition: Focus on productive rules

As suggested in section 1.1, linguistic theory in the generative tradition has been dominated by the idea that the magic of language lies in its ability to create an unlimited number of novel structures from a limited set of items. This perspective has led to an emphasis on the productive, rule-governed aspects of language.

The ideology that has emerged from this tradition is that all structure (or all "interesting" structure) comes from applying productive rules to items stored in the lexicon, thereby creating novel structures that are *not* in the lexicon. The lexicon itself is unstructured, or as Bloomfield (1933: 274) puts it, "a list of basic irregularities." Consequently, in the generative tradition, rules are where the real action is, and words are regarded as just a matter of lexicography.

Of course, rules are part of one's knowledge of language, so they have to be stored as well. But since they are so different in character from lexical items, one might want to say the lexicon and the grammar are stored in different metaphorical "places," or even in different *literal* places in the brain (as has in fact been claimed by Michael Ullman (2015)).

Chapter 1 questioned this sharp dichotomy between unstructured lexicon and productive rules. It does work pretty well for syntax. But, as observed in section 1.1, it is not at all comfortable in tackling morphology. Words often don't lend themselves to productive rules, yet they certainly *look* as though they have rule-governed internal structure. The resulting tension reveals itself time after time in the morphological literature. For instance, DiSciullo and Williams (1987: 4) say:

> [A] view we reject is the idea that the lexicon has structure…[I]t is simply a collection of the lawless, and there neither can nor should be a theory directly about it, for it can only be understood in terms of the laws it fails to obey.

Yet DiSciullo and Williams do accord structure to morphologically complex items such as *hydroelectricity* (p. 72), whose meaning is surely not predictable by rule.

Similarly, Lieber (1992) says:

> Certain things almost go without saying: that…a theory [of word formation]…should be based on observations about living, productive patterns of word formation, rather than unproductive, moribund patterns (p. 1)…. [A measure of productivity is necessary in order to] help to determine which processes of word formation the theory

The Texture of the Lexicon. First edition. Ray Jackendoff and Jenny Audring © Ray Jackendoff and Jenny Audring 2020. First published in 2020 by Oxford University Press. DOI: 10.1093/oso/9780198827900.001.0001

need not be responsible to (p. 2)....I assume the existence of a lexicon which lists all idiosyncratic information about listemes. I assume...that this repository of listemes is not structured (p. 21).[1]

And yet, shortly thereafter she says: "I assume...that bound roots such as *path* (as in *psychopath* or *pathology*) have lexical entries as any other morphemes do" (p. 23). But morphological combinations with *path* are extremely idiosyncratic and certainly unproductive, so according to the quote above, the theory need not take them into account.

Here is Aronoff (1976: 22–3):

I do not view [word formation] rules as applying every time the speaker of a language speaks. They are rules for making up new words which may be added to the speaker's lexicon...[The theory] remov[es] from consideration all matters pertaining to words already in the dictionary.

Yet most of his evidence for word formation rules comes from the structure of existing words.

Finally, here is Spencer (2013: 3):

...much of the derivational morphology discussed in the literature is...of the occasional, accidental kind, and therefore of comparatively little interest to grammar writers (though it may be of interest to lexicographers, historians, psycholinguists, language teachers, and others).

The upshot is that the moment an item deviates from full predictability, it is no longer very important.

Related views are not uncommon elsewhere in the literature. For instance, in response to the connectionists, who deny the need for rules and representations altogether, Pinker (1999) proposes a "dual-route" or "words and rules" theory in which productive phenomena are the responsibility of rules, but irregular patterns are a matter of unprincipled association and analogy. Kay (2012), in a Construction Grammar framework, argues that the grammar should pertain only to fully productive phenomena, and he consigns the rest to what he calls "meta-grammar," which likewise works basically by association and analogy.

The unspoken assumption behind all of these views is made explicit by Chomsky (1965: 218):

It must be borne in mind that the general rules of a grammar are not invalidated by the existence of exceptions....It is for this reason that the discovery of peculiarities and exceptions (which are rarely lacking, in a system of the complexity of a natural

---

[1] We are not sure whether Lieber is claiming it is individual listemes that are unstructured, or the repository as a whole.

language) is generally so unrewarding and, in itself, has so little importance for the study of the grammatical structure of the language in question...

This gives the impression that the "exceptions" are a minor matter. But in morphology they are everywhere: they are less like a grammatical "leak" (to use Sapir's term) and more like a raging torrent. A responsible theory of knowledge of language cannot simply declare them "unrewarding" and of "little importance": it should include an account of their irregularities and subregularities.

Chomsky redeems the situation with a caveat:

> ...unless, of course, it [i.e. the discovery of peculiarities and exceptions – RJ/JA] leads to the discovery of deeper generalizations.

But consider: if, as advocated, one disregards peculiarities and exceptions, one will never find out if they lead to any deeper generalizations. They might or they might not.[2] In this chapter we propose to show that indeed there are deeper generalizations to be found, encompassing both the productive and the irregular facets of language. Lawfulness is not an all-or-nothing matter. The lexicon is full of structure, in which the systematic and the unsystematic are deeply interwoven—in an unsystematic fashion, no less!

A brief guide to where we are headed: In order to first pay our dues to productive patterns, section 2.2 shows how declarative schemas of the sort proposed in Chapter 1 can be used in a *generative role* to account for the phenomena traditionally attributed to productive rules. The question then arises of whether rules and schemas are simply notational variants. Sections 2.3 and 2.4 argue that they are not, and that traditional rules face a number of difficulties in dealing with morphology in general, as well as with idioms in particular. Expanding the responsibility of the theory beyond productive patterns, section 2.5 introduces *nonproductive* schemas to capture partial regularities. These schemas function in a *relational role*, more or less parallel to traditional lexical redundancy rules. Section 2.6 shows that productive schemas too can be used in a relational role. This observation blurs the traditional strong distinction between partial regularity "in the lexicon" and full regularity "in the grammar," and it solves the problems for rules raised in sections 2.3 and 2.4. Sections 2.7 through 2.10 discuss the treatment of productivity and give reasons to include nonproductive schemas in the grammar, rather than (or in addition to) associative and analogical relations. Section 2.7 and especially sections 8.1 and 8.2 show that many of the same considerations apply in phrasal syntax, both strengthening the evidence for the architecture in Figure 1.4 and bringing us closer to an integrated theory of language.

Section 2.11 puts all these pieces together and shows how they lead to a surprising reconceptualization of linguistic theory, hinted at in section 1.1: the main focus of

---

[2] Spencer (2003) makes a similar methodological argument against prejudging the relation of morphology and syntax.

inquiry expands to include not just the productive patterns of languages, but also all the partial regularities and idiosyncrasies. We show that this conception indeed "leads to the discovery of deeper generalizations," and we conclude that the study of "peculiarities and exceptions" is not at all in vain.

2.2 The generative function of schemas

Chapter 1 introduced schemas as an alternative to traditional rules. We now compare them in more detail.

A traditional rule is procedural: "Put *this* together with *this* to create *this*" or "Change *this* into *this*." (1) (= (10b) in Chapter 1) informally paraphrases a procedural word formation rule for the *-ish* suffix. It has an "input" and an "output," and it applies in sequence with other rules to perform derivations.

(1) *Procedural rule:*
     "Take a noun that means 'X' as input, and add /ɪʃ/ to its phonology, outputting an adjective that means 'like X.'"

Such a rule can be understood in two ways. The more concrete interpretation sees it as modeling a psychological process, an active computation. The more abstract interpretation sees it as simply a way of defining a set of grammatical structures, rather like the way the Peano postulates recursively define the set of integers. By the time of *Aspects* (1965), though, it had become clear that the concrete interpretation was unsustainable: the procedural rules of MGG could not be understood as modeling mental processes. Rather, falling back on the competence-performance distinction, MGG's derivations came to be uniformly understood as abstract or "metaphorical."

In contrast, a schema is a declarative template for a structure—"*This* is a possible structure." It has no "input" or "output." (2) (= (10a) in Chapter 1) paraphrases the *-ish* schema in such a way as to bring out its declarative character. This general characterization is shared by many other schema- and constraint-based frameworks such as LFG, HPSG, Cognitive Grammar, Construction Grammar, and Construction Morphology.

(2) *Declarative schema:*
     "An adjective ending in /ɪʃ/ can mean 'like X,' where the meaning 'X' is expressed by a noun whose phonology precedes /ɪʃ/."

This is meant to model a template stored in memory. However, we would also like to use it to model the procedure of constructing a word or sentence, whether in production or comprehension. But how can a procedure be accomplished by a template?

The answer is that a procedural rule can be pried apart into two components. One component specifies the elements being combined (the input) and the resulting structure (the output); these can be stated in terms of declarative templates—in present terms, schemas. The other component contributes the procedural character of the rule: it actively manipulates pieces of structure, turning a structure that satisfies the "input template" into one that satisfies the "output template."

The Parallel Architecture, like other schema- and constraint-based theories, adopts the attractive hypothesis that this combinatorial procedure is uniform across the grammar, and that all the differentiation lies in the declarative templates, which specify what is to be combined and what the result is. This single procedural rule is *unification*, in effect a Boolean union of structures (Shieber 1986). Unification *superimposes* one structure on another, preserving the unique parts of both without doubling the shared parts. For example, if we unify the strings ABCD and CDEF, the result is ABCDEF, which maintains the relation of CD to both AB and EF.

The Minimalist Program (Chomsky 1995) embraces a similar hypothesis, claiming that the only procedural rule (of interest) in the grammar is Merge, an operation that concatenates any two constituents to form a larger constituent. However, if we use Merge to combine ABCD and CDEF, the result is ABCDCDEF (or CDEFABCD, or, in more austere expositions such as Berwick and Chomsky (2016: 10), the set {ABCD, CDEF}). Hence unification and Merge are not notational variants.

To be sure, unification is a more complex operation than Merge. However, it is a plausible combinatorial principle not only for linguistic structure, but also for a variety of other cognitive domains. For instance, in perceiving an object through vision and touch at the same time, one has to unify information about its size and shape (derived from both modalities) with color (from vision only) and temperature (from touch only) (see section 1.2 and Jackendoff 2011). Neither visual nor haptic representations can be derived from the other. Given this cross-faculty generality, we conclude that the relative complexity of unification is a matter to be accounted for with respect to the mind as a whole, not just in the language faculty per se. What makes language special is not so much its means for combining units as the content of what is combined: phonological, syntactic, and semantic structures rather than, say, visual or haptic representations.[3] (We return to the issue of cross-domain generality in section 8.6.)

The principal application of unification in the PA is to instantiate variables in schemas. Consider the English plural schema. Its syntax requires its morphosyntactic variable to be satisfied by a noun, and its meaning requires its semantic variable to be a singular count entity. In order to encode these restrictions, we elaborate slightly the

---

[3] This contrasts with the Minimalist Program's view of Merge as *the* central evolutionary innovation in the faculty of language. See Pinker and Jackendoff (2005), Jackendoff and Pinker (2005), in response to Hauser, Chomsky, and Fitch (2002) and Fitch, Hauser, and Chomsky (2005).

Berwick and Chomsky (2016: 175) argue in passing (and without documentation) that "[unification] is Turing-complete, so there is *no* formal limit on the kinds of grammars it can describe." Without knowing what characteristics of unification they have in mind, we cannot address this criticism. Here, we retain our informal characterization in order to explore the formal scope of this operation within the present theory. We take the degree of complexity required by unification for the purposes of natural language to be an empirical and partly theory-dependent matter. In any event, our hypothesis is that the constraints on possible languages will turn out to be a consequence of constraints on (declarative) representations and constraints on the processing of representations, rather than on the formal operation that combines representations.

For more extensive discussion of differences between unification and Merge, see Jackendoff (2011).

notation for schemas introduced in Chapter 1, marking the variables with underlines, as in (3).

(3) *Plural schema*
     Semantics: $[\text{PLUR}\,([\underline{\text{INDIVIDUAL}}]_x)]_y$
     Morphosyntax: $[\underline{\text{N}}_x\,\text{PL}_1\,]_y$
     Phonology: $/\underline{...}_x\,\text{s}_1\,/_y$

The underlined material in (3) may be thought of as stipulating selectional restrictions (or output constraints): whatever putatively instantiates the variables has to be able to unify with them. Hence (3) unifies successfully only with nouns that denote individuals, such as *cat*. (4a) is the entry for *cat*, and (4b) shows the result of unifying it with (3) to form *cats*.

(4)   a. *cat*   b. *cats*
     Semantics: CAT_2 $[\text{PLUR}\,([\text{CAT}]_2)]_3$
     Morphosyntax: N_2 $[\text{N}_2\,\text{PL}_1\,]_3$
     Phonology: $/\text{kæt}/_2$ $/\text{kæt}_2\,\text{s}_1\,/_3$

Let us unpack this operation.

- In the semantics, CAT in (4a) unifies with the variable INDIVIDUAL in (3), yielding CAT in (4b) (since a cat is inherently an individual).
- In morphosyntax, N in (4a) unifies with N in (3), yielding N in (4b).
- In phonology, /kæt/ in (4a) unifies with the featureless variable in (3) to yield /kæt/ in (4b).
- In addition, the interface links of *cat*, notated with coindex 2, unify with the variable coindices x in the schema, yielding coindex 2 in (4b).
- Since this is now a fully specified word, coindex 3 replaces variable coindex y in the schema.

On the other hand, (3) cannot unify with a semantic/morphosyntactic plural, to form, for instance, **cattles* and **polices*, whose meanings conflict with INDIVIDUAL. And for the same reason, (3) either fails to unify with mass nouns, as in **nitrogens*, or coerces them online into an individuated 'portion of' or 'kind of' reading, as in *how many beers did you drink* ('portions of beer') or *how many beers do they serve here* ('kinds of beer'). (Plural does of course unify with, say, *family* to form *families*, because *family* denotes a singular group composed of plural members.)

In short, schemas plus unification can play the role usually assigned to procedural rules, namely building novel structures from stored parts. As Shieber (1986: 23) puts it, "this systematic relationship between static identity and dynamic unification… allows a declarative formalism to have a procedural interpretation." We will call this procedure the **generative** function of schemas. It applies not only in morphology, but also in syntax, leading to the construction of syntactic trees.

One might still think there is nothing new here, that we are merely proposing a notational variant of traditional generative rules. Why should one abandon rules in favor of schemas? How are they different? We now show that there is more to the story, and that schemas have important advantages over generative rules.

2.3 Schemas vs. rules

As observed in sections 1.3 and 1.4, there is a major difference between generative rules and schemas. A rule-based theory takes for granted two independent constructs, a lexicon and a grammar. In contrast, in a schema-based theory, words and schemas are both made of pieces of semantic, morphosyntactic, and phonological structure, connected by interface links. Hence there is no need to separate the theoretical constructs of "lexicon" and "grammar." This is not a minor tweak: it coalesces the two traditional big components of language into one. As we will continue to demonstrate, this proves not to be just a difference in elegance.

Another major difference concerns the sequence in which stored lexical items are combined to produce novel utterances. In standard generative theories, the rules build an utterance by applying in a determinate order, either from the top down (all generative theories from *Syntactic Structures* through Principles and Parameters), or from the bottom up (the Minimalist Program). From the point of view of a competence grammar, understood abstractly, this might be perfectly satisfactory. But from the perspective of psycholinguistics, it is problematic, in that neither order of derivation bears any relation to the order in which sentences are processed, in either comprehension or production. One does not comprehend or produce a sentence top-down, first building a syntactic tree and then populating it with words. Nor does one do it bottom-up, first selecting a bag of words from the lexicon and then building them into a syntactic tree that gets sent off to semantics and phonology.

Word formation rules in morphology likewise are often taken to be applied sequentially. Inner affixes are attached to stems before outer affixes; in some approaches (e.g. Lexical Phonology: Mohanan 1986), certain aspects of morphology "happen" "before syntax," and others "after." As in syntax, this ordering has little to do with how speakers actually process complex words.

By contrast, schema- or constraint-based theories involve no inherent order of derivation: structures can be assembled from the bottom up, from the top down, from left to right, from phonology to semantics (in language comprehension), or vice versa (in language production), as long as each part of the result is licensed by some word or schema. This free order of assembly lends itself to being directly implemented in contemporary opportunistic theories of language processing. In other words, it is possible to view schemas as psychologically real—to understand them literally rather than metaphorically—presumably a theoretical desideratum. (See Sag 1992; Jackendoff 2002, 2007a; Sag and Wasow 2011; Chapter 7 takes this issue up in detail.)

The fact that schemas are in the same format as words has another advantage: it makes an account of their acquisition formally more straightforward. Every theory of acquisition needs a mechanism that detects parallelisms among stored items and that uses these parallelisms as the basis for positing a tentative rule. In a traditional architecture, such a posited rule is a procedure—an entirely different sort of entity from a lexical item. Hence, as observed by Bybee (1995), the acquisition process must, so to speak, cross a transcendental gap from word format to rule format.[4]

A mechanism for forming schemas, in contrast, simply creates a new lexical item—the schema—by copying the parts of the parallel instances that are the same, and replacing with variables the parts that are different among the instances. For instance, the plural schema (3) has constants coindexed 1 where *cats*, *umbrellas*, and *hurricanes* are the same, and variables where they are different. In other words, the schema can be derived directly from the lexical items that motivate it. The same sort of procedure has been advocated for phrasal schemas such as the VP schema (= (5b) in Chapter 1) by, among others, Tomasello (2003) and Culicover and Nowak (2003). We take this to be an immediate formal advantage of schemas, and another respect in which they are not simply a notational variant of traditional rules. (We return to schema acquisition in sections 2.8.2 and 7.7 to 7.9.)

2.4 Problems with rules

The differences do not stop there. Traditional generative rules face a number of snags in accounting for simple morphological phenomena. Here are some of them.

Problem 1: Nonproductive patterns. Some families of words have perfectly predictable phonology and meaning, but have to be listed anyway. An example is the family of deadjectival verbs illustrated in (5). These are all based on monosyllabic adjectives that end in an obstruent, and they all mean '(cause to) become (more) X.' This regularity might be captured by a traditional word formation rule like (6).

(5)   whiten, thicken, dampen, brighten, harden, sicken (+ about 50 more examples)

(6)   Rule: A + -*en* → V

Some adjectives fail to form -*en* verbs because they do not satisfy the schema's phonological requirements. For example, *greenen is out because *green* doesn't end in an obstruent. However, there are other adjectives that satisfy the phonological criteria perfectly but do not form -*en* verbs: we don't find *louden, *safen, *balden, *colden, or *crispen.[5] The simplest way to distinguish the forms that exist from those that don't is

---

[4] Such a switch in format can be seen for instance in Albright and Hayes's (2003) formalization of past tense acquisition, which otherwise is very much in tune with our approach; see sections 2.8.1 and 7.8.

[5] Granted, some of the words that we cite as nonexistent may be found in small numbers somewhere in some large corpus. The *Oxford English Dictionary* does list some of them, but places them in frequency ranges described as "extremely rare" or "unknown to most people" (OED.com, consulted February 24, 2019). If we

to list the forms that exist. But that means that the regularity of the pattern cannot be captured by a rule along the lines of "Add *-en* to an adjective that means 'X' to create a new word that means 'become X.'" The output of such a rule is by definition *outside* the lexicon, but the resulting derived words have to be *inside* the lexicon.

Similarly, Dutch has several hundred adjectives with the suffix *-(e)lijk*, e.g. those in (7).[6] This regularity could be stated as a word formation rule along the lines of (8).

(7) Dutch:
   Verb base: gruwelijk 'gruesome', sterfelijk 'mortal'
   Noun base: lichamelijk 'bodily', mannelijk 'male'
   Adjective base: bangelijk 'fearful', lief(e)lijk 'lovely'

(8) Rule: V/N/A + *-(e)lijk* → A

However, the pattern is not synchronically productive (de Haas and Trommelen 1993: 294–9). Potential forms such as **kopelijk* ('buyable'), **angstelijk* ('fearful'), and **langelijk* ('elongated') do not exist, despite their perfectly transparent form and meaning (note that German has the equivalents *käuflich, ängstlich*, and *länglich*). Hence (8) has to be prevented from overgenerating nonexistent forms. The simplest way, again, is to list the forms that actually exist. But in that case there is no way for a generative rule to capture their commonality.

As mentioned in section 1.6, a widely accepted approach to nonproductivity is Chomsky's (1970) Lexicalist Hypothesis. The idea is that regular, predictable patterns belong to syntax, while more idiosyncratic patterns fall under the purview of **lexical redundancy rules** (or simply **lexical rules**), which apply before words are inserted into syntactic structures. One conception of lexical rules is that they are "presyntactic" generative procedures (e.g. Halle 1973; Aronoff 1976; Mohanan 1986; Pollard and Sag 1987; Hale and Keyser 2002). Alternatively, they have been viewed as ways of establishing relations among stored items (Jackendoff 1975; Bochner 1993; Booij 2010). The effect of the Lexicalist Hypothesis has been to further bolster the strict distinction between lexicon and grammar, by removing from the syntactic component all traces of idiosyncrasy. At the same time, by adding rules inside the lexicon, it undermines the ideology of keeping grammar and lexicon separate.[7]

---

ourselves were faced with them on a lexical decision task, we would vote no. Nor would we use them except as a joke. In other words, these words are not part of our personal knowledge of English. Perhaps other speakers would have different judgments. We are modeling speakers' knowledge, not the corpus or the dictionary.

[6] The CELEX lemma list contains more than 700 instances, including compounded forms (http://celex.mpi.nl, consulted February 24, 2019).

[7] Two other ancient proposals: Halle's (1973) grammar generated all possible words, and passed them through a "filter" that admitted only the actual words. Alternatively, Lakoff (1970) invoked "minor rules," which required a list of all the bases that undergo them to form derived words. The term "governed rules" was also common during that early period, with approximately the same sense, and this device is retained in Distributed Morphology (e.g. Embick 2015). These proposals amount to indirect ways of listing the existing forms. We propose simply to list them in the lexicon directly; the next section discusses how to capture their partial generality.

Chomsky himself seems to have reverted to his earlier view of the lexicon as simply a repository of irregularity, or of "syntactic atoms," and he has subsequently paid the lexicon little attention. Berwick and *(Continued)*

It should be added that limited productivity is usually considered a pet problem of morphology. However, it is also found in phrasal syntax, in constructions like *day after day* and *such a story*, as we will see in section 8.1.

Problem 2: Complex forms without lexical bases. Less attention has been paid in the literature to complex items with a nonword base—so-called bound roots or cranberry morphs, as in (9).

(9)   a. *Compounds:* cranberry, iceberg, nightmare, nickname, cobweb
      b. *Derived forms:* commotion, tradition, scrumptious, impetuous, modify, ramify
      c. *Inflected forms:* scads of X, oodles of X

Such words are far from rare. English has hundreds of adjectives that end in *-ous* and lack a lexical base, e.g. (10a), plus a huge number of such verbs that end in *-ate* (10b). Chomsky (1970: 220–1, note 37) lists dozens of adjectives in *-able/-ible* without lexical bases (10c).

(10)   a. delicious, gorgeous, hideous, meretricious, raucous, stupendous, supercilious
       b. abdicate, accelerate, accumulate, aggravate, agitate, alleviate, amputate, attenuate
       c. audible, compatible, delectable, eligible, feasible, irascible, incredible, indelible

These words conform to patterns that appear rule-governed. Yet they cannot be built by rule from smaller parts, since one of the parts has no independent existence—there is no base to build the word from.[8]

We reject the possibility that these words are simply monomorphemic, lacking internal structure. That would in effect say that *scrumptious, impetuous,* and *tedious* are as unsystematic as *crocodile, broccoli,* and *hurricane.* A possible alternative is that these words have lexically listed roots which are, however, constrained to appear with only one particular suffix. But the information in such an entry would just be an indirect and complicated way of listing the word itself, in effect: "I am a word pronounced *commote,* but I can only be inserted into a tree if I am adjoined to *-ion.*" We prefer simply to list the word directly. But then it is impossible to generate it by rule and thereby capture its relation to other *-ion* words.

Problem 3: Semantic idiosyncrasy despite formal regularity. Another well-known problem for generative rules is that they do not always account for the semantics of complex words that they (allegedly) generate. Consider the assorted examples in (11).

Chomsky (2016: 90) refer to these "atomic elements" as "the minimal meaning-bearing elements of human languages—wordlike, but not words" (which sounds a lot like traditional morphemes) and they say these elements "pose deep mysteries…. Their origin is entirely obscure, posing a very serious problem for the evolution of human cognitive capacities." A very curious position: the essence of language is Merge, but the things that get Merged, namely wordlike atomic elements, are a mystery?

   [8] Plag (2003) notes the importance of examples like these, in particular the difficulty they pose for morpheme-based views of morphology. Hay (2001) presents experimental evidence that words based on nonlexical roots are perceived as less clearly structured than words with lexical bases, a result congenial to our account. See further discussion of the processing of such words in section 7.5.

(11) a. ručka 'ballpoint pen,' '(door) handle' (lit. 'hand-DIM')   (Russian)
      b. telefoontje 'phone call' (lit. 'telephone-DIM')   (Dutch)
      c. finnes 'to exist' (lit. 'find-PASSIVE')   (Norwegian Bokmål)
      d. strings 'group of players of string instruments in the orchestra'   (English)
          (lit. 'string-PL'); note that a single player of a string instrument
          cannot be referred to as a *string*

In each of these, the morphosyntax and phonology are entirely regular: (11a,b) are diminutive nouns, (11c) is a passive verb, and (11d) is a regular plural. Therefore, on the traditional view, they should be generated by the relevant rules rather than being listed. But since their meanings are partly or fully noncompositional and cannot be predicted from the meanings of their parts, these words must be stored in the lexicon. Hence the theory is conflicted.

This issue appears in phrasal syntax as well. As observed in sections 1.1 and 1.3, an idiom like *call the shots* ('exert authority in choosing an action') looks syntactically as though it has been generated by the regular VP and NP rules. But because of its noncompositional interpretation, it has to be listed in the lexicon. Hence its apparent VP-hood can only be a convenient accident. Mainstream Generative Grammar has for the most part been evasive about this problem, despite its having been pointed out as early as Weinreich (1969) (see also van Gestel 1995). But idioms are no peripheral matter: languages have thousands of them.[9]

This problem with idioms leads to a further difficulty within morphology, raised already in section 1.1. The idioms in (12a) contain plurals of existing nouns but with an idiosyncratic interpretation; those in (12b) have plurals of bases that cannot be used in the singular, at least not with the same interpretation (what is a cahoot?).

(12) a. call the shots, raining cats and dogs, shake hands, a can of worms, music to
          my ears, go great guns, make ends meet
      b. make amends, odds and ends, give NP the creeps, in cahoots, best regards

These are fixed expressions and therefore must be stored in the lexicon; so the plural rule "in the grammar" cannot have generated them. Again, the problem is that as soon as an item shows any degree of idiosyncrasy, it has to be imprisoned in the lexicon, inaccessible to grammar, despite all its regular properties. (More such lexicalized plurals appear in Bauer, Lieber, and Plag 2006: 206.)

---

[9] Nediger (2017) is a recent attempt to treat idioms in Minimalist terms. If we understand the proposal correctly, the idea is that an idiom is first generated by normal syntactic processes, and then its literal meaning is replaced by a noncanonical interpretation, just in case the generated syntax and phonology match those of a stored idiom. In turn, the stored idioms consist of composed phonological, syntactic, and semantic structures—essentially the same information the PA would store in an idiom's lexical entry. (Chomsky (p.c.) has informally proposed a similar account.) What is not explained by this proposal is where these composed structures—complete with idiomatic interpretations—come from, since they are not generated by Merge, by hypothesis the sole source of combinatorial structure.

Problem 4: Stored regular forms. Think of all the phrases and even sentences that one stores in memory: poems, song lyrics, slogans, catch phrases, "prefabs" such as *I (don't) think (so), I'm (so) sorry, without further ado, there is a sense in which…*, and so on, plus even long memorized texts such as one's lines in a play or the entire Koran. Most of these memorized passages have internal structure that conforms perfectly to the productive rules of grammar. Yet the only way that generative rules can capture their regularity is to generate them from their parts rather than listing them in the lexicon.

The same issue arises in morphology. *Hopeful* has the components *hope* and *-ful*, and its meaning is transparently related to that of its components. If the grammar captures this relationship through a rule that generates *hopeful* from its components, the implication is that this word is not listed in the lexicon. Alternatively, if it *is* listed as a word of English (as we believe it is), its lawful structure cannot have been created by a generative rule. This recurring dilemma is a consequence of what Langacker (1987) calls the "rule-list fallacy": the methodological assumption that if something is generated by rule, it cannot also be listed.

From a psycholinguistic perspective, the problem becomes more acute. In production, does a speaker always build up complex words such as *hopeful* and *rapidly* from minimal stored parts? This might seem an attractive option in a system geared to minimal or efficient storage. But speech needs to be fast. If one wants to say *shoes*, it is surely quicker to pull up the complete word, should it happen to be listed, than to take *shoe* out of the lexicon and apply a plural rule to it. Moreover, nothing should prevent the mind from memorizing the outcome of a computation, especially if this item occurs frequently. Indeed, the experimental literature has amassed evidence for the listing of compounds, derivations, and inflected forms, including even regular inflections such as *cats* that are perfectly computable by rule. We return to the psycholinguistic issues in Chapter 7.[10]

In all of these scenarios—non-productivity, complex words with non-lexical bases, semantic idiosyncrasy, and stored regulars—the conclusion is the same: items with apparently rule-governed structure nevertheless have to be stored in the lexicon. But if the grammar and the lexicon are separate components of language (whether metaphorically in the theory or literally in the brain), storing items in the lexicon entails that they are not generated by the grammar. The upshot is that a huge proportion of morphologically complex patterns are disowned.

We now develop a schema-theoretic approach that remedies these problems.

2.5 Nonproductive schemas and the relational role

In order to capture nonproductive morphological patterns, we introduce **nonproductive schemas**, which do the work that the Lexicalist Hypothesis assigns to lexical redundancy rules. These schemas are not used generatively to produce novel forms. Rather, they

---

[10] The strongest and best-documented evidence for this position comes from surface frequency effects: the processing time of many complex forms correlates with their frequency, which is only possible if the complex forms are stored (e.g. Baayen, Dijkstra, and Schreuder 1997; Alegre and Gordon 1999; Baayen et al. 2002; Baayen 2007; Gagné 2009).

express the commonalities among items listed in the lexicon. The English A-*en* verbs and the Dutch -*(e)lijk* adjectives must be listed, so they fall under such schemas. The literature refers to the relationship between the listed instances and their pattern as "motivation" (e.g. Goldberg 1995, 2006; Booij 2017) and treats it in terms of "inheritance" (e.g. Pollard and Sag 1994; Goldberg again). For the moment, we keep the notion of motivation somewhat vague; we explore it in detail in Chapter 3.

To be a bit more concrete, (13) shows the relation between *hard* and *harden*, and (14) is a first approximation to the schema under which this relation falls—again a triplet of linked structures in semantics, syntax, and phonology. (We refine this schema in section 4.1.)

(13) Semantics: a. HARD_4 b. $[\text{BECOME}\,(\text{HARD}_4)]_5$
      Morphosyntax: A_4 $[_V A_4 \, \text{aff}_6]_5$
      Phonology: $/\text{hard}/_4$ $/\text{hard}_4 \, \text{ən}_6 /_5$

(14) Semantics: $[\text{BECOME}\,(\underline{X}_x)]_y$
      Morphosyntax: $[_V \underline{A}_x \, \text{aff}_6]_y$
      Phonology: $/\underline{\ldots}_x \, \text{ən}_6 /_y$

Paralleling our treatment of the -*ish* schema in Chapter 1 and the plural schema earlier in this chapter, (14) says that an adjective—whatever its meaning ('X') and whatever its pronunciation—can be the base of a verb that means 'become X' and that has the suffix /ən/ following the base. The suffix is constant throughout all instances, so it is encoded with a constant numerical coindex 6. This coindex denotes a relational link between the affix in the schema and the same affix in all its instances. As in the previous examples, the variable coindices x and y allow this schema to be related to any word such as *harden* or *widen* that has a corresponding pattern of coindexation. The variables thereby have relational links to each of their instances.

(14) is a nonproductive schema, and it functions in what we will call a **relational role**. It captures a pattern among items stored in the lexicon, but it does not "generate" them, and it is not expected to apply to every potential base. Rather, an item such as *crispen*, which *could* fall under the schema, simply is not listed and therefore is not used.

It is important that (14), like all the schemas we have seen so far, is in the same format as words: it is a lexical entry made up of linked pieces of semantic, morphosyntactic, and phonological structure. Thus we can dispense with a special category of lexical redundancy rules, with its own proprietary format. Nonproductive schemas are simply lexical items containing variables. However, this leaves open the question of how they can be distinguished from productive schemas, which are also lexical items that contain variables. We defer this question to section 2.7.

Actually, one might wonder whether the pattern could be more simply expressed in terms of the phonology shared across *harden*, *widen*, *darken*, and so on. The answer is that the commonality among them runs deeper than just the fact that they end with the same phonological string: they all are verbs with an adjectival base and an inchoative ('become X') meaning. The suffix is merely the phonological marker of that configuration. Schema (14) captures all the aspects of this commonality.

Unlike a generative rule, a nonproductive schema does not have to specify every property of the items it relates. It just picks out commonalities, whatever they may be. We saw this in the treatment of *-ish* words in section 1.4. The schema specifies that *piggish* means 'like a pig', but it does not specify that *piggish* means 'like a pig in sloppiness and greed' rather than, say, 'like a pig in color', nor that *childish* means 'like a child in (bad) behavior' rather than 'like a child in height.' These idiosyncratic aspects of meaning must be learned word by word; they are bits of structure that a traditional generative rule necessarily misses.

Nonproductive schemas thus give a way of dealing with the existence of nonproductive patterns (Problem 1 above). They also give us an approach to complex words that lack a lexical base (Problem 2). For instance, (15) shows the lexical entries of *gorgeous* and *tremendous*.

(15) Semantics: a. BEAUTIFUL_7 b. VERY LARGE_9
      Morphosyntax: $[_A - \text{aff}_8]_7$ $[_A - \text{aff}_8]_9$
      Phonology: $/\text{gɔɹdʒ əs}_8/_7$ $/\text{trəmɛnd əs}_8/_9$

These differ from *harden* in that *gorge (in the appropriate sense) and *tremend are not independent words. Hence they have no behavior in phrasal syntax that could be used to assign them to a syntactic category. We therefore notate their morphosyntax with a dash or a gap, i.e. unspecified. *Gorge and *tremend also do not correspond to any identifiable part of the words' meanings, so there is no interface link between them and the semantics. Thus the only parts of these words that are linked internally are the morphosyntax and phonology of the affix. As a result, the base is not a morpheme in the traditional sense of a minimal meaningful unit. However, the words are still legitimate instances of the *-ous* schema, which they fit in terms of phonology and syntactic category.

In fact, since there are many *-ous* words with nonlexical bases, this pattern might have a schema of its own, as in (16).

(16) Semantics: $\underline{\text{PROPERTY}}_z$
      Morphosyntax: $[_A - \text{aff}_8]_z$
      Phonology: $/\underline{\dots} \text{ əs}_8/_z$

This says that an adjective that expresses a property (as all adjectives do) can end in an affix pronounced /əs/, whatever the preceding phonology. Allowing this kind of schema solves the problem posed by families of words with nonword bases, as in (10). We take these cases up again in section 4.2.

2.6 Productive schemas used in a relational role

Let us explore further how a schema-theoretic approach deals with the difficulties encountered by generative rules. Consider again idioms. Because of their noncompositional meaning, they must be stored somehow in the lexicon. The Lexicalist Hypothesis, with its split between "syntactic" and "lexical" rules, therefore has to claim that they are accounted for in terms of the latter—despite the fact that they are bigger than words. Yet, as is well known, virtually all idioms conform to existing syntactic phrase structure rules (Weinreich 1969; Fraser 1970; Nunberg, Sag, and Wasow 1994; Culicover, Jackendoff, and Audring 2017). The issue extends to regular "prefabs" and other stored regular forms as well: If they are the product of lexical redundancy rules, why do they look just like freely generated forms?

In the face of this situation, Jackendoff (1975) argues that there shouldn't be two identical sets of rules, "syntactic" rules for ordinary phrases outside the lexicon, and "lexical" rules for idiomatic phrases inside the lexicon. He suggests instead that phrase structure rules can also double as lexical redundancy rules, expressing "passive" generalizations among items in the lexicon. Conversely, the lexical redundancy rules that capture the relationships among lexicalized compounds such as *salami sandwich* and *watchdog* can also be used creatively, to produce novel compounds such as *crab quesadilla*, *kimchi burrito*, and *guard llama* (we didn't make these up!).

The conclusion is that, although "the normal mode for syntactic rules is creative and the normal mode for lexical rules is passive," there is not "a strict division between phrase-structure rules and morphological redundancy rules ....The only difference between the two types of rules is...in their normal modes of operation" (Jackendoff 1975: 668). Aronoff (1976: 31) makes a similar point, focusing on morphology: "... while the rules as rules of word formation are rules for generating forms, the *same rules* of word analysis can be viewed as redundancy rules [our emphasis – RJ/JA]. They can be used to segment a word into morphological constituents, though the word may not be strictly generable from these constituents." Bybee and Slobin (1982) and Mohanan (1986: 53) also recognize this duality.[11]

Within the theoretical framework of the 1970s and 1980s, it was hard to make sense of this proposal, since generative rules and lexical redundancy rules were understood to be in different components of the grammar—and in some approaches, in entirely different formats. The present approach, however, encounters no such obstacle, because it treats all rules as schemas in the lexicon. We need only to add one innovation: *productive schemas can also function in a relational role.* For instance, Figure 2.1 shows a taxonomy of the uses of the regular English plural schema.

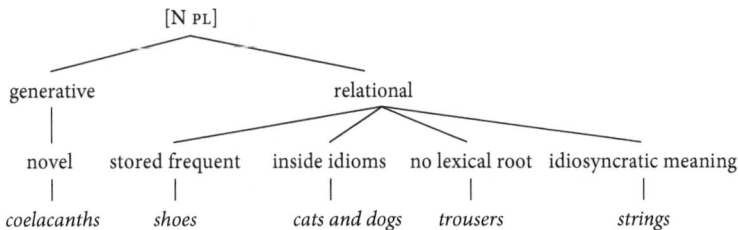

Figure 2.1 Uses of the regular English plural

---

[11] Alas, Halle (1973) does not recognize it. Observing that many morphologically complex forms must be listed in his "dictionary," he hesitantly concludes that "From the viewpoint of performance one might say that the role played by the rules of syntax and phonology differs fundamentally from that played by the rules of word formation. The knowledge represented by the latter might be said to be more passive than that represented by the former."

In its generative role, the plural schema unifies with singular nouns to generate novel plurals such as *coelacanths* and *wugs*. But in addition, it functions in a relational role: it motivates the pattern of perfectly regular but stored plurals such as *eyes* and *shoes* (if they are frequent enough). This solves the problem of stored regulars (Problem 4 above).

Next, recall that nonproductive schemas, which are used relationally, do not have to predict everything about their instances. We can now extend this property to productive schemas when they are used relationally. For instance, the plural schema motivates the morphological structure of lexicalized plurals like *trousers*, plural nouns with idiosyncratic meanings such as *strings*, and the idiomatic *cats* in *raining cats and dogs*. But it does not predict their meaning. Nevertheless, it is the same schema, just used in a different role. This solves the problem of regular forms with idiosyncratic interpretations (Problem 3).

Similarly, one encounters and coins novel compounds all the time. Hence the compound schema has to function in a generative role to create these new structures. But at the same time, there are thousands of lexicalized compounds that conform to the compound schema, yet have idiosyncratic interpretations (Jackendoff 2010 and references therein). These too fall under the compound schema, but in its relational role.

The same is true in phrasal syntax. As argued in section 1.3, the VP schema $[_{VP}$ V NP] is stored in the lexicon, and it is used generatively (i.e. productively) to create novel verb phrases, along the lines discussed in section 2.2. But it can also function relationally, encoding the syntactic pattern of lexicalized VP idioms such as *call the shots* and *shoot the breeze*. Again, it is the same schema, just used differently.[12]

2.7 How to distinguish productive from nonproductive schemas

To sum up our progress so far: The last three sections have shown that the schema-theoretic approach of Relational Morphology is not a notational variant of traditional generative rules, and that it is in fact superior in some nontrivial respects. To flesh out our analysis, we now have to address the question: How can we tell productive and nonproductive schemas apart? This question leads to the further question of what is meant by productivity. This section and the next three discuss these issues. Sections 2.11 and 2.12 step back and reflect on what the system looks like from this new vantage point.

At the moment we face a curious situation. The Lexicalist Hypothesis runs into trouble because it makes too strong a distinction between productive syntactic rules

---

[12] Spencer (2013: 414) says "It's extremely important for linguistic theory to recognize that the mechanisms and principles deployed for describing completely regular patterns [our generative function – RJ/JA] will not always be appropriate for describing completely irregular, semantically opaque patterns [our relational function]...." Similarly, Blevins (2006, 2016) makes a distinction between "constructive" theories, which assume procedures that resemble our generative use of schemas, and "abstractive" theories," which evoke our relational use. We are claiming not only that these mechanisms coexist, but that in fact they can use the *very same schemas*, just in a different way.

and nonproductive lexical redundancy rules: despite their similarity, they are in entirely different components of the grammar. Ironically, we now have the opposite problem: productive and nonproductive schemas are formally indistinguishable. They are both in the lexicon, in exactly the same format, as can be seen by comparing the nonproductive schemas (14) and (16) with the productive plural schema (3). Nothing in the formalism (so far) tells us that (3) can be used generatively and (14) and (16) cannot.

On the other hand, the formal similarity of the two kinds of schemas is actually an advantage. It means that nothing prevents a productive schema such as the plural from being used relationally as well, for instance applying it to the lexicalized forms *strings*, *trousers*, *shake hands*, *oodles*, and even the perfectly ordinary but relatively frequent *shoes*. The problem is only how to prevent nonproductive schemas such as [$_V$ A-*en*] from being used generatively.

An easy solution is to mark each schema with a feature that signals whether it is productive or not. Booij (2010) takes this approach. In a similar spirit, Lakoff (1970) made a distinction between "major" rules, which are productive, and "minor" rules, which apply only to listed bases. Depending on how productivity is defined, this feature might be categorical (±productive) or gradient (productive to such-and-such a degree). For the moment we assume it is a binary distinction; section 2.9 discusses some other options.

We propose a more fine-grained alternative: productivity is marked not on a schema as a whole, but rather on its *variables*. For instance, the variables in the plural schema (3) are to be marked productive (or **open**), and those in the [$_V$ A-*en*] schema (14) are to be marked nonproductive (or **closed**). In other words, productivity amounts to the openness of the variable, where we take openness to mean the degree to which it accepts new instantiations.

This sounds superficially like a notational variant of marking entire rules or schemas for productivity. But it opens up an interesting loophole: a schema might contain one variable that is open and another that is closed. And indeed such schemas exist. For instance, English has four different patterns for toponyms (names of geographical features), shown in (17a-d). The italicized words denote the type of geographical feature.

(17)   a. Arrowhead *Lake*, Loon *Mountain*, Wissahickon *Creek*, Laurel *Hill*, Sugar *Island*
       b. *Mount* Everest, *Lake* Michigan, *Cape* Cod
       c. the Indian *Ocean*, the Black *Sea*, the Hudson *River*, the White *Mountains*, the San Andreas *Fault*
       d. the *Bay* of Fundy, the *Gulf* of St. Lawrence, the *Cape* of Good Hope, the *Isle* of Wight

The schemas for these patterns contain two variable slots: one for the name and one for the type of geographical feature. The choice of name is completely productive: if we want to name a mountain for Morris Halle, we have no hesitation in calling it *Morris Mountain* (like (17a)) or *Mount Morris* (like (17b)). On the other hand, the variable for the type of geographical feature is not productive. One has to learn which words go in which patterns; for instance one would not say *Mountain Morris* (like (17b)) or *the Mount of Halle* (like (17d)). Hence the schemas for these patterns have one variable of each type, as shown in (18). We notate the open variable—the actual name—with a double underline, and we notate the closed variable—the type of geographical feature—with a single underline; *the* and *of* in (18c,d) are fixed constants. All four have the same semantics, just mapped differently onto syntax and phonology.[13]

(18)   Semantics: $[\underline{\text{GEOGRAPHICAL FEATURE}}_x; \text{Name: } \underline{\underline{Y}}_y]_z$

  a. Morphosyntax: $[_N \underline{\underline{N}}_y \underline{N}_x]_z$ [e.g. *Loon Lake*]
     Phonology: $/\underline{\underline{\ldots}}_y \underline{\ldots}_x/_z$

  b. Morphosyntax: $[_N \underline{N}_x \underline{\underline{N}}_y]_z$ [e.g. *Mount Washington*]
     Phonology: $/\underline{\ldots}_x \underline{\underline{\ldots}}_y/_z$

  c. (Morpho)syntax: $[_{NP} \text{Det}_{10} [_N \underline{\underline{N}}_y \underline{N}_x]]_z$ [e.g. *the Lehigh River*]
     Phonology: $/ðə_{10} \underline{\underline{\ldots}}_y \underline{\ldots}_x/_z$

  d. Syntax: $[_{NP} \text{Det}_{10} \underline{N}_x [_{PP} P_{12} [_{NP} \underline{\underline{N}}_y]]]$ [e.g. *the Gulf of Mexico*]
     Phonology: $/ðə_{10} \underline{\ldots}_x əv_{11} \underline{\underline{\ldots}}_y/_z$

Such a situation cannot be encoded by marking the distinction between productive and nonproductive on the schema as a whole. Nor is it very natural within the Lexicalist Hypothesis, in which the name is inserted "in the grammar" but the choice of pattern, determined by the type of geographical feature, is "in the lexicon."

The schemas in (18c,d) contain three types of constituents: constants, closed variables, and open variables. This distinction is also helpful in thinking about phrasal idioms, many of which also contain all three types. One such case, pointed out by Bybee (2010), is the idiom (or collection of idioms) in (19).

(19) $[_{VP}$ drive NP crazy/mad/insane/nuts/bananas/up the wall/out of Pro's mind/ off Pro's rocker/…]

The verb in this idiom is fixed, the direct object is completely open, and the final phrase has to denote some form of craziness. However, even within these constraints, the final phrase is not entirely open. For instance, although RJ recognizes *meshuga* and *(going) postal* as denoting kinds of craziness, his idiolect excludes *drive NP *meshuga* and *drive NP *postal* (even if they may be present in other speakers' mental lexicons). This suggests that the relevant variable is nonproductive—one learns the available instances one by one. So the schema looks like (20), with a fixed part (the

---

[13] The patterns in (17)-(18) offer another piece of evidence for the continuity of morphology and phrasal syntax, discussed in section 1.6. On one hand, (17a,b) look like compounds. For example, they can be preceded by adjectival modifiers—*beautiful Arrowhead Lake, forbidding Mount Everest*—so (18a,b) assigns them to the category N. On the other hand, (17c,d) extend into the phrasal domain, because they have a determiner that can be followed by a modifying adjective: *the majestic Hudson River, the dangerous Bay of Fundy*; moreover, the items in (17d) have an *of*-phrase, characteristic of phrasal NP structure. Hence (18c,d) assign these to the category NP. We are not forced to form the first two "in the lexicon" and the other two "in the grammar," or to derive any of them from the others. Rather, all four of the schemas in (18) are in the lexicon: (18a,b) are morphosyntactic; (18c), in which the two nouns still form a compound, is a mixed morphosyntactic and phrasal schema; and (18d) is purely phrasal.

verb), a productive variable (the direct object), and a nonproductive variable (the term denoting craziness).[14]

(20) Semantics: $[\text{CAUSE} (\underline{X}, [\text{BECOME} (\underline{Y}_y, \underline{\text{CRAZY}}_z)])]_w$
 Syntax: $[_{VP} V_{13} \underline{NP}_y \text{ AP/NP/PP}_z]_w$
 Phonology: $/\text{drajv}_{13}\underline{\dots}_y\dots_z/_w$

A similar case (even in its semantics, oddly enough) is the German idiom *jemandem auf Det X gehen* 'to get on somebody's nerves'. In addition to *die Nerven* 'the nerves', a wide variety of items can be found in the Det X position. Yet no overall semantic or formal pattern is discernible (though some words, such as *Eier*, appear to be euphemisms for certain body parts, and neuter nouns are rare). A selection is given in (21).

(21) German:
 Sie geht meinem Bruder auf… 'She's getting on my brother's…'
 – die Nerven 'the nerves'
 – den Sack 'the sack'
 – den Keks 'the cookie'
 – den Wecker 'the alarm clock'
 – die Eier 'the eggs'
 – die Ketten 'the chains'
 – den Docht 'the wick'
 – den Trichter 'the funnel'
 – den Zeiger 'the pointer/ the clock hand'
 – den Senkel 'the shoelace'
 – das Schwein 'the pig'

The verb *gehen*, the preposition *auf*, and the definite determiner are constants (aside from the determiner's number and gender values), and cannot be changed. The first NP slot (coindex *y*) is open: any semantically appropriate NP can fill it. The second NP slot, however, is a closed variable, with a learned list of possible fillers (coindex *u*). The schema thus looks something like (22).[15]

(22) Semantics: $[\text{CAUSE} (\underline{X}, [\text{BECOME} (\underline{Y}_y, \text{IRRITATED})])]_z$
 Syntax: $[_{VP} [\underline{NP}, \text{DAT}]_y [_{PP} P_{14} [_{NP, ACC} \underline{[\text{Det}, \underline{\text{DEF}}]}_w \underline{N}_u]] V_{15}]_z$
 Phonology: $/\underline{\dots}_y \text{ auf}_{14} \dots_w \dots_u \text{ ge}_{15}/_z$

In short, by marking each variable for openness or closedness, the behavior of a schema can be described in more fine-grained detail than by stating productivity as a property of the entire schema.

---

[14] We put off till Chapter 5 the question of how the verb in this schema comes out *drove* in the past and *driven* in the past participle.

[15] In (22), X in the semantics maps to the subject, and /ge/ in the phonology maps to the verb stem (coindex 15). We finesse the issue of verb position (V1, V2, or V-final); (22) notates the verb as clause-final. We put off the phonological realization of the gender- and case-marked determiner until Chapter 4, and that of the verb till Chapter 5. Notice also that unlike (19), where all the predicates in the list denote some form of craziness, none of the listed nouns other than *Nerven* have much to do with irritation. Hence the second NP is not coindexed to the semantics.

2.8 Do we really need nonproductive schemas?

In spite of our invocation of nonproductive schemas, one might still question the need for them in the theory. Why couldn't we get by with a simpler position, such as Pinker's (1999) "words and rules" approach, in which regular phenomena are indeed rule- (or schema-) governed, but irregular phenomena hang together only by association or analogy? This section addresses this question, offering two ways that nonproductive schemas are useful: first, as an aid in organizing storage in the lexicon, and second, as an aid in the acquisition of new instances. We defer to Chapter 7 a third way they are useful, namely for their role in language processing.

2.8.1 Nonproductive schemas in the organization of the lexicon

A word can be related to other words in endless ways—along one dimension with one word (e.g. initial syllable), along another dimension with another word (meaning), along a third dimension with a third word (final syllable), and so on. Schemas, on the other hand, codify a more systematic pattern of similarity among their instances. For a simple illustration, based on an argument by Albright and Hayes (2003), let us compare two possible toy lexicons, an "associationist" lexicon (23) and a "schema-style" lexicon (24). (Albright and Hayes's terms are "variegated similarity" and "structural similarity.")

(23) Associationist lexicon
      ("Variegated similarity")
      a. A B C
      b. D B C
      c. A D C
      d. A B D

(24) Schema-style lexicon
      ("Structural similarity")
      a. A B C
      b. A D E
      c. A F G
      d. A H I

In terms of raw similarity, each item in (23) shares two symbols with another item; furthermore, three items have A in first position, three have B in second position, and three have C in third position, and there are only four different units altogether, A through D. In contrast, the items in (24) all have A in first position, but they are otherwise unlike, and there are nine different units. And yet the structure of (24) strikes us as more cohesive. Although each item in (23) is like the others in one respect or another, and although those in (24) are overall less alike, the latter are alike in *exactly the same respect.* The similarity among the items in (24) items is structured or factorized (in the sense of Spencer 2010), and its structure jumps out immediately in intuition. This cohesion in (24) can be characterized readily with a schema [A X̲ Y̲], while (23) can only be characterized in terms of a looser family-resemblance type of organization.

Put in present terms, Albright and Hayes's point is that a schema explicitly captures relevant dimensions of similarity among a set of items, whereas an account that relies purely on associations among individual items may result in heterogeneous classes with no constant relation among their members. Albright and Hayes support their argument with a computational model of learning the English past tense system, showing that only a schema-based approach correctly captures the desired generalizations—even in a system riddled with irregularity. The broader argument is that schema-style generalizations are ubiquitous in human language, and hence that the brain not only tolerates but seeks such organization.[16]

2.8.2 Nonproductive schemas in acquisition

A further reason for allowing nonproductive schemas in the lexicon is their potential role in acquisition. Looking ahead to Chapter 7: An essential part of language acquisition is constructing (or discovering) the productive rules of the language. They are not present in the primary linguistic input. You can't hear variables! Rather, the procedure for learning morphology must involve observing some number of words with similar phonological and semantic structures, and formulating a hypothesis about the general pattern they instantiate (Culicover and Nowak 2003; Tomasello 2003).

What is the form of such a hypothesis? In a rule-based theory, the creation of a rule has to "cross over" from the lexically stored information to the grammar, taking on a different character in a different "place." Within the PA and other constructionist theories, the process is simpler: a hypothesis has the form of a tentative schema added to the lexicon, in the same format as words; its constants reflect the similarities among the words, and its variables reflect the differences among them. This is already an improvement.

Now here is a crucial point of logic. Learners have no way of knowing in advance whether a pattern they observe—and hence the hypothesized schema—will be fully productive or not. So they will inevitably create a lot of tentative schemas that fail the criteria for productivity, whatever these criteria may be (for suggestions, see sections 2.9 and 7.9). What happens to a failed schema? If there is no such thing as a nonproductive schema, it must be immediately expunged, since it's not a rule.

One might suggest that the learner holds off building a putative rule until all the evidence is in. This won't work. The learner can never know when all the evidence is in. There is no signal to flag the last piece of evidence. Moreover, there is no way for the learner to even identify evidence, without knowing what it is evidence *for*—namely a hypothesis, which in present terms takes the form of a tentative schema.

Relational Morphology offers a more nuanced story: Productive and nonproductive schemas are in the same format. If a learner extracts a pattern as a schema, it might or might not be a productive one, and the next job is to determine whether this

---

[16] This is not to say association-style categories are not also found, especially in semantics. The case for such "family resemblance" categories was first made by Wittgenstein (1953) in his famous analysis of the word *game*. Such categories also appear, for instance, in Rosch's (1978) treatment of prototypes, in Lakoff's (1987) "radial categories," and in Jackendoff's (1983) "preference rule systems." See also Jackendoff (2002: section 11.6.2) and references there.

schema is productive or not. This choice is not a transcendental distinction between a rule "in the grammar" and one "in the lexicon," as in the Lexicalist Hypothesis, or between a rule and the absence of a rule, as in Pinker's (1999) "words and rules" approach (a difficulty pointed out by Bybee 1995). It is just a matter of determining the proper diacritic on the schema's variable: closed vs. open (or, if gradient, degree of openness). Formally, this is a relatively small and local issue—which we take to be a good thing. Moreover, there is no need to discard failed hypotheses. Rather, we should expect to find the lexicon littered with failed hypotheses that still survive as nonproductive schemas. And if a schema is found to be productive, it still does not have to relinquish its status as a lexical redundancy rule. Rather, it retains its relational function of capturing generalizations among stored items.[17]

We conclude that there are interesting reasons to admit nonproductive schemas into the theoretical apparatus; further reasons appear in Chapter 7 and section 8.1. In particular, RM's uniformly declarative theory can still maintain the distinction between productivity and nonproductivity that the Lexicalist Hypothesis and the "words and rules" hypothesis are meant to capture. But the distinction is not whether there is a lexicon-grammar distinction, or whether there are rules or not. It is simply how the variables in the rule are marked for productivity.

2.9 More on productivity

We have been treating the distinction between productive and nonproductive as if it is straightforward. This section addresses some more subtle considerations.

The literature offers many definitions and many different criteria for productivity (cf. the discussions in Spencer 1991, Plag 2003, Barðdal 2008, and Haspelmath and Sims 2010). The measure we are most concerned with is how willing speakers are to extend the pattern to new instances (Aronoff 1976; Baayen and Lieber 1991; O'Donnell 2015). By a productive pattern, we mean one that speakers use freely and systematically in novel instances, and that hearers interpret without particular attention, for instance English regular plurals and the suffixes *-ly* and *-ness*. In contrast, patterns like [$_V$ A-*en*] in (5) and Dutch [$_A$ X-*elijk*] in (7) are not productive: despite their perfect regularity in meaning, speakers do not use novel instances such as *louden* and *kopelijk*, and hearers do not accept them.

In between the extremes of freely extendable patterns such as [$_N$ A-*ness*] and closed patterns such as [$_A$ X-*elijk*] are patterns such as *-ify* that lend themselves to occasional improvisation of new items, such as *dutchify* and *Trumpification*.[18] Lexicographers

---

[17] A similar point can be made with respect to historical change. When a pattern changes from productive to nonproductive, or the reverse, the grammar does not have to shift this pattern from one component to another. It only has to change the openness of the relevant variable.

[18] *Dutchify*: Coined by JA to describe RJ's putting Dutch-style handlebars on his bicycle, as in *send me a picture of your bike when it's dutchified* (p.c., April 17, 2014). *Trumpification*: From a headline in *The Washington Post*, September 13, 2016: *The Trumpification of Mike Pence*.

might call them coinages: they call attention to themselves, and hearers notice them ("Oh yes, clever!"). In contrast, a new use of a productive affix, say *picturesqueness*, is more likely (in the right context) to slide right by without drawing attention, and it probably would not be thought of as a coinage. For these in-between sorts of cases, it might make sense to talk about "partial productivity" or "degree of productivity." For now, we leave open the question of whether there is a strict distinction between completely open patterns, completely closed patterns, and these in-between cases; the differences may be gradient. Pending a resolution of the issue, we will reserve the term "productive" for the fully productive patterns and refer to the rest as "nonproductive."

Let us sketch some of the considerations that bear on the notion of productivity. First, it is not entirely a matter of frequency. On one hand, the *-elijk* words are highly frequent (both in type and token), yet the set is not productively extended. And on the other hand, consider the English pattern *(all) X-ed out* 'worn out from too much X', as in *all coffee'd out, knitted out, Olympic'd out, historied out* (the latter two encountered by RJ in conversation; for many more examples, see Hugou 2013). As these examples illustrate, this construction allows a wide range of novel instances. Yet it is highly infrequent: one encounters it perhaps two or three times per year, and, unless one is a linguist and makes a point of it, one cannot consciously recall instances one has heard previously. One thing that might aid in the retention of the pattern is the semantic and morphosyntactic structure it shares with the family of lexical items that mean about the same: *tired out, worn out, burned out, pooped out*, and so on. But the existence of this related nonproductive pattern does not predict that the pattern with a random noun or verb in the variable position is productive.

Another place where frequency and productivity can diverge is in *defaults*: patterns one follows if all else fails. A default need not be the most frequent option. Marcus et al. (1995) and Pinker (1999) argue that the German *-s* plural, despite its relatively limited set of instances compared to the other six possible plural patterns of German, is the default form and therefore productive—a form for which one does not have to memorize instances. This is what Corbett and Fraser (2000) call an "exceptional case default."[19]

Other factors also play a role in the intuitive notion of productivity. An important one is *transparency* (stressed by e.g. Clark 1993). In a transparent pattern, it is easy to identify the base of the derived word, and it is possible to determine the meaning, given the base and the context. Transparency is a prerequisite for free extendability: without it one could not understand a new use.[20] Still, transparency alone is not sufficient for willingness to extend a pattern's use to new items: a large proportion

---

[19] We caution that the analysis of *-s* as the default form for plural in German is not universally accepted (e.g. Köpcke 1998; Wegener 1999; Gaeta 2008).

[20] Transparency is sometimes a matter of the immediate context of utterance: consider the classic spontaneous example of *bike girl* 'girl who left her bike in the vestibule' (Downing 1977) or the one-off example *theremin filibuster* (uttered by S. Jay Keyser on November 1, 2016; RJ cannot recall the context, but it made sense then!).

of the *-elijk* adjectives are transparent and all of the A-*en* verbs are, yet these patterns are nonproductive.

Another criterion for productivity is the relative absence of exceptions and of competition from other patterns (for the latter, see Aronoff and Lindsay 2014). This criterion, sometimes called *regularity*, is a central preoccupation of Yang (2016), which we discuss in section 7.9.

Yet another factor in the intuitive notion of productivity is the relative breadth of the schema's variable: a pattern that allows a wide range of bases might be considered more productive than one with a narrow range. Barðdal (2008) calls this factor *generality*. However, generality and productivity are not always correlated. For instance, Dutch allows adjective-noun compounds, which present a large space of possibilities; that is, the pattern is quite general in Barðdal's sense. But the pattern has many fewer instances than the closely related German compound pattern; that is, it is less extendable (Hüning 2010).

Alternatively, a pattern can be limited in range (i.e. less general) but productive. For instance, the pattern of English denominal verbs in the limited space of fastener names, such as *tape*, *nail*, *glue*, and *screw*, was extended immediately to the novel fastener *velcro*. Moreover, a very general but not highly productive pattern may have within it a less general but fully productive pattern. For example, Hüning (2009) observes that Dutch noun-to-verb conversion is not especially productive, but any name for a sport can be converted into a verb, as in words like *tennissen* 'to play tennis', *volleyballen* 'to play volleyball', or *golfen* 'to play golf'. The same goes for computer-related activities such as *gamen*, *computeren*, *skypen*, and *whatsappen* (Geert Booij, p.c.). Thus these little semantic niches are productive, within a more general but less productive range of possibilities.

Similarly, anticipating the next section, a rule/schema that marks all words for female persons as feminine gender is more general than one that marks all names of domestic trees as feminine. Yet in either case, a speaker will extend the pattern to newly introduced words, so long as they conform to the schema's selectional restriction. That is, the schemas may be equally productive. In fact, a pattern's range may be so exquisitely narrow that all possibilities are exhausted by actual instances, for instance the pattern [X-*day*] for the days of the week. This pattern is exceptionless, yet non-extendable. For such cases, the notion of productivity ceases to be very useful.

The situation can be still more convoluted. For instance, there is an unlimited set of ordinal numbers ending in *-th* (e.g. *fourth*, *twenty-sixth*, *three thousand and seventeenth*, *eight billionth*), and speakers freely create new instances. But its variable is restricted to numerals, and in fact only fifteen forms have to be learned in order to master the pattern.[21] Hence, despite the fact that novel forms such as *seven hundred*

---

[21] *Fourth, fifth, sixth, seventh, eighth, ninth, tenth, eleventh, twelfth, -teenth, -tieth, hundredth, thousandth, -illionth*, and (for some speakers) the mathematical expression *nth*. RJ finds the potential word **googolth* very odd.

and twelfth are readily produced and accepted, it is unclear whether to call the pattern productive.

Finally, we suspect that the freedom to produce novel instances of a pattern is partly a matter of fashion. In Dutch, the *-fie* of *selfie* came to be reanalyzed as a suffix meaning 'photo of oneself with/at X', as in the attested examples in (25). (For many more, see the "selfictionary," http://ivdnt.org/onderzoek-a-onderwijs/webrubrieken/ gelegenheidswoordenboekjes/1045-selfictionary.)

(25)   Dutch:
       stemfie 'photo of oneself voting', from *stemmen* 'vote'
       fietsfie 'photo of oneself biking', from *fietsen* 'ride a bike'
       domfie 'photo of oneself in front of the cathedral', from *dom* 'cathedral'
       brilfie 'photo of oneself wearing glasses', from *bril* 'glasses'
       vliegfie 'photo of oneself, flying', from *vliegen* 'fly'
       reünifie 'photo of selves celebrating a reunion'
       panorafie 'photo of oneself in front of a panorama'

For a period of time, around 2010–2014, this pattern was highly extendable, especially in social media. It is our impression, though, that in more recent years the flood has reduced to a trickle. Nothing *structural* about the pattern has changed, but the novelty has apparently worn off. In contrast, *X-gate*, for a political scandal with cover-up, has held on tenaciously, if less frequently, since the 1972 burglary of the Watergate hotel by Richard Nixon's operatives.

A diagnostic for productivity in a corpus comes from Baayen and colleagues (Baayen 1989, 1992, 1993; Baayen and Lieber 1991): If a pattern is truly productive, that is, if speakers are making up new instances on the spot, it will have a large number of instances that appear only rarely, possibly only once. Based on this reasoning, the criterion for productivity is taken to be the existence of a significant number of hapax legomena (words that occur only once in a corpus) that exemplify the pattern in question.[22] O'Donnell (2015) refines this criterion, basing a measure of productivity on the frequency spectrum of an affix's instances. Section 7.9 comes back to these proposals.

All of these factors converge in distinguishing stereotypically productive patterns like the English regular plural from stereotypically nonproductive patterns like the *-th* in *warmth* and *width*. But, as we have seen, these factors come apart in a number of different ways when dealing with nonstereotypical cases. In other words, the intuitive concept of productivity is probably a "family resemblance" notion of the classic sort (see note 16). This should not be a surprise, given that lots of concepts are like this.

A major question that we leave open is how, over time, a pattern becomes productive in a speech community—or ceases to be—whether through competition from other forms (Aronoff and Lindsay 2014), change in fashion (as in the *-fie* forms), or

---

[22] Note, though, that multiple instances of a rare word in a corpus may well be independent coinages by different speakers. So counting hapaxes likely underestimates the amount of creativity going on.

other grammatical and social factors. We will not speculate on whether Relational Morphology can lend insight to this question.

2.10 An illustrative case: Grammatical gender

To illustrate the approach to schemas developed so far, we briefly consider principles that assign grammatical gender to nouns. In traditional morphology, gender hangs uncomfortably between the grammar and the lexicon, because of its mixture of systematicity and idiosyncrasy in many languages. The perspective of Relational Morphology helps resolve at least some of the tensions.

In the literature on gender assignment, "much scholarly ingenuity is displayed in suggesting rules" (Enger 2009: 1290). Many of them are plausible "core rules" in that they cover a sizeable portion of the noun vocabulary,[23] and in that they recur in various languages or reflect distinctions recognized in other parts of grammar. They may be based on semantics, phonology, or morphology. Well-known rules discussed in the literature (Corbett 1991) include the following:

(26) a. *Semantically based:*
Nouns denoting female persons are feminine.   (e.g. in Diyari (Pama-Nyungan), Austin 1981; Corbett 1991: 11)

b. *Phonologically based:*
Nouns ending in an accented vowel are feminine.   (e.g. in Qafar (East Cushitic), Parker and Hayward 1985; Corbett 1991: 51)

c. *Morphologically based:*
Nouns belonging to inflectional class I are masculine.   (e.g. in Russian, Corbett 1991: 36)

In all three cases, the properties involved are straightforward and general; the rule covers a substantial number of nouns, especially when paired with a default rule accounting for the remainder.

At the other end of the spectrum, we find rules that Enger (2009) terms "crazy rules." Here are some of his examples, all semantically based:

(27) a. Nouns denoting dairy products are masculine in Norwegian.
b. Nouns denoting domestic trees are feminine in Scandinavian.
c. Nouns denoting alcoholic drinks tend to be masculine in German (though *Bier* 'beer' is neuter, and *Piña colada* and *Margarita* are feminine for phonological reasons)

---

[23] Enger (2009: 1290) formulates this criterion in a different way: "A plausible rule should cover a reasonable share of the possible candidate nouns." However, it is possible for a rule to cover most or all of its candidate instances and still be questionable. For example, the names of the seasons are masculine in German almost without exception (including the lesser-used word *Lenz* 'spring', but excluding the compound *Frühjahr* 'spring', which is neuter due to its second constituent). Yet the pattern involves only half a dozen nouns at most, and therefore a rule would be of doubtful generality, much like the days of the week and the ordinal numbers mentioned in the previous section.

d. Nouns denoting "functional hollows" (whatever they are) are neuter in German.

e. Nouns denoting cars are feminine in Italian.

f. Nouns denoting phenomena that naturally occur pair-wise are feminine in Norwegian.

Rules of this type are sometimes found in pedagogical grammars, and also in the linguistic literature; famous examples are Köpcke's (1982) account of German gender assignment and Tucker, Lambert, and Rigault (1977) on French. Such rules are language-specific and small in scope, and they involve properties that are not commonly found relevant in grammar. Hence their status has met with doubt. Do speakers actually internalize such rules? How can they be acquired when they are based on generalizations that might be quite irrelevant to children (Comrie 1999; Plaster and Polinsky 2010)? The concern is often raised that such rules amount to "postfactum rationalizations" (Comrie 1999: 461), devoid of psychological reality.

In the context of the PA and Relational Morphology, the issues appear in a different light. Since gender is a lexical feature, we can assume it is stored within the morpho-syntax of the noun's lexical entry. Still, the generalizations of gender assignment can be captured by schemas. For instance, productive schemas encoding (26a,b) would look like (28a,b) respectively. (A treatment of (26c) depends on a treatment of inflectional classes, which we develop in Chapter 5.) The double underlines indicate that the patterns are productive.

(28) a. Semantics: $[\underline{\underline{\text{PERSON; FEMALE}}}]_x$
     Morphosyntax: $[\underline{\underline{\text{N}}}, \text{FEM}]_x$
 b. Morphosyntax: $[\underline{\underline{\text{N}}}, \text{FEM}]_y$
    Phonology: $/[_\omega \underline{\underline{\dots [\text{V}, +\text{stress}]}}]/_y$

The "crazy rules" in (27) would look just the same as (28a), except that their semantics would be far more limiting and eccentric, and perhaps their variables would be nonproductive.

Now consider how these schemas are used. Since gender is stored lexically on nouns, gender schemas rarely are called upon to assign gender to novel items; the main occasions are genderless loanwords and neologisms. However, in the present framework, gender schemas can still exert their influence through their relational function: they motivate the gender value of designated groups of nouns. Nouns can in fact fall under more than one schema, resulting in either competition or alignment. Generally, patterns have the tendency to align with each other. For instance, the phonological rules of Qafar largely align with semantics, such that nouns for female persons tend to end in an accented vowel (Corbett 1991: 52). Such patterns lead to greater cohesion across the lexicon.

The important point is that a schema's justification need not depend on its generality. Narrow and idiosyncratic generalizations like (27) may be just as valid as broad-based generalizations like (26). In some respects, schemas over restrictive domains might even be more reliable than global schemas, in that they might have fewer exceptions. As long as the schema helps to reduce arbitrariness in the lexicon, it is doing some useful work. In this light, it is probably a matter of psycholinguistics, not linguistic theory, to determine whether the brain actually detects "crazy" patterns like (27) and constructs schemas for them. Indeed, individuals may differ in (a) the richness of their vocabulary, and thus their potential for making generalizations, and (b) how adept (or relentless) their brains are at picking out and making use of such small and offbeat patterns. (On individual differences, see Chapter 3, note 18 and Chapter 7, note 19.)

2.11 Reframing the goals of linguistic theory: The Relational Hypothesis

At this point we have arrived at (or perhaps stumbled into) a radical conclusion, hinted at in section 1.1. We have encountered two kinds of schemas: productive schemas, which can be used both generatively and relationally, and nonproductive schemas, which can only be used relationally. It is logically possible that there also exist schemas that are used only generatively. Indeed, that is the way traditional rules are conceived. But in fact this is a highly unlikely situation. Why? First, it would involve either (a) erasing from memory all the instances that motivated such schemas in the first place, or (b) leaving the instances in the lexicon without acknowledging their generality, since by hypothesis these schemas cannot be used relationally. Second, it would require not remembering any of the words produced by the schema in its generative role, despite the fact that anything that is generated online can be committed to memory. Again, if these words are remembered, they too would have to fall under the schema's relational role. Hence our taxonomy of schemas can be framed as what section 1.1 called the *Relational Hypothesis*:

> *All* schemas can be used relationally. A particular subset of them, the productive ones, can *also* be used generatively.

In other words, we can think of productive schemas as "ordinary" schemas that have so to speak "gone viral."

This reframing leads us to a major reconceptualization of the linguistic enterprise. Humboldt's "infinite use of finite means"—Berwick and Chomsky's "Basic Property"— is only one part of the picture. It characterizes only the generative use of that particular subset of schemas that happen to be productive. For us, the relational use of schemas is not a relatively uninteresting add-on to the all-important productive grammar. Rather, schemas in their relational role encode all the partial regularities of the language, and even completely productive schemas—both morphological and phrasal—can play this role. Thus if anything is an add-on, it is the *generative* role of schemas, which is restricted to a subset of schemas in a speaker's repertoire. Only some schemas allow it. We might add this corollary to the Relational Hypothesis:

The generative property of language, the "infinite use of finite means," emerges from and rides on top of the system of lexical relations.

In this context, we return to Chomsky's (1965) methodological advice, cited at the beginning of this chapter: "…the discovery of peculiarities and exceptions.…is generally…unrewarding and, in itself, has…little importance for the study of the grammatical structure of the language in question, unless, of course, it leads to the discovery of deeper generalizations." We believe the Relational Hypothesis and its corollary are just such a deeper generalization. They undermine the overwhelming emphasis in linguistic theory on productive phenomena.

In short, instead of a powerful "generative engine" that operates on an unsystematic lexicon, the central construct of Relational Morphology is a highly structured lexicon, with a relatively thin overlay of generative capacity. To understand the generative aspects of language, then, it is necessary to understand the texture of the lexicon. As a bonus, though, the Relational Hypothesis opens up the whole domain of nonproductive patterns to systematic and principled investigation, fully integrated with productive phenomena. We take this to be progress.

2.12 Conclusions

Here is how far we have come: The Parallel Architecture leads us to view a lexical item as an interface construct, linking pieces of phonology, syntax, and semantics. This enables us to break down the distinction between words and rules. Traditional procedural rules are replaced by declarative schemas (a.k.a. constructions), which, like words, are pieces of linguistic structure. A lexical item is more schema-like to the extent that it contains variables. In this respect the PA concurs more or less with other constraint-based and constructionist frameworks.

This chapter has further explored the properties of schemas. Section 2.1 observed the tensions between the traditional lexicon-grammar dichotomy and the partial regularities endemic in morphological structure. Section 2.2 showed how declarative schemas plus the general procedure of unification fulfill the function of traditional generative rules, again concurring with the other constraint-based and constructionist theories. Sections 2.3 and 2.4 pointed out difficulties with the traditional notion of generative rules, some well-known, others less so. Section 2.5 then introduced the notion of nonproductive schemas, all of whose instances have to be listed in the lexicon. They function *relationally*, doing the work traditionally attributed to "lexical redundancy rules," thereby solving the difficulties that are posed for generative rules by nonproductive patterns and complex forms without lexical bases. Section 2.6 extended the relational role to productive schemas, allowing us to account both for idiosyncratic and regular stored instances.

Section 2.7 then asked how the distinction between productive and nonproductive schemas is to be formalized. We concluded that it is not encoded on the schema as a whole, but rather on its variables. In particular, a single schema may have a mixture of open and closed variables. This further unifies productive and nonproductive patterns, and allows us to account for even very idiosyncratic and limited patterns. We explored ramifications of this position in sections 2.8–10.

All these considerations led us to reframe the typology of schemas as the Relational Hypothesis: *all* schemas can be used relationally, but only some—the productive schemas—can be used generatively. This conclusion moves generativity from its traditional dominant position in linguistic theory to a more balanced partnership with lexical relations.

It therefore emerges that the relational use of schemas is an absolutely central notion of our theory. So far, though, we have not offered more than a rather vague account of this notion. Chapter 3 is devoted to fleshing it out.

3

Motivation in the lexicon

3.1 Lexical relations and motivation

Chapter 2 argued that, in their relational role, schemas capture generalizations among more highly specified lexical items. However, we said nothing very concrete about what it means to "capture a generalization"; we threw the term about rather loosely. This chapter develops an account of how a schema *supports* or *motivates* the structure of its instances, thereby capturing the generalization among them. We explore the notion of **inheritance**, often appealed to as an implementation of motivation, and we develop a number of refinements and extensions that better suit the needs of morphological description. We also work through the implications of this account of motivation for the form of lexical entries. The outcome is an interpretation of motivation in terms of **relational links**, which encode shared structure among lexical items.

The notion of motivation is invoked widely in Cognitive Grammar (e.g. Lakoff 1987; Radden and Panther 2004), Construction Grammar (Goldberg 1995), and Construction Morphology (Booij 2017). In fact, the term goes back to de Saussure, who introduces it as an important amendment to his more famous doctrine of the "arbitrariness of the sign": "Some signs are absolutely arbitrary; in others we note [...] degrees of arbitrariness: *the sign may be relatively motivated*" (de Saussure 1959 [1915]: 131; his italics).

In de Saussure's account, a sign is motivated by the existence of another sign that shares some of its structure, reducing its arbitrariness. For instance, the adjective *joyous* shares structure with the noun *joy* and with the family of -*ous* words. In present terms, *joyous* has relational links to *joy* and to the [$_A$ N-*ous*] schema; the latter captures what all the -*ous* words have in common. Thus no part of *joyous* is left unaccounted for. For a different case, consider an item like *scrumptious*, whose base is not an independent word. In de Saussure's terms, its suffix is motivated by the family of -*ous* words, but its base is arbitrary. In our terms, following the discussion in section 2.4, the suffix has a relational link to the [$_A$ – *ous*] schema (Chapter 2, ex. (16)), but the phonology of *scrumpt*- is unlinked. Still, *scrumptious* is less arbitrary than, say, *newt*, which does not share structure with anything else in the lexicon and hence has no relational links. While *newt* is shorter than *joyous* and *scrumptious*—and perhaps easiest to process—it is the least connected to the rest of the lexicon.

More generally, the idea is that if A motivates B, it does not necessarily *predict* or *determine* B, but it provides some hints toward guessing what B might be. For instance, as discussed in section 1.4, *pig* plus the affix -*ish* together motivate the meaning 'like a pig in some respect'—but they don't tell us in *what* respect, namely in sloppiness or greed. Similarly, *column* plus the affix -*ist* tells us that a columnist is someone who

The Texture of the Lexicon. First edition. Ray Jackendoff and Jenny Audring © Ray Jackendoff and Jenny Audring 2020.
First published in 2020 by Oxford University Press. DOI: 10.1093/oso/9780198827900.001.0001

does something that has to do with columns. But it does not tell us the whole story, namely that it's someone who *writes* columns for a *newspaper*. It could just as easily be an architect whose specialty is designing columns for buildings, where *columns* is understood in a different sense. These extra idiosyncratic bits of meaning do not have relational links to the schema, so they remain arbitrary.

Motivation has an important cognitive function. Since it decreases arbitrariness, it also decreases uncertainty: even if a word is not entirely predictable, parts of its form and meaning may make better sense in the light of other known items. If we believe that one of the main tasks of the mind is making sense of the world, then it ought to be a priority of the brain's to discover motivation in the lexicon—not to mention in other sorts of memory.[1]

3.2 Motivation as inheritance

Motivation is commonly explicated in linguistics in terms of **inheritance**: item B inherits some of its properties from item A. For instance, Goldberg (1995: 70, citing Lakoff 1987) says: "A given construction is motivated to the degree that its structure is inherited from other constructions." Motivation is seen here as proceeding from general to specific, from schema to instantiation. This conception of motivation appears also in Construction Morphology: "a word formation schema motivates an individual complex word to the extent that it predicts its properties" (Booij 2017).

The usual practice is to notate inheritance in terms of a taxonomy, in which inheritance passes down the branches. For example, Figures 3.1 and 3.2 are two (sort of common-practice) inheritance hierarchies in morphology, from Booij (2010: 26).

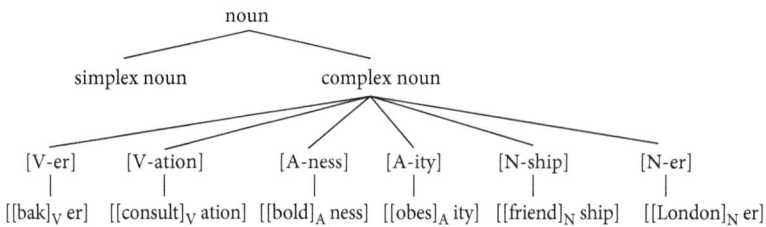

Figure 3.1 An inheritance hierarchy

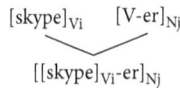

Figure 3.2 Multiple inheritance

---

[1] Another possible interpretation of "motivation" is diachronic. We still *hang up* a phone because telephones used to be hung on a wall; and the irregular alternation *sing/sang* is motivated by virtue of having been a regular pattern in some earlier stage of Indo-European. Many such cases are cited by Radden and Panther (2004). Although this is an important way of describing the development of language over time, it is not the sense of motivation we are concerned with here. Language learners don't know anything about the history of the language; they learn based just on what they hear. We are interested in the structure of what they have learned.

Figure 3.1 is meant to represent the fact that, for instance, *baker* inherits all the properties of agentive -*er* nominals, and these nominals inherit all the properties of morphologically complex nouns (such as headedness). In turn, complex nouns inherit all the properties of nouns, in particular their ability to occur in noun positions in syntax, and, in languages that mark case, their requiring case-markers. In Figure 3.2, *skyper*, like *baker*, inherits all the properties of agentive nominals ending in -*er*, but in addition its base inherits properties from the verb *skype*. This is a case of so-called *multiple inheritance*. (The verb *skype* in turn inherits from the noun *skype*.) All the derived words in Figure 3.1 of course inherit from their bases as well, although this is not shown.

In Construction Grammar, HPSG, LFG (Asudeh and Toivonen 2014), and the Parallel Architecture, not only words but also syntactic constructions can inherit properties from more general constructions. Figure 3.3 is an inheritance hierarchy for the English NPN construction (more detail in section 8.1.6; Jackendoff 2008); Figure 3.4 is a hierarchy for English wh-relative clauses (Sag 1997; see also Culicover 2013 for a reformulation).

Figure 3.3 says that the NPN construction is ancestor to a small list of idioms, plus five subconstructions with different prepositions. Instances include *day by day, dollar for dollar, week after week, student upon student*, and *face to face*. Each subconstruction has its own peculiar properties, but they share the same idiomatic syntactic form.

Turning to Figure 3.4, its details are not essential to our purposes, but the basic idea is that each of the three types of wh-relative clauses (in bold italics) inherits

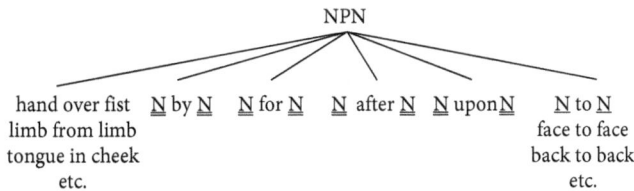

Figure 3.3 Inheritance hierarchy for the NPN construction

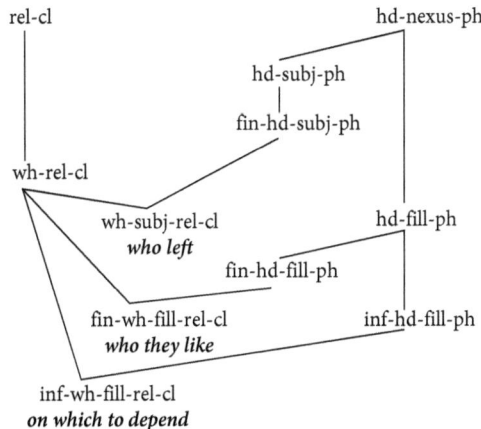

Figure 3.4 Inheritance hierarchy for wh-relative clause constructions

various of its properties from more general constructions. Like Figure 3.2, this involves multiple inheritance. (Not all the branches are shown. For example, all the constructions on the right-hand side of Figure 3.4 are ancestors to other constructions as well.)

One reason that inheritance hierarchies are attractive for morphology is that they are not domain-specific: they also play an important role in the organization of concepts in semantic memory. Figure 3.5 is an early example from Collins and Quillian (1969), hearkening back to Linnaean taxonomy. Figure 3.6 is a version of a similar taxonomy invoking multiple inheritance; for instance *dog* inherits from both *pet* and *mammal* (Jackendoff 2002: 185). (These hierarchies are clearly crude and are meant only to illustrate common descriptive practice.)

Figure 3.5 also illustrates the notion of default inheritance: one of the properties of (typical) birds is that they can fly. But ostriches and penguins, exceptionally, cannot. So the idea is that descendants inherit properties from their ancestors *unless marked otherwise*; the marked property overrides or supplants the inherited one.

More broadly, inheritance has been a preoccupation in psychological studies of concepts, where it is often characterized as an *IS-A* relation between nodes in a semantic network (Raphael 1968; Miller and Johnson-Laird 1976: 276; Smith and

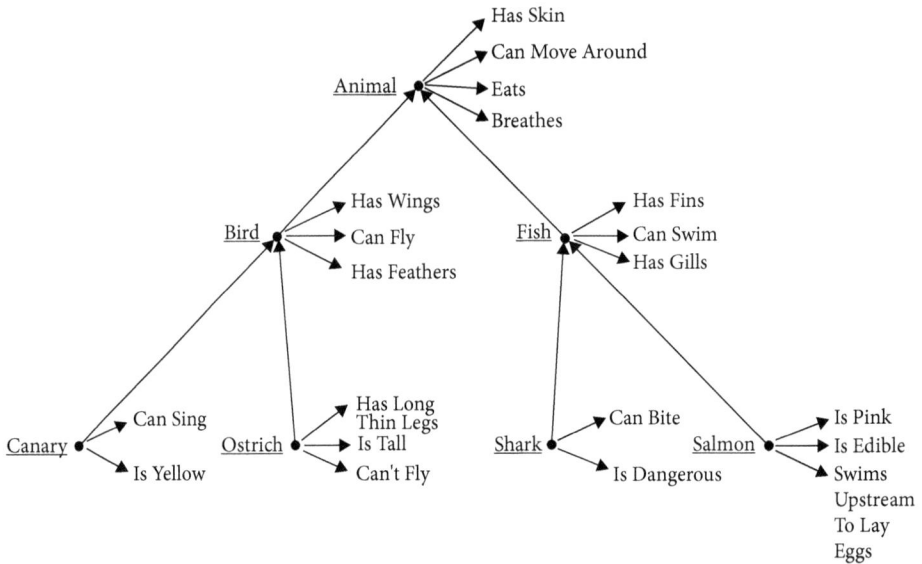

Figure 3.5 Inheritance hierarchy for concepts

Source: Collins and Quillian (1969)

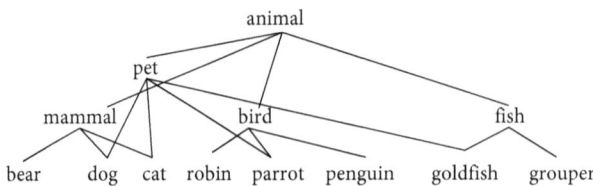

Figure 3.6 Multiple inheritance in animal concepts

Medin 1981; for a survey, see Murphy 2002, especially chapter 7). Inheritance has also played a major role in computational linguistics (e.g. Shieber 1986; Daelemans, Gazdar, and De Smedt 1994) and computer languages (e.g. Touretzky 1986).

Intuitively attractive though the notion of inheritance is, it raises some fundamental questions. What exactly does it mean to "inherit" a property from a higher node? Exactly what do the lines in Figures 3.1–3.6 signify? What is encoded in the nodes joined by the lines? Booij (2010) offers two possible answers, differing in the form they posit for lexical entries. The first of them is what Jackendoff (1975) terms an *impoverished entry theory*: "[t]he formal implication of using 'inheritance' is that for individual words only those properties need to be specified that are not inherited from dominating nodes" (Booij 2010: 25). The other alternative is a *full entry theory*: "the individual lexical entries are fully specified, and the inheritance mechanism serves to compute which of this information is redundant information" (Booij 2010: 27).

Along with Jackendoff (1975), Miller and Johnson-Laird (1976: 679), and Booij (2010), we will argue that full entry inheritance is superior to impoverished entry inheritance. We will show, however, that neither yields a full explication of motivation. We develop our own alternative, *relational motivation*, based on the notion of relational links introduced in the previous chapters.

3.3 Motivation as impoverished entry inheritance

In impoverished entry inheritance, descendants in an inheritance hierarchy systematically omit all information that can be supplied from their ancestors. This approach arises from the same impulse as the emphasis on productivity discussed in Chapter 2: the assumption that knowledge of language should be economical, efficient, and therefore reduced to a minimum number of symbols. For instance, Chomsky (1965) and Chomsky and Halle (1968) argue that a theory should be chosen in which the correct linguistic generalizations result in a reduction of the length of the grammar. Similar notions of simplicity and efficiency are widespread in cognitive science at large (for a survey, see Chater and Vitányi 2003). In computational linguistics, the formal language DATR (Evans and Gazdar 1996) involves a treatment of inheritance that "can be used to squeeze out redundancy from lexical descriptions" (DATR webpages, www.datr.org.uk). DATR in turn is used to formally implement the theory of Network Morphology (Brown and Hippisley 2012; Brown 2019), which is similarly committed to describing inflectional paradigms with a bare minimum of symbols (or nodes in the network).

A simple illustration of this type of approach: The word *baker* is a descendant of *bake*. Therefore its lexical entry does not list the phonology, morphosyntax, or semantics of *bake*; it simply needs a pointer to the lexical entry of *bake*. Furthermore, because *baker* is also a descendant of the [$_N$ V-*er*] agentive nominal schema, it does not list the phonology, morphosyntax, or semantics of the suffix either. Hence the entry of *baker* reduces to a sequence of two pointers, thereby simplifying the lexicon, as in (1).

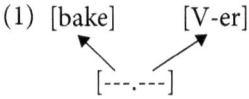

(1) [bake]   [V-er]

       [---.---]

Baker contrasts with a word such as *butcher* (2a), which inherits from the agentive nominal schema, but whose base is not inherited from anything; it is another case like *commotion* and *scrumptious*. And both *baker* and *butcher* contrast with *king* (2b), which has the semantics of an agentive nominal (parallel to *ruler* and *governor*), but whose phonology is completely arbitrary. Thus, given the rest of the lexicon, *baker* "costs" less—it requires fewer unpredictable bits of information—than *butcher*, which in turn "costs" less than *king*.

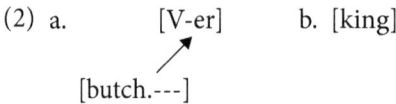

(2) a.   [V-er]   b. [king]

       [butch.---]

This notion of inheritance can be extended to the treatment of idioms and collocations in phrasal grammar. For example, *kick the bucket* inherits all its syntactic and phonological content from the lexical entries for *kick*, *the*, and *bucket*. The only thing it has to specify in its lexical entry is the meaning DIE, which overrides the inherited compositional meaning. Hence, it "costs" less than, say, *by dint of* 'because of', which contains the unmotivated item *dint*.

As observed in Chapter 2, this view of the lexicon as maximally nonredundant is urged, for instance, by Chomsky (1965) (citing Sweet and Bloomfield as antecedents), and by Chomsky and Halle (1968), who wish the lexicon to list only completely unpredictable information. For example, Chomsky and Halle observe that all three-consonant syllable onsets in English begin with /s/. From this, they conclude that it is unnecessary to actually specify the features of this position: *spray* can be listed as /Cpray/, omitting from the initial consonant the features [-voice, +continuant, +alveolar, +strident].[2]

Nonredundancy of the lexicon is also a desideratum in HPSG (e.g. Pollard and Sag 1987: Chapter 8), instantiated in terms of inheritance. Here is a representative quote from Pollard and Sag (1994: 36–7):

> …[a] lexical entry for the word *gives* might specify that it inherits all constraints imposed by the two generic entries *ditransitive* and *third-singular-finite*…; thus the only specific information about *gives* that has to be stipulated is the phonology of the base form, the semantic relation of its CONTENT value, and the assignment of semantic roles to grammatical relations.

---

[2] Just to be careful: Chomsky and Halle do not invoke the notion of inheritance per se. For them, an impoverished lexical entry is reconstituted by procedural rules rather than by features trickling down through an inheritance hierarchy. Nevertheless, what is crucial for them, just as for advocates of impoverished entry inheritance, is the assumption that anything predictable is to be removed from the lexicon.

The idea of a maximally nonredundant lexicon appears even in an attempt to incorporate word formation into the Parallel Architecture. Fernández-Domínguez (2016: 145–6) proposes that "in [the PA] the lexicon stores the syntactic, phonological and semantic information that cannot be recovered from word formation....The characteristics that can be reconstructed online will be dealt with by word formation, and those that need to be stored will be handled by the lexicon."

This treatment of inheritance is shared as well by Collins and Quillian (1969). For instance, the node for *bird* in Figure 3.5 does not list 'has skin,' 'eats,' 'moves,' and 'breathes'; and the node for *canary* does not list 'has wings,' 'has feathers,' and 'can fly.'[3] Similar notions of inheritance appear in computer science, in discussions and implementations of knowledge representation (e.g. Sowa 1991).

In this approach, then, inheritance can be thought of as a means of "data compression": the lexicon lists only what it is absolutely necessary to list (Chater and Vitányi 2003). Inheritance decreases the demands on storage, increases economy, and reduces redundancy. The links or pointers provide the explicit route by which descendants inherit information from their ancestors, and by which descendants can be reconstituted when the need for them arises.

We have identified a number of difficulties with (at least the strongest form of) the impoverished entry theory, in particular with the assumption that the lexicon is nonredundant, and that properties that can be determined by inheritance (or rules) from an ancestor are not listed in its descendants. (See also Bochner 1993: 30–9.) We caution the reader that many of our arguments rely on taking seriously the interpretation of lexicon and grammar as psychological constructs. They do not necessarily apply if the lexicon and grammar are understood as an abstract model of "competence," in which "economy" is only a matter of formal elegance.

Objection 1: Suppose *baker* is listed as in (1). In order to access it in production or comprehension, first its parts have to be accessed individually, and then they have to be assembled into the full word. Thus it should take longer to process *baker* than its base *bake*, and similarly for all other morphologically derived words. A multimorphemic word such as *adaptationist* should require multiple stages of lookup and assembly, while a monomorphemic word such as *affidavit* can be retrieved all at once. Similarly, since an English regular plural noun is completely predictable from its singular plus the plural schema, the impoverished entry theory claims that it is not stored (or at best is stored as a set of pointers). But, as observed in Chapter 2, psycholinguistic evidence suggests that speakers do store entirely redundant lexical entries for sufficiently frequent words. For instance, *eyes* is accessed just as fast as *eye*, perhaps because it is

---

[3] Collins and Quillian do however recognize that this is not always the case: "[P]eople surely store certain properties at more than one level in the hierarchy. For example, having leaves is a general property of trees, but many people must have information stored about the maple leaf directly with maple, because of the distinctiveness of its leaf. In selecting examples, such hierarchies and instances were avoided. However, there will always be [subject]s for whom extensive familiarity will lead to the storing of many more properties (and sometimes supersets) than we have assumed" (1969: 242).

more frequent. This could not be the case if it were always assembled online from *eye* plus the plural (Baayen, Dijkstra, and Schreuder 1997; Alegre and Gordon 1999; Nooteboom, Weerman, and Wijnen 2002; see also references in Chapter 7).[4]

Similarly, the impoverished entry theory predicts that an idiom such *kick the bucket* could not be identified without first accessing the lexical entries for *kick*, *the*, and *bucket*. An idiomatic reading therefore should take at least as long as a literal interpretation. But experimental results show that idiomatic meanings may actually be accessed faster than literal readings (in comprehension: Swinney and Cutler 1979; Gibbs 1985; Glucksberg 1993; in production: Sprenger 2003).

Objection 2: The impoverished entry theory results in a fragile system. Suppose the *animal* node or the [V-*er*] node is impaired, so that its features are not accessible—either temporarily, e.g. in momentary forgetfulness, or more drastically, as in aphasia. Then every node that descends from it is similarly impaired. In other words, whole families of concepts can be compromised by damage to one point in the network. To us this seems unlikely (though to our knowledge it awaits experimental confirmation).

Next come three related objections.

Objection 3: A schema such as [$_N$ V-*er*] can only be acquired on the basis of generalizing over some collection of individually learned instances. The schema's properties have to be derived from what the instances have in common, namely that they are all agentive (semantics), nouns (syntax), and end in /ɹ/ (phonology). A strict impoverished entry theory would demand that once the schema is created, the shared information immediately has to be erased from all the instances in order to eliminate their redundancy, perhaps by a "garbage collection" function that removes material that is no longer needed. We are not aware of any proposals of such a function.

Objection 4: A similar problem arises with learning new instances of an existing schema. In order to see if some new word (or concept) is an instance of a schema, it has to be encoded in a form that allows it to be checked against the properties stipulated by the schema ("Does this have wings? Can it fly?" "Does this end in -*er*?"). In other words, it has to look for the very properties that will be rendered redundant by an inheritance link to the schema. Again, a strict impoverished entry theory would require that once the link is established, the shared information is erased from the new instance. (Notice the parallel of this argument and the previous one to our argument about the acquisition of schemas in section 2.8.2.)

---

[4] Ironically, Collins and Quillian (1969) actually report experiments that confirm this prediction of the impoverished entry theory. For example, their subjects were quicker to assent to 'a bird can fly,' a property attached to the *bird* node, than to assent to 'a bird breathes,' which requires going up the hierarchy to the *animal* node. These results were later accounted for in terms of the psychological priority of basic-level categories (Rosch 1978; Murphy 2002).

Objection 5: Similarly, suppose one adds a new intermediate level in the network, say by discovering that there is a category 'mammal' that groups together some animals such as cats and dogs but not robins or goldfish. Then the content of each of its descendants (e.g. *dog, monkey, giraffe,...*) has to be changed, eliminating all the newly redundant mammalian features; and all the links between particular mammals and 'animal' have to be rerouted through the new node. Again, all this erasure and rewriting in the interest of preserving nonredundancy seems at least inconvenient, not to mention psychologically implausible.

Objection 6: Finally, the idiosyncratic properties of a daughter node often cannot be articulated without making use of information that is listed only in the mother node. For instance, going back to the quote from Pollard and Sag: "...[a] lexical entry for the word *gives*...inherits all constraints imposed by the two generic entries *ditransitive* and *third-singular-finite*... [T]he only specific information about *gives* that has to be stipulated is the phonology of the base form...and the assignment of semantic roles to grammatical relations." The difficulty is that semantic roles cannot be assigned to grammatical relations without appealing to the word's three argument slots, which by hypothesis are specified not in the entry for *gives*, but only in the entry for *ditransitive*. Specifying ditransitivity in the lexical entry of *gives* would be redundant. In other words, the entry does not have enough structure to allow a further property to be connected to it, because what it is a property *of* is only encoded on a higher node.

A more graphic example of the same problem comes from conceptual inheritance: RJ's concept of his late cat Peanut can't specify the color of her paws without linking it to her paws. But by hypothesis, the fact that she had paws is inherited from his concept of cats in general, and is not a direct part of his concept of Peanut. In other words, according to the impoverished entry theory, the concept of Peanut per se contains nothing that the color can be the color *of*. As Bybee (2001: 7) puts it (citing Langacker 1987 and Ohala and Ohala 1995), "if predictable properties are taken away from objects, they become unrecognizable." *Something* redundant has to be retained in the concept for idiosyncratic properties to be attached to.

Going a bit further afield, consider poetic forms such as limericks. A text counts as a limerick if it conforms to a particular metrical pattern and a particular rhyme scheme; in addition, a large subclass of limericks begin with the text *There once was an X from Y, who....* An impoverished entry treatment of redundancy in memory suggests that all redundant information in a memorized limerick should be absent from its memory trace, and inherited from the general limerick schema. As with Peanut's paws, it is hard to specify the exact form of such a denatured text. In particular, the rhyming parts of the second and fifth lines can be predicted from the first line. But how can these redundant parts be absent in memory? Even worse, the number of syllables in each line is supposed to be inherited from the schema; but how could the number of syllables be eliminated from the text? (See section 8.5 for a brief discussion of poetic schemas.)

These observations make it evident that the impoverished entry theory faces serious challenges, despite its intuitive plausibility (and its usefulness in computational applications).

We now turn to the alternative.

3.4 Motivation as full entry inheritance

3.4.1 Exemplar theories

We have just seen that the impoverished entry theory, by eliminating too much of lexical entries, encounters problems with respect to processing, acquisition, and the treatment of idiosyncrasy. On the opposite extreme are a variety of *exemplar* theories, which posit that one's brain stores every input one has experienced. The theories differ in how much is stored beyond individual tokens. Some approaches claim that token inputs are *all* that one stores (Latent Semantic Analysis: Landauer and Dumais 1997; Bybee 2001; Bybee and McClelland 2005). Some allow the inputs to be categorized or otherwise grouped (Smith and Medin 1981; Bybee 2010). Still others posit abstract schemas of our sort in addition to the mass of stored inputs (Bod 2006; Taylor 2012; Goldberg 2019).

A first response to these theories—and, we think, a plausible one—is incredulity. To be sure, memory capacity is prodigious. Not only does one store vast amounts of linguistic knowledge, one also recognizes vast numbers of objects, people, tunes, and geographical locations (see section 8.6). But do you store a memory of every cup of coffee you've ever drunk, of every doorknob you've ever turned, of every time you've shaken hands with someone? Or in language, every time you've said *good morning* or *the*? This seems wildly excessive.[5]

A second concern involves what might be called "granularity": What size units does one store? If one stores a memory of each cat one has encountered, does one also store a separate memory of its tail, so that one can form a category of tails, classified in turn as cat tails, lizard tails, peacock tails, and so on? Similarly, if one stores entire sentences and discourses, does one also separately store every single token of their words, every single token of their phonological segments, and/or every acoustic trace of the utterance, including speaker's voice and tone of voice, all in full detail?[6]

For those versions of exemplar theory that deny the existence of categories or schemas, there is a further logical problem: how does one store experiences? You can't simply copy sunsets or horses or vowels into your head. There has to be a format of

---

[5] Some advocates of exemplar theory, when pressed, claim only that every utterance one encounters "leaves a trace" in memory, leaving unspecified what that trace is. (Bybee 2010 might be interpreted this way.) If "leaving a trace" amounts to having some effect on memory, we agree: an input that matches a previously stored item affects that item's resting activation or "lexical strength" (section 7.3.1). But this is far from storing every exemplar individually.

[6] See McQueen, Cutler, and Norris (2006) for experimental evidence against exemplar theories of word learning. Further abroad, Smith (2014) develops computational simulations of category learning, comparing a prototype-based approach (a close analogue to our schemas) to an exemplar-based approach. On a variety of assumptions about category structure, the prototype-based approach was the more successful of the two, albeit moderately so.

storage—some repertoire of features and/or analog dimensions of similarity and vari-ation, in terms of which one's experiences are encoded. But a feature defines a category of things that have that feature; and a dimension of variation likewise is an abstraction over the instances. In other words, a category- and abstraction-free coding of experi-ence is impossible.

In the face of these problems, we set exemplar theories aside.

3.4.2 Full entry inheritance and redundant storage

We turn instead to a third possible treatment of lexical storage, the *full entry* theory. Unlike the exemplar theory, lexical items are stored only once. But unlike the impov-erished entry theory, lexical items are spelled out in detail, whether redundant or not. They contain enough information to enable them to be built directly into sentences, without any appeal to other nodes higher up in the inheritance hierarchy. The assump-tion behind this approach is that rather than seeking to minimize redundancy in the lexicon, the brain *welcomes* and *thrives on* redundancy; redundancy has the effect of making mental computation more robust (Libben 2006: 6).

This view of the status of redundancy in the brain receives support from the visual system, where for instance there are multiple cues for depth perception—how far away objects are perceived to be. These cues include lens accommodation (how much the lenses have to be squeezed to bring an object into focus), eye convergence (how much the eyes have to be crossed to align with the same object), stereopsis (how much the images in the two eyes differ), occlusion (what is behind what), perspective, and high-level knowledge of how large particular objects should be (Neisser 1967; Marr 1982). In many situations these cues overlap, complementing each other; in other situations perhaps only one or two are applicable. The result is a more flexible and robust system. And of course language contains similar redundancies, such as the possibility of signaling thematic roles simultaneously by word order, case-marking, and verb agreement, and the possibility of signaling voicing phonetically with voice onset time, length of closure, and length of the preceding vowel. Hence the redun-dancy countenanced by the full entry theory is arguably more "in the style of the brain" than the sparse lexical representations of the impoverished entry theory. (Van de Velde 2014 develops this point under the term "degeneracy," and he draws further parallels to nonlinguistic domains, including even basic metabolic functions such as thermoregulation.)

In the full entry approach, both *bake* and *baker* are listed in full in the lexicon, des-pite their considerable overlap. What it means for *baker* to inherit properties from *bake* and from [$_N$ V-*er*] is that it is redundant with these items. In these terms, the notion of "cost" of a lexical item is not to be cashed out in terms of the number of symbols it takes to specify it, as in (1)-(2). Rather, its "cost" is to be measured in terms of its arbitrariness, or the number of *nonredundant* symbols—or as Jackendoff (1975) puts it, in terms of its "independent information content," perhaps to be measured in bits. Section 3.8 briefly develops this notion of "cost"; Chapter 7 discusses other ways in which redundancy can aid in processing and acquisition.

A full entry theory of inheritance immediately solves the six objections to the impoverished-entry theory posed in the previous section.

Answer to Objection 1: Since morphologically complex entries and idioms are listed in full, there is no need to reassemble them from their parts in the course of lexical access. Therefore it is not logically necessary that a complex item is accessed more slowly than its base. In particular, as observed experimentally, if a complex item is more frequent than its base, it can be accessed at least as quickly. Moreover, as we will discuss further in Chapter 7, there need not be a conflict between interpreting *baker* via the whole word's lexical entry and interpreting it componentially in terms of *bake* and the *-er* affix. Both strategies can be going on simultaneously, as in the visual system, and since they yield the same result, redundantly, they can reinforce each other.

Answer to Objection 2: In a full entry theory, if a node is impaired or deleted, all its daughters retain their content, just less redundantly, and therefore less robustly.

Answer to Objection 3: A schema is constructed in memory on the basis of shared structure among previously learned instances. Once it is constructed, there is no need for a "garbage collector" to erase the information in its instances: this information remains as part of their full entries.

Answer to Objection 4: Similarly, when a new instance of a schema is being learned, its properties are checked against those of the schema. But there is no need to eliminate the properties from the instance once they are checked off. They are redundant and therefore "cost" less, but they are there.

Answer to Objection 5: Likewise, if a new intermediate node such as 'mammal' is added, nothing has to be deleted from its daughters; it simply increases their redundancy in the network. In particular, there is no need to eliminate the link between 'dog' and 'animal.' Rather, new inheritance links to 'mammal' are simply added, again increasing the redundancy in the network.

Answer to Objection 6: In a full entry theory, a lexical entry contains all the predictable structure that is needed to attach the idiosyncratic features. *Gives* is marked directly as ditransitive, so there is no problem identifying argument slots. Peanut's paws are included in the conceptual entry for Peanut, so their color can be attached to them. Nevertheless, because of the structure shared with the general concept of CAT, her paws are not completely arbitrary features of her anatomy. Similarly, memorized limericks are coded in full; there is no problem of how to evacuate all the redundant content and to restore it whenever the limerick is recited. Nevertheless, because of the redundant content, a limerick is less arbitrary and therefore easier to learn and remember than a random text of the same length.

3.4.3 How full should a full entry lexicon be?

In spite of its advantages over the impoverished entry theory, the full entry theory as formulated so far is somewhat too extreme. If full entries were uniformly and thoroughly full, this would entail that every bit of information about a lexical item must be stored, no matter how predictable. For example, every verb would specify not only its argument structure, but also the totally general fact that it requires a subject and that it allows every possible kind of (semantically acceptable) adjunct. Similarly, every noun would specify that it requires a determiner and allows prenominal adjectives, postnominal PPs, relative clauses, and so on. (A version of such a theory is proposed by MacDonald, Pearlmutter, and Seidenberg 1994, though apparently without noticing the consequences. See Jackendoff 2007a for discussion.)

In a different sphere, one might ask whether the full entry theory requires lexical entries to include phonological variants of the same word, say *working* and *workin'*, or, even more extreme, for the same word spoken with focal and non-focal intonation, with different accents, or even in different tones of voice.[7] Our intuition for both these cases is that some of this knowledge is general enough and easy enough to generate on the fly, and it need not be stored. (And even if it is stored, each version needs only to be stored once, not as a cluster of exemplars.)

A similar issue arises with conceptual inheritance. According to the full entry theory, Peanut's paws are included within RJ's conceptual entry for Peanut, even though having paws is a (default) property of cats in general. This gives the concept of Peanut something to attach the color of Peanut's paws to. On the other hand, Peanut has other properties that seem less likely to be included in RJ's Peanut concept per se, for example that she has a liver. This property feels intuitively like an inference about Peanut, derived from her belonging to the category of cats and ultimately to the category of animals. Pushing this point further, the fact that she'll fall if you drop her probably isn't listed in her conceptual entry; it is inherited from her being a physical object. This suggests that perhaps only the most useful and/or observable properties of Peanut are listed in her conceptual entry, while other properties may be derived inferentially. (Miller and Johnson-Laird (1976: 246) make a similar distinction between *A poodle is a dog*, which is relatively direct, and *A poodle is a mammal*, which has much more the flavor of an inference.)

Part of the way to escape these difficulties is to recognize the distinction between what *can* be stored and what *must* be stored. Anything at all *can* be stored, from a regular inflected form such as *eyes* to the peculiar way that RJ's childhood clarinet teacher pronounced the word *nuances* (*nuancences*), or to Henry Gleitman's theatrical pronunciation of the phrase *the sophisticated monkey* in an introductory psychology lecture. What *can* be stored but *need not* be are forms that are completely predictable from other lexical forms plus productive rules—that is, forms a speaker doesn't have

---

[7] There is evidence that inflected forms may differ in sub-phonemic detail from their bases, and that this information is stored (Kemps et al. 2005). But is this information stored with every word?

to learn. This includes all regular forms in an inflectional paradigm, all regular derivational forms (e.g. *large-toed*), all regular phonological and prosodic variants, and
phonological/phonetic details such as aspiration, insofar as they are predictable. What
must be stored are idiosyncratic form-meaning associations such as the association of
/kæt/ with the meaning CAT, instances of nonproductive schemas (*synonymous,
harden, refusal*), and instances of productive schemas that have idiosyncratic meanings (*honeymoon*, *shoot the breeze*). There are even cases in which one has to list idiosyncratic prosody, such as the specific low-high-mid intonation of the colloquial
American sarcastic use of *hello?* ('are you paying attention?').

Our sense, therefore, is that memory is heterogeneous; a properly nuanced full
entry theory should not insist on *everything* being listed in *every* lexical entry. One
can store information at any level of generality, from fine-scale phonetics to the
highest-level schema, including predictable properties and predictable forms. But
that doesn't mean that one *does* store it all. Rather, the lexicon stores some opportunistic mixture of specific and general items, redundant or not, and it tolerates
(and even welcomes) redundancy among items that share structure. Within these
parameters, determining what is *actually* stored by a particular individual or
by members of a speech community is more likely a matter for psycholinguistics
than for linguistic theory. (Di Sciullo and Williams (1987: 7) arrive at a similar
conclusion.)

3.4.4 Morphological problems with full entry inheritance

Leaving these general questions aside, section 3.4.2 has shown how a full entry theory
of inheritance is an improvement on the impoverished entry theory, at least for the
purposes of morphology. Still, the full entry theory too encounters difficulties that
stem from the notion of inheritance. Under the customary conception, inheritance is
an asymmetrical, "vertical" relation, in which (in the impoverished entry theory) the
ancestor contains information that "trickles down" to its descendants, or that (in the
full entry theory) renders its descendants partly redundant and hence less costly. For
instance, Radden and Panther (2004) analyze motivation as asymmetric, proceeding
from a "source" to a "target." But this conception is too limited for the work we wish
motivation to be able to do. Here are four objections, which pertain to impoverished
entry theories as well. The first two are perhaps only issues of terminological discom-
fort; the remaining two are more substantive.

Objection 7: There is a certain unnaturalness in the conventional inheritance hierarchy in (2) (*skyper*) or (3).

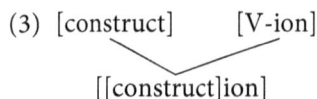

(3) [construct]   [V-ion]

         [[construct]ion]

This diagram suggests that *construction* is "below" the *-ion* schema, in the sense that it is an instantiation of the variable in the schema, and hence it is less abstract than the schema. (3) also suggests that *construction* is "below" its base *construct*. But *construction* is an elaboration of *construct*—it contains *construct* within it. One might therefore have the intuition that it should be "above" rather than "below" *construct*.

Furthermore, the inheritance relations in (3) are not the same as inheritance in conceptual hierarchies: A dog is a type of animal; dogs are a subset of animals; here verticality might be meaningful. But *construction* is neither a type nor a subset of *construct*, and it is not clear whether it ought be regarded as a type or subset of $[_N$ V-*ion*] (it's a subset of the set of *-ion* words, but the schema is not that set). In other words, on closer examination, it is not so obvious that the notion of inheritance in morphology should be entirely assimilated to conceptual inheritance.

Objection 8: Pushing the issue of verticality a little further, let us ask what motivates what. Traditionally, a schema such as $[_N$ V-*ion*] is thought of as motivating instances such as *construction*, *creation*, and *dedication*. But in the course of acquisition, the instances are the evidence for positing the schema, so in a sense the instances motivate the schema rather than (or in addition to) vice versa. Similarly, not only does *bake* make *baker* less arbitrary, the reverse is the case as well: *bake* is in a sense supported by *baker*. In other words, we would like a more neutral notion of motivation than the asymmetric relation implied by traditional inheritance.

Objection 9: The problem with verticality becomes more acute when we observe that many pairs of words such as (4) are related symmetrically, or "horizontally," or "paradigmatically" (where "paradigmatically" is understood in the broad sense, not restricted to inflectional paradigms).

(4) ambition ~ ambitious
    contagion ~ contagious
    ostentation ~ ostentatious
    sedition ~ seditious

The paired words share material, but strictly speaking it does not make sense to say that either one inherits from the other. Which is the "base" form, and which the "derived" form? Phonologically, neither is contained in the other. Semantically, one could gloss *ambitious* as 'having ambition'; but one could also gloss *ambition* as 'what one has when one is ambitious.' There seems to be no fact of the matter as to which inherits from which.[8]

There are of course similar pairs where both can inherit from a simpler base, such as (5).

(5) flirt ~ flirtation ~ flirtatious
    vex ~ vexation ~ vexatious

---

[8] Blevins (2016: 132) discusses other situations where there is no evidence as to the directionality of a morphological relation. He couches this problem in the context of "rules of referral."

One might therefore be tempted to claim that, by analogy, both *ambitious* and *ambition* inherit part of their meaning and pronunciation from an "abstract" or "virtual" lexical item **ambit*. This account is essentially in the spirit of Halle's (1973) proposal that there is a lexical item *ambit*, to which a "special filter" supplies the feature [−lexical insertion] or [+bound], and from which *ambition* and *ambitious* can be derived.[9] In addition to the theoretically questionable nature of this entry, there is the further question of its exact phonological form. Should it be *amb+ition*, *ambi+tion*, or *ambit+ion*? We would prefer to account for this case by weakening the requirement that inheritance is top-down, and by allowing items of equal complexity to motivate each other "horizontally." We develop such an approach in the next section.

For a similar case, consider an umlaut alternation like *goose/geese*. Given the very limited number of items that undergo this alternation, it is suspicious to account for this alternation in the style of *Sound Pattern of English*, with a rule or rules that convert *goose* into *geese* in the context of a plural number feature. Alternatively, traditional inheritance requires us to posit an abstract form *gVse* in the lexicon, from which the actual forms inherit everything but the frontness and rounding of their vowels, which are conditioned on plurality. Again, we would like to avoid such abstract forms wherever possible (which does not necessarily mean always! See Chapter 5).

Objection 10: Finally, there are cases where the "direction of derivation" is conflicted.

(6) a. assassin ~ assassinate
     b. chemist ~ chemistry
     c. critic ~ criticize
     d. linguist ~ linguistics

Morphologically, the second member of each pair is based on the first, e.g. *assassinate* is "built from" *assassin*. But the semantic relation goes in the other direction. An assassin is someone who assassinates people; that is, the noun's meaning is built on the verb's. If the morphology and the semantics were properly aligned, the noun would be **assassinator*. Similarly, a chemist is someone who does chemistry, a critic is someone who criticizes (the noun should be *criticizer*), and a linguist is someone who does linguistics (nonprofessional acquaintances sometimes want to call us *linguisticists*). In short, on the phonological and morphosyntactic planes, the second member should inherit from the first; but on the semantic plane, the first member should inherit from the second. (Booij 2019: 7 points out similar examples in Dutch.)

The relations in these examples pose a paradox for the standard notion of inheritance, in either a full or an impoverished entry approach. They cannot be captured with vertical links among items, because *assassin* is both "above" and "below"

---

[9] Such a solution is also proposed in essence by Baeskow (2004). A related claim is made by Distributed Morphology: bases are "uncategorized roots" which acquire a syntactic category only when they are instantiated as a word. In the present case, it is unclear what distinguishes √*flirt*, which has a realization as a monomorphemic word, from √*ambit*, which does not. We would surmise that the difference is that one is listed in the Dictionary and the other is not.

assassinate. A notion that incorporates "horizontal" inheritance can be more forgiving, as we will see in a moment.

The upshot of these last four points is that the standard notion of inheritance—even a full entry version—is too rigidly asymmetric to be able to express the full range of lexical relations. We would like a theory of lexical relations that does not require one element of a related pair always to be "above" the other, and that allows items of equal complexity to be related symmetrically.

3.5 Motivation as relational linking

Toward such a theory, we retain full entries in the lexicon, thereby gaining the advantages of the full entry theory over the impoverished entry theory. But, as proposed at the outset of this chapter, instead of using asymmetric inheritance relations, we explicate motivation in terms of the relational links introduced in Chapters 1 and 2: explicit associations between those parts of linked lexical entries that are deemed to be the same.

To make the proposal more concrete, here are lexical entries and links for the examples in (1) and (2). (We keep semantics very informal; more details in Chapter 4. In particular, we have omitted all the alternative readings of *-er*, which have their own schemas.)

(7) a. *bake*
Semantics: $[\text{BAKE (Agent: X, Patient: Y}_2)]_1$
Morphosyntax: $[_{VP}\, V_1\, NP_2\,]$
Phonology: $/\text{bejk}/_1$

   b. *baker*
Semantics: $[\text{PERSON [WHO BAKES BREAD/PASTRY]}_1\,]_3$
Morphosyntax: $[_N\, V_1\, \text{aff}_4\,]_3$
Phonology: $/\text{bejk}_1\, \text{r}_4\,/_3$

   c. *-er schema*
Semantics: $[\text{PERSON [WHO DOES X]}_x\,]_y$
Morphosyntax: $[_N\, V_x\, \text{aff}_4\,]_y$
Phonology: $/...{}_x\, \text{r}_4\,/_y$

   d. *butcher*
Semantics: $[\text{PERSON [WHO SELLS MEAT]}\,]_5$
Morphosyntax: $[_N\, -\, \text{aff}_4\,]_5$
Phonology: $/\text{bʊtʃ}\, \text{r}_4\,/_5$

   e. *king*
Semantics: $[\text{PERSON [WHO RULES COUNTRY]}\,]_6$
Morphosyntax: N_6
Phonology: $/\text{kɪŋ}/_6$

These entries reflect the intuitions behind (1) and (2). *Baker*, *butcher*, and *king* have similar semantics: they all denote a person who does something: bakes bread and/or pastry, sells meat, or rules a country. *Baker* has a relational link to *bake* (coindex 1). It also has links to parallel parts of the *-er* schema (7c): coindex 4 identifies the affix; coindex 1 matches *x* in the schema; and coindex 3 matches *y* in the schema. Hence *baker* is maximally motivated. In contrast, *king* (7e) has only the interface links notated with coindex 6; it has no relational links.[10]

In between is *butcher* (7d): it has a relational link to the schema (coindex 4 for the suffix again, and coindex 5 matching *y* in the schema). This much is motivated. But there is no base verb: **butch* is phonologically unmotivated, i.e. arbitrary. As with *gorgeous* and *tremendous* ((15a,b) in Chapter 2), we notate this with a dash where the base would be expected to be. Since this piece of the morphosyntax is not a word, it has no identifiable syntactic category and no independent meaning. Hence it has no interface link to the phonology and semantics, and no relational link to a base verb or to the verb position in the schema. Thus we can think of *butcher* as only partially parsed morphosyntactically, and its motivation is intermediate between that of *baker* and *king*.

Crucially, the relational links in (7) are symmetrical, so motivation is mutual. For instance, coindex 1 connects *bake* and *baker* nondirectionally; each motivates the other. The sense of directionality comes from the fact that the entire entry of *bake* is included in the entry for *baker*. But, as we have seen with *ambition/ambitious* in (4) and *assassin/ assassinate* in (6), complete inclusion is only one way items can be related.

This approach immediately addresses most of the objections to full entry inheritance:

Answer to Objection 7: The distinction between elaboration of a base and instantiation of a variable is inherent in the notation. *Baker* directly contains *bake*, with a common coindex, so it is an elaboration of *bake*, or "built on" it. *Baker* also matches the variable coindices in the *-er* schema and instantiates its variables. There is no metaphor of "up" and "down" in the relations among items.

Answer to Objection 8: There is no problem saying that a schema is motivated by its instances, especially in the course of acquisition. Nothing requires motivation to go from general to specific. Relational links go both ways, and hence so does motivation.

Answer to Objection 9: Pairs like *ambition/ambitious* can be related directly, without an intervening root from which they are both derived. We call such configurations **sister links**: there is no "mother" that they both inherit from. The coindexation notation enables us to be quite precise about the respect in which items are related. Here are first approximations to the entries for *ambition* and *ambitious*.[11]

---

[10] Alternatively, the semantics of *king* does have a relational link to that of other agentive nouns, but only on the semantic level, whether morphologically marked (*baker, trombonist, senator*) or not (*pilot, boss, nurse*).

[11] DESIRE is of course an approximation. Ambition is a desire *to do something*. And there is more: one may simply have a desire to visit The Hague; but if one has an *ambition* to visit The Hague, somehow more is at stake. A better gloss of *ambition* might be 'desire to do something that will increase one's (self-)esteem.'

(8)   a.   *ambition*
        Semantics: $[\text{DESIRE}]_7$
        Morphosyntax: $[_N - \text{aff}_9]_7$
        Phonology: $/\text{æmbɪʃ}_8 \text{ən}_9 /_7$

   b.   *ambitious*
        Semantics: $[\text{HAVING } [\text{DESIRE}]_7]_{10}$
        Morphosyntax: $[_A - \text{aff}_{11}]_{10}$
        Phonology: $/\text{æmbɪʃ}_8 \text{əs}_{11} /_{10}$

Let us unpack this notation. Each of the words has its own overall interface link: 7 for *ambition* and 10 for *ambitious*. They partially share meaning: coindex 7 serves also as a relational link across the semantics. The phonological bases also share the phono-logical string /æmbɪʃ/ (coindex 8). However, as with *butcher*, the base *ambit* is not a word, so it has no part of speech. Hence this part is morphosyntactically blank in both words, and it is unlinked to phonology and semantics. Finally, the affixes of the two words are linked by 9 and 11 to the schemas for *-ion* and *-ious* (not shown here) respectively.

The important point here is that relational links are more flexible than inheritance. In canonical cases such as *bake/baker*, the two are more or less equivalent. But in the case of *ambition/ambitious*, relational links make it possible to associate two words directly as "sisters" and to pinpoint their similarities.

For the moment we leave two issues open: the treatment of the *goose/geese* alter-nation (section 3.7) and the indeterminate segmentation of *ambition* and *ambitious* (section 6.8).

Answer to Objection 10: The flexibility of relational links becomes still clearer in the case of pairs of sisters with mixed directions of inheritance. Here are the entries for *assassin* and *assassinate* (with *very* approximate semantics).

(9)   a.   *assassin*
        Semantics: $[\text{PERSON } [\text{WHO MURDERS POLITICIAN})]_{13}]_{14}$
        Morphosyntax: N_{14}
        Phonology: $/\text{əsæsən}/_{14}$

   b.   *assassinate*
        Semantics: $[\text{MURDER POLITICIAN})]_{13}$
        Morphosyntax: $[_V N_{14} \text{ aff}_{15}]_{13}$
        Phonology: $/\text{əsæsən}_{14} \text{ejt}_{15} /_{13}$

The semantics of *assassinate*, coindexed 13, has a relational link to part of the semantics of *assassin*. Meanwhile, the phonology of *assassin*, coindexed 14, has a relational link to part of *assassinate*. (Coindex 15, which identifies the affix, is shared with the *-ate* schema, not shown here.) Beyond this, there is no need to say which word is derived from which; *assassin* and *assassinate* motivate each other.

To sum up so far, we propose to replace (or broaden, or tweak—take your choice) the notion of inheritance, and to explicate motivation in terms of shared structure— the parts of two or more fully specified items that are taken to be the same. Shared structure is encoded in the form of relational links. In the noncanonical cases of motivation seen in (8)-(9), the relational links and the coindexing notation make it possible to correlate phonology, syntax, and semantics independently. In more canonical cases in which one word is effectively contained in another, this approach replicates the directionality of traditional inheritance.

Going to the most mechanistic level of explanation, it is altogether unclear to us how shared structure is implemented in the brain. However, we do not consider this cause for despair. For one thing, the neural implementation of an impoverished entry lexicon is equally mysterious. But more fundamentally, at the time of this writing, it seems to be completely unclear to *everyone* how *any* sort of structure, shared or otherwise, is implemented in the brain (cf. Jackendoff 2002: section 3.5; Poeppel and Embick 2005). With no serious candidates on the horizon, the best we can do on this front is to be as true to the linguistics as we can, while keeping our eyes open for promising developments in neuroscience.

3.6 Do we need relational links?

An important question immediately arises in response to our analysis: Does the theory really *need* relational links such as those between *bake* and *baker* (7a,b)? Couldn't lexical relations be entirely implicit? That is, couldn't it be enough that the structure of *baker* incorporates the structure of *bake*? Why is it necessary for the brain to actually spell this fact out in a relational link?[12]

In response to these questions: We regard a relational link as an explicit association in memory that connects two pieces of structure that the mind *judges* or *considers* to be the same (consciously or unconsciously). Crucially, judging that two items are alike *adds information* to the lexicon. Like any other information added to memory, this information comes at a cost. But at the same time it also confers a benefit: it renders the lexicon less arbitrary, and, as we will argue, it facilitates lexical processing. What one knows about *bake* helps one understand and use *baker*, and vice versa.

To illustrate the effect of a relational link, we step outside of morphology for a moment and put relational links in a larger context. Consider Figure 3.7.

A single Necker cube is ambiguous between two readings. An array of two Necker cubes therefore ought to be four ways ambiguous. But it isn't: we can't help seeing the

---

[12] This is related to the question in section 2.8 of why we need nonproductive schemas. There we proposed that relational links are the mechanism by which schemas are related to their instances. Hence the question in this section is why such a mechanism is necessary.

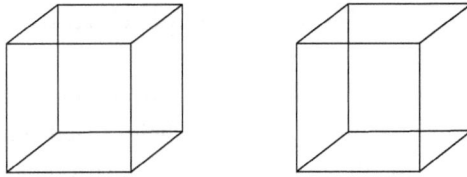

Figure 3.7 Two identical Necker cubes

two of them in the same aspect. If one switches, so does the other. (Or at least it's very difficult to disengage them.) Why should this be?

Culicover and Jackendoff (2012) propose that visual cognition connects the two cubes with (in present terms) a relational link, which says explicitly that they are the same. This link forces us to perceive their similarity not only in their surface patterns but also in the way they are understood. In other words, visual cognition encodes Figure 3.7 not just as two cubes but as two cubes *that have the same structure*. Their being the same is extra information about the array beyond the visible parts, in other words an explicit link—one that is not consciously perceived but which affects the character of conscious perception.

A second argument for explicit relational links pertains specifically to morphology. We will call it the Same Verb Problem. Consider the irregular verbs of English. The grammar has to specify their stem allomorphy, for instance that the past tense of *sing* is *sang*. The problem is that this allomorphy can cut across multiple lexical entries that contain what is apparently the same verb. The past tense of the main verb *take* is *took*, but it is also *took* in the past tense of idioms like *take part* and *take a chance*, as well as in the past tense of the verbs *undertake, mistake,* and *partake*. Similarly, the past of *do* is *did*, whether as a light verb (*did a dance*), a main verb (*did the job, did well on the exam*), or a meaningless auxiliary (*he didn't win*). So the question is: How does the grammar say that these uses in some sense involve the same verb? We need a way to say that although their meaning is different, not only their phonology but their *inflectional patterns* are the same. This requires an explicit link of some sort between distinct lexical entries, a link that records the fact that this parallelism in inflectional structure is principled. In the present framework, relational links serve this function: they connect the items in question directly by coindexation.[13] The overall point is that linked lexical items co-constrain each other's structure in the same way as the interpretations of the linked Necker cubes. Section 5.6 will show how this is accomplished.

Again, a relational link explicitly marks corresponding parts of two or more lexical items that are the same. Judgments of sameness, both conscious and unconscious, are not specific to morphology or even to language: they occur everywhere in cognition, including paired Necker cubes.

---

[13] These verbs present another situation in which asymmetrical inheritance is problematic: which use is the "basic" one from which the others inherit their inflectional properties? In the present approach, this issue does not arise, because relational links have no inherent directionality.

3.7 The same-except relation

But there is more to sameness than that. As Culicover and Jackendoff (2012) observe, along with an intuition of sameness comes a heightened sensitivity to differences between items that are *nearly* the same. They describe this phenomenon in terms of a domain-general cognitive relation that they call **same-except**.

Same-except is illustrated most easily in terms of visual perception. It creates intuitive judgments spontaneously, evaluating similar objects in terms of the properties they share (the *same*) and those they do not (*except*). Figures 3.8 and 3.9 illustrate two basic cases.

In Figure 3.8, the two wugs are immediately seen as the *same, except* for the presence of a head decoration on one of them. Culicover and Jackendoff call this case *elaboration*. In Figure 3.9, the wugs are seen as the same, except for their different head decorations. This case is called *contrast*. The same two cases of same-except can be experienced not only with objects, but also with actions, musical motives, and even foods ("These two bowls of soup taste the same, except this one is a little saltier"), poetry (two words rhyme if they are the same except to the left of the main-stressed vowel), and analytic argument ("This case is the same as that one, except for such-and-such a factor").

The same-except relation and its two cases were noticed by William James (1890, Vol. 1: 490–1), who characterizes them like this:

> In many concrete objects which differ from one another we can plainly see that the difference does consist simply in the fact that one object is the same as the other *plus* something else [elaboration – RJ/JA], or that they both have an identical part, to which each adds a distinct remainder [contrast – RJ/JA].

How is the same-except relation established? Gentner and Sagi (2006) characterize the process in terms of comparing the structures of the relata and seeking maximal alignment. Alignment pertains not only to the parts but to the relations among the parts. Thus two shapes do not count as the same if they consist of the same parts, but in a different configuration. This requirement extends also to "except" constituents: it matters that the different decorations on the wugs in Figure 3.8 are in parallel places, namely on their heads. If one wug's decoration is on its head and the other wug's

Figure 3.8 Elaboration   Figure 3.9 Contrast

Figure 3.10 Wugs with elaborations in different places

decoration is on its body, as in Figure 3.10, these are more likely viewed as independent elaborations rather than contrast. (Alternatively, they are seen as double contrast: different decorations in different places.)

Culicover and Jackendoff show that the same-except relation lies behind the semantics of a wide variety of linguistic phenomena, including contrastive stress, anaphora, VP ellipsis, gapping, and (of course) the meanings of words such as *same*, *similar*, *alike*, *except*, *aside from*, and *instead*. Here we wish to show how same-except can help characterize relational links more carefully. We will conclude that the kinds of relational links found among lexical items are not specific to language, but follow from more general properties of human cognition.

We first must compare same-except to *analogy*, which morphological theorists often cite as the relation that motivates new forms. Analogy is typically represented as 'A is to B as C is to D', for instance 'bird is to air as fish is to water'. In the usual examples, such as this one, A and C are unrelated. The crucial part in the analogy is the relation that the two pairs have in common, in this case, 'birds <u>move around in</u> air, and fish <u>move around in</u> water', and the point of the analogy is to evoke this unexpressed relation.

The same-except relation can be thought of as an extremely constrained case of analogy. For instance, Figure 3.9 could be described as 'The double curl is to the wug on the left as the single curl is to the wug on the right'. But there is more to say. First, the relation between the two wugs is that, apart from their respective head-curls, they are identical. Second, the common relation between each decoration and its respective wug is that the double curl is *a part* of the left-hand wug, and the single curl is *a part* of the right-hand wug. Third, these parts are *in the same place* on their respective wugs. This complex of relations appears in every case of same-except. An elaborative same-except relation such as Figure 3.8 is further constrained: there is a part on one wug with nothing in the corresponding place on the other. So same-except can be thought of as a variety of analogy—but of an extremely limited sort. We believe that this very constrained relation is sufficient for all the cases where analogy has been invoked in morphological theory.

The basic applications of same-except to morphology are simple. A pair like *construct* and *construction* is related in the same way as the wugs in Figure 3.8: *construct* is like the plain wug and *construction* is like the decorated one. Hence we can think of *construction* as an elaboration of *construct*: it has all the parts of *construct* plus something else. So elaboration captures the stereotypical cases of affixation, i.e. the syntagmatic dimension of morphology.

The contrast relation is clearest in the case of paradigmatic or "sister" relations. *Ambitious* and *ambition* in (8), like the wugs in Figure 3.9, share the same "body"—the meaning DESIRE and the phonology /æmbɪʃ/—but differ in their "decorations"—syntactic category and affix. Notice that the relation in Figure 3.9 does not presume the existence of an unadorned wug. This is consistent with our decision to reject an abstract *ambit that underlies both forms.[14]

In the pair *ambition/ambitious*, the phonological forms can be (fairly) neatly factored into the part that is the same, i.e. /æmbɪʃ/, and the parts that contrast, /ən/ vs. /əs/.[15] In other cases, such as *goose/geese*, the contrasting part is *inside* the part that is the same, perhaps a bit like Figure 3.11 where the difference between the two wugs lies within the body. Again, this does not presume the existence of an eyeless wug that shares exactly what the two have in common!

For such cases we introduce a special notation, which we will need extensively in what is to follow. In order to motivate it, we first return to the example of *sheep* from section 1.4. (10a) is the stem (which in English is identical to the singular), and (10b) is the plural (= chapter 1, example (7); see also section 4.3).

(10)   a. *sheep (stem)*   b. *sheep (plural)*

	a. *sheep (stem)*	b. *sheep (plural)*
Semantics:	SHEEP_{17}	$[\text{PLUR}(\text{SHEEP}_{17})]_{18}$
Morphosyntax:	N_{17}	$[\text{N}_{17}\ \text{PL}]_{18}$
Phonology:	$/\text{ʃip}/_{17}$	$/\text{ʃip}/_{17,18}$

Walking through this example:

- The three components of the stem are linked by interface coindex 17; the three components of the plural form are linked by coindex 18.
- In the semantics, coindex 17 serves as a relational link between SHEEP in (10a) and (10b).[16]

Figure 3.11 Internal contrast

---

[14] This analysis depends to some extent on context. If there were 100 wugs with different head decorations, we would be inclined to posit a wug schema with a variable in the place of the head decorations (if we only knew how to draw visual variables).

[15] To be slightly more careful: /ə/ in principle could count as belonging to the "same" part. It is only in the context of other *-ion* and *-ious* words that it is better to treat the schwa as belonging to the affix.

[16] One might ask why the semantics of the stem is not, say, [SINGULAR (SHEEP)], parallel to the plural. The answer is that SHEEP denotes a physical object. Since physical objects are inherently single entities, there is no need for an additional singular marking in semantics. However, the plural (10b) needs the PLUR operator in semantics in order to denote a collection of such objects.

- In the morphosyntax, coindex 17 serves as a relational link between the stem and the base of the plural.
- In the phonology, (10b) has an interface link 18 to its syntax and semantics, but it also has a relational link 17 to the phonology of the singular, marking the two as the same. There is no need for a "zero morpheme" in the phonology.

Now consider *goose/geese*. This pair has the same configuration as *sheep/sheep*, aside from one thing: the internal umlaut in the phonology. We notate this difference by enclosing in stars the parts of the sequence that differ. For a simplified example, (11a) and (11b) share a relational coindex 1 and therefore count as the same. However, they actually differ in that (11a) has *C* where (11b) has *D*. The stars pick out the difference.

(11)   a. $[A *C* B]_1$ b. $[A *D* B]_1$

Similarly, *goose* and *geese* count as phonologically the same, except for the vowels surrounded by stars.

(12)   a. *goose (stem)*   b. *geese*

	a. *goose (stem)*	b. *geese*
Semantics:	$GOOSE_{20}$	$[PLUR (GOOSE_{20})]_{21}$
Morphosyntax:	N_{20}	$[N_{20}, PL]_{21}$
Phonology:	/g *uw* s/$_{20}$	/g *i* s/$_{20,21}$

(12a,b) are entirely parallel in their coindexation to (10a,b), with the exception of the starred segments. Coindex 20 marks an interface link among the three components of *goose*. But it also marks a relational link between the phonology /guws/ in (12a) and /gis/ in (12b): it says the two words are the same, except that one has /uw/ where the other has /i/.[17]

For the purposes of morphology, we need to supplement elaboration and contrast with a third case of same-except, not mentioned by William James or by Culicover and Jackendoff: the instantiation of variables in a schema. For instance, consider the relation between *baker* and the $[_N V$-*er*$]$ schema. We don't have a convenient way to visualize this relation as we did for the other two cases: we don't know how to draw a variable part of a wug. From a formal point of view, though, we can think of the relation as a kind of internal elaboration: *baker* adds information to the features of the variable verb in the schema. Alternatively, we can think of their relation as a kind of contrast: *baker* and $[_N V$-*er*$]$ have the same ending and morphosyntactic structure, but *baker* has a real word inside of it, with a phonological realization and a meaning,

---

[17] And actually the difference is less than that, since they are both high vowels. In more detail, the stars would only have to mark differences in backness and rounding.

An alternative notation for the phonology in (12) would separate the relational coindices from the interface coindices 20 and 21, introducing a coindex 22 specifically for the relational link:

(i)   a. /g *uw* s/$_{20,22}$ b. /g *i* s/$_{21,22}$

See section 4.13 for further discussion of such notational alternatives.

where [$_N$ V-*er*] has variables. At least for now, it doesn't matter too much what we call it, so we will simply set instantiation apart as a separate case.

A schema itself also expresses a same-except relation, of course: it relates a whole family of lexical items, registering that they are the same in some respects—the constants in the schema—and different in others—the variables. Moreover, the variables have a definite location within the overall structure of the schema, so they determine that the contrasting parts of the instances are in the same structural position, as required by same-except. And, as observed in section 2.8.2, the acquisition of a schema depends on observing what putative instances have in common and where they differ—in other words, the same-except relations among them.

We conclude that relational links are not only explicit in memory, as argued in section 3.6: they embody a version of the domain-general relation same-except. Recall that part of the appeal of inheritance as an account of morphological motivation is its domain-general character. We are now suggesting that motivation in terms of relational links is equally domain-general. In this sense, the visual counterparts in Figures 3.7–3.11 are not just metaphors that help understand the application of same-except to morphology—they illustrate the *very same cognitive relation*.

3.8 The "cost" of lexical entries

We next must ask what relational links are good for. Just adding relations among lexical items is not enough: there must be a cognitive benefit to doing so. Intuition suggests three potential benefits: (a) they make items they relate easier to learn; (b) once learned, related items are easier to retain in memory; (c) an item with relational links is easier to retrieve in the course of comprehension and production. Here we briefly discuss a way of thinking about (b), the cost of lexical memory; we put off discussion of the other two until Chapter 7.

We can think of the cost of a stored lexical item as having two components. The more obvious component is the item's information content. Other things being equal, a longer item (say *salamander*) has more bits than a comparable shorter item (say *newt*), and therefore it should "use up" more space in memory. A second (possible) component is the cost of stipulating that there is such an item, whether predictable or not. We might think of this as an "entrance fee" or "cover charge." We do not know how to quantify this amount; if it turns out to be zero, that will be fine. We just don't want to *assume* that it is zero.

Relational links do not affect the "entrance fee"; this factor applies to each item individually. However, lexical relations can affect the cost of an item's content. Jackendoff (1975) proposes a metric of "cost" that considers not information content as such, but *independent* information content—the amount of nonredundant, unpredictable information in the lexicon. An extension of this proposal appears in Bochner (1993); a similar and statistically more sophisticated measure in terms of "entropy" is proposed by Moscoso del Prado Martín, Kostić, and Baayen (2004) and endorsed by

Blevins (2016), though only for inflectional systems. To put these proposals in present terms, the presence of relational links makes lexical items "less costly" because they mark structure as shared, redundant, and predictable. Pieces of structure connected by relational links are registered as the *same*: anything one knows about one of them, one automatically knows about the other. Thus the cost of information content is shared between them.

Under this conception, *baker* shares part of its structure with *bake* and *bakery*, and the rest with the *-er* schema, so for a first approximation, its cost is reduced by (some proportion) of the bits in the shared portions. *Butcher*, however, only shares structure with the schema (disregarding the verb *butcher*, for purposes of illustration). Hence its cost is the entrance fee plus the bits in *butch-*. *King*, like *newt* and *salamander*, shares with nothing (except in semantics), so its cost is the entrance fee plus all the bits in the word. This parallels the intuitions about cost in the impoverished entry theory, but in terms of different formal machinery.

For inflectional forms in a paradigm, predictability can be so high that their cost is reduced to zero or close to zero: if one knows there is a verb, one does not have to learn whether it has a past tense third person plural form—or if it's regular, what its phonological realization is (assuming that the paradigm does not involve arbitrarily assigned inflectional classes or any type of defectiveness). Yet, storing a regular item still involves an entrance fee, perhaps creating a pressure against storage, which has to be overcome by frequency. The result would be that only relatively frequent regular inflected forms are stored.

Another component of storage cost is the cost of relational links themselves. Section 3.6 argued that establishing a relational link between two items adds information to the lexicon; the fact that two items share structure is information about them that has to be acquired or computed. For instance, a student of RJ's once confessed that he hadn't realized that *torrent* and *torrential* are related; a more widespread case might be *heal/health*. Similarly, RJ's granddaughter at the age of three was reported to have had a sudden realization that *owner* is connected to *own*. These anecdotes suggest that a relational link doesn't come entirely for free. The benefit of paying this cost, of course, is a saving in the amount of independent information (or a lower entropy) in the linked items, so it can be worthwhile to establish a link. In addition, this cost might act as a pressure against "frivolous" links such as *rub/rubbish* that don't save much independent information. We will discuss some such cases in Chapter 7.[18]

A further piece to the story is the cost of a schema. Consider the *-er* schema. Its semantic, morphosyntactic, and phonological constants are shared with all its instances, so they come without cost. What is left is the "entrance fee" (it is a lexical item, after all), plus the cost of its variables (which are independent information content), plus the

---

[18] There is some evidence for significant individual differences in how readily people draw analytic connections among lexical items (Gleitman and Gleitman 1970; Reifegerste, Meyer, and Zwitserlood 2017; Dąbrowska 2018). This is reflected, for instance, in how sensitive they are to root frequency in accessing morphological complex items. These differences might be incorporated in the theory by setting the cost of a link differently: highly analytic people might have cheaper links, and therefore establish them more readily.

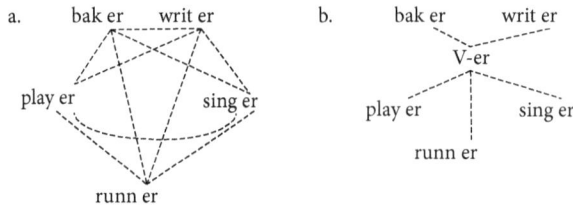

Figure 3.12 Relational links (a) without and (b) with a schema

cost of the relational links to its instances. However, the presence of the schema may alleviate the need to maintain relational links *among* its instances: instead of *baker* being directly related to *writer*, *player*, *singer*, and so on, and each of them being related to the others, as in Figure 3.12a, a comparable degree of motivation may be achieved by simply linking each of them to the schema, as in Figure 3.12b. The schema might then serve as a relational "hub." In this case, the overall cost of a schema might even be negative. We leave the question open.

Of course, even if a schema has a positive cost, it might nevertheless have benefits, in particular aiding processing and facilitating acquisition of further items, which we discuss in Chapter 7.

We submit that these proposals are speculative. The notion of independent information content, measured in bits, is at best a mathematical formalization of something about the mind that we don't yet know how to characterize more concretely. In fact, we doubt that the brain is overtly calculating independent content or entropy. We would prefer an account in which these effects followed implicitly from the architecture of memory. However, as with all other aspects of linguistic representation, at the present we have no way to connect this to actual neural storage and computation. Any sort of experimental procedure depends on activating lexical items one way or another, so it depends ultimately on ease of processing. Nevertheless, these factors seem relevant to us as groundwork for future research.

3.9 Conclusions

This chapter has explored the notion of motivation in the lexicon. It has often been assumed without question that motivation can be explicated in terms of inheritance hierarchies. Sections 3.2 and 3.3 demonstrated that the most popular version of inheritance, the impoverished entry theory, encounters a number of empirical and conceptual difficulties. Section 3.4 showed that these objections are met by another version of inheritance, the full entry theory, in which motivation (or "cost") is measured in terms of degree of redundancy rather than in terms of minimum description length. However, section 3.4 also presented further objections that pertain to both versions of inheritance, based on the necessary asymmetry of the relation 'item X inherits feature F from item Y.'

Section 3.5 proposed that these objections are overcome by the relational links introduced in Chapters 1 and 2, which establish symmetrical relations among items. They therefore provide a more suitably nondirectional account of motivation or nonarbitrariness. Sections 3.6 and 3.7 made the case that relational links constitute one embodiment of a domain-general relation, same-except. Hence they are not just something we (or nature) have made up in order to account for morphology. Finally, section 3.8 started to work out a more concrete measure of the benefits of relational links and schemas to the storage of lexical items, in terms of independent information content.

For the present, we have run this thread of inquiry as far as we can. Further progress in understanding motivation, we think, must lie in connecting it more closely to the character of neural storage—memory in general—perhaps through appropriate computational modeling.

Going back to the big picture, this chapter has deepened our overall view of knowledge of language. The lexicon is not just an unstructured list of exceptions. It is a richly textured network made up of fully specified items of all sizes, with relational links among them. This chapter has highlighted the nature of relational links, not only between words, but also between words and schemas; Chapter 4 will add relational links between two or more schemas. These results amplify the conclusions of Chapter 2: the productive uses of language are not a transcendentally different and "higher" form of linguistic knowledge; they are a natural outgrowth of the schemas and relational links in the lexicon.

PART II
USING AND REFINING THE TOOLS

4

Formalizing morphological phenomena

The development of Relational Morphology in Chapters 1–3 was based on a relatively small sample of morphological phenomena. Most of these involved a straightforward correspondence between semantics, morphosyntax, and phonology. For instance, *harden* is easily decomposed into *hard+en* in all three levels, in keeping with the traditional notion of the morpheme. However, we also began to dip into less canonical cases such as *sheep* and *geese*. Such mismatches between the structure of form and that of meaning are of course altogether routine in morphology. Accordingly, Chapters 4–6 look at a broader range of phenomena, canonical and noncanonical, representative of the sorts of issues that arise in morphological theory. In most of these cases, the complexity turns out to lie in the interface between morphosyntax and phonology.

This chapter deals primarily (but not exclusively) with derivational morphology; Chapter 5 addresses inflectional morphology and paradigms; Chapter 6 is about the effects morphology can have on the phonological form of the base, as in pairs like *harmony ~ harmonious*. In each case, the questions we address are:

- What is the lexical entry for such-and-such a morphologically complex word?
- What structure does it share with other lexical entries?
- Is there a schema for this shared structure?
- What tools do we need to add to the theory, if any, in order to account for the structures involved?

4.1 The simplest, most canonical cases

We begin by reviewing the simplest cases from Chapters 1–3. Here again are the lexical entries for *wide*, *widen*, *dark*, *darken*, and the [$_V$ A-*en*] schema. X in the semantics of (1b), (2b), and (3b) is the semantic argument position that comes to be occupied by the subject of the verb. The other semantic argument can be either a property ('wide') or a comparative property ('wider'); section 4.4 will add a causative option ('cause X to become wide'). We use angle brackets < > to denote optionality; to avoid typographical clutter, we omit underlining of variables except when they impose selectional restrictions and/or extend over multiple constituents, as they do in (3b).

The Texture of the Lexicon. First edition. Ray Jackendoff and Jenny Audring © Ray Jackendoff and Jenny Audring 2020.
First published in 2020 by Oxford University Press. DOI: 10.1093/oso/9780198827900.001.0001

(1)   a. *wide*   b. *widen*

     Semantics: WIDE_1 $[\text{BECOME (X, <MORE> WIDE}_1)]_2$

     Morphosyntax: A_1 $[_V A_1 \text{ aff}_3]_2$

     Phonology: $/\text{wajd}_1/$ $/\text{wajd}_1 \text{ ən}_3 /_2$

(2)   a. *dark*   b. *darken*

     Semantics: DARK_4 $[\text{BECOME (X, <MORE> DARK}_4)]_5$

     Morphosyntax: A_4 $[_V A_4 \text{ aff}_3]_5$

     Phonology: $/\text{dark}_4/$ $/\text{dark}_4 \text{ ən}_3 /_5$

(3) $[_V A\text{-}en]$ *schema*

     Semantics: $[\text{BECOME (X, [<MORE> PROPERTY]}_x)]_y$

     Morphosyntax: $[_V A_x \text{ aff}_3]_y$

     Phonology: $/ \underline{/\sigma [\text{-son}]}/_x \text{ ən}_6 /_y$

Reviewing the interpretation of the coindices in these examples:

- Coindex 1 in (1a) marks an interface link that ties together the three levels of the word *wide*. We'll call this the **outer interface link** or just **outer link**.
- Coindex 2 in (1b) serves the same function for the word *widen*.
- Coindex 1 also ties together the three levels of the base within *widen*. We'll call this the **inner interface link** or **inner link**.
- Coindex 1 additionally marks a relational link between the whole word *wide* and the base of *widen*, encoding the fact that they are the same. It will often be necessary to distinguish the base of *widen* from the word *wide* itself, and therefore we'll refer to the word *wide* as the **lexical cognate** or the **related free form**.
- Coindices 4 and 5 mark similar functions in *dark* (2a) and *darken* (2b).
- Coindex 3 in (1b) marks an interface link between the morphosyntactic affix and its phonological realization /ən/. This affix is the same in *wide*, *dark*, and the schema, so coindex 3 also marks a relational link between them. (We discuss in section 4.13 why coindex 3 does not appear in the semantics.)
- In schema (3), the **variable coindices** *x* and *y* mark interface links between the three levels of the schema.
- The underlined parts of (3) are selectional constraints on the base—structure that the base must satisfy. In particular, the phonology in (3) reflects the constraint that the related free form must be monosyllabic; its final phoneme is an obstruent that syllabifies with the affix.

The upshot of all this coindexing is that *widen* and *darken* are fully motivated. Their bases are related to free forms, and their affixes and their overall structure are the same as schema (3). Hence their informational cost in the sense of section 3.8 is basically just the "entrance fee" for the lexical entry—the knowledge that the word exists—plus the cost of their relational links to *wide*, *dark*, and the schema.

Notice that in semantics, the meaning of the affix is a function, and the meaning of the base is its argument. However, in phonology, the affix simply follows the base in linear order. This is a special case of the more general fact that hierarchical structure in semantics tends to be flattened out in phonology. (But see sections 4.7 and 4.11 for cases in which the affix cannot be linearized with respect to the base.)

Reviewing section 3.5, a similar pattern of linkage, but with a different semantic configuration, appears in the entries for *bake*, *baker*, *write*, *writer*, and the agentive $[_N V\text{-}er]$ schema.

(4) a. *bake*
       Semantics: $[\text{BAKE (Agent: X, Patient: Y)}]_6$
       Morphosyntax: V_6
       Phonology: $/\text{bejk}_6/$
   b. *baker*
       Semantics: $[\text{PERSON}^\alpha; [\text{BAKE (Agent: } \alpha, \text{Patient: INDEF)}]_6]_7$
       Morphosyntax: $[_N V_6 \text{ aff}_8]_7$
       Phonology: $/\text{bejk}_6\,\text{r}_8/_7$

(5) a. *write*
       Semantics: $[\text{WRITE (Agent: X, Patient: Y)}]_9$
       Morphosyntax: V_9
       Phonology: $/\text{rajt}_9/$
   b. *writer*
       Semantics: $[\text{PERSON}^\alpha; [\text{WRITE (Agent: } \alpha, \text{Patient: INDEF)}]_9]_{10}$
       Morphosyntax: $[_N V_9 \text{ aff}_8]_{10}$
       Phonology: $/\text{rajt}_9\,\text{r}_8/_{10}$

(6) $[_N V\text{-}er]$ *schema*
       Semantics: $[\text{PERSON}^\alpha; [\text{F (Agent: } \alpha, \ldots)]_z]_w$
       Morphosyntax: $[_N V_z \text{ aff}_8]_w$
       Phonology: $/\ldots_z\,\text{r}_8/_w$

Beginning with the semantics: The transitive verb *bake* (4a) has two semantic arguments, an Agent and a Patient (or Undergoer), which are to be filled in by phrasal composition.[1] In (4b), the Patient of *baker* does not have to be expressed in syntax, so it is an unlinked indefinite. The semantic head is PERSON; the function BAKE is a modifier; we notate its status by setting it off with a semicolon. The α superscript on

---

[1] Note that there are other affixes with the same phonology but different meaning, as in *diner* ('place where one dines'), *two-pounder* ('something that weighs two pounds') and *Londoner* ('inhabitant of London').

The stipulation of thematic roles is a notational convenience. In a more fully articulated semantic theory, thematic roles reduce to structural positions in Conceptual Structure: Theme is the first argument of GO or BE, Goal is the argument of the Path-function TO, and so on (see Jackendoff 1983, 1990, 2002, 2007b). Another approach invokes Dowty's (1991) proto-roles, in which thematic roles are treated as collections of features. Practitioners of other semantic frameworks are welcome to substitute their own notation, as long as it makes the requisite distinctions.

PERSON connects it to the Agent argument of BAKE, encoding the fact that they are the same individual.[2] This yields the desired reading: a baker is a person who is the Agent of baking.[3] *Write* and *writer* are related similarly. In schema (6), the semantics abstracts away from the content of the individual verb meanings, replacing BAKE and WRITE with an unspecified function F. The only thing the schema specifies about F is that one of its thematic roles is an Agent.

The coindexation in (4)-(6) parallels (1)-(3). Coindex 7 links the three levels of *baker*. Coindex 6 marks the outer link of *bake*, the inner link of *baker*, and the relational link between them. Coindices 10 and 9 do the same for *write* and *writer*. Coindex 8 links the morphosyntax and phonology of the affix within the two words, and also marks a relational link between them.

Turning to schema (6), the outer variable link (coindex w) connects the three levels of the whole schema, and also marks a relational link to *baker* and *writer*. The inner variable link (coindex z) connects the three levels of the base, and also marks a relational link to the bases of *baker* and *writer*. Hence the bases of *baker* and *writer* are motivated by their relation to the independent words *bake* and *write*, and their affixes are motivated by the $[_N \text{ V-}er]$ schema.[4]

Again, these are canonical cases: their semantic composition is mirrored in both their morphosyntax and their phonology. Patterns like these motivate the traditional conception of the morpheme as the "smallest meaningful unit." Relational Morphology, along with Construction Morphology, insists that if one wants to think of an affix as a "morpheme," it involves not just phonology, but semantics and morphosyntax as well, complete with variables, plus the links between the three, as in (3) and (6). If there is a "smallest meaningful unit," it is this entire complex.

4.2 Morphological complexity without full motivation

We now explore numerous variants of this canonical pattern, beginning with situations in which morphologically complex items are not fully motivated.

One relatively rare and little-remarked type of morphological relation involves pairs of words that are morphologically related, but whose relationship is unique. For

---

[2] This treatment is a semantic counterpart of traditional syntactic control, with α playing the role of PRO and its binding to a controller. See Culicover and Jackendoff (2005: 375) for discussion of this use of the α notation and its extension to binding more generally. An alternative notation, more in the style of formal semantics, would invoke lambda-abstraction: $\lambda x \exists y. [\text{PERSON}x \ \& \ \text{BAKE}xy]$.

[3] More precisely, a baker is a person who bakes things habitually or professionally. Following Busa (1997) and Jackendoff (2010), this can be encoded as an "action modality" applied to the event of baking. We will not formalize it here. This action modality is not a special property of *-er* nominals: it also occurs in the meaning of morphologically simple nouns that denote the agent of a particular activity. For instance, the difference between *slut* and *whore* is in whether the relevant activity is habitual or professional.

[4] This treatment is easily extended to compounds such as *truck driver*. In these cases, the semantics of the first noun serves as the Patient argument of the second, yielding the structure in (i).

(i) Semantics: [PERSON$^\alpha$; [DRIVE (Agent: α, Patient: TRUCK)]]

We conjecture that a treatment along similar lines can be constructed for Noun Incorporation (section 1.6).

instance, *laughter* is clearly related to *laugh*, both semantically and phonologically, and the *-ter* in *laughter* looks like a suffix. Yet this suffix (if that is what it is) is sui generis: it is found in no other words.[5] Here are a few such pairs; others appear in Raffelsiefen (2010).

(7) a. laugh ~ laughter
     b. hate ~ hatred
     c. compare ~ comparison
     d. bomb ~ bombard
     e. hero ~ heroine
     f. know ~ knowledge
     g. proud ~ pride
     h. bequeath ~ bequest
     i. expert ~ expertise
     j. Glasgow ~ Glaswegian

(8) illustrates the relation of *laughter* to *laugh*. It parallels precisely the relation of *widen* to *wide*. The only difference is that the lexicon contains no schema for $[_N \text{ V-}ter]$. Hence coindex 3 is only an item-internal interface link; this part of *laughter* is unmotivated. (For convenience, we restart numbering of coindices at 1, and likewise in subsequent sections.)

(8)   a. *laugh*
     Semantics: $[\text{LAUGH (Agent: X)}]_1$
     Morphosyntax: V_1
     Phonology: $/\text{læf}_1/$

                         b. *laughter*
     Semantics: $[\text{ACT-OF/SOUND-OF } ([_\text{LAUGH (Agent: INDEF)}]_1)]_2$
     Morphosyntax: $[_N V_1 \text{ aff}_3]_2$
     Phonology: $/\text{læf}_1 \text{ tr}_3 /_2$

Should *-ter* be considered a morpheme in the traditional sense? It's unclear—but there is no reason to have to decide. The main point is that *laugh* and *laughter* are related, but without the support of a schema.

In contrast, consider how this case would be treated in a more traditional framework. If the lexicon is regarded as just a "collection of the lawless," it cannot express the clear relation between *laugh* and *laughter*. To capture this relation, *-ter* could be treated like a morpheme on a par with, say, *-tion*. But it would have to be constrained to occur only in the single word *laughter*—it would be a sort of "cranberry suffix." Alternatively, one could devise a very narrow word formation rule that applies only to *laugh* and converts it into *laughter*. But such a treatment makes no sense: a rule that

---

[5] A pair with a nearly identical relation is *slay ~ slaughter*, with stem allomorphy. However, to contemporary ears, the noun *slaughter* is probably more closely related to the homophonous verb *slaughter*.

applies to just one item is no rule at all. By comparison, the RM treatment says just what needs to be said about this configuration.

Far more numerous than words with cranberry suffixes are words whose *bases* are cranberry morphs (a.k.a. bound roots). These came up sporadically in Chapters 2 and 3, and we review them here. English has hundreds of such items. (9) lists a very small selection, as well as a few examples from Dutch in (9f); many examples from German appear in Hüning (2018).

(9) a. scrumptious, jealous, gorgeous, impetuous, surreptitious, voluptuous, ...
     b. qualify, modify, ramify, petrify, magnify, ...
     c. commotion, contraption, ovation, duration, constellation, ...
     d. butcher, doctor, tailor, soldier, ...
     e. aggravate, irritate, expurgate, annihilate, separate, ...
     f. (Dutch) sprookje 'fairy tale' (*sprook), akkefietje 'tiff, chore' (*akkefie(t)), plunje 'clothes' (*plun), flensje 'small pancake' (*flens)

Although these words have recognizable suffixes (including the hugely productive diminutive *-(t)je* in (9f)), their bases do not have related free forms such as **scrumpt*, **qual*, **commote*, **butch*, **aggrave*, or **sprook*.

(10) shows how we encode *scrumptious*. (Parallel cases such as *butcher* and *gorgeous* appeared in sections 2.5 and 3.5.)

(10) *scrumptious*

Semantics:	TASTY_4
Morphosyntax:	$[_A - \text{aff}_5]_4$
Phonology:	$/\text{skr}\Lambda\text{mpt}\int \text{əs}_5 /_4$

Like all words with the affix *-ous*, this word is an adjective. As in previous cases, the outer coindex 4 links the three levels of the word together, and coindex 5 links aff to the phonology of the suffix. However, consider the base. Normally, the base's syntactic category matches that of the related free form. But there is no free form to which *scrumpt-* can be matched. Therefore, as argued in Chapter 2, it has no syntactic category either. In effect, this part of the word remains unparsed in morphosyntax. We notate this with a dash.[6] The upshot is that the phonology $/\text{skr}\Lambda\text{mpt}\int/$, lacking an inner link, is unmotivated, and lexical storage has to "pay for it." In other words, *scrumpt-* does not fit the description of a canonical morpheme. To use Anderson's (1992) term, *scrumptious* is partly "a-morphous"—it is only partly structured.

(11) (= (16) in Chapter 2) is the schema that motivates the affix shared by *scrumptious* and the other items in (9a).

---

[6] Booij (2010: 30) would notate the morphosyntax of *scrumptious*, for example, as $[_A \text{ X aff}]$. We are reserving this notation for cases like *-ery*, which (typically) requires a base with a lexical cognate but which is indifferent as to its category (see (58) in section 4.9.2). In contrast, (11) notates a situation in which the base has no lexical cognate at all.

(11) $[_A$ -ous] *schema*

    Semantics: $[\underline{\text{PROPERTY}}]_y$

    Morphosyntax: $[_A - \text{aff}_5]_y$

    Phonology: $/\ldots \text{əs}_5/_y$

The schema, like its instances in (9a), has no inner link, because the base has no syntactic category that can be linked. And since the base has no independent meaning, the semantics cannot be factored into the meaning of the base plus the meaning of the affix.

Of course *-ous* can also be attached to bases with a related free form, for instance *joyous, glorious, mischievous,* and so on. The bases of all of these are nouns, suggesting a schema with fully parsed morphosyntax, along the lines of (3) and (6). We could write this as a separate schema, connected by relational links to (11). Alternatively we can combine the two, using angle brackets to demarcate optional specifications of the variable, as in (12).

(12) $[_A$ <N>-ous] *schema*

    Semantics: $[_{\text{Property}} \underline{<\text{PERTAINING TO X}_x>}]_y$

    Morphosyntax: $[_A <\text{N}_x> \text{aff}_5]_y$

    Phonology: $/\ldots_{<x>} \text{əs}_5/_y$

This says that the base of an *-ous* adjective may or may not have a related free form. If there is a related free form, it is a noun, and the *-ous* adjective means 'pertaining to X,' where 'X' is the meaning of the noun. For instance, *joyous* means 'pertaining to joy' (plus any idiosyncratic features). Alternatively, if the material in angle brackets is omitted from (12), we are back to the situation in (11), and it is impossible to segment out a distinct meaning for the suffix *-ous*.

A more extreme case is presented by the sizable family of adjectives in (13).

(13)   vivid, rancid, fluid, fetid, flaccid, hybrid, lucid, lurid, . . .

All these adjectives end with *–id,* and they all have penultimate stress. Nearly all are bisyllabic, with exceptions such as *intrepid* and *insipid.* However, virtually none of them has a related free form (*pale ~ pallid* is a possible exception). One might legitimately wonder if there should be a schema for this family at all; their similarity might be just coincidental. On the other hand, these words are intuitively more closely related than, say, the words in (14), which bear only phonological similarity.

(14)   sheepish, vanish, varnish, radish, lavish, anguish, vanquish, . . .

This difference provides at least intuitive justification for a schema along the lines of (15), which is parallel in structure to (11). (16a,b) are among its instances. The phonology of the affix is shared among the three items (coindex 6). The variable in the phonology of (15) encompasses an initial syllable plus an optional onset for the syllable ending in /ɪd/. However, these pieces of phonology have no interface links to other levels; on their own they have no semantics or morphosyntax.

(15) $[_A$ -*id*$]$ *schema*
    Semantics: $[\text{PROPERTY}]_z$
    Morphosyntax: $[_A - \text{aff}_6]_z$
    Phonology: $/\sigma <\text{C}> \text{ɪd}_6 /_z$

(16) Semantics: a. VIVID_7 b. RANCID_8
    Morphosyntax: $[_A - \text{aff}_6]_7$ $[_A - \text{aff}_6]_8$
    Phonology: $/\text{vɪ v ɪd}_6 /_7$ $/\text{ræn s ɪd}_6 /_8$

Morphological structure is still more attenuated in the family in (17).

(17)   million, billion, trillion,…; zillion, kajillion, godzillion

The pattern is easily recognizable and can be creatively extended, as in the last three examples. But the morphological status of -*illion* is problematic. If it is a suffix, then *m-*, *b-*, *z-* and so on must be bound roots, each of which occurs only in these words. This analysis is suspicious, given that English doesn't have other bound roots that consist of a single consonant. Alternatively, if -*illion* is itself a root, the preceding consonants have to include nonce prefixes *m-*, *b-*, *z-*, and so on, which do not occur anywhere else in the language.

    Instead of settling for either of these unsatisfactory analyses, we can treat these words as simply lacking internal morphosyntactic structure. The phonological string -*illion* is associated with a meaning: in the strict numerical sense, 'power of 1000', and in the jocular sense, 'very large number.' But there is no associated morphosyntactic decomposition. (18a) shows an entry for *trillion*, and (18b) is a possible -*illion* schema for the strict sense.

(18)   a. *trillion*   b -*illion schema*
    Semantics: $10^{12}{}_{11}$ POWER OF 1000_x
    Morphosyntax: Numeral_{11} Numeral_x
    Phonology: $/ \text{tr ɪljən}_{12} /_{11}$ $/… \text{ɪljən}_{12} /_x$

(18a) treats *trillion* as simply a morphosyntactic numeral with no internal morphosyntactic structure. Schema (18b) says that a power of 1000 can be expressed by a syntactic numeral whose pronunciation ends in /ɪljən/. Coindex 12 connects the schema to its instances only in the phonology, not in morphosyntax as in previous cases. If the semantics is loosened to something like VERY LARGE NUMBER, this schema is available for coining jocular number words such as *kajillion*. So this is a fully a-morphous example in Anderson's sense.

    A similar approach can be applied to the much larger family of town names ending in -*ton*, -*bury*, and -*ville*, such as *Littleton, Waterbury, Danville*, and so on. It can also be applied to phonaesthemic patterns such as the *gl-* in *glimmer, glow, glitter, gleam*, and so on. These words too have no internal morphosyntactic structure, but some part of their phonology is systematically linked to part of their meaning. (However, Bloomfield (1933) thinks there is morphosyntax in phonaesthemes, and he cites several further instances. For a recent discussion, see Kwon and Round (2015). Many more examples of complex words without lexical roots, including town names, appear in Booij and Audring (2018b).)

A different sort of partial motivation occurs with constituents of compounds that are actual words, but whose meanings have nothing to do with the meaning of the compound. These might be called "strawberry morphs": *straw* has little to do with the (synchronic) meaning of *strawberry*, and similarly for the underlined portions of *polka dot*, *dogwood*, *sidekick*, *water moccasin*, *civil engineer*, *skinflint*, and *honeymoon*. (19) shows the structure of *honeymoon* and its two constituents. The crucial point is that relational links appear only in morphosyntax and phonology; semantics is not connected.

(19)

	a. *honey*	b. *moon*	c. *honeymoon*
Semantics:	$HONEY_{13}$	$MOON_{14}$	$[POST\text{-}WEDDING\ JOURNEY]_{15}$
Morphosyntax:	N_{13}	N_{14}	$[_N\ N_{13}\ N_{14}\ ]_{15}$
Phonology:	$/h\Lambda ni/_{13}$	$/mun/_{14}$	$/h\Lambda ni_{13}\ mun_{14}\ /_{15}$

This treatment can be easily extended to phrasal idioms. As is well known, most idioms are composed of existing words arranged in normal syntactic patterns, but (much of) their meaning is independent of their words and their syntactic structure. The coindexing notation allows us easily to capture the disconnect between linguistic structure and meaning. Here are lexical entries for *chew the fat* ('converse idly') (20a) and for its constituents (20b-f).

(20)

	a. *chew the fat*
Semantics:	$[CONVERSE\ (X)]_{16}$
Syntax:	$[_{VP}\ V_{17}\ [_{NP}\ Det_{18}\ N_{19}\ ]_{20}\ ]_{16}$
Phonology:	$/t\int uw_{17}\ \eth\partial_{18}\ fæt_{19}\ /_{16}$

	b. *chew*	c. *the*	d. *fat*
Semantics:	$[CHEW\ (X,Y)]_{17}$	DEF_{18}	FAT_{19}
Syntax:	V_{17}	Det_{18}	N_{19}
Phonology:	$/t\int uw_{17}/$	$/\eth\partial_{18}/$	$/fæt_{19}/$

	e. *VP schema*	f. *NP schema*
Syntax:	$[_{VP}\ V_x\ NP_y\ ]_z$	$[_{NP}\ Det_u\ N_v\ ]_w$

The coindexation between (20a) and (20b,c,d) links not the whole words, but just their phonology and syntax. The meaning in (20a) is not coindexed to the semantics of any of these components, and therefore it floats free of the individual word meanings, just as desired in an idiom.[7]

---

[7] A recurring preoccupation in the study of idioms is why some idioms such as *spill the beans* allow syntactic variants such as passive, and others such as *chew the fat* do not (e.g. *The beans have been spilled* but **The fat was being chewed*). We cannot offer an account here (after all, this is a book about morphology), but a generally accepted answer is that passive is possible when the relevant parts of an idiom have metaphorical interpretations. For instance, *beans* is interpreted as 'secret', but *fat* has no independent interpretation. See Jackendoff (1997: section 7.6) for a PA formulation of this approach.

In addition, the syntactic structure of (20a) is coindexed with the lexical entries of the phrase structure schemas for VP (20e) and NP (20f), which are being used here in their relational role (section 2.6). Thus the only thing that the idiom has to "pay for" is its noncanonical meaning and its relational links to its lexical cognates: it does not have to pay for its phonological words and its canonical syntactic structure. (In contrast, a syntactically noncanonical idiom such as *How about XP?* does have to pay for its syntactic structure.)

We should add that nothing here precludes a literal interpretation of *chew the fat*, e.g. in *He cut off some meat, chewed the fat, and swallowed it*. This can be generated online, by unifying (20b-f) in standard fashion (section 2.2), complete with meanings.

We see, then, that morphological patterns can involve various degrees of motivation, all the way from full motivation in *harden* to minimal motivation in *vivid, trillion*, and *glimmer*, with many varieties in between.

4.3   Conversions and other zero morphology

We next look at patterns whose morphosyntactic structure is not linked to phonology—so-called zero morphology.

For a first case, consider an English zero plural such as *sheep*, already mentioned in section 1.4. Despite the phonological identity between the singular and the plural, they obviously have to differ in semantics. They also have to differ in morphosyntax, in order to control determiner and verb agreement (*this sheep is…*vs. *those sheep are…*). The stem and plural form of *sheep* are shown in (21) (= Chapter 1, ex. (7)). We get to the singular and the status of stems in a moment. (Again we restart coindex numbering at 1.)

(21)   a. *Stem*   b. *Plural*

	a. *Stem*	b. *Plural*
Semantics:	$SHEEP_1$	$[PLUR\,(SHEEP_1)]_2$
Morphosyntax:	N_1	$[_N\,N_1\,PL]_2$
Phonology:	$/\text{ʃip}/_1$	$/\text{ʃip}/_{1,2}$

Coindex 2 marks the outer link of the plural noun; coindex 1 does the same for the stem. Coindex 1 also marks interface links within the plural noun, as well as relational links between the plural noun and the stem. However, PL in morphosyntax is not linked to phonology. Hence the phonology of the base is the same as that of the whole word, and this is indicated by the double coindexation 1,2. This will be our standard way of treating "zero morphemes." We do not have to stipulate a "zero morpheme"; such structures simply have no phonology to go with their morphosyntax and morphosemantics.

Sheep is of course not alone in having a zero plural. Other animal names such as *deer* and *fish* share this feature. We can capture the generalization among them with schema (22).

(22) *Zero plural schema (restricted to animals)*
     Semantics: $[\text{PLUR}(\text{ANIMAL}_x)]_y$
     Morphosyntax: $[_N\,N_x\,\text{PL}]_y$
     Phonology: $/\ldots/_{x,y}$

This says that the plural of a noun denoting an animal can be expressed by the same phonological string as the noun stem, with no further phonological affix.

The question arises of why the form **sheeps* is not licensed as well, by the regular plural schema. In response, we appeal to the usual notion of blocking (a.k.a. Pāṇini's Principle or the Elsewhere Condition (Kiparsky 1982; Anderson 1992)): a listed example takes precedence over a generated form that shares the same semantics and morphosyntax. However, there is nothing to categorically prohibit multiple listed forms, as we do find both *fish* and (in certain contexts) *fishes*. The Elsewhere Condition crops up in many contexts to follow. It is a linguistic counterpart of an exception that overrides default inheritance, for instance the flightlessness of ostriches overriding the default that birds fly (section 3.2).

Turning to the singular: Again, in order to properly control agreement, singular *sheep* has to carry a number feature SG in its morphosyntax. However, it proves useful to distinguish the singular from an uninflected stem that appears in words like *sheep-ish*, *sheepskin*, *sheep-herding*, and so on. In English, the singular is phonologically identical to the stem. This is not the case in, say, Italian, where singular and plural share a stem but have divergent affixes (e.g. singular *clarinetto* vs. plural *clarinetti*). For English, we can write a schema (23) that assigns the stem and singular the same phonology; in effect treating singular as another "zero morph." (For further discussion of the status of stems, see section 5.5.)

(23) *Identity of noun stem and singular*
     Semantics: $X_{z,w}$
     Morphosyntax: $[_N\,N_z\,\text{SG}]_w$
     Phonology: $/\ldots/_{z,w}$

The variables in (23) are productive, unlike the very similar (22), which is confined to listed instances. (Chapters 2 and 3 notated this difference by underlining nonproductive variables and double underlining productive variables. In the interest of avoiding clutter, we omit this notation.)[8]

Next consider conversions such as the verb *butter* 'spread butter on.' It denotes an action that involves the substance butter, so it incorporates the meaning of the noun *butter*, in exactly the same way as *widen* incorporates the meaning of *wide*. However, in this case the two words are phonologically identical. (24a) and (24b) show the verb and noun respectively.

---

[8] An alternative analysis would treat PL as a privative feature and singular as the unmarked case, as in Stump's (2016) Identity Function Defaults. Number agreement would then be singular by default, unless PL is present. This would eliminate the need for a separate stem form and for schema (23). For languages like Italian, though, a separate stem form is necessary in any event.

(24)   a. *butter*$_N$ b. *butter*$_V$

    Semantics: BUTTER$_3$ [SPREAD (Agent: X, Patient: BUTTER$_3$, ON Y)]$_4$

    Morphosyntax: N$_3$ [$_V$ N$_3$]$_4$

    Phonology: /bʌɾɪ/$_3$ /bʌɾɪ/$_{3,4}$

The morphosyntax of (24b) differs from the cases we have looked at so far, in that it contains no constituent aff. Rather, the morphosyntax is simply a verb made up of a noun. We could in principle introduce an aff constituent here to preserve uniformity. However, this aff would do no work, since there is no phonology for it to link to, and, unlike plurality, it has no effect on syntax. (Readers who are more comfortable with an aff here are welcome to interpolate it; section 4.8 offers an alternative treatment that more clearly does away with aff.)

A general schema for zero denominal verbs appears in (25). It has abundant lexicalized instances such as *paint, bottle, hammer,* and *glue.* But it is also easily extended to novel uses (Clark and Clark 1979), so its variable is productive.

(25)   *Zero denominal verb schema*

    Semantics: [F (Z$_z$)]$_w$

    Morphosyntax: [$_V$ N$_z$]$_w$

    Phonology: /.../$_{z,w}$

(25) says that a verb can contain a noun as its sole morphosyntactic constituent, and that the verb's phonology is identical to the noun's. The verb's meaning is some function *F* of the noun's; each individual instance has to specify what that function is. (24b) is an instance of this schema, in which coindex 3 links to the inner variable coindex *z* and coindex 4 links to the outer variable coindex *w*.

Clark and Clark cite many cases where the function *F* is dependent on context and presumed mutual knowledge. However, in denominal verbs such as *butter, paint,* and *saddle,* the function *F* comes from the meaning of the noun, specifically from the noun's "proper function" (Millikan 1984) or "telic quale" (Pustejovsky 1995). The proper function of butter, for instance, is to be spread on things like bread and pans, and this specifies the semantics of (24b) by formal means that we will not explore here.

Zero causative verbs in English receive a similar analysis. (26) shows intransitive (inchoative/unaccusative) *break,* transitive (causative) *break,* and the schema that relates them.

This schema also relates intransitive and transitive *bake* and many other such verbs.

(26)   a. *Intransitive (inchoative, unaccusative) break*

    Semantics: [BREAK (Undergoer: X)]$_5$

    Morphosyntax: V$_5$

    Phonology: /brejk/$_5$

   b. *Transitive (causative) break*

      Semantics: [CAUSE (Agent: Y, [BREAK (Undergoer: X)]$_5$)]$_6$

      Morphosyntax: [$_V$ V$_5$]$_6$

      Phonology: /brejk/$_{5,6}$

   c. *Causative schema*

      Semantics: [CAUSE (Agent: Y, [F (Undergoer: X)]$_u$)]$_v$

      Morphosyntax: [$_V$ V$_u$]$_v$

      Phonology: /.../$_{u,v}$

Causative *break*, with outer coindex 6, contains the semantics of inchoative *break*, coindexed 5. Since (26a) and (26b) have identical phonology, both coindices appear on the phonology of (26b). In the absence of an affix in (26b), we end up with the morphosyntax [$_V$ V]—a verb dominating a verb, which may seem a bit mysterious. However, it does make sense in the context of the morphology: the inner V is the base, and the outer V is the resulting morphologically complex word.[9] Schema (26c) abstracts away from the phonology of the verb and from the particular event that is being caused, again listing only an unspecified semantic function *F*.

On this treatment, it is not necessary to choose whether the causative is *derived* from the inchoative or vice versa, as would be required by an account in terms of generative word formation rules. Rather, (26c) simply says that a causative and homophonous inchoative are related, and that the cost of the pair is correspondingly reduced, compared to a pair with comparable semantics but no phonological relation, such as *kill* and *die*.

4.4 Digression: Causatives without homophonous inchoatives

Return to the [$_V$ A-*en*] verbs. So far we have analyzed their meaning as inchoative 'become X.' However, many of them also have a causative reading: alongside (27a) we have causative (27b). In fact, quite a few, such as *dampen*, *sadden*, and *sweeten*, have *only* a causative reading and lack a corresponding inchoative, as seen in (27c,d).

(27) a. The soup thickened (as it cooked).   ('became thick')

      b. Bill thickened the soup (with cornstarch). ('caused to become thick')

      c. *The ground dampened (as the rain fell).   ('became damp')

      d. The rain dampened the ground.   ('caused to become damp')

A traditional derivation based on word formation rules would derive intransitive *thicken* from the adjective *thick*; it would then "causativize" intransitive *thicken* to derive transitive *thicken*. But for a word like *dampen*, such a derivation has to pass through a stage that is not a word: *damp*$_A$ > **dampen*$_{intrans}$ > *dampen*$_{trans}$. In this approach,

---

[9] One way of avoiding the V inside V configuration would be to use double coindexation in morphosyntax as well as phonology, i.e. V$_{5,6}$ in (26b) and V$_{u,v}$ in the schema. For another alternative, see section 4.8.3.

then, the grammar somehow has to countenance word forms that play a role in derivations but are not themselves lexical words.

In the RM framework, this issue does not arise. Here is the structure of *dampen*.

(28) *dampen*

Semantics: $[\text{CAUSE (Agent: Y, [BECOME (Undergoer: X, DAMP}_7)]_8)]_9$

Morphosyntax: $[_V [_V A_7 \text{ aff}_3]_8]_9$

Phonology: $/ \text{dæmp}_7 \text{ ən}_3 /_{8,9}$

The whole word is linked together by the outer coindex 9. Its base /dæmp/ is linked (coindex 7) to the adjective *damp* (not shown in (28)). The affix, coindexed 3, is relationally linked to the $[_V$ A-*en*] schema ((3) above). The crucial point, though, is the status of the inner verb, coindexed 8. Internally, it is motivated by the $[_V$ A-*en*] schema. However, it is also motivated by the causative schema: it is linked to the constituent in (26c) with the variable coindex *u*. Thus all the parts of (28) are relationally linked to schemas, and there is no need for a word *dampen*_{intrans} to mediate between *damp* and *dampen*_{trans}. If there were such a word, it would provide additional motivation for the inner verb constituent, but this is not necessary. We have thus combined the effects of the $[_V$ A-*en*] schema and the zero causative schema, without recourse to a traditional step-by-step or recursive derivation. (A similar problem, with a similar solution, is proposed within Construction Morphology by Booij 2018b.)

4.5 Phonology without corresponding semantics

Section 4.3 dealt with cases where semantics and morphosyntax are linked, but without corresponding phonology. The reverse is also possible: phonological material that is unlinked to semantics. Some well-known examples are thematic vowels, as in Italian *and-**a**-re* 'to walk' vs. *dorm-**i**-re* 'to sleep'; Persian *ezafe*, linking nouns to postnominal modifiers (Ghomeshi 1997); and linking elements in compounds (see Szczepaniak and Kürschner (2013) for Germanic; Booij (2019: Chapter 5) for Dutch; Botha (1968) for Afrikaans). In each case, the presence of the linking element is syntactically or morphosyntactically conditioned, but the linker itself has no morphosyntactic category and no meaning.

Here are some Dutch compounds with no linking element (29a), linking element /s/ (29b), linking element /ə/ (29c), and linking element /ən/ (29d).

(29) a. waterfles 'water bottle', cameratas 'camera bag', boekbinder '(book) binder', vloerverwarming 'underfloor heating', strandcafé 'beach cafe'

  b. gezin**s**hoofd 'head of the family', schei**d**srechter 'referee', varken**s**vlees 'pork', voorjaar**s**avond 'spring evening', leven**s**verzekering 'life insurance'

  c. ap**e**trots 'very proud (lit. ape-proud), drink**e**broer 'drunkard (lit. drink-brother)', lach**e**bek 'smiley face', kost**e**loos 'for free (lit. cost-less)'

  d. brill**en**koker 'glasses case', leeuw**en**deel 'lion's share', her**en**huis 'manor', fless**en**hals 'bottle neck'

For example, the structure of the compound *dorpskroeg* 'village café' is shown in (30). Its linking element /s/ is present in phonology but is unlinked to morphosyntax and semantics.

(30) *dorpskroeg*
       Semantics: $[CAFE_1; IN (VILLAGE_2)]_3$
       Morphosyntax: $[_N N_2 N_1]_3$
       Phonology: $/dɔrp_2 s krux_1/_3$

More generally, (31) states four variants of the compound schema, corresponding to the four possibilities illustrated in (29). They share semantics and morphosyntax; they differ only in the choice of linking element in the phonology. (The semantics says only that the meaning of the compound is some function of the meanings of the constituent nouns. See Jackendoff (2010) for much more detail from the perspective of the Parallel Architecture.)

(31)   *Compound schema with linking segment*
        Semantics: $[F (X_x, Y_y)]_z$
        Morphosyntax: $[_N N_x N_y]_z$
        a. Phonology: $/..._x ..._y/_z$ (*No linking element*)
        b. Phonology: $/..._x s ..._y/_z$ (*Linking element /s/*)
        c. Phonology: $/..._x ə ..._y/_z$ (*Linking element /ə/*)
        d. Phonology: $/..._x ən ..._y/_z$ (*Linking element /ən/*)

An alternative approach might treat the absence of a linking element segment in (31a) as productive, hence the unmarked case. The presence of a linking element would then count as more highly specified, thereby blocking (31a) by some version of Pāṇini's Principle (a.k.a. the Elsewhere Condition).[10]

4.6 One-many and many-one links between morphosyntax and phonology

In canonical cases such as $[_V A-en]$ and $[_N V-er]$, a morphosyntactic affix is linked uniquely to a phonological affix. Sections 4.2–4.5 have dealt with cases where some of

---

[10] The choice of linking element is not entirely random. Various factors have been identified that help determine which of the linking elements is appropriate in any particular case. For instance, there is a tendency for compounds with the same first noun to have the same linking element, as in (i). On the other hand, many Dutch nouns occur with multiple linking elements, as in (ii).

(i)   a. dorp**s**kroeg 'village cafe', dorp**s**oudste 'village elder', dorp**s**straat 'village street'
      b. paard**en**staart 'pigtail, lit. horse's tail', paard**en**vlees 'horse meat', paard**en**stal 'horse stable'
(ii) a. schaa**p**herder 'shepherd', scha**pen**wol 'sheep's wool', schaa**p**skooi 'sheep's pen'
      b. zon**w**ering 'awning', zon**nen**scherm 'awning', zon**s**verduistering 'solar eclipse'

For other factors, see Booij (2019) and the section on linking elements in Taalportaal <http://taalportaal.org/taalportaal/topic/pid/topic-13998813295824921>.

this linkage is absent. We now consider cases where there is *multiple* linkage between morphosyntax and phonology, both one-to-many and many-to-one.

The first case is cumulative exponence (or portmanteau affixes), where a phonological affix expresses more than a single morphosyntactic feature. A very simple case is German verb inflection, which collapses person and number marking into a single suffix. (32a) shows the morphosyntax and phonology of *machtest* 'make.PAST.2.SG'; (32b) shows the schema that licenses the linkage of person and number to the suffix *-est*. (We defer details of inflectional morphosyntax to Chapter 5.)

(32) German: a. *machtest*[11]   b. *2d person singular schema*

Morphosyntax: $[_V{}_1 \text{ PAST}_2\ 2_3\ \text{SG}_4\ ]_5$ $[_V{}_x \text{ TENSE}_y\ 2_3\ \text{SG}_4\ ]_z$

Phonology: $/\text{max}_1\ t_2\ \text{əst}_{3,4}\ /_5$ $/\ldots_x \ldots_y\ \text{əst}_{3,4}\ /_z$

Here again we use double subscripting: the phonology is linked to both the person and number features in morphosyntax. If we were to notate (32a) in terms of association lines instead of coindices, it would look like (33), in which two features in morphosyntax converge on a single affix in phonology.

(33) Morphosyntax: [V PAST 2 SG]
                     | | \ /
      Phonology: / max   t   əst /

(34) offers three German determiners with more complex morphosyntax.

(34) a. German: *dem* 'the' (+ agreement features)

Morphosyntax: $[_\text{Det} \text{ DEF SG}_7 \text{ MASC/NEUT}_8 \text{ DAT}_9\ ]_{10}$

Phonology: $/\text{dem}_{7,8,9}\ /_{10}$

b. German: *deinem* 'your' (possessive + agreement features)

Morphosyntax: $[_\text{Det}\ [_\text{Pro}\ 2 \text{ SG POSS}]_{11} \text{ SG}_{13} \text{ MASC/NEUT}_{14} \text{ DAT}_{15}\ ]_{12}$

Phonology: $/\text{daın}_{11}\ \text{əm}_{13,14,15}\ /_{12}$

c. German: *ihrem* 'her' (possessive + agreement features)

Morphosyntax: $[_\text{Det}\ [_\text{Pro}\ 3 \text{ FEM SG POSS}]_{16} \text{ SG}_{13} \text{ MASC/NEUT}_{14} \text{ DAT}_{15}\ ]_{17}$

Phonology: $/\text{ı:r}_{16}\ \text{əm}_{13,\ 14,15}\ /_{17}$

In (34a), the word expresses at once number, person, and case as well as definiteness. (34b) has embedded morphosyntactic structure. The inner brackets give the inherent features of the base *dein-*, and the affix *-em* agrees in number, gender, and case with the determiner's head noun. (34c) makes the embedding more evident: the base is feminine and the affix is masculine or neuter, agreeing with the head noun. The two gender markers are kept separate, thanks to the embedding.

Another type of cumulative exponence extends into phrasal syntax, for instance German *am*, a portmanteau of the preposition *an* and the determiner *dem* (35a). The

[11] We take /t/ to be the phonology of the past tense suffix; other analyses are possible (see e.g. Schäfer 2018: 303).

ellipsis in the syntax stands for the rest of the NP, including its head noun. (35b) shows the same thing in terms of a syntactic tree and association lines. (The solid lines show syntactic constituency; the dashed lines are the interface links to phonology.)

(35) *German: am*
    a. Syntax: $[_{PP} P_{18} [_{NP} [_{Det} SG_{13} MASC/NEUT_{14} DAT_{15}]_{19} \ldots]]$
       Phonology: $/am/_{18,19}$

    b. Syntax:

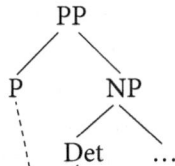

       Phonology: /am/

The portmanteau *I'm* in English is similar (though specifying its syntax involves assumptions about auxiliaries that we don't wish to engage with here).

The reverse of cumulative exponence is multiple exponence, when the same morphosyntactic feature is realized in two or more positions in the phonology. A simple case, again from German, is the circumfix past participle. (36a) is *gemacht*, the past participle of the verb *machen*, and (36b) is the general schema (which we will revise in section 5.4.5).

(36) German: a. *gemacht*   b. *past participle schema*
    Morphosyntax: $[V_1 PTCP_{20,21}]_{22}$ $[V_z PTCP_{20,21}]_w$
    Phonology: $/gə_{20} max_1 t_{21}/_{22}$ $/gə_{20} \ldots_z t_{21}/_w$

4.7 Is there linear order in morphosyntax?

The treatment of circumfixes raises a more general issue about morphosyntax. So far we have notated aff and inflectional features as if they have inherent linear order with respect to the base. This treatment is perfectly natural when dealing with prefixes and suffixes, because the linear order in morphosyntax can mirror the phonology. But the phonological form of a circumfix falls on both sides of the base, so it has no single natural position in morphosyntax. The situation is still more vexing in the case of infixes (which we discuss in section 4.11), because it makes no sense to think of inserting aff inside of N or V.

This problem is not confined to circumfixes and infixes. When two or more inflectional features converge on a single piece of phonology, as in the German words in (33) and (34), there is no evidence for the order of the two morphosyntactic features. For that matter, when dealing with zero affixation, as in plural *sheep*, there is no evidence for any ordering of morphosyntactic plural with respect to its base. Perhaps the most striking case is Semitic morphology, where the phonology of the base and of the affixes are intercalated, as in (37), for instance.

(37)   Hebrew: /mɛlɛx/ 'king' ~ /məlaxim/ 'kings'; /jɛlɛd/ 'boy' ~ /jəladim/ 'boys'

The singular schema for this class of nouns is /CɛCɛC/; the plural is /CəCaCim/. It is impossible to justify placing the inflection in morphosyntax either before or after the stem.

A solution for these cases is to eliminate linear order from morphosyntax— potentially, not just for these cases, but everywhere—that is, treating morphosyntactic structure as simply an unordered set of morphosyntactic objects. It can still link in the very same way to phonology, where linear order remains in force. For instance, we could rewrite (36a) as (38), where the curly brackets indicate that V and PTCP are considered simply elements of a set.

(38)   *German past participle circumfix with unordered morphosyntax*
       Morphosyntax: $\{V_1, \text{PTCP}_{20,21}\}_{22}$
       Phonology: $/\text{gə}_{20} \text{ max}_1 \text{ t}_{21}/_{22}$

In this approach, morphosyntax doesn't care whether an affix is realized as a suffix, a prefix, a circumfix, or an infix. That choice is made not by morphosyntax itself, but by its mapping into phonology.[12]

Such an approach has antecedents in syntactic theory. Traditional phrase structure rules of course determine both constituency and linear order, just as we have been assuming for morphosyntax up to this point. But schools of thought as different as GPSG (Gazdar et al. 1985), the Minimalist Program (Chomsky 1995; Hornstein 2018) and Simpler Syntax (Culicover, in preparation) have proposed separating linear order from dominance (= set inclusion) in syntactic grammars. Thus we are not making a totally unprecedented move. In the present framework and its sibling Simpler Syntax,

---

[12] The literature has discussed some cases in which affixes display alternative orders. One type of example: Noyer (1994) and Kim (2010) cite a completive affix in Huave (an isolate spoken in Oaxaca, Mexico) that is normally a suffix by default (i.a). But if the verb stem happens to be both vowel-initial and consonant-final, the completive marker appears as a prefix (i.b).

(i)   a.   [mojk-   o]-   t
           face.down-themevowel-compl
           's/he lay face down'
      b.   t-   [e-mojk-   o-   r]
           compl-2-face.down-themevowel-2.intr
           'you (sg.) lay face down'

We see no reason why the morpho*syntax* should be any different in these two cases. The difference between them is most easily accounted for if the completive affix in morphosyntax is unordered with respect to the verb stem, and the position of the affix is determined only by phonology.

Bickel et al. (2007) discuss the case of Chintang, which has free order of certain verbal prefixes, and Newbold (2013) discusses variable affix order in Kuna (Chibchan, Panama). Ryan (2010) discusses several other cases, including Tagalog. For further discussion of alternative affix orders, see Woodbury (1996), Haspelmath (2011: 43), and Blevins, Ackerman, and Malouf (2019).

(Culicover and Jackendoff 2005), the principles of linear order can be encoded in interface links between syntax and phonology, if desired.

One place where an unordered version of morphosyntax seems especially attractive is sign language morphophonology, in which a potentially large number of constituents are executed simultaneously. These constituents may include a verb of motion; a classifier handshape that agrees with the entity in motion; the beginning and end position of motion, agreeing with source and goal; and aspectual markers such as iterativity and distributivity (Klima and Bellugi 1979; Napoli 2019). Except for beginning and end position, the phonology is not linearly ordered, so there is no motivation at all for linear ordering in the morphosyntax. Hence the curly bracket notation is just right for this case. However, we also need a way to notate the simultaneous performance of all these quasi-morphemes. One possibility is to extend the curly bracket notation to phonology, where it would mean not lack of order but simultaneity. The result might look something like (39). (Note that initial position and final position *are* linearly ordered with respect to the rest.)[13]

(39) *ASL verb schema (grossly oversimplified):*

Morphosyntax: $\{_{\text{Vinflected}} \, V_{15}, \text{classifier}_{16}, \text{source agreement}_{17}, \text{goal agreement}_{18}, \text{aspect}_{19} \}_{20}$

Phonology: $/ \, \text{initial position}_{17}, \{ \, \text{motion}_{15}, \text{handshape}_{16}, \text{manner of motion}_{19} \}, \text{final position}_{18} \, /_{20}$

For the moment, we set the differences between these two formalisms aside and continue to use our customary notation, with the understanding that it may be *interpreted* like (38) whenever appropriate (which might be always—we leave the question open). Section 5.1 will make the case that inflectional morphology is better treated in terms of unordered features, while derivational morphology makes use of the separate constituent aff, whether ordered or unordered with respect to the base.

4.8 Sister words and sister schemas

4.8.1 Sister words

In the canonical lexical relations discussed in section 4.1, a morphologically complex word such as *widen* or *baker* has a base with a lexical cognate such as *wide* or *bake*. We next turn to relations between words in which neither word can serve as lexical cognate for the other.

Sections 3.4 and 3.5 mentioned two such situations. One involves one-off relations like those in (40). Here the phonology of the first member of each pair is identical

---

[13] We are grateful to Naomi Caselli, Rabia Ergin, Ryan Lepic, and the late Irit Meir for much discussion of sign language morphology. Lepic and Occhino (2018) develop a treatment of sign morphology in a Construction Morphology framework.

with the base of the second member, but the semantics of the second is contained in that of the first. For instance in (40a), an assassin is someone who assassinates people.[14]

(40) a. assassin ~ assassinate
      b. chemist ~ chemistry
      c. critic ~ criticize
      d. linguist ~ linguistics

(41) repeats the lexical entries of *assassin* and *assassinate* from section 3.5, formalizing the binding relation in the semantics along the lines of *baker* in section 4.1.

(41) a. *assassin*

Semantics:	$[[\text{PERSON}^{\alpha}; [\text{MURDER (Agent: } \alpha, \text{ Patient: POLITICIAN)}]_1]_2$
Morphosyntax:	N_2
Phonology:	$/\text{əsæsən}/_2$

      b. *assassinate*

Semantics:	$[\text{MURDER (Agent: X, Patient: POLITICIAN)}]_1$
Morphosyntax:	$[_V N_2 \text{ aff}_3]_1$
Phonology:	$/\text{əsæsən}_2 \text{ ejt}_3 /_1$

As in section 3.5, the entire semantics of *assassinate* is linked to part of the semantics of *assassin*, and part of the phonology of *assassinate* is linked to the entire phonology of *assassin*. Hence *assassin* and *assassinate* motivate each other, without needing to say which word is derived from which. We will call the relation between the two a **sister relation**: they share structure, but neither contains all of the other.

A more widespread case of sister relations also appeared in sections 3.4–3.5: pairs of words such as (42) that share a base but lack a related free form. Again there is no way to decide which is "derived" from the other.

(42) a. ambition ~ ambitious
      b. contagion ~ contagious
      c. ostentation ~ ostentatious
      d. sedition ~ seditious
      e. hilarity ~ hilarious
      f. cognition ~ cognitive

(43) repeats the lexical entries of *ambition* and *ambitious*. Individually, they are like *scrumptious* in (10), but they share the unparsed stretch of their phonology (coindex 7) and part of their meanings (coindex 4).

---

[14] We note that the first member of each pair in (40) is an occupation and the second member the activity associated with that occupation. (They are among the "personal nouns" of Spencer 1988.) We do not know if there is any systematic connection between their semantics and their unusual morphology.

(43)   a. *ambition*   b. *ambitious*

    Semantics: DESIRE_4 $[\mathrm{HAVING}\,(\mathrm{DESIRE}_4)]_6$

    Morphosyntax: $[_N - \mathrm{aff}_8\,]_4$ $[_A - \mathrm{aff}_5\,]_6$

    Phonology: $/\text{æmbɪʃ}_7\,\text{ən}_8\,/_4$ $/\text{æmbɪʃ}_7\,\text{əs}_5\,/_6$

In addition, *ambitious* is further motivated by the -*ous* schema (11) (coindex 5), and *ambition* is motivated by the -*ion* schema (coindex 8, schema not yet stated).

4.8.2 Sister schemas

A very important case of sister relations involves not just relations between *words* but relations between *schemas*. For instance, Booij (2010) cites the relation between an ideology or set of practices (X-*ism*) and one of its adherents or practitioners (X-*ist*), illustrated by the pairs in (44). (Similar observations are made by Di Sciullo and Williams 1987: 21, Bochner 1993: 80–6, and Nesset 2008.)

(44)   a. behaviorism ~ behaviorist, impressionism ~ impressionist,
        minimalism ~ minimalist, communism ~ communist, terrorism ~ terrorist
    b. pacifism ~ pacifist, atheism ~ atheist, pessimism ~ pessimist

The pairs in (44a) have a related free form; the pairs in (44b) do not. But even when there is a related free form, the -*ist* term is typically closer to the meaning of the -*ism* term than to that of the free form. For example, a *communist* is a follower of communism, not someone who lives in a commune. (For a more complex case, an *impressionist* is either a practitioner of impressionism or someone who does impressions (imitations) of public figures.)

    Within each pair, the relation between its members can be captured by a sister relation like the one in (43). However, Booij points out that in addition, all these pairs exhibit the *same* sister relation. In order to encode this generalization, we have to bump the sister relationship up a level and state it as a relation between the *schemas* for the -*ism* words and the -*ist* words, as in the upper relation in (45).

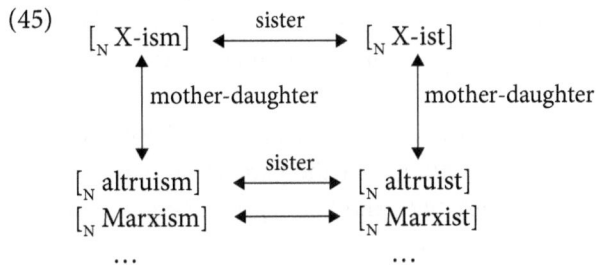

(45)

    $[_N \text{ X-ism}] \xleftrightarrow{\text{sister}} [_N \text{ X-ist}]$

    $\downarrow$ mother-daughter $\downarrow$ mother-daughter

    $[_N \text{ altruism}] \xleftrightarrow{\text{sister}} [_N \text{ altruist}]$
    $[_N \text{ Marxism}] \longleftrightarrow [_N \text{ Marxist}]$
    ...   ...

Booij (2010) (also Kapatsinski 2007; Nesset 2008; Booij and Masini 2015; Booij and Audring 2017) calls this sort of configuration a "second-order schema"; Plag (2003) refers to it as a "cross-formation."

In order to formalize this configuration, we first state the schemas separately, in (46). The base noun is optional; for simplicity we omit it. (It would add optional material along the lines of (12), the $[_A <N>\text{-}ous]$ schema.)

(46)   a. $[_N \text{-}ism]$ *schema* b. $[_N \text{-}ist]$ *schema*
      Semantics: IDEOLOGY$_x$ [ADHERENT (IDEOLOGY)]$_z$
      Morphosyntax: $[_N - aff_9]_x$ $[_N - aff_{10}]_z$
      Phonology: $/\ldots \text{ızəm}_9/_x$ $/\ldots \text{ıst}_{10}/_z$

(46a) says that there is a class of nouns ending in *-ism* that denote an ideology; (46b) says that there is a class of nouns ending in *-ist* that denote adherents of an ideology. What's missing from (46) is acknowledgment that these classes are correlated: if a noun N_1 that ends in *-ist* has the same phonological base as another noun N_2 that ends in *-ism*, and if N_2 denotes an ideology, then N_1 quite likely denotes an adherent of that ideology—and vice versa.

In order to say this formally, we need to establish a relational link between the *variables* in (46a) and (46b): the ideology in (46b), whatever it may be, is the same as that in (46a), and the phonology of the base in (46b), whatever it may be, is the same as that in (46a). So far we have treated each variable coindex as distinct from all the others. Now we wish to be able to say that a variable in one schema and a corresponding variable in another schema are in fact the very *same* variable. We do this by introducing the notion of **linked variable coindices**, which express a relational link between variables in two or more schemas. We notate linked variable coindices with Greek letters, giving us (47) in place of (46).

(47) *Linked [-ism] and [-ist] schemas*
      Semantics: a. IDEOLOGY$_\beta$ b. [ADHERENT (IDEOLOGY$_\beta$)]$_z$
      Morphosyntax: $[_N - aff_9]_\beta$ $[_N - aff_{10}]_z$
      Phonology: $/\ldots_\alpha \text{ızəm}_9/_\beta$ $/\ldots_\alpha \text{ıst}_{10}/_z$

In (47), α marks the phonological link between the variables in the two schemas, and β marks the semantic link. β also marks an outer variable link between the three levels of (47a). A comparison with (43), the sisters *ambition* and *ambitious*, shows a precise structural parallelism. Where *ambition* and *ambitious* share the phonology of the base (coindex 7), the *-ism* and *-ist* schemas share the (variable) phonology of their base (coindex α); and where *ambition* and *ambitious* share part of their semantics (coindex 4), so do X-*ism* and X-*ist* (coindex β).

Booij notates second-order schemas with a $\approx$ between the two relevant schemas. The coindexing notation used here better brings out the parallelism between sister schemas like (47) and sister *words* like (40), (42), and (44), again taking advantage of the fact that words and rules are in the same format.[15]

---

[15] Booij (2010) and Bochner (1993: 84–5) treat cases like *ambition/ambitious* by positing second-order schemas. They do not have a way of stating direct relations between sister words. Rather, for them, the relation between sister words is always mediated by sister schemas.
   From our perspective, the "rules of referral" in realizational theories of morphology (e.g. Blevins 2016: 127) can be recast as a particular variety of sister schemas. Blevins (2016: 132) mentions troublesome cases where the proper direction of rules of referral cannot be determined. This issue does not arise in Relational Morphology, because the sister relation is by definition nondirectional.

The relation in (47) appears to be open-ended. Existing *-ism* ideologies are regularly paired with *-ist* adherents or practitioners. And should a new ideology come on the scene, say *Trumpism*, then there is no hesitation in calling its adherents *Trumpists*. On the other hand, an expected regular form can be blocked by a lexical competitor. For instance, a practitioner of *cynicism* is not a **cynicist* but a *cynic*, and in the other direction, a *casuist* is a practitioner not of **casuism* but of *casuistry*. This parallels exactly the behavior of, say, the English regular plural, which is productive but blockable by the Elsewhere Condition.

(48) illustrates two more patterns that involve sister schemas.

(48) a. Dutch:
        werker 'worker' ~ werkster 'female worker'
        bewoner 'inhabitant' ~ bewoonster 'female inhabitant'
        reiziger 'traveler' ~ reizigster 'female traveler'
      b. candid ~ candor, fervid ~ fervor, horrid ~ horror, languid ~ languor,
        pallid ~ pallor, splendid ~ splendor, squalid ~ squalor, torpid ~ torpor,
        (*possibly*) stupid ~ stupor

(48a) illustrates a productive pattern in Dutch, relating agentive human nouns in *-er* to their female counterparts (Van Marle 1985; Booij 1997b, 2010). An important example is *reizigster*, which has to be related most directly to the noun *reiziger*, because there is no related free form **reizig* on which it could be based—hence it has to be motivated by a sister relation.

On the other hand, the sister schemas in (48b) are nonproductive. Not all *-id* adjectives have an *-or* counterpart, e.g. *vivid ~ *vivor, tepid ~ *tepor*; nor do all *-or* nouns have an *-id* counterpart, e.g. *vigor ~ *vigid, terror ~ *terrid*. In fact (48b) lists about all the instances there are.[16]

4.8.3 Can all patterns be sister schemas?

Many of the schemas we have developed up to this point can be reformulated in terms of sister schemas. For instance, (49) restates the $[_V$ A-*en*] schema (3) in terms of sister-hood to the base's lexical cognate. The linked variables are notated with the coindex δ.

(49) *Linked Adjectival and* $[_V$ *-en*] *schemas*

	a.	b.
Semantics:	PROPERTY$_δ$	[BECOME ([<MORE> PROPERTY]$_δ$)]$_y$
Morphosyntax:	A$_δ$	[$_V$ A$_δ$ aff$_3$]$_y$
Phonology:	/$_σ$ ... [-son] /$_δ$	/ /σ [-son]/$_δ$ ən$_3$ /$_y$

---

[16] *Fervid ~ fervor* also has the sister *fervent; horrid ~ horror* also has sisters *horrible, horrific, horrendous, horrify*, and perhaps *abhor; languid ~ languor* also has the sisters *languorous* and possibly *languish; stupid ~ stupor* also has the sister *stupefy. Humid* and *humor* are probably related historically, but not synchronically, as their meanings are unrelated; the same might go for *rigid* and *rigor*.

Informally, this says "If you have an adjective pronounced /…/ that denotes a property, there is likely to also be a verb pronounced /…ən/ that denotes an event of acquiring that property, and vice versa."

Sister schemas also offer an attractive alternative to the treatment of conversions in section 4.3. In that analysis, (24) embedded $butter_N$ in its entirety into $butter_V$. (50) instead treats the two as sisters: they are a noun and a verb that share phonology and part of their semantics. The apparent "direction of derivation" comes only from the semantics, where the meaning of the noun is embedded in that of the verb.

(50) a. $butter_N$ b. $butter_V$

Semantics:	$BUTTER_{11}$	$[SPREAD (Agent: X, Patient: BUTTER_{11}, ON Y)]_{12}$
Morphosyntax:	N_{11}	V_{12}
Phonology:	$/bʌɾɹ̩/_{11}$	$/bʌɾɹ̩/_{11,12}$

In these terms, schema (25) for zero denominal verbs is recast as the sister schemas in (51).

(51) *Zero denominal verb sister schemas*

Semantics:	a. $Z_ε$	b. $[F (Z_ε)]_w$
Morphosyntax:	$N_ε$	V_w
Phonology:	$/…/_ε$	$/…/_{ε,w}$

And the zero causative in (26c), with its questionable $[_V V]$, is recast as (52).

(52) *Zero causative sister schemas*

Semantics:	a. $[F (Undergoer: X)]_ζ$	b. $[CAUSE (Agent: Y, [F (Undergoer: X)]_ζ)]_v$
Morphosyntax:	$V_ζ$	V_v
Phonology:	$/…/_ζ$	$/…/_{ζ,v}$

Given these options, one might ask if *all* morphological relations should be stated in terms of sister schemas; this would make the theory more uniform. In fact, Jackendoff (1975), Bochner (1993), Haspelmath and Sims (2010), and others do state all morphological patterns in essentially these terms. However, there is at least one important situation where the approach does not work: items whose bases lack a related free form. For instance, suppose that the structure of *joyous* is motivated through a pair of sister schemas that together relate it to *joy*. Then there is no way to account for the partial structure of *scrumptious*, since there is no lexical item that its base can be related to. In contrast, our single-term schema (11) simply says "There are adjectives ending in *-ous* that denote properties," a sort of "morphotactic" principle. The schema relates *scrumptious* to all the other *-ous* adjectives, but there is no requirement that its base be related to an independent word.[17]

---

[17] Single-term schemas parallel the "product-" or "output-oriented" generalizations of Bybee (1985). Of the two schemas in a sister relationship, one (such as (49a)) can sometimes be thought of as "source-" or "input-oriented" and the other (such as (49b)) as "output-oriented"—with the caveats that (a) there is no derivation involved and (b) in many cases, such as *-ism* ~ *-ist*, it is impossible to think of one as "input" and the other as "output."

Booij observes that sister schemas open the door to stating paradigmatic relations, including ablaut and other forms of stem allomorphy. We will encounter many such phenomena in what is to come.

At this point, then, the theory needs relations between words and words (i.e. sister words), between words and schemas, and between sister schemas. An important feature of the theory is that these constructs are formally all of a piece. Single-term schemas have the same form as words, except that they contain variables. Similarly, the formal relation between sister schemas is exactly the same as the relation between sister words, except for the use of linked variables. This again brings out the continuity between words and rules that is central to the PA/RM approach.

4.9 Patterns that fragment the base: Blends and truncations

In the patterns treated so far, the base of a derived word preserves the related free form, if there is one. For instance, the base of *harden* is identical to the free form *hard*. But there are also many patterns in which the free form is no longer intact in the derived item, for example truncation, umlaut, and stress and tone shift. Many morphologists (e.g. Anderson 1992) have taken such patterns as strong evidence for what Inkelas (2014: 81–3) calls "process morphology," in which the alternation in question cannot be localized in a phonological affix (i.e. there is no identifiable "morpheme"), and in which the phonological form of a stem is altered by procedural rules.

The procedural rules of process morphology are not available in RM. We will instead develop an account of such patterns in terms of sister relations. This section and the next two look at blends, truncations, umlaut, infixes, reduplication, and some cases of stem allomorphy. Chapter 5 brings this treatment to bear on inflectional patterns, and Chapter 6 deals with alterations of stress and segmental quality, as in *human ~ humanity*.

4.9.1 Blends

Consider blends like those in (53).

(53) a. spork (= spoon+fork)
      b. composium (= compose+symposium) (*Boston Globe*, December 16, 2014)
      c. Spanglish (= Spanish+English)

Spork is obviously built from the onset of *spoon* and the rhyme of *fork*. Its meaning, 'object that serves both as a spoon and a fork', is built pragmatically from the meanings of the two words. However, it has no internal morphosyntax: neither *sp* nor *ork* is a word, an affix, or an instance of a schema. Rather, each part is like the *scrumpt-* in *scrumptious* or the *tr-* in *trillion*, which section 4.2 treated as unsyntactified pieces of phonology. This leads to an a-morphous structure along the lines in (54), where the relevant phonological substrings in *spoon* and *fork* are coindexed with (i.e. marked the same as) the corresponding parts of *spork*.

(54) Semantics: a. SPOON$_1$ b. FORK$_2$ c. [SPOON$_1$ + FORK$_2$]$_3$
      Morphosyntax: N$_1$ N$_2$ N$_3$
      Phonology: /sp$_4$ uwn/$_1$ /f ɔrk$_5$/$_2$ /sp$_4$ ɔrk$_5$/$_3$

Coindices 1, 2, and 3 are the outer links for the three levels of *spoon*, *fork*, and *spork* respectively. In the semantics, coindices 1 and 2 also serve as relational links from the meanings of *spoon* and *fork* to the meaning of *spork*. The interest lies in the phonological level. Coindex 4 links the onsets of *spoon* and *spork*, and coindex 5 links the rhymes of *fork* and *spork*. Importantly, the phonological parsing of *spoon* and *fork* is present only to support their relation to *spork*, and has no significance to semantics or morphosyntax. Hence there are no interface links between the phonological sequences /sp/ and /ork/ and the meanings SPOON and FORK, respectively. In other words, the coindexed segments simply show what is "borrowed" into the blend. For clarity, (55) shows the relational links in phonology in terms of association lines.[18]

(55) spoon   fork

          sp ork

The composition of the two parts is more complex in *composium* and *Spanglish*, because the constituents overlap. There is no reason to say that /mpoʊz/ comes exclusively from either *compose* or *symposium*, and there is no reason to say that /ɪʃ/ comes from either *Spanish* or *English*. Accordingly, we wish to coindex these stretches to both components.

We need a notation for this sort of overlap. Up till now, we have coindexed a span of phonology just at its right-hand end, and we have left a space before the left-hand end of the string. However, now we must explicitly mark the beginning of a coindexed string as well as its end, because parts of the string belong to another string as well. (56) illustrates. Coindex 6 in (56c) links a stretch of *composium* to the corresponding stretch in *compose*, and coindex 8 connects part of *composium* to the parallel part of *symposium*. The brackets below informally pick out the extent of the overlap. Again, coindices 6 and 8 in (56c) are purely relational indices, marking shared substrings that are of no significance to morphosyntax or semantics.

(56) Semantics: a. COMPOSE$_6$ b. SYMPOSIUM$_7$
      Morphosyntax: V$_6$ N$_7$
      Phonology: /$_6$kəmpoʊz$_6$ /sɪ $_8$mpoʊziəm$_8$ /$_7$

      Semantics: c. [SYMPOSIUM$_7$ ABOUT COMPOSING$_6$]$_9$
      Morphosyntax: N$_9$
      Phonology: $_9$/$_6$kə $_8$mpoʊz$_6$ iəm$_8$ /$_9$

---

[18] This is actually a bit too simple. The same machinery could be used to license improbable blends such as *forsp* and *orkoon*, which also combine phonological substrings of the two base words. A more complete story would add a requirement that the blended parts maintain their roles in syllabic structure: /sp/ has to remain

Spanglish is still a bit more complex, as it contains two disjoint parts of *Spanish*. This is shown in (57). The two fragments of *Spanish* have coindices 12 and 13; the latter of these overlaps with a longer fragment of *English* (coindex 14).

(57) Semantics: a. SPANISH_{10} b. ENGLISH_{11}

  Morphosyntax: N_{10} N_{11}

  Phonology: $_{10}/\ _{12}\text{spæ}_{12}\ \text{n}\ _{13}\text{ɪʃ}_{13}\ /_{10}$ $_{11}/\ \text{ɪ}\ _{14}\text{ŋglɪʃ}_{14}\ /_{11}$

  Semantics: c. $[\text{MIXTURE OF SPANISH}_{10} + \text{ENGLISH}_{11}]_{15}$

  Morphosyntax: N_{15}

  Phonology: $_{15}/\ _{12}\text{spæ}_{12}\ _{14}\text{ŋgl}\ _{13}\ \text{ɪʃ}_{13,14}\ /_{15}$

There is actually more overlap than notated in (56) and (57), in that *composium* maintains the prosody of its constituents, and *Spanglish* maintains not only prosody but also the nasality in the /n/-/ŋ/ segment.

A similar approach accounts for the German portmanteau *am* mentioned in section 4.6, a blend of the preposition *an* and the determiner *dem*. The /a/ comes from the nucleus of *an*, and the /m/ from the coda of *dem*. In addition, the /n/ and /m/ overlap in phonological features, aside from place of articulation.[19]

4.9.2 A blend with a derivational suffix

Blending is not confined to one-off situations like these. It can also be involved in more "hardcore" morphology. Consider nominals containing the suffix *-ery*. This suffix attaches to nouns, verbs, and adjectives alike. The examples in (58a) look like normal concatenation, adding *-ery* to the base. However, in (58b), the base ends in a nonmorphemic *-er*, and instead of the expected two *er*'s, there is only one, an instance of haplology.

(58) a. *Noun bases*: buffoonery, knavery, slavery, snobbery
  Verb bases: forgery, mockery; *Sandwich Meltery* (name of establishment in Boston's South Station)
  Adjective bases: bravery, drollery
  b. butchery (butcher), delivery (deliver), discovery (discover), embroidery (embroider), flattery (flatter), recovery (recover)

---

an onset, and /ork/ has to remain a rhyme. *Forsp* attempts to combine two onsets, so its /sp/ does not count as the same as the /sp/ in *spoon*. Similarly, *orkoon* attempts to combine two rhymes.

  This constraint still does not exclude the potential blend *foon* (which does in fact appear here and there). We suspect that part of the appeal of blends is that, as it were, they wear their hearts on their sleeves: the components are readily identifiable. And this is less true of *foon* than of *spork*: /f/ could be anything, but / ɔrk/ is a strong giveaway. Still less plausible are possible blends that are already existing words, such as *spook*. We leave these considerations unformalized (see Arndt-Lappe and Plag (2013) for more discussion).

  [19] An irresistible example: When rumors swirled about the possible resignation of then-US Secretary of State Rex Tillerson, the anticipated event was referred to as *Rexit* (Daily Kos Recommended, July 25, 2017), not only blending *Rex* and *exit*, but also evoking the contemporaneous *Brexit*, itself a blend of *Britain* and *exit*.

This alternation is not purely phonological: it depends specifically on the affix -*ery*. The agentive -*er* does not trigger this alternation. For example, someone who discovers something is a *discoverer*, not a *discover. Similarly, the comparative of *clever* is *cleverer*, not *clever.

Traditional word formation rules would have to say one of two things: either -*ery* has an allomorph -*y* that occurs after -*er*, or else -*ery* attaches to *flatter* to form *flatter-ery*, and one copy of -*er* deletes. In the latter case, though, it is impossible to determine which of the -*er*'s deletes. The alternative we propose is that -*ery* blends or overlaps with *flatter*, as in (59b), using the notation employed in *composium* above.

(59)   Semantics: a. FLATTER_{16} b. $[\text{ACT-OF } (\text{FLATTER}_{16})]_{17}$
       Morphosyntax: V_{16} $[_N \; V_{16} \; \text{aff}_{18}]_{17}$
       Phonology: $/\text{flæɾɾ}_{16}/$ $_{17}/\;_{16}\text{flæɾ}\;_{18}\text{ɾ}_{16}\;\text{i}_{18}/_{17}$

The novelty here is that the -*er*- stretch of *flattery* belongs to both the base and the affix.[20]

(60) states sister schemas for -*ery*. (60a) is the related free form, (60b) is the unblended case, and (60c) is the blended case. (60b,c) are almost identical, so they are connected as sisters by the relational link δ. The difference between them is in where the base ends. In (60b), it ends in the usual place, before the suffix; but in (60c) the base ends with -*er*, which overlaps with the suffix. (The syntactic category X in (60) stands for a choice of N, V, or A; we have notated only one of the possible meanings for the affix, and we won't pursue the semantics further.)[21]

(60)   *Sister schemas for* -ery: *No overlap*   *Overlap*
       Semantics: a. Y_α b. $[\text{ACT-OF } (Y_\alpha)]_\delta$ c. $[\text{ACT-OF } (Y_\alpha)]_\delta$
       Morphosyntax: X_α $[_N X_\alpha \; \text{aff}_{18}]_\delta$ $[_N X_\alpha \; \text{aff}_{18}]_\delta$
       Phonology: $/\;_\alpha\cdots_\alpha/$ $/\;_\alpha\cdots_{\alpha\;18}\text{ɾi}_{18}/_\delta$ $/\;_\alpha\cdots_{18}\text{ɾ}_\alpha \text{i}_{18}/_\delta$

Pāṇini's Principle (a.k.a. the Elsewhere Condition) stipulates that the larger, more highly structured option (60c) applies whenever possible. It is not entirely clear how to apply it in this case, but the idea is that if the affix can overlap with the base, it must do so. Otherwise, the free form is simply concatenated with the affix. The result is that *flattery* overlaps but *mockery* does not.

---

[20] Other instances of -*ery* have no related free form: *mystery, chicanery, skulduggery*. Still others share a non-lexical base with a sister: *misery* ~ *miserable, sorcery* ~ *sorceror, surgery* ~ *surgeon*, parallel to *ambition* ~ *ambitious*. None of these bear on the issue of blending, so we set them aside. We also set aside the condition that, with very few exceptions, -*ery* is preceded by a stressed syllable.
   Notice that *butchery* is polysemous. One reading, based on the noun *butcher*, is 'place where a butcher works', parallel to *nunnery*. The other, based on the verb *butcher*, is 'act of butchering', parallel to *flattery*. In the latter case, 'butchering' can apply to people as well as animals, as in *the butchery of Native Americans*.
[21] A more traditional approach to (60b,c) would develop an abbreviation that collapsed the two into a single formula, on the grounds that the generalization demands squeezing as many bits as possible out of the lexicon. However, given RM's full entry theory of lexical storage, what is important about generalizations is that they increase redundancy. In the present case, the relational link coindexed δ has the desired effect, and also has the virtue of separating the schemas so they are easier to read.

Such a situation, where a stretch of phonology is linked simultaneously to parts of two other words or schemas, cannot be described in theories that are based on the decomposition of complex items into morphemes, since they require contradictory decisions about morpheme boundaries. In the present approach, the internal structure of a lexical item is determined by its relation to other lexical items. The /ɪʃ/ in *Spanglish* is linked both to *Spanish* and *English*, and the /ɾ/ in *flattery* is linked to /ɾ/s in both *flatter* and *-ery*. Relational links thus provide a flexible way of notating multiply motivated structures of this sort. Section 6.8 presents further examples of affixes that blend with their bases. (For more on multiple motivation, see Booij and Audring 2018b.)

4.9.3 Truncations

Next consider some cases of truncation. (61) gives a selection of chemical names.

(61)   a. sulfur ~ sulfate, nitrogen ~ nitrate, phosphorus ~ phosphate,
          bromine ~ bromate
       b. silicon ~ silicate, manganese ~ manganate, arsenic ~ arsenate

In (61a), what precedes the *-ate* affix in each case (let's call it the "trunc") is the initial syllable of the lexical cognate plus the onset of its next syllable. In (61b), the trunc retains an unstressed second syllable. The relation between *sulfur* and *sulfate* can be formalized as (62).

(62)   Semantics: a. $SULFUR_1$ b. $[ION/COMPOUND\ CONTAINING\ (SULFUR_1)]_2$
       Morphosyntax: N_1 $[_N N_1\ aff_3\ ]_2$
       Phonology: $/sʌlf_4\ ɾ\ /_1$ $/sʌlf_4\ ɛɪt_3\ /_2$

This looks like normal affixation, except for the fact that only part of the phonology of (62a)—the trunc—is coindexed to (62b). The end of the word remains unlinked.

It might seem artificial to divide up *sulfur* into the trunc *sulf-* and the remainder *-ur*. However, just as with blends, although the relational link coindexed 4 in (62) divides up the phonology of *sulfur*, it has no relation to the syntax and semantics. Hence the link is not relevant to *sulfur* in isolation, only to the phonological relation of *sulfur* to *sulfate*.

Generalizing to the class of words in (61a), we can state a pair of sister schemas as (63). (C_1 stands for one or more consonants.)

(63)   *Sister schemas for chemical terms in -ate*
       a. Semantics: $CHEMICAL\text{-}ELEMENT_α$
          Morphosyntax: $N_α$
          Phonology: $//σ\ C_1\ /_β ...\ /_α$

          Example: *sul- f - ur*

b. Semantics: $[\text{ION/COMPOUND CONTAINING (CHEMICAL-ELEMENT}_\alpha)]_\gamma$
   Morphosyntax: $[_N \, N_\alpha \, \text{aff}_3 \,]_\gamma$
   Phonology: $// \sigma \, C_1 /_\beta \, \varepsilon \text{It}_3 /_\gamma$

   Example: *sul- f - ate*

The semantics and morphosyntax of (63a,b) are altogether normal, just like any pair of sister schemas. Again the interest is in the phonology: only *part* of the free form (63a) is linked to the base of (63b) by coindex β. The rest of the free form simply has no counterpart in the complex form. In other words, (63) accomplishes relationally what a traditional procedural rule would bring about by deletion. ((63) can be extended to the examples in (61b) by including an optional unstressed syllable; we will not formalize it here.)

   (63) is in fact not so different from a schema for blends. One can equally think of *sulfate* as a truncation of *sulfur* to *sulf* plus the suffix, or as a blend of *sulfur* with the suffix, along the lines of *spork*. (63) in effect says that these amount to the same thing.

   Truncation is also involved in the classic case of nicknames (or hypocoristics: Lappe 2007; Alber and Arndt-Lappe 2012; Booij and Audring 2017; and, for Japanese, Tsujimura and Davis 2018). (64) gives some canonical pairs in English. (We'll get to the variant with final /i/ in a moment.)

(64)   David ~ Dave, Daniel ~ Dan, Jennifer ~ Jen, Elizabeth ~ Liz, Ezra ~ Ez,
       Thomas ~ Tom, Barbara ~ Barb, Amy ~ Ame

The structure of a typical pair is shown in (65). (For the Register feature, see section 8.3.)

(65)   Semantics: a. DAVID_5 b. $[\text{DAVID}_5; \text{Register: INFORMAL})]_6$
       Morphosyntax: Proper Noun$_5$ Proper Noun$_6$
       Phonology: $/\text{d}\varepsilon\text{Iv}_7 \, \text{Id}/_5$ $/\text{d}\varepsilon\text{Iv}/_{7,6}$

Again the relations in semantics and morphosyntax are straightforward. We note only that this time the "derived" form has no internal morphosyntactic structure; it is simply a Proper Noun. The phonology is where the interest lies: only part of *David* is linked with *Dave*, hence the appearance of truncation.

   The sister schemas (66) that license this form for nicknames again identify the trunc as the stressed syllable plus the following onset; in the nickname, this consonant syllabifies as a coda. In order to include *Elizabeth/Liz* and perhaps others, (66a) allows a syllable before the trunc. A similar analysis appears in Booij and Audring (2017). ($\acute{\sigma}$ denotes a stressed syllable.)

(66)   Semantics: a. $[X]_\alpha$ b. $[X_\alpha; \text{Register: INFORMAL})]_z$
       Morphosyntax: $[\text{Proper Noun}]_\alpha$ $[\text{Proper Noun}]_z$
       Phonology: $/ \ldots / \acute{\sigma} \, C /_\beta \ldots /_\alpha$ $/ \, [_{\acute{\sigma}} \ldots C] \, /_{\beta,z}$

       Example: *E - li z - abeth*   *Li - z*

A similar pair of sister schemas yields clippings like *mathematics* ~ *math, psychology* ~ *psych, chemistry* ~ *chem, economics* ~ *ec*, and the authors' favorite private coinage, *morphology* ~ *morf*. In these cases, the trunc is like that in *sulfate*: simply the first syllable plus the initial consonant of the second.[22]

The bisyllabic variant of nicknames has /i/ attached at the end of the nickname, as in *Freddy, Suzie*, and *Jenny*. (67) is the relevant schema. It is similar to (66), but adds the final /i/ as a suffix.

(67) Semantics: a. $[X]_\alpha$ b. $[X_\alpha; \text{Register: INFORMAL}]_w$
      Morphosyntax: $[\text{Proper Noun}]_\alpha$ $[\text{Proper Noun}_\alpha \text{aff}_8]_w$
      Phonology: $/\ldots/\acute{\sigma}\,C_1/_\beta\,\ldots/_\alpha$ $//\acute{\sigma}\,C_1/_\beta i_8/_w$

      Example: *Jenn - ifer*   *Jenn   -y*

This pair of schemas is applicable even if the formal name in (67a) is monosyllabic, as in *John* ~ *Johnny, Beth* ~ *Bethie*. In addition, since the nickname schemas in (66b) and (67b) are both sisters of the name schema in (66a)/(67a), they are also sisters of each other. This means that they can relate alternative nicknames for which there is no corresponding formal name, such as *Sparky* ~ *Spark* (in RJ's lexicon).

Looking briefly at "hard-core" morphology again, consider the affix *-ify*, which must be immediately preceded by main stress. It unifies smoothly with final-stressed bases like *diverse* and *intense*, forming *diversify* and *intensify*. With other bases it shifts stress: *pérson* ~ *persónify, húmid* ~ *humídify*, etc. (see section 6.7 for the comparable case of *-ity*). But with still others, it uses everything in the base up to the onset of the post-stress syllable, which therefore looks like a trunc.

(68)   *deity* ~ *deify, calcium* ~ *calcify, liquid* ~ *liquefy, stupid* ~ *stupefy*

The sister schemas for this use of the affix are (69a,b). (C_0 stands for zero or more consonants.)

(69) Semantics: a. X_α b. $[\text{BECOME}\,(X_\alpha)]_z$
      Morphosyntax: $[\text{N/A}]_\alpha$ $[_V \text{N/A}_\alpha\,\text{aff}_9]_z$
      Phonology: $//\acute{\sigma}\,C_0/_\beta\ldots/_\alpha$ $//\acute{\sigma}\,C_0/_\beta \text{əfaj}_9/_z$

      Example: *stu-p - id*   *stu-p - efy*

This schema, like many others we have looked at, is almost like ordinary affixation. The sole difference is in the phonology, where only the beginning of the lexical cognate is linked to the complex form. So again we get the appearance of truncation having taken place, but without appealing to a *process* of truncation.

---

[22] Of course, not all nicknames conform to the pattern in (66). *Robert* ~ *Bob* and *William* ~ *Bill* do not share the initial consonant; *Susan* ~ *Sue* and *Joseph* ~ *Joe* do not share the second consonant. And some nicknames have nothing to do with their formal counterpart, for example (in RJ's lexicon) *Harry* ~ *Sparky*. But this sort of variation is to be expected in lexical relations.

4.10 Umlaut and other stem allomorphy; the star notation

Section 3.7 discussed the umlaut alternation of *goose* and *geese*. We treated this alternation in terms of the ***same-except*** relation: phonologically they are taken to be the same, except for their vowels. We drew a parallel between them and the wugs in Figure 4.1 (= Figure 3.11), which are perceived as the same, except for their contrasting eyes.

With this parallel in mind, we can analyze *geese* in much the same way as zero plurals like *sheep*. The only difference is that in this case the phonological relation to the singular is not complete identity. Section 3.7 introduced the ***star notation*** to express such a configuration. Applying this notation to the phonology of *goose* and *geese*, we get (70).[23]

(70) Semantics: a. GOOSE_1 b. $[\text{PLUR}\,(\text{GOOSE}_1)]_2$
      Morphosyntax: N_1 $\{\text{N}_1, \text{PL}\}_2$
      Phonology: $/\text{g}\,{*}\text{uw}{*}\,\text{s}/_1$ $/\text{g}\,{*}\text{i}{*}\,\text{s}/_{1,2}$

In (70b), coindices 1 and 2 are configured in the usual fashion for a zero inflection. The crucial innovation is yet again in the phonology, where the relational link coindexed 1 is modulated by the stars. The interpretation is that *geese* is pronounced the same as *goose*—except for the contrasting vowels, which are starred.

There are two other instances of this particular alternation, namely *tooth ~ teeth* and *foot ~ feet*. We suspect that these three are not enough to warrant a pair of sister schemas. Similarly for the exceptional alternations in *long ~ length* and *strong ~ strength*. Nevertheless, the relation between the members of each of these pairs can be captured with lexical entries like those in (70).

A more robust candidate for a same-except *schema* is the *f-v* alternation in *wife ~ wives, life ~ lives, wolf ~ wolves, half ~ halves*, etc., which has a substantial collection of instances. Here is the pair *wolf ~ wolves*.

(71) Semantics: a. WOLF_3 b. $[\text{PLUR}\,(\text{WOLF}_3)]_4$
      Morphosyntax: N_3 $\{\text{N}_3, \text{PL}_5\}_4$
      Phonology: $/\text{wʊl}\,{*}\text{f}{*}/_3$ $/\,/\text{wʊl}\,{*}\text{v}{*}/_3\,\text{z}_5\,/_4$

Figure 4.1 Internal contrast

[23] For discussion of the absence of SG in (70a), see sections 4.3 and 5.5.

Here, *wolv-* in the plural is the same as *wolf* in the stem (coindex 3), except for the final consonant—more precisely, except for the voicing feature in the final consonant. Notice that the /f/ is retained in the possessive *wolf's* and the verb (*He <u>wolfs</u> down his food*). This shows that the alternation is morphologically conditioned by the plural and is not just a matter for phonology.

A pair of schemas for the *f/v* plural alternation is (72). These say that a noun that ends in /f/ may have a plural that ends in /vz/. (*House ~ houses* may be a one-off extension to an alveolar.)

(72) *Sister schemas for f-v alternation in plural*

Semantics:	a. X_α	b. $[\text{PLUR}\,(X_\alpha)]_\gamma$
Morphosyntax:	N_α	$[N_\alpha\ \text{PL}_1]_\gamma$
Phonology:	$/...{*}f{*}/_\alpha$	$//...{*}v{*}/_\alpha\,z_1/_\gamma$

What makes this different from the regular plural schema (Chapter 2, example (2)), is the phonology: the material in (72a) and (72b) with coindex α counts as the same, except for the difference between /f/ and /v/ (to be more precise, their voicing feature).

A more complex example of the star notation comes from the Latinate prefix-stem verbs of English, many of which undergo stem allomorphy in the context of *-(t/s)ion*. (73) gives a few examples. (Other such examples appear in Booij 1997a.)

(73) a. propel ~ propulsion
      b. resolve ~ resolution
      c. adhere ~ adhesion
      d. receive ~ reception

We would like to say that *propul(s)-* is the same as *propel*, except for the second vowel. Accordingly, we notate (73a) as (74). (It is not clear whether the /s/ is part of the base or part of the affix; for simplicity we will assign it to the affix. But see section 6.8.2.)

(74)

	a. *propel*	b. *propulsion*
Semantics:	PROPEL_6	$[\text{ACT-OF}\,(\text{PROPEL}_6)]_7$
Morphosyntax:	V_6	$[_N\,V_6\,\text{aff}_8\,]_7$
Phonology:	$/\text{prəp}\,{*}ɛ{*}\,l/_6$	$//\text{prəp}\,{*}ʌ{*}\,l/_6\,\text{ʃən}_8\,/_7$

We next note that most of the *-pel* words have the same allomorphy.

(75) propel ~ propulsion
      expel ~ expulsion
      compel ~ compulsion
      repel ~ repulsion
      although:
      impel ~ *impulsion ~ impulse
      dispel ~ *dispulsion

Should this call for a schema, (76) does the job.

(76) *Sister schemas for -pel ~ -pul alternation*

Semantics:	a. X_α	b. $[ACT\text{-}OF\,(X_\alpha)]_y$
Morphosyntax:	V_α	$[_N\,V_\alpha\,aff_8\,]_y$
Phonology:	$/...p\,{*}\varepsilon{*}\,l/_\alpha$	$//...p\,{*}\Lambda{*}\,l/_\alpha\ \int\!\partial n_8\,/_y$

Aronoff (1976) and Bochner (1993) observe that if a Latinate verb has an allomorph with *-ion*, it tends to use the same allomorph with *-ive*, as seen in (77). This pertains even to the one-off alternation in (77d).[24]

(77) a. repel ~ repulsion ~ repulsive, compel ~ compulsion ~ compulsive,
       expel ~ expulsion ~ expulsive
    b. receive ~ reception ~ receptive, deceive ~ deception ~ deceptive,
       perceive ~ perception ~ perceptive
    c. adhere~ adhesion ~ adhesive, cohere ~ cohesion ~ cohesive
    d. destroy ~ destruction ~ destructive

Aronoff and Bochner propose to capture this generalization (in our terms) by a pair of sister schemas, one for *-ion* and one for *-ive*, which equate all the phonology preceding the suffix, from whatever source, allomorphic or not.

(78) Morphosyntax: a. $[_N\,V_\alpha\,aff_9\,]_y$ b. $[_A\,V_\alpha\,aff_{10}\,]_z$
    Phonology: $/..._\alpha\,\partial n_9\,]_y$ $/..._\alpha\,IV_{10}\,]_z$

These schemas operate independently from those like (76), which determine the proper allomorph of the base. If a verb happens to have *-ion* and *-ive* forms, (78) says they will have the same form of the base. So, for instance, if the phonology in the *-ion* form happens to be /prəpʌl/, (78) says that its sisters' instances will come out as *propulsion* and *propulsive*. If it happens to be /rəcɛpt/, the sisters will come out as *reception* and *receptive*.[25] In other words, motivation for the pair *propulsion ~ propulsive* comes from two independent pairs of sister schemas: (76), which determines the form of the stem allomorph, and (78), which motivates uniformity of allomorph choice across the two affixes.[26]

4.11 More fragmentation: Infixation and reduplication

The previous two sections have discussed morphological patterns in which there is a related free form, but the base is not entirely identical to it. We now turn to further cases where the base is a mangled version of the related free form: infixation and reduplication.

---

[24] For Aronoff, this relationship is directional, giving one form priority over the other. This is unnecessary in the RM analysis; the two forms are sisters.

[25] For discussion of the /ʃ/ ~ /t/ alternation in *recep/ʃ/ion ~ recep/t/ive* and parallel alternations in (77), see section 6.8.

[26] Further fine details of Latinate prefix-stem morphology, as discussed by Aronoff, Bochner, and others, are beyond the scope of the present study. Hüning (2018) deals with similar allomorphy in the German affixes *-ieren*, *-isieren*, and *-ifizieren*, including cases in which the boundary between the stem and the affix is ambiguous, much like English *reception*.

4.11.1 Infixation

Infixation is a converse of circumfixation: instead of a base surrounded by two pieces of an affix, an affix is surrounded by two pieces of a base. A well-known citation is the Tagalog Agent Focus infix *-um-*, as in (79) (from Crowhurst 1998).

(79) Tagalog:
> a. súlat 'write'   s**um**úlat 'write (Agent focus)'
> b. yáman 'become rich'   y**um**áman 'become rich (Agent focus)'
> c. bilí 'buy'   b**um**ilí 'buy (Agent focus)'
> d. gradwet 'graduate'   gr**um**adwet 'graduate (Agent focus)'
> e. tawag 'call'   t**um**awag 'call (Agent focus)'

We wish to express the intuition that *sumulat* in (79a) is just the word *sulat*, with *-um-* stuffed into its middle. To capture this intuition, we have to address two issues. First, just as in circumfixation, it is impossible to justify a linear ordering of the base and the affix in morphosyntax. Rather, we have to state the morphosyntax in the unordered set notation {V, aff}.

Second, and more difficult, it is necessary to get the infix inside the base. To accomplish this, we again appeal to the same-except relation: we regard *sumulat* as the same as *sulat*, except for an elaboration *-um-*. However, because the elaboration is internal to the word, it can't be simply tacked onto the beginning or end of the word. The star notation comes to the rescue. This is shown in (80) (adopting Crowhurst's notation for the phonology).

(80) Semantics: a. WRITE_1 b. $[\text{WRITE}_1; \text{Agent focus}]_2$
>   Morphosyntax: V_1 $\{_V\, V_1, \text{aff}_3\}_2$
>   Phonology: $/\text{sulat}/_1$ $/\text{s}\,{}^*\text{um}_3{}^*\,\text{ulat}\,/_{1,2}$

The links in semantics and morphosyntax are perfectly ordinary for an affixed form. The novelty is once more in the phonology. The trick is in coindex 1. It links /sumulat/ to /sulat/, saying they are the same—except for the starred /um/. In turn, the starred /um/ is coindexed to the morphosyntax of (80b), exactly like a suffix. The effect is that infixation is exactly like suffixation, except for the unusual position of the affix.

The infix itself is notated as a pair of sister schemas, one for the verb stem, and one for the infixed form, as in (81). (81b) places the infix after the first consonant of the base. As usual, coindex α marks correlated variables across the two schemas.

(81) *Sister schemas for Tagalog Agent focus reduplication*
>   Semantics: a. $[\text{F}\,(\text{X},\ldots)]_\alpha$ b. $[\text{F}\,(\text{X},\ldots)_\alpha; \text{Agent focus}]_\gamma$
>   Morphosyntax: V_α $\{V_\alpha, \text{aff}_3\}_\gamma$
>   Phonology: $/\ldots/_\alpha$ $/\text{C}\,{}^*\text{um}_3{}^*\,\ldots\,/_{\alpha,\gamma}$

The only difference between (81) and our treatment of suffixes in terms of sister schemas, e.g. (49), lies in the phonology of (81b). It breaks the base into its initial consonant and everything else; the infix is located between them. This precisely mirrors our intuition about the structure of infixation.

Inkelas (2014) discusses crosslinguistic constraints on possible positions for infixation, e.g. after the first consonant, after the first syllable, preceding the stressed syllable (as in English expletive infixation: *abso-bloomin-lutely*, McCarthy 1982) and so on, as well as prosodic constraints on the infix itself. In the present framework, this amounts to constraints on possible versions of the phonology in schemas like (81b).

4.11.2 Reduplication

A final challenge for this chapter is reduplication, where in place of an affix with fixed phonology, we find a copy of the base or of a part of it. For instance, Warlpiri expresses plural of some nouns with full reduplication of the base, as in (82) (from Marantz (1982), citing Nash (1980)).

(82) Warlpiri:
    kurdu 'child'   kurdukurdu 'children'
    kamina 'girl, maiden'   kaminakamina 'girls, maidens'
    mardukuja 'woman, female'   mardukujamardukuja 'women, females'

Accounts of reduplication typically focus on its phonological constraints in various languages. However, reduplication constructions also have a morphosemantics, one that overlaps substantially with that of ordinary affixation (Moravcsik 1978; Ghomeshi et al. 2004; Rubino 2013). Hence, if at all possible, reduplicative constructions should be treated the same way as affixal morphology—in RM, as lexical items with variables. What makes them different is that the phonology of the reduplicative morpheme is not a constant but a bound variable, linked to the phonology of its host.

(83) is a possible representation for such examples. The semantics and morphosyntax are identical with the English plural, but the N node has a double connection to the phonology. Thus it is sort of an upside-down version of portmanteaux. The morphosyntactic PL itself has no direct connection to phonology; plurality is associated with the formal pattern as a whole.[27]

(83) Semantics: $[\text{PLUR (CHILD}_1)]_2$
      Morphosyntax: $\{N_1, \text{PL}\}_2$
      Phonology: $/\text{kurdu}_1 \text{ kurdu}_1 /_2$

The general schema is (84). The noun in morphosyntax is linked to two identical phonological strings, both subscripted *x* (a Greek letter would also be possible).

---

[27] Alternatively, PL could link to one or both of the identical segments of (83). If only one, this raises the question of which copy is the base and which the reduplicant in (83). In some cases this may be clear from the phonology, say if the reduplicant is a reduced form of the base. We need not decide here whether PL is linked or not. For our purposes, it suffices to show that the tools of Relational Morphology afford several possible accounts, differing in small details.

(84) *Warlpiri plural schema*
    Semantics: $[\text{PLUR}(X_x)]_y$
    Morphosyntax: $\{N_x, \text{PL}\}_y$
    Phonology: $/\ldots_x \ldots_x/_y$

Coindex 1 in (83) assigns interface links between the morphosyntax and both copies of the base in the phonology. The question arises of whether this coindex might instead (or also) designate a relational link between the two occurrences of *kurdu*—here, a relational link *inside* a lexical item. This possibility emerges in a more complex case of reduplication such as (85), from Mangarayi, in which the reduplicant is a copy of only part of the base, and it is moreover infixed (Merlan 1982; McCarthy and Prince 1995; Inkelas 2014).[28]

(85) *Mangarayi plural*

	Singular	Plural	
a.	gabuji	g-**ab**-abuji	'old person(s)'
b.	yirag	y-**ir**-iragji	'father(s) and child(ren)'
c.	waŋgij	w-**aŋg**-aŋgij	'child(ren)'
d.	jimgan	j-**img**-imgan	'knowledgeable person(s)'
e.	guryag	g-**ury**-uryagji	'lily/having a lot of lilies'

                      [a different meaning expressed by reduplication]

For this case we have to invoke the machinery for infixation from the previous subsection. But instead of the infix being a phonological constant like Tagalog *-um-*, it is a copy of a fragment of the base. Here are the morphosyntax and phonology for the pair of words in (85a). Crucially, coindex 6 marks a relational link *inside* the item, linking the /ab/ in (86a) with two copies in (86b).

(86) Morphosyntax: a. N_4 b. $\{_N N_4, \text{PL}\}_5$
      Phonology: $/\text{g ab}_6 \text{ uji}/_4$ $/\text{g }^*\text{ab}_6{}^* \text{ ab}_6 \text{ uji }/_{4,5}$

Notice the role of coindex 4 in the phonology: it says that /gababuji/ in (86b) is the same as /gabuji/ in (85a)—except for the extra /ab/. This creates the appearance of reduplication.

    The general pattern found in (86) is captured by the sister schemas in (87).

(87) *Sister schemas for Mangarayi plural*
    Morphosyntax: a. N_α b. $\{_N N_\alpha \text{ PL}\}_y$
    Phonology: $/\text{C VC}_\beta\ldots/_\alpha$ $/\text{C }^*\text{VC}_\beta{}^* \text{VC}_\beta\ldots/_{\alpha,y}$

---

[28] Merlan (1982) segments the phonology by syllables, which results in strange rules of reduplication. We follow Inkelas and McCarthy and Prince in seeing the reduplicant as following the initial consonant and crossing syllable boundaries.
    Tsujimura and Davis (2018) cite cases of reduplication in Japanese in which there is no related non-reduplicated form. This speaks in favor of choosing an analysis for reduplication in which the presence of a lexical noun is inessential, and the crucial element is the relational link between the two identical pieces of phonology.

The phonology of (87b) is divided into four pieces: the initial consonant, the reduplicant, the segment that is to be reduplicated, and the rest of the word. Greek subscript β links the reduplicated parts of (87b) to the relevant part of the related free form (87a); subscript α links the entire phonology of (87b) to that of the related free form: they are the same except for the starred intrusion.

In principle, this formalization allows the reduplicant to copy any chunk at all of the base, and for it to be placed anywhere—before, after, or anywhere within the base. Again, the constraints discussed at length by Inkelas (2014) can be stated in terms of what is a permissible structural description for the phonology in reduplicative sister schemas. We have stated the constraints in (87) simply in terms of strings of consonants and vowels, but we do not mean to preclude statements in terms of more sophisticated prosodic units, as discussed by Inkelas and by McCarthy and Prince.

In any event, the coindexing formalism of RM captures the relation of the reduplicant to its base directly and explicitly. We see no need to generate a partial reduplicant as a full copy, then reduce it, as in Inkelas and Zoll (2005), or to generate an infixed reduplicant outside the base and move it in in order to satisfy various prosodic conditions, as in McCarthy and Prince (1995). We take this to be a useful consequence of the RM approach.

4.12 Summary

This chapter has explored a wide range of morphological phenomena that differ primarily in how morphosyntax is linked to phonology.[29] In canonical cases such as *harden* and *baker*, each morphosyntactic constituent corresponds to a discrete and continuous segment of phonology, and the base has a related free form with the same phonology. Such cases underlie the appeal of the classical notion of the morpheme as the "minimal meaningful unit." However, all the other phenomena we have considered involve various noncanonical linkings across the morphosyntax-phonology interface. For example, the very same morphosyntax of the plural (88) allows widely varying phonological realizations (89a-g).

(88) Morphosyntax: [N PL] or {N, PL}

(89) a. Phonology: /cats/   (Regular affixal plural)
      b. Phonology: /sheep/   (Zero plural: (21))
      c. Phonology: /geese/   (Umlaut: (70))
      d. Phonology: /wolves/   (Stem alternation: (71))
      e. Phonology: /məlaxim/   (Semitic intercalation: (37))
      f. Phonology: /kurdukurdu/   (Warlpiri full reduplication: (84))
      g. Phonology: /gababuji/   (Mangarayi infixed partial reduplication: (87))

---

[29] One important thing we have not addressed is polysynthetic morphology. Baker (2018) develops a treatment of the polysynthetic languages Wubuy and Ngalakgan in a Construction Morphology framework, using a formalism quite close to that of RM.

At the same time, each of these types of linking can be used with other patterns of affixation. For instance, zero morphology also appears in English denominal verbs such as *butter*, and vowel alternation also appears in English past tenses such as *sang*.

One of the important deviations from the canonical morpheme is found in words like *scrumptious* and *commotion*, which have an identifiable affix but whose base has no lexical cognate. We have analyzed these as partially a-morphous, in that they lack a lexical base in morphosyntax. Their affix is a classical morpheme, but their base is not. Further out on the fringe are classes of words like *candid*, *splendid*, and *rancid*, for which it is not clear whether even the shared portion should count as a morphosyntactic affix (although counting it as an affix makes it possible to recognize the relation to *candor*, *splendor*, etc.). At the extreme are cases like *trillion* and *glimmer*, which contain some degree of phonological and semantic compositionality, but which offer no evidence for morphosyntactic structure—and hence are fully a-morphous.

Our toolkit for expressing lexical structure and lexical relations has involved two kinds of links: interface links and relational links. *Interface* links connect semantic, syntactic, and phonological constituents of the same lexical item, for instance the meaning HARD, the syntactic category Adjective, and the phonology /hard/. The outer interface link unifies the three structures into a lexical entry; this link serves the function that is traditionally notated by large square brackets.

Relational links connect constituents of the *same* level. Usually the linked constituents are in different lexical items. However, in reduplication, a relational link connects the reduplicant and what it is a copy of, within the same lexical entry.

We have introduced four kinds of relational links:

- Two or more constants can be marked as identical. We notate this by marking them with identical numerical coindices. For instance, the word *wide* and the base of *widen* are linked with a numerical coindex, as are the suffix in *widen* and the suffix in the [$_V$ A-*en*] schema.
- A constant can be marked as an instance of a variable. We notate this by assigning the constant a numerical coindex and assigning the variable a variable coindex (*x*, *y*, etc.). For instance, the base of *widen* has a numerical coindex, and the variable it satisfies, namely the adjective in [$_V$ A-*en*], has a variable coindex. (See section 4.13 for some further discussion of the notation for this.)
- Variables in different schemas can be marked as identical, forming linked sister schemas. We notate this by coindexing them with Greek letters. For instance, the variables in the -*ism* and -*ist* schemas run in parallel, giving us *pacifism* ~ *pacifist*, *optimism* ~ *optimist*, and so on.
- When two phonological constituents are marked as identical by a relational link, they may still differ with respect to some interior contrast or elaboration. The differing part is marked with stars, as in *g*oo* se* ~ *g*ee* se* and *gabuji* ~ *g*ab* abuji*.

As discussed in Chapters 1–3, many morphological theories account for regularities in terms of sequences of procedural rules that change one form (the underlying form) into another (the surface form). In contrast, Relational Morphology (along with Construction Morphology and Bybee's (1995) Network Model) does not countenance procedural rules or underlying forms. Therefore it requires a mechanism that produces the effects typically attributed to procedural derivations. The notion of sister schemas does the desired work. Rather than changing one schematized structure S_1 into another schematized structure S_2, we have two schemas S_1 and S_2 that are linked through a shared part. Where the procedural rule effects a change, the paired schemas codify the relation in terms of the differences between the two schemas. For instance, instead of turning *-ism* words into *-ist* words by adding *-ist* and deleting *-ism*, the two schemas simply say that *-ism* and *-ist* are parts that the two schemas do not share. There is no need to establish a direction of derivation. This is a good consequence of the approach, because, as we have shown, there are cases like *linguist ~ linguistics* where "direction of derivation" is conflicted. In addition, we have shown how some of the parade cases of process morphology, such as truncation, reduplication, and infixation, can be described in terms of sister schemas.

One of the intuitions behind rule-based morphology is that words can be built up step by step, for instance adding *-ure* to *proceed* to get *procedure*, then adding *-al* to get *procedural*, and finally adding *-ly* to get *procedurally*. Section 4.4 showed how to achieve the same effect by relating each "step" of the "derivation" to a separate schema, without implying any order of application. Section 4.9.2, discussing the morphology of *mockery* vs. *flattery*, showed how schemas can apply in overlapping fashion, so that some phonological segments of a word are associated with two morphosyntactic constituents at once. This is impossible in a rule-based derivation, where such a configuration can only be simulated by deleting one of the doubled segments. (Further examples appear in section 6.8; Audring, Booij, and Jackendoff (2017) develop another example of this situation.)

Finally, we again wish to stress the formal parallelism between words and schemas in Relational Morphology. Every schema is based on words, simply replacing parts of the words' content with variables. Some other approaches to morphology, especially Bochner (1993) and Booij (2010), are based on this parallelism. However, here we are pushing this policy as far as we can, in particular bringing out the parallel between sister words and sister schemas. We hope to have shown that this is a fruitful approach.

4.13 Appendix: Alternatives in the notation

In developing a notation for Relational Morphology, we have had to make a lot of difficult choices, often finding it necessary to balance formal rigor with readability. We have tried to spare the reader the agony behind the development of the notation; we have presented only what we hope is a reasonably finished product. However, a few issues seem important enough to mention. This section discusses three of them.

4.13.1 Separating interface and relational indices

The notation we have adopted here requires many coindices to do double duty, simultaneously marking interface and relational links. We recognize that this policy is not always perspicuous. Consider again the relation between *wide* and *widen* in (90) (= (1)).

(90) Semantics: a. WIDE_1 b. $[\text{BECOME (X, WIDE}_1)]_2$

     Morphosyntax: A_1 $[_V A_1 \text{ aff}_3]_2$

     Phonology: /wajd$_1$/   /wajd$_1$ ən$_3$ /$_2$

Coindex 1 here marks simultaneously the outer interface link of *wide* (90a), the inner interface link for the base in *widen* (90b), and the relational link between these two. A more rigorous notation would keep these functions distinct. In particular, it would be useful to make a notational distinction between interface links and relational links, which are quite different in what they link.

(91) shows one possible way of doing this. Interface links are notated as before with subscripted numeral indices 1, 2, 3, 4, 5. Relational links are notated with presubscripted letters *a*, *b*, *c*, *d*, *e*. There are three distinct relational links *a*, *b*, and *c* between *wide* and *widen*, one for each level, plus relational links *d* and *e* that connect to the $[_V \text{ A-}en]$ schema.

(91) Semantics: a. $_a\text{WIDE}_1$ b. $[\text{BECOME (X, }_a\text{WIDE}_4)]_2$

     Morphosyntax: $_bA_1$ $[_V \,_bA_4 \,_d\text{aff}_3]_2$

     Phonology: /$_c$wajd$_1$/   /$_c$wajd$_4$ $_e$ən$_3$ /$_2$

The relation between singular and plural *sheep* then looks like this (compare to (21)):

(92) Semantics: a. $_f\text{SHEEP}_5$ b. $[\text{PLUR (}_f\text{SHEEP}_7)]_6$

     Morphosyntax: $_gN_5$ $[_N \,_gN_7 \,_i\text{PL}]_6$

     Phonology: /$_h$ʃip$_5$/   /$_h$ʃip/$_{7,6}$

And the relation between the sisters *ambition/ambitious* comes out like this (compare to (43)):

(93) Semantics: a. $_k\text{DESIRE}_8$ b. $[\text{HAVING (}_k\text{DESIRE})]_9$

     Morphosyntax: $[_N - \,_l\text{aff}_{10}]_8$ $[_A - \,_o\text{aff}_{11}]_9$

     Phonology: /$_n$æmbɪʃ $_m$ən$_{10}$ /$_8$ /$_n$æmbɪʃ $_p$əs$_{11}$ /$_9$

This becomes rather messy. The outer coindex for *ambition* is 8; that for *ambitious* is 9. Coindex 10 ties together the morphosyntactic affix and its phonology in *ambition*, and coindex 11 does the same in *ambitious*. The two occurrences of DESIRE are linked by relational coindex *k*; the two occurrences of /æmbɪʃ/ are linked by coindex *n*. Relational coindices *l* and *m* connect the affix in *ambition* to that in the $[_N \text{ -}ion]$ schema; and coindices *o* and *p* connect the affix in *ambitious* to the $[_A \text{ -}ious]$ schema.

Well. This is indeed formally more precise than the notation we have been using. But one is at the risk of drowning in subscripts. Since we are writing for human readers (including ourselves), and not for a computational implementation, which would require maximal explicitness, we have decided to retain the simpler notation for expediency, while recognizing that it is not the ultimate in formalization.

4.13.2 The treatment of variable instantiation

We have been a bit casual in our treatment of the relation between schemas and their instances. Here is the $[_V$ A-*en*$]$ schema again.

(94) Semantics: $[\text{BECOME } (X, [<\text{MORE}> \text{PROPERTY}]_x)]_y$
      Morphosyntax: $[_V A_x \text{ aff}_3]_y$
      Phonology: $//\sigma \, [\text{-son}]/_x \, \text{ən}_3 /_y$

Comparing this to its instance (90b), we see that coindex *x* corresponds to coindex 1 in (90b); coindex *y* corresponds to coindex 2 in (90b), and coindex 3—the constant in the schema—corresponds to coindex 3 in (90b).

The reason that we introduced variable subscripts in the schema is that they have to correspond to different subscripts in each of the schema's instances: *x* corresponds to 12 and *y* corresponds to 13 in *darken* (95) (= (2b)).

(95) Semantics: $[\text{BECOME } (X, \text{DARK}_{12})]_{13}$
      Morphosyntax: $[_V A_{12} \text{ aff}_3]_{13}$
      Phonology: $/\text{dark}_{12} \, \text{ən}_3 /_{13}$

Hence we said that the relational links between the schema and its instances are established by virtue of parallel structure between them.

One way to be more precise is to notate individual relational links between the schema and each of its instances. Using the pre-subscripting notation suggested above, schema (94) and its instances *widen* and *darken* could be notated as in (96). Notice that each piece of the schema has separate relational links to the corresponding parts of *widen* and *darken*, followed by an ellipsis that stands in for all the other instances.

(96) Semantics: a. $_{t,w,...}[\text{BECOME } (X, \, _{a,o,...}[\text{PROPERTY}]_{14}) \,]_{15}$
      Morphosyntax: $_{u,x,...}[_V \, _{b,p,...} A_{14 \, d,r,...} \text{aff}_{16}]_{15}$
      Phonology: $_{v,y,...}/ \, _{c,q,...}/[\sigma \, [\text{-son}]/_{14 \, e,s,...} \text{ən}_{16} /_{15}$

      Semantics: b. $_t[\text{BECOME } (X, \, _a \text{WIDE}_4)]_2$
      Morphosyntax: $_u[_V \, _b A_4 \, _d \text{aff}_3]_2$
      Phonology: $_v/ \, _c \text{wajd}_4 \, _e \text{ən}_3 /_2$

      Semantics: c. $_w[\text{BECOME } (X, \, _o \text{DARK}_{12})]_{13}$
      Morphosyntax: $_x[_V \, _p A_{12} \, _r \text{aff}_{14}]_{13}$
      Phonology: $_y/ \, _q \text{dark}_{12} \, _s \text{ən}_{14} /_{13}$

This traces all the relational links individually, which is good. It just happens to be impossible to use. So again, we retain our less precise formalism in the interest of sanity.

Nevertheless, there is one point of theoretical interest in this notation. Schema (96) carries subscripts for each of its instances. This is perfect for the relational use of a schema: its instances are directly connected to it. However, a productive schema has to be open to new instances never encountered before. And here a variable subscript seems absolutely appropriate. Section 2.7 argued that the difference between productive schemas such as the English plural and nonproductive schemas such as $[_V$ A-*en*] is coded in the variable. There we regarded this difference as a diacritic on the variable, and we noted this diacritic in terms of underline (nonproductive) vs. double underline (productive). The notation in (96) offers the possibility of defining a productive variable as one that has a variable coindex in addition to its list of constant coindices. However, in the face of the fearsome notation, we continue to leave this point unformalized.

4.13.3 An interface link between aff and semantics?

We have systematically notated an interface link between morphosyntactic affixes and the corresponding phonology, for instance coindex 3 in *widen* (90) and *darken* (95). Intuitively, on grounds of uniformity, one might expect this link to extend to semantics as well. The most obvious way of achieving such uniformity is illustrated in (97), in which coindex 3 is also subscripted to BECOME.

(97) Semantics: $[BECOME_3 (X, WIDE_1)]_2$
      Morphosyntax: $[_V A_1 \, aff_3 \,]_2$
      Phonology: $/wajd_1 \, \partial n_3 \, /_2$

However, this notation will not work in general, because the semantic structure associated with the affix is not always a coindexable constituent. Consider *baker* ((98) = (4b)). The parts of the semantics that correspond to the meaning of the affix have a wavy underline.

(98) Semantics: $[\underline{PERSON}^\alpha; [BAKE (\underline{Agent: \alpha}, Patient: INDEF)]_6]_7$
      Morphosyntax: $[_N V_6 \, aff_8 \,]_7$
      Phonology: $/bejk_6 \, r_8 \,]_7$

These underlined portions do not form a constituent to which a subscript can be attached. Similarly for causative *dampen* (99) (= (28)): should one put coindex 3 on CAUSE, or on BECOME?

(99) Semantics: $[\underline{CAUSE} (Agent: Z, [\underline{BECOME} (Undergoer: X, DAMP_8)]_9)]_{10}$
      Morphosyntax: $[_V [_V A_8 \, aff_3 \,]_9 \,]_{10}$
      Phonology: $/dæmp_8 \, \partial n_3 \, /_{9,10}$

The underlying reason these cases don't work is that the meaning of the affix is a function, *including the variables that constitute its arguments*. BECOME alone in (97) makes no sense—only BECOME (X,Y) does. Similarly, in (98), it is impossible to coindex the wavy underlined portion to the base. What has to be coindexed is [PERSON^a; [F (Agent: α, Patient: INDEF)]], with a variable function F.

One way to remedy this problem is to coindex aff with the entire semantic expression, as in (100), where coindex 3 falls all the way on the outside of the semantics.

(100) Semantics: $[\text{BECOME (X, WIDE}_1)]_{3,2}$
       Morphosyntax: $[_V A_1 \text{ aff}_3]_2$
       Phonology: $/ \text{ wajd}_1 \text{ ən}_3 /_2$

However, this makes it look as though WIDE is part of the meaning associated with the affix.

An uglier alternative separates the variable (which comes from the meaning of the affix) and its instantiation (which comes from the meaning of the base), as in (101).

(101)
$$\left[\begin{array}{c} [\text{BECOME (X, Y)}]_3 \\ | \\ \text{WIDE}_1 \end{array} \right]_2$$
       Semantics:

       Morphosyntax: $[_V A_1 \text{ aff}_3]_2$
       Phonology: $/\text{wajd}_1 \text{ en}_3 /_2$

For a different approach, instead of adding an interface link to semantics, we could achieve uniformity by eliminating aff altogether, as in (102).

(102) Semantics: $[\text{BECOME (X, WIDE}_1)]_2$
       Morphosyntax: $[_V A_1]_2$
       Phonology: $/\text{wajd}_1 \text{ ən} /_2$

The idea behind this notation is that the phonological suffix is an overt marker for the entire pattern, so no further marking is needed in morphosyntax.

We see two problems with this notation. First, we cannot eliminate inflectional features from morphosyntax, because they have to interact with phrasal syntax. For instance, plural agreement in English cannot be keyed to its wide variety of phonological realizations (including zero!): a morphosyntactic plural feature is required to draw all these cases together. Second, this notation has the consequence that items that lack a related free form are completely a-morphous. For instance, instead of (103) (= (10)) we would have (104), which parallels a-morphous cases like *billion*. More generally, it runs together affixal morphology and conversion.

(103) Semantics: TASTY_4
       Morphosyntax: $[_A - \text{aff}_5]_4$
       Phonology: $/\text{skrʌmptʃ əs}_5 /_4$

(104) Semantics: TASTY$_4$
       Morphosyntax: $[_A -]_4$ (*or simply:* A$_4$)
       Phonology: / skrʌmptʃ əs /$_4$

We are not sure we wish to accept this consequence.

Given the difficulties associated with each of these alternatives, the notation adopted throughout the rest of the book appears to us to be a reasonably optimal combination of rigor and practicality.

5

Formalizing Inflection

Our survey of morphological patterns in Chapter 4 included both derivation (word formation) and inflection, and we did not worry too much about the differences between them. This chapter concentrates on inflectional morphology. We first address the issue of how inflection and derivation are different. We then offer detailed accounts of two inflectional systems: English verb inflection as a warmup, followed by German verb inflection for a more complex case. We conclude with a discussion of some further general phenomena.

5.1 What's special about inflection?

In some respects, inflection and derivation are difficult to distinguish, and the criteria are not always entirely clear. So the question arises: What makes inflection and derivation different?[1]

The difference is not in their morphophonology. Inflection and derivation involve basically the same morphophonological resources: affixation, zero morphology, reduplication, stem allomorphy (including umlaut and ablaut), and so on. Both inflection and derivation include nonproductive morphophonological patterns (forms like *sang* in inflection and *harden* and *song* in derivation) as well as productive ones (forms like *cats* and *happily*). Hence the machinery developed in the previous chapters for the interface between morphosyntax and morphophonology applies equally to inflection and derivation. As Aronoff (1994: 15) puts it, "the morphology [here, specifically morphophonology – RJ/JA] of inflection and derivation seem to be very similar to a great extent in most languages that have been investigated in any depth."

Turning to semantics, inflection and derivation convey somewhat different ranges of meanings. Inflection typically marks tense, aspect, mood, evidentiality, person, number, gender, semantic role, and so on, while the semantics of derivation is considerably more varied. Both inflection and derivation are often polysemous. Just as *construction* can denote either the process of constructing or its result, English present tense can denote not only present time but also generic (1a), scheduled future (1b), casual narrative past (1c), and conditional (1d).

(1) a. Cows eat grass.
     b. We leave tomorrow.
     c. …and then she says to me…
     d. If he comes,…

[1] This section draws freely on similar discussions in Anderson (1992), Aronoff (1994), Stump (1998), Haspelmath and Sims (2010), Booij (2012), and Spencer (2013).

The Texture of the Lexicon. First edition. Ray Jackendoff and Jenny Audring © Ray Jackendoff and Jenny Audring 2020. First published in 2020 by Oxford University Press. DOI: 10.1093/oso/9780198827900.001.0001

Some inflections contribute nothing to meaning, for example structural case and, in non-pro-drop languages, subject-verb agreement. But some derivational patterns are meaningless too, for instance verbs vs. their derived process nominals ((2a) vs. (2b)),[2] manner adjectives vs. manner adverbs (also (2a) vs. (2b)), and passive participles vs. passive adjectives ((3a) vs. (3b)). Such semantic parallelisms are often subsumed under the label of *transpositions* and discussed as problems for the inflection-derivation divide (Haspelmath 1996; Spencer 2010, 2013).

(2) a. She sneezed. He died. They constructed the building rapidly.
     b. her sneeze; his death; the rapid construction of the building

(3) a. This outcome was not [$_{V,PTCP}$ expected] by anyone.
     b. an un-[$_A$ expected] outcome

Derivation of course abounds in stored items that have idiosyncratic meanings. Such items are considerably rarer in inflection, but as observed in section 2.4, they do exist, for instance *brains* in the sense 'intelligence', *troops* in the sense 'soldiers' rather than 'groups of soldiers', and *strings* in the sense 'players of string instruments in an orchestra'. We also pointed out idiomatic collocations containing plurals such as *make amends*, *shake hands*, and *odds and ends*. In short, semantics offers no bright line between inflection and derivation.

Another possible difference between the two might be in their status in the architecture of the grammar. For instance, in the so-called split morphology hypothesis (Anderson 1982; Perlmutter 1988), word formation (= derivation) takes place in the lexicon, before words are inserted into syntactic structures; inflection is applied afterward, as part of or as a result of syntactic operations. This division has been criticized in the literature (e.g. Booij 1996; Bickel and Nichols 2007), and in any event it is not an option available to us here. In Relational Morphology, inflection and derivation are both encoded in morphosyntactic representation, and this level of representation interfaces with phrasal syntax, semantics and phonology all at once (or atemporally). There is no derivation with a "before" and "after."[3]

Having eliminated phonology, semantics, and the order of application in the grammar as possible loci of differences between inflection and derivation, about the only place left is in the morphosyntax, as observed by Anderson (1992), for instance. Two important differences arise, which we take up in turn.

The first difference is that inflection comes in *paradigms*. Derivational patterns are more or less catch-as-catch-can—there is no overall template that determines what

---

[2] If there is a meaning difference between verbs and their process nominals, it is subtle. They share semantic argument structure and affordances for semantic modification. What differences there are seem to be connected with different affordances for syntactic modification, e.g. verbal tense (*paid* vs. *past payment*) and nominal quantification (*all payment stopped* vs. *stopped paying everything*).

[3] Haspelmath and Sims (2010: 103–5) contrast split morphology with what they call a "single-component architecture," in which morphosyntactic representation feeds a component called "word-formation + inflection," which in turn feeds phonology. This too differs from RM in being sequential. In particular, their phonological component does not have direct access to (or influence on) morphosyntax. In RM, morphosyntactic representation incorporates both derivation and inflection, and it is connected to phonology by a nondirectional interface.

sorts of derivational affixes can or must occur. In contrast, the grammar of a language has to designate certain syntactic categories as inflected. These are usually nouns, pronouns, determiners, verbs, and/or adjectives, but other categories may require inflection as well (Corbett 2006). For each category, the grammar has to stipulate the features it inflects for, such as gender, number, or case; the grammar further determines the range of values for each feature: how many genders there are, how many numbers, and how many cases. When a category requires more than one inflectional feature, these features are expected to be orthogonal to each other. The result is the familiar matrix of cells in a paradigm. Each dimension in the matrix corresponds to an inflectional feature, and each cell in the matrix corresponds to a unique set of values of the inflectional features. For example, the German determiner paradigm can be represented as a three-dimensional matrix of three genders by two numbers by four cases, in which each cell specifies a value in each dimension, such as feminine.plural.accusative.

Each cell in the matrix has to specify the corresponding phonology. In the canonical case, each member of an inflected syntactic category is expected to have a set of inflected forms that together fill out the entire paradigm. It is a surprise when a paradigm is defective, i.e. when expected forms are missing, either for one or more lexical items, or for individual cells or a larger stretch of the paradigm (Halle 1973; Baerman, Corbett, and Brown 2011; Sims 2015).

Realizational morphology (e.g. Anderson 1992; Stump 2001, 2016; Blevins 2016) encodes the relation between the morphosyntax of inflection and the associated phonology in terms of procedural rules that map each combination of inflectional features into its phonological realization. Relational Morphology replaces realization rules with nondirectional interface links between morphosyntax and phonology.

The second major difference between inflection and derivation is that inflection has a much richer interaction with phrasal syntax. For example, phrasal syntax determines which contexts require a finite verb and which require an infinitive or a participle. Among the inflectional features, some are *inherent* to the words of a particular category—either determined by the lexical entry of the word (e.g. grammatical gender) or freely chosen in accordance with the semantics of the sentence (e.g. tense). Other features are *contextual*, determined by agreement in phrasal syntax (this terminology from Booij 1996). For contextual features, phrasal syntax has to stipulate what has to agree with what, and in what syntactic configuration. For English and German, for example, the relevant features include:

- Tense on finite verbs is determined by the semantics of the sentence.
- The number value on nouns is normally determined by the semantics of the sentence, though it is also lexically marked in words like *police, people, cattle,* and (in British English) *team*.[4] But on determiners, adjectives, and verbs, number is contextual, determined by agreement.

---

[4] *Team* in this variety is actually more complicated, as it determines singular agreement on its determiner (*this/*these team*) and plural agreement on its verb (*the team are...*). We set this detail aside.

- In German, gender on nouns is an inherent lexical property; but gender on determiners and attributive adjectives is contextual, determined by agreement.
- In German, case on nouns and their modifiers is determined either by the syntactic context in which the noun phrase falls or, for "quirky case," by a verb or preposition that stipulates the case of one of its arguments.

Derivational morphology has nothing like this—no paradigms that need to be completely filled out, no features with a variety of values, no multiple orthogonal dimensions, no rich interaction with phrasal syntax.[5] This is a major difference that has to be negotiated in any theory of morphology.

5.2 Formalization of inflection vs. derivation

One might further ask whether inflection and derivation differ in their morphosyntactic representation, and if so, how. We propose that they do differ, at least in the Relational Morphology formalism. To establish a basis for comparison, we first examine the morphosyntax of derivation, then see how it has to be modified to be suitable for inflection.

Following the treatment in the preceding chapters, a stereotypical derived word such as *fearless* looks like (4). Extracting the general pattern for the morphosyntactic component of a derived word, we get (5a), or, in the unordered variant suggested in section 4.7, (5b). In either alternative, the base has a syntactic category X, and the word as a whole has a syntactic category Y, which may or may not be the same as that of the base.[6]

(4) Semantics: $[\text{LACKING (FEAR}_1)]_2$
     Morphosyntax: $[_A \text{N}_1 \text{ aff}_3]_2$
     Phonology: $/\text{fir}_1 \text{ ləs}_3 /_2$

(5) a. Morphosyntax: $[_Y \text{ X aff }]$
     b. Morphosyntax: $\{_Y \text{ X, aff}\}$

Now consider what happens when there are *two* derivational affixes, as in *fearlessness* (6). The general pattern for the morphosyntax is (7a), or if unordered, (7b).

(6) Semantics: $[\text{STATE OF }([\text{LACKING (FEAR}_1)]_2)]_4$
     Morphosyntax: $[_N [_A \text{N}_1 \text{ aff}_3]_2 \text{ aff}_5]_4$
     Phonology: $/ / \text{fir}_1 \text{ ləs}_3 /_2 \text{ nəs}_5 /_4$

---

[5] Cases that might straddle the border between inflection and derivation would include evaluative morphology, i.e. diminutive and augmentative patterns, and comparative and superlative patterns (Scalise 1984). These might be considered derivational but paradigmatic.

[6] For this reason, Williams (1981), Selkirk (1982), and Lieber (1992) call the affix the head of the composite word. In RM, what determines the category of the composite word is not the affix per se, but the schema containing the affix. Note that a derivational schema need not have a different syntactic category from its base. The two categories are the same in schemas such as $[_V \text{ re-V}]$ (*rebuild*), $[_N \text{ N-ery}]$ (*nunnery*), and $[_N \text{N-ist}]$ (*clarinetist*).

(7)   a. Morphosyntax: $[_Z [_Y X \text{ aff1}] \text{ aff2}]$
        b. Morphosyntax: $\{_Z \{_Y X , \text{ aff1}\}, \text{ aff2} \}$

The morphosyntax in (6) has an embedded (i.e. hierarchical) structure, in which the inner derived form *fearless* serves as base for the word as a whole. This embedding parallels the semantics, as can be seen in (6): in both morphosyntax and semantics, *fear* (coindex 1) is embedded in *fearless* (coindex 2), and *fearless* in turn is embedded in *fearlessness* (coindex 4). Thanks to this embedding, if both affixes are either prefixes or suffixes, the inner affix will normally be closer to the base than the outer affix in the phonology.[7]

   One more point concerns the status of aff. It typically combines with an X^0 category to form a set (whether ordered or unordered).[8] On the premise that a set should contain elements of the same type, aff should belong to a (morpho)syntactic category as well. Following section 1.5, we will therefore regard aff as a morphosyntactic category that does not appear in phrasal syntax. In order to be usable as part of a word, it has to be dominated by some X^0 category in morphosyntax. A counterpart in phrasal syntax might be a functional category such as Det, which has to be dominated by NP in order to be usable as part of a sentence.[9]

   With these details of derivation in mind, we turn to inflectional morphosyntax. Suppose, for instance, that we treat a plural noun along the lines of (4) (as we did in Chapter 2). The result is (8).

(8)   Semantics: $[\text{PLUR (CAT}_6)]_7$
        Morphosyntax: $[_N N_6 \text{ PL}_8]_7$
        Phonology: $/\text{kæt}_6 \text{ s}_8 /_7$

An important respect in which this differs from derivation is that the morphosyntactic operator is not just the undifferentiated element aff, but a specific value of an inflectional feature. In another respect, the morphosyntax of (8) is somewhat suspicious, in that the label N occurs twice, apparently redundantly. Unlike in derivation, where the two labels may be different, in inflection the two labels will always be the same: an inflected noun is always still a noun. Can either of the labels be eliminated? (9) shows the two possibilities.

---

[7] This provides a natural account of Baker's (1988) Mirror Principle. For the most part, the embedding in semantics is reflected in phrasal syntax. Therefore phrasal embedding and morphological embedding will tend both to align with the semantics, and hence with each other as well. There is no need to account for this alignment by *deriving* morphological embedding from phrasal embedding, as Baker does.
   On the other hand, see Stump (2019a,b) and references there for examples where such correspondences between morphosyntax and semantics fail to hold: "the notion that a word form is morphotactically isomorphic to its semantic structure is directly disconfirmed by a vast array of empirical evidence" (2019b: 287); see also Booij and Masini (2015).
[8] However, this is only the canonical situation, because aff stands on its own in words whose base is not an X^0 category, such as *scrumptious*, and because it is occasionally concatenated with something other than a single X^0 category, as in *three-toed* (two X^0 categories plus the affix *-ed*) and *stick-to-itiveness* (a phrasal category plus two affixes).
[9] A different parallel, inspired by Selkirk (1982) and Lieber (1992), might extend X-bar theory down into morphology. On this approach, aff in *fearless* (4) could be regarded as an A^{-1} head that takes an N^0 complement, the combination resulting in an A^0. This would be a morphological counterpart of phrasal syntax, in which an X^0 head combines with a YP complement to form an XP.

(9) a. *Eliminating inner N:* $[_N \text{PL}_8]_7$
b. *Eliminating outer N:* $[N_6 \text{PL}_8]_7$

(9a) doesn't make a lot of sense. For one thing, it appears to represent a morphosyntactic noun that consists only of a plural feature. For another, it is not clear how to coindex (9a) to the semantics and phonology: where would coindex 6, which identifies the word as *cat*, be attached in (9a)?

(9b) shows more promise, if we are careful about its interpretation. One of the innovations of Chomsky (1970) was to regard syntactic category as a feature or combination of features.[10] Following this line of reasoning, we can regard N as just a value of the category feature, so that both N and PL are values of features.

However, what does it mean for the outer bracket of (9b) to be unlabeled? In particular, if the bracket is unlabeled, what is the syntactic category of (9b)? We propose that the syntactic category of (9b) is 'plural noun,' that is, its category is the entire feature set. This construal has a nice consequence: when it comes to accessibility to phrasal syntax, inflectional features are just as "visible" as part-of-speech features, e.g. 'plural noun' is just as "visible" as 'noun.' This is exactly what we need in order to state principles of agreement and case-marking in phrasal syntax.

Next consider a configuration with multiple contextual inflections, say marking of gender, number, and case on German prenominal adjectives. The three inflectional features are orthogonal dimensions of variation, which is why their interaction can be represented as a three-dimensional matrix. Since adjectival inflection is contextually determined, these features contribute nothing to meaning. Hence, unlike the multiple derivational affixes in (6), semantics offers no motivation for hierarchical structure. Moreover, the three inflectional features are gathered together phonologically into a single portmanteau suffix such as *-es*, so there is no evidence from phonology for linear order among them (aside from the order of the stem and the suffix).

Thus on the simplest treatment of this pattern, the morphosyntax consists of an unordered collection of features, as in (10a). For comparison, (10b) illustrates what the structure is *not*—binary branching and recursive. (11) makes the difference visually clearer, by renotating the morphosyntax of (10a,b) in tree notation.[11]

(10) German: *grosses* 'big' (+ agreement features)

Semantics: a. $[\text{BIG}]_9$
Morphosyntax: $\{A_9, \text{NEUT}_{10}, \text{SG}_{11}, \text{NOM}_{12}\}_{13}$
Phonology: $/\text{gros}_9 \, \text{əs}_{10,11,12}/_{13}$

Semantics: b. $[\text{BIG}]_9$
Morphosyntax: $[[[A_9 \, \text{NEUT}_{10}] \, \text{SG}_{11}] \, \text{NOM}_{12}]_{13}$
Phonology: $/\text{gros}_9 \, \text{əs}_{10,11,12}/_{13}$

---

[10] This is what made X-bar theory possible: syntactic rules, like phonological rules, could cut across categories by referring to the features they have in common.

[11] The inflectional structure is not always entirely flat. Spencer (2013: 354–6) cites a more complex case from the language Awngi, in which genitive case on possessor nouns agrees with the number and gender of the possessum, and adds the case-marker of the possessum, setting up the possibility of embedding in the inflectional structure. Hierarchical inflectional features also showed up in the treatment of German *deinem* in section 4.6. See also Nikolaeva and Spencer (2012).

(11)   a. *(this:)*   b. *(not this:)*

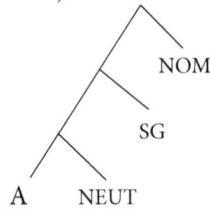

A similar situation arises in the German verbal system, in which finite verbs are inflected for tense, person, and number. Again, there is no semantic priority among these dimensions: each of the three can vary independently without affecting the others (though see Bybee (1985) for crosslinguistic tendencies in the ordering of verbal inflectional affixes, based on greater or lesser semantic relevance to the stem). For German, there is no evidence for a hierarchy among them. In the phonology, person and number are always realized either as a single suffix or as zero, and tense is realized in some cases as a suffix, in other cases as zero, and in still others as ablaut. Hence, apart from tense preceding person and number, there is no consistent evidence for morphosyntactic linear order across the paradigm. Accordingly, (12) represents a typical inflected form, in which the morphosyntax is simply a set consisting of a category feature and three inflectional features. (Section 5.4 works out the verbal paradigm in more detail.)

(12)   *machtest*[12] '(you) made'

Semantics: [PAST ([MAKE (Agent: ADDRESSEE$_{17}$, SG$_{18}$; Patient: Y)]$_{14}$)]$_{15}$
Morphosyntax: {V$_{14}$, PAST$_{16}$, 2$_{17}$, SG$_{18}$ }$_{15}$
Phonology: /max$_{14}$ t$_{16}$ əst$_{17,18}$ /$_{15}$

On this story, then, what distinguishes inflection from derivation in morphosyntax (in addition to paradigms) is that derivation assigns a syntactic category to the combination of the base and the affix, resulting in a different word (or lexeme); whereas inflection adds one or more features to the syntactic category of its base.[13] This difference is notated simply by the presence or absence of a category label on the outer bracket of the morphosyntax (compare (10a) and (12) to (6)).[14]

However, we are not yet quite out of the woods: we need to consider combinations of inflection and derivation within the same word. The typical situation is when a derived form is inflected, for instance in *instructions*. (13) shows the morphosyntax and phonology of *instruction* and the plural schema. (We notate the phonology in

---

[12]   As mentioned in section 4.6, note 11, we take /t/ to be the phonology of the past tense suffix.
[13]   Aronoff (1994: 126) puts it like this: "…inflection is the morphological realization of syntax, while derivation is the morphological realization of lexeme formation." We think he is trying to say the same thing as we are.
[14]   This distinction offers an attractive account of the minimal morphosyntactic difference between verbal and adjectival passive participle in English: in structure (i) it behaves like a verb, in (ii) like an adjective, with no difference in phonology, but different possibilities for syntactic position and for further inflection such as agreement.
(i)   {V, PTCP}   (verbal participle, no label on outer bracket)
(ii) [$_A$ {V, PTCP}]   (adjectival participle, label on outer bracket)

ordinary orthography, in order to finesse phonological issues to be discussed in Chapter 6, in particular the source of /ʃ/.)

(13) a. *instruction* b. *Plural schema*

Morphosyntax: $[_N V_{19} aff_{20}]_{21}$ $\{N_x, PL_8\}_y$

Phonology: $/instruct_{19} ion_{20}/_{21}$ $/..._x s_8/_y$

In (13a), N on the bracket stands for the category of a hierarchical structure, composed of V and aff. But in (13b), N stands for a value of a feature. How can the noun (13a) be unified with the N in (13b)?

To resolve this difficulty, we adopt a practice of GPSG (Gazdar et al. 1985) and HPSG (Pollard and Sag 1994): *we allow syntactic features to have internal structure.* What this amounts to in our terms is that N in (13a) is the top node of a tree, dominating V and aff. But at the same time, it also can be unified with the feature N in (13b) to form the structure (14).

(14) *instructions*

Morphosyntax: $\{[_N V_{19} aff_{20}]_{21}, PL_8\}_{22}$

Phonology: $/ /instruct_{19} ion_{20}/_{21} s_8/_{22}$

In conformance with the plural schema, (14) has no label on the outer curly brackets. Hence the two constituents of the outer brackets, N and PL, are construed as features that mark the whole word as a plural noun. However, the feature N also has internal structure: a verb and an affix.

This construal of (14) is somewhat unorthodox. However, we believe it says exactly what we want it to say. In particular, notice that V in (14) is not a maximal X^0—only N is. Thus the phrasal syntax cannot "see" V, which is precisely as desired for the contrast between inflectional and derivational morphology.

For a more complex example, the German derived adjective *weib-lich-es* 'female (NEUT.SG.NOM)' has contextual inflectional features just like *gross-es* in (10a), resulting in the structure in (15).

(15) German: *weibliches*

Morphosyntax: $\{[_A N_{31} aff_{32}]_{33} NEUT_{10}, SG_{11}, NOM_{12}\}_{34}$

Phonology: $/ /vaɪb_{31} lɪç_{32}/_{33} əs_{10,11,12}/_{34}$

The constituents of the outer brackets are an adjective part-of-speech feature plus the three inflectional features. The constituents of the inner brackets are a noun and a derivational affix.

The treatment of categories as features with internal structure leaves open issues of interpretation that go beyond the scope of this book. Readers who retain metaphysical qualms should rest assured that we share them. However, this approach gives us enough machinery to deal with the morphosyntax of inflection in the cases we study here, and to that end we set doubts aside for the time being.

5.3 The English verb paradigm

In order to gradually build up our tolerance for inflectional complexity, we begin with the relatively simple English verb paradigm, then move on to the more challenging German verbs.

5.3.1 Morphosyntax

The morphosyntax defines the repertoire of possible inflected forms in the language. We assume that each member of this repertoire can be distinguished only if it has a dedicated phonological reflex and/or a dedicated syntactic function. For English, the repertoire includes six forms, which can be treated as a simple list. PRES and PAST are to be thought of as values of the feature T (TENSE); 3 is a value of the feature PERSON; SG is a value of the feature NUMBER.[15]

(16) *Finite forms*
  a. present: $\{V, [_T \text{ PRES}]\}$
  b. present, 3 sing: $\{V, [_T \text{ PRES}], [_{PERS} 3], [_{NUM} \text{ SG}]\}$
  c. past: $\{V, [_T \text{ PAST}]\}$

  Nonfinite forms
  d. infinitive: $\{V, \text{INF}\}$
  e. present participle: $\{V, \text{PRESPT}\}$
  f. past participle: $\{V, \text{PTCP}\}$

The choice among these morphosyntactic forms is conditioned by their position in phrasal syntax. (17) sketches a few of the syntactic schemas in which various verb forms appear. These schemas can be considered part of the syntax-morphology interface. Since it doesn't matter what the verb means or how it is pronounced, these schemas are purely (morpho)syntactic, and say nothing about the relation of the patterns to associated semantics or phonology.[16]

(17) a. Tensed verb in full S, no auxiliary, e.g. *Amy walks*
        $[_S \ldots [_{VP} \{V, T\} \ldots]]$
     b. Infinitive in *to VP*, e.g. *Ezra wants to walk*
        $[_{CP} \text{ to } [_{VP} \{V, \text{INF}\} \ldots]]$
     c. Infinitive with modal, e.g. *Levi will walk*
        $[_S \ldots [\text{Aux}_M] [_{VP} \{V, \text{INF}\} \ldots]]$
     d. Present participle with progressive auxiliary, e.g. *They are walking*
        $[_{S/VP} \ldots \text{Aux}_{prog} [_{VP} \{V, \text{PRESPT}\} \ldots]]$

---

[15] One could certainly expand the paradigm in (16) into a traditional full matrix of person and number. But aside from the verb *be*, all such further distinctions would do no work in the grammar. Things are quite different in the much more articulated German paradigm, which we take up in the next section.

[16] Hence these schemas would not be possible in the versions of CxG that postulate that every construction is a Saussurean sign, i.e. is linked to a meaning.

These schemas give rise to an important question. (17a) licenses a tensed verb as the head of a VP. What stops such a VP from appearing after a modal auxiliary, e.g. *John might walked*? The answer is that another schema, (17c), also licenses the configuration of a modal followed by a VP. (17c) is more specific than (17a), in that its environment stipulates more structure. Hence again we can appeal to the Elsewhere Condition (Anderson 1977, 1982): a more highly structured schema constitutes an exception to a less highly structured one, and therefore takes precedence over it. For a similar case, $\{[_T \text{ PRES}], 3, \text{SG}\}$ is more specific than unadorned present tense. Hence, when both are applicable, (16b) takes precedence over (16a).[17]

5.3.2 Morphophonology of regular verbs

We now have to work out the morphophonology—the interface between morphosyntax and word phonology. For each combination of morphosyntactic features in (16), there has to be an interface schema that specifies its phonological counterpart, the *exponents* of that combination of features. These interface schemas play essentially the same role that realization rules play in realizational morphology. However, as previously noted, instead of being viewed as procedures for mapping morphosyntax into phonology, interface schemas are nondirectional relations between these two levels.

If life were simple, each cell in a morphosyntactic paradigm would specify a single counterpart in phonology, and that would be the end of it. In a sense, this would be one of Corbett's (2007) *canonical* inflectional systems. However, life in the morphological world is rarely simple. Among the many sorts of deviations from this ideal is the possibility of multiple *inflectional classes*, such that each class realizes the exponents of inflection differently from the others. For both English and German, the verbs are customarily divided into inflectional classes of regular (or weak) verbs and irregular (or strong) verbs, the latter in turn encompassing numerous smaller subclasses. A word's membership in a particular class is often encoded in terms of a feature, say [±strong] or [+class 1], and realization rules are keyed to this feature. As our story develops, we will propose a somewhat more flexible account.

We begin with the relatively straightforward morphophonology of English regular verbs. For simplicity, we assume there is an uninflected *stem* form, stored in the lexicon, to which inflectional exponents are applied; section 5.5 revisits this assumption and arrives at a more nuanced position. For now, we take the stem form for a regular verb such as *walk* to have structure (18).

(18) *walk (stem form)*
    Semantics: $[\text{WALK (X)}]_1$
    Morphosyntax: V_1
    Phonology: $/\text{wɔk}/_1$

---

[17] This treatment, in which a more specific schema takes precedence over a less specific one, is also employed in other frameworks, e.g. Paradigm Function Morphology (Stump 2001: 22–4) and Network Morphology (Brown and Hippisley 2012; Brown 2019).

The inflectional paradigm of *walk* can then be stated as (19). Each of the six entries corresponds to one of the morphosyntactic patterns in (16). As a group, they constitute a set of sisters related through a shared stem (coindex 1).

(19) *Inflectional paradigm of* walk

	a. *Present*	b. *Present 3 singular*
Semantics:	$[\text{PRES} ([\text{WALK} (X)]_1)]_2$	$[\text{PRES} ([\text{WALK} (3_4; \text{SG}_5)]_1)]_6$
Morphosyntax:	$\{V_1, \text{PRES}_3\}_2$	$\{V_1, \text{PRES}_3, 3_4, \text{SG}_5 \}_6$
Phonology:	$/\text{wɔk}/_{1,2}$	$/\text{wɔk}_1 \text{s}_{3,4,5}/_6$

	c. *Past*	d. *Infinitive*
Semantics:	$[\text{PAST} ([\text{WALK} (X)]_1)]_7$	$[\text{WALK} (X)]_{1,9}$
Morphosyntax:	$\{V_1, \text{PAST}_8\}_7$	$\{V_1, \text{INF}\}_9$
Phonology:	$/\text{wɔk}_1 \text{t}_8 /_7$	$/\text{wɔk}/_{1,9}$

	e *Present participle*	f. *Past participle*
Semantics:	$[\text{WALK} (X)]_{1,11}$	$[\text{WALK} (X)]_{1,13}$
Morphosyntax:	$\{V_1, \text{PRESPT}_{10} \}_{11}$	$\{V_1, \text{PTCP}_{12} \}_{13}$
Phonology:	$/\text{wɔk}_1 \text{ɪŋ}_{10} /_{11}$	$/\text{wɔk}_1 \text{t}_{12} /_{13}$

Notice that the present tense and infinitive add no phonological content to the stem. We therefore treat them in the manner adopted in section 4.3 for zero affixation: the phonology is coindexed both with the base and with the whole word (coindices 1 and 2 in the case of the present tense, and 1 and 9 in the infinitive). Similarly in the semantics, only present and past tenses have contentful meanings; the infinitive and participles therefore coindex the semantics to both the whole word and the base (coindices 1 and 9 in the infinitive, 1 and 11 in the present participle, 1 and 13 in the past participle).[18]

Extracting the contribution of *walk* to (19), we arrive at the schemas in (20) for the regular inflectional paradigm. These schemas unify with the lexical entry for the stem *walk* (18) in the usual way, resulting in the forms in (19). (We omit the allomorphy of *s/z/əz* in PRES.3.SG and of *t/d/əd* in past and past participle.)

(20) *Inflectional paradigm for English regular verbs*

	a. *Present*	b. *Present 3 singular*
Semantics:	$[\text{PRES} ([\text{F} (...)]_\alpha)]_x$	$[\text{PRES} ([\text{F} (3_4; \text{SG}_5)]_\alpha)]_y$
Morphosyntax:	$\{V_\alpha, \text{PRES}_3 \}_x$	$\{V_\alpha, \text{PRES}_3, 3_4, \text{SG}_5\}_y$
Phonology:	$/...\ /_{\alpha,x}$	$/...\ _\alpha \text{z}_{3,4,5} /_y$

	c. *Past*	d. *Infinitive*
Semantics:	$[\text{PAST} ([\text{F} (...)]_\alpha)]_z$	$[\text{F} (...)]_{\alpha,w}$
Morphosyntax:	$\{V_\alpha, \text{PAST}_8\}_z$	$\{V_\alpha, \text{INF}\}_w$
Phonology:	$/...\ _\alpha \text{d}_8 /_z$	$/...\ /_{\alpha,w}$

---

[18] The participles do contribute to constructional meaning in the context of particular syntactic configurations. For instance, tensed *have* plus past participle expresses perfect, while *be* plus past participle expresses passive. Similarly, the imperative construction stipulates the use of the infinitive form.

	e. *Present participle*	f. *Past participle*
Semantics:	$[\mathrm{F}\,(\ldots)]_{a,v}$	$[\mathrm{F}\,(\ldots)]_{a,u}$
Morphosyntax:	$\{V_a, \mathrm{PRESPT}_{10}\}_v$	$\{V_a, \mathrm{PTCP}_{12}\}_u$
Phonology:	$/\ldots_a \, \mathrm{I}\eta_{10}\,/_v$	$/\ldots_a \, d_{12}\,/_u$

Some remarks on these schemas: First, section 5.1 observed that morphosyntactic present tense can be used to express a variety of semantic operators—not just present time, but generic, conditional, scheduled future, and casual narrative past. Similarly, morphosyntactic past can express not only past time but also past generic (*In his youth, he smoked*) and what might be called hypothetical conditional (*If he came tomorrow,...*). These require further schemas that substitute various other semantic operators for PRES and PAST in (20a,b,c). We discuss the consequences in section 5.6.

Second, notice that the verb stems in (20a-f) are all subscripted a. This indicates that these schemas are sisters, this time a set of six, rather than the sets of two we saw in Chapter 4. If the sister relation is productive (as this one is), the shared variable stipulates that a verb that participates in one of the schemas participates in all of them. In other words, we have used sister schemas to model the traditional notion of an inflectional paradigm, as suggested by Booij (2010).

Third, the present and the infinitive have identical phonology, as do the past tense and past participle of regular verbs. We would like the grammar to express these syncretisms. One way to do this is to add a relational link between the members of each pair. This link pertains only to phonology, as the semantics and morphosyntax of the two forms are distinct. In the case of the present and the infinitive, such a link is already present: the a in the phonology says that these forms are identical to each other—as well as to the stem. In the case of the past and the past participle, there is no such preexisting relational link, but we can add one. (21) shows the relevant parts of (20), with the added link marked by coindex β. This says that whatever way the past is pronounced, the participle is as well, and vice versa.

(21) *Syncretism of past tense and past participle with regular verbs (revision of (20c,f))*

Morphosyntax:	c. $\{V_a, \mathrm{PAST}_8\}_z$	f. $\{V_a, \mathrm{PTCP}_{12}\}_u$
Phonology:	$/\ldots_a \, d_8\,/_{\beta,z}$	$/\ldots_a \, d_{12}\,/_{\beta,u}$

In this conception of paradigms, it is strictly speaking unnecessary to store uninflected stem forms like (18) in long-term memory. One could just as well store any of the forms in (19) and derive the rest online as needed, with the help of the stored paradigm (20). In other words, we should not think of the past tense as uniformly "derived" from the stem or the present tense, as in procedural theories of inflection (and much of the psycholinguistic literature). Rather, the relation between them is symmetrical: when operating in generative mode, given the past form of a verb, the schemas can just as readily be used to obtain the present or any of the other forms. We return to this issue in section 5.5, developing some details of how this is accomplished.

5.3.3 Irregular past tenses

We next turn to the English verbs with irregular past tenses, which splinter into a multitude of inflectional classes, each of which contrasts in a different way with the inflectional class of regular verbs. We say "splinter" because the classes are quite small, each containing anywhere from one to about two dozen members.

We note first that, aside from *be, have,* and *do,* irregular verbs behave just like regular verbs except in the past tense and past participle forms, and therefore it is only for these cells in the paradigm that we need distinct schemas. In other languages, of course, inflectional classes may involve larger collections of cells. But in English we can keep things relatively simple (but only relatively!).

First consider an inflectional class with only one member: the total suppletion of *go/went.*[19] The semantics and morphosyntax of the two forms are straightforward, but the phonological forms of the two items are totally unrelated. (22a) shows the stem form, (22b) the present, and (22c) the past.

(22)   a. *Stem*
      Semantics: $[GO\,(X, Path)]_{16}$
      Morphosyntax: V_{16}
      Phonology: $/goʊ/_{16}$

                   b. *Present tense*   c. *Past tense*
  Semantics: $[PRES\,([GO\,(X, Path)]_{16}\,)]_{17}$ $[PAST\,([GO\,(X, Path)]_{16}\,)]_{18}$
  Morphosyntax $\{V_{16}, PRES_3\}_{17}$ $\{V_{16}, PAST_8\}_{18}$
  Phonology: $/goʊ/_{16,17}$ $/wɛnt/_{18}$

Four points are of interest here. First, coindex 16 ties together all three forms, identifying them as versions of the same verb.[20] Second, there is no phonological string within *went* that specifically expresses past tense. Hence the PAST feature in morphosyntax is not linked to phonology: only the entire word is (coindex 18). (Coindex 8, however, does link PAST to its occurrences in other past tense verbs and in schema (20c).) Third, the phonology /wɛnt/ as a whole is not linked to either the verb stem or the PAST feature. Since it does not share structure with anything else, it must "pay full freight" for storage in the lexicon. Fourth, since this case is one-off, like *laugh* and *laughter* in Chapter 4, the two forms are not related by a schema—they are just sisters.[21]

---

[19] One might resist calling a singleton such as *go/went* an inflectional class of its own. If so, two questions arise: first, what *should* one call this case, and second, how many instances does a pattern need before it counts as an inflectional class? We have opted for terminology that sidesteps these question. Readers should feel free to substitute their own preferred terms. Corbett (1991: 161) discusses this issue in the context of distinguishing agreement classes, under the heading "the maximalist problem."

[20] This collection of three forms—or what the forms have in common—is what other approaches call a *lexeme.* The lexeme as an independent theoretical construct is usually understood as an abstraction, not as a piece of stored structure (Spencer 2018). Hence we avoid the term, except informally.

[21] Note how this is a sort of upside-down version of idioms, whose syntax and phonology are motivated but whose semantics is unmotivated. Here the semantics and morphosyntax are motivated but the phonology is sui generis.

A considerably larger inflectional class consists of verbs that end in alveolar stops and have a zero past tense, e.g. *put, cut, rid,* and *spread.*[22] All are monosyllabic except for *forecast* and *upset,* whose first syllable is evidently a prefix. The sister schemas are shown in (23). (For convenience, we show the stem (23a) but not the present tense. Also, the argument structure in the semantics is entirely unspecified; we don't care how many arguments the verb has.)

(23) *Stem and past tense sister schemas for verbs with zero past tense (e.g.* put*)*

Semantics:	a. $[F (...)]_\gamma$	b. $[PAST ([F (...)]_\gamma)]_z$
Morphosyntax:	V_γ	$\{V_\gamma, PAST_8 \}_z$
Phonology:	$/[_\sigma ... [-cont, +alv]]/_\gamma$	$/[_\sigma ... [-cont, +alv]]/_{\gamma,z}$

This schema has the same general shape as our previous instances of zero morphology: the coindex γ ties the variables of the two schemas together, and the phonology of (23b) bears indices for both the base and the whole word. The schema is nonproductive: all its instances have to be listed individually. This prevents potential past tenses like **pet* and **flit,* which fit the phonological pattern but are not listed instances of the schema. At the same time, because (23b) is more highly specified than (20c), it blocks regular pasts such as **putted.*

More interesting are the inflectional classes of verbs whose past tenses involve ablaut. We encountered a similar vowel alternation in the pair *goose/geese* in sections 3.7 and 4.10, treating the two forms as sisters in a same-except relation. Following that analysis, (24) shows a typical instance of verbal ablaut, *sing/sang.*

(24) *Stem and past tense sister entries for* sing *and* sang

Semantics:	a. $[SING (X)]_{19}$	b. $[PAST ([SING (X)]_{19})]_{20}$
Morphosyntax:	V_{19}	$\{V_{19}, PAST_8 \}_{20}$
Phonology:	$/s *ɪ* ŋ/_{19}$	$/s *æ* ŋ /_{19,20}$

As with *put/put,* the two words are marked as the same in phonology (here, coindex 19). However, the starred vowels mark a deviation from complete identity. Hence in this case what has to be "paid for" is the choice of vowel.

Looking at ablaut past tenses more generally, about 115 English verbs have different vowels in their present and past tense. Among these, there are about thirty-seven different patterns of vowel contrast, listed in Table 5.1 (words with alternate forms are in parentheses). Sixteen of these occur in only one verb (e.g. *choose/chose*), and many of the patterns are only slightly less marginal. Among the thirty-seven patterns, every present tense vowel corresponds to between two and five past tense vowels, and every past tense vowel corresponds to between one and five present tense vowels. There are even pairs whose vowels alternate in opposite directions: *hang/hung* vs. *run/ran.* Adding past participle ablauts would fragment the classes still further; see section 5.4.5. (A similar table for Dutch appears in Booij 2019: 54.)

---

[22] Twenty-one of these end with /t/: *beat, bet, burst, cast, cost, cut, fit, forecast, hit, hurt, let, put, quit, set, shut, slit, spit, split, thrust, upset,* and *wet.* The remaining four of them end with /d/: *bid, rid, spread, wed.*

Table 5.1 English ablaut verbs

Vowel alternation	Example	Other instances (Items in parentheses have alternate forms.)
i/ej	eat/ate	---
i/ɛ	bleed/bled	breed, creep, deal, (dream), feed, feel, flee, keep, (kneel), lead, (leap), leave, mean, meet, (plead), read, sleep, speed, sweep, weep
i/o	speak/spoke	freeze, steal, weave
i/ʌ	sneak/snuck	---
i/ɔ	seek/sought	teach [*difference in Coda as well as Nucleus*]
ɪ/ej	give/gave	forgive
ɪ/æ	drink/drank	begin, ring, (shrink), sing, sink, sit, (spit), spring, (stink), swim
ɪ/ɾ	hear/heard	---
ɪ/ʌ	cling/clung	dig, fling, (shrink), sling, slink, spin, stick, sting, (stink), string, swing, win, wring
ɪ/ɔ	bring/brought	think [*difference in Coda as well as Nucleus*]
ej/ɛ	say/said	---
ej/o	break/broke	(a)wake
ej/u	slay/slew	---
ej/ʊ	take/took	forsake, mistake, partake, shake, undertake
ɛ/a	get/got	forget, (tread)
ɛ/o	sell/sold	tell
ɛ/ɔ	bear/bore	swear, tear, wear
æ/ʊ	stand/stood	understand, withstand [*difference in Coda as well as Nucleus*]
æ/ʌ	hang/hung	---
æ/ɔ	catch/caught	--- [*difference in Coda as well as Nucleus*]
aj/ɪ	bite/bit	hide, light, slide
aj/ej	lie/lay	---
aj/aw	bind/bound	find, grind, wind
aj/o	drive/drove	arise, (dive), ride, rise, (shine), smite, stride, strive, write
aj/u	fly/flew	---
aj/ʌ	strike/struck	---
aj/ɔ	buy/bought	fight [*difference in Coda as well as Nucleus*]
o/ɛ	hold/held	withhold
o/u	blow/blew	grow, know, throw
u/ɪ	do/did	---
u/a	shoot/shot	---
u/o	choose/chose	---
u/ɔ	lose/lost	---
ʌ/ej	come/came	become
ʌ/æ	run/ran	---
ɔ/ɛ	fall/fell	---
ɔ/u	draw/drew	withdraw

As with *go/went*, the singletons do not merit schemas of their own: the stem and the past tense are simply sisters. And as usual, it is not clear how many instances of a pattern it takes in order to warrant a schema. Two instances hardly seem enough (e.g. *break/broke* and *wake/woke*); four intuitively begins to sound plausible (e.g. *bind/bound*, *find/found*, *grind/ground*, *wind/wound*).

However, all these cases fall under an overall generalization that should be captured by a schema, namely that English has ablaut verbs. (25) states the sister schemas that express the possibility of ablaut in general. We can think of (25) as defining an umbrella inflectional class with numerous little subclasses.

(25) *Stem and past tense sister schemas for ablaut past*
      Semantics: a. $[\mathrm{F}(\dots)]_\delta$ b. $[\mathrm{PAST}([\mathrm{F}(\dots)]_\delta)]_x$
      Morphosyntax: V_δ $\{V_\delta, \mathrm{PAST}_8\}_x$
      Phonology: $/[_\sigma \dots {}^*\mathrm{Nuc}^* \mathrm{Coda}]/_\delta$ $/[_\sigma \dots {}^*\mathrm{Nuc}^* \mathrm{Coda}]/_{\delta,x}$

This says that the past tense of a monosyllabic verb can be phonologically identical to the verb stem, with the exception of the syllabic nucleus. However, it does not specify what the nuclei in question are. These have to be learned on a verb-by-verb basis. This is surely true of the many singletons such as *eat/ate* and *hang/hung*.

On the other hand, some ablaut patterns are not quite so restricted. For instance, the *sing/sang* pattern has ten verbs, and the *string/strung* pattern has thirteen. Both these patterns are constrained to ending with a nasal (*swim/swam*), a velar stop (*dig/dug*), or both (*sink/sank*), with *sit/sat* as an outlier. In the heyday of the past tense debate, these patterns were shown to be strong targets for generalization to nonce forms such as *spling/splung* (Bybee and Moder 1983; Pinker 1999). This suggests that they probably do deserve their own subschemas, along the lines of (26), which is itself a special case of the more general ablaut schema in (25). (26a) delimits the possible stem forms with /ɪ/, and (26b) shows their past tenses with /æ/. The *swing/swung* pattern is identical to (26b) except for having /ʌ/ instead of /æ/. (N in (26) stands for the nasal and C_{vel} stands for the velar consonant.)

(26) *Sister schemas for the family of verbs with the* sing/sang *alternation*
      Semantics: a. $[\mathrm{F}(\dots)]_\varepsilon$ b. $[\mathrm{PAST}([\mathrm{F}(\dots)]_\varepsilon)]_y$
      Morphosyntax: V_ε $\{V_\varepsilon, \mathrm{PAST}_8\}_y$
      Phonology: $/[_\sigma \dots {}^*\mathrm{I}^* <\mathrm{N}> <C_{vel}>]/_\varepsilon$ $/[_\sigma \dots {}^*\mathrm{æ}^* <\mathrm{N}> <C_{vel}>]/_{\varepsilon,y}$

For another case, the *buy/bought* pattern has the seven instances *buy, bring, catch, fight, seek, teach,* and *think*. If this pattern is worthy of a schema, it stipulates that the stem and the past tense share only their syllabic Onset. The rhyme of the stem is completely unspecified, while the rhyme of the past tense is the constant /ɔt/. We won't formalize it here.

An important feature of this analysis is that the regular past (20c) and the irregular schemas (23b), (25b), and (26b) are identical in their semantics and morphosyntax. They differ only in their phonology. In other words, what makes an inflected form regular or irregular depends entirely on the morphosyntax-phonology interface.

Notice also how inflectional classes can be picked out by the Greek subscripts on the base of the schemas. For instance, in (26), the relational coindex ε pairs up stems that have the vowel /ɪ/ with past tenses that have the vowel /æ/—just the effect that an inflectional class feature is supposed to accomplish. In addition, all instances of (26) are also instances of the general ablaut schema (25), whose marker is the coindex δ. Hence we achieve the effect of inflectional subclasses without introducing new kinds of features—just new uses of the existing formal tools.

5.4 The German verb paradigm

5.4.1 Defining the paradigm

We now turn to the somewhat more complex German verbal paradigm. As in English, the morphosyntax stipulates the dimensions of the paradigm. Finite verbs vary in three independent dimensions: tense, person, and number. Tense and number have two possible values each; person has three. In addition, there are three nonfinite forms: infinitive, present participle, and past participle.[23] We can lay the paradigm out as (27), where the verb is an open variable, and tense, person, and number are closed variables.

(27)   a. {V, T, Pers, Num}   (finite verb)
      b. {V, INF}   (infinitive)
      c. {V, PRESPT}   (present participle)
      d. {V, PTCP}   (past participle)

We then have the slightly tedious task of enumerating the possible values of tense, person, and number, filling out the $2 \times 3 \times 2$ matrix of cells in the finite part of the paradigm, as in (28a-c).

(28)   a. Tenses: $[_T \text{PRES}]$, $[_T \text{PAST}]$
      b. Persons: $[_{\text{Pers}} 1]$, $[_{\text{Pers}} 2]$, $[_{\text{Pers}} 3]$
      c. Numbers: $[_{\text{Num}} \text{SG}]$, $[_{\text{Num}} \text{PL}]$

Within the finite forms, the value of tense is free-choice, determined by the semantics; person and number are determined contextually, through agreement with the subject. As in English, the syntactic configuration determines which of the forms in (27) is appropriate. For instance, finite forms are required for a main verb; infinitives are required after the complementizer *zu* and in the complement of certain verbs; past participles are required in perfect and passive constructions.

5.4.2 The weak paradigm

The morphosyntactic paradigm now has to be linked to phonology. This linkage is where all the complexity lies. (29) is a traditional matrix for the finite and infinitive forms of the German regular (or **weak**) paradigm, with the verb *machen* 'make.' (We treat the realization of PAST as -*t*-; for convenience we omit the participles.)

---

[23] We set aside mood, whose values are indicative, imperative, and subjunctive. The imperative always conforms to the verb stem plus a number suffix, and, in the contemporary language, the subjunctive is mostly restricted to auxiliary verbs.

    The periphrastic tenses (e.g. future, perfect, and pluperfect) are phrasal constructions with an auxiliary and a non-finite form of the main verb. For the purposes of phrasal syntax and semantics, these tenses naturally have to be defined. But the morphological component is responsible only for the insides of the auxiliary and main verbs; the relation of auxiliary and main verb is determined by phrasal syntax (Ackerman and Webelhuth 1999). However, the morphology of the auxiliaries themselves fall under our treatment here, as the periphrastic tenses involve a present tense (for the future and perfect) or a past tense (for the pluperfect).

(29) *Weak paradigm*

PRESENT	SG	PL		PAST	SG	PL
1	mach-e	mach-en		1	mach-t-e	mach-t-en
2	mach-st	mach-t		2	mach-t-est	mach-t-et
3	mach-t	mach-en		3	mach-t-e	mach-t-en
INFINITIVE	mach-en					

Each cell in this matrix stands for an interface link between a set of morphosyntactic features and the associated phonology. The position of the cell in the matrix determines its morphosyntactic features, and the content of the cell determines the associated phonology.

In order to translate this matrix into RM notation, we need a representation of the stem, shown in (30). As proposed in section 5.2, the morphosyntax of the stem has only syntactic category features; it lacks inflectional features. This entails a lexical entry that never surfaces alone, i.e. the stem is necessarily a bound form. (For readers who disapprove of this analysis—an issue on which the authors waver—we develop a treatment in section 5.5 that allows but does not require storage of bound stems.)

(30) *machen (stem)*
    Semantics: $[\text{MAKE (X, Y)}]_{11}$
    Morphosyntax: V_{11}
    Phonology: $/\text{max}/_{11}$

Two representative forms from matrix (29) are spelled out in (31); the other eleven are similar. They have relational links to the stem and to each other (coindex 11). PRES is not linked to phonology, but PAST is. Person and number are both linked to the final suffix. (To keep things simple, we omit semantics.)

(31)   a. *mache*   b. *machten*
    Morphosyntax: $\{V_{11}, \text{PRES}_4, 1_1, \text{SG}_6\}_8$ $\{V_{11}, \text{PAST}_5, 3_3, \text{PL}_7\}_9$
    Phonology: $/\text{max}_{11}\,ə_{1,6}/_8$ $/\text{max}_{11}\,t_5\,ən_{3,7}/_9$

We next need to state the schemas that support the inflections for *machen* and other weak verbs. We first lay out an overall template for their structure in (32). This says that the basic order in phonology for a finite weak verb is the verb stem (variable coindex *x*) followed by the tense (coindex *y*), followed by a portmanteau of the person and number features (coindices *z* and *w*). In order to account for zero morphology in present tense, the relevant portion of the phonology is optional, notated with < >.

(32) *Inflectional template for finite weak verbs*
    Morphosyntax: $\{V_x, T_{<y>}, \text{PERS}_z, \text{NUM}_w\}_v$
    Phonology: $/\ldots_x <\ldots_y> \ldots_{z,w}/_v$

Next come the schemas for the individual suffixes. (33) shows two of them, again the present 1st singular and the past 3rd plural; the rest of the schemas are similar. Each of these schemas is a special case (or subschema) of template (32). The stems of the schemas are tied together by the Greek coindex α; this is what makes the collection of schemas serve as a paradigm.

(33)   a. *PRESENT 1 SG schema*   b. *PAST 3 PL schema*

       Morphosyntax: $\{V_\alpha, \text{PRES}_4, 1_1, \text{SG}_6\}_x$ $\{V_\alpha, \text{PAST}_5, 3_3, \text{PL}_7\}_y$

       Phonology: $/\ldots_\alpha\, \partial_{1,6}/_x$ $/\ldots_\alpha\, t_5\, \partial n_{3,7}/_y$

These schemas unify with the stem *mach-* (30) to form the inflected verbs in (31).

A further generalization is that the present tense is always zero and the past is always *-t-*. This can be expressed with the schemas (34a,b). (33a,b) are among their respective instances.[24]

(34)   a. *Present tense schema*   b. *Past tense schema*

       Morphosyntax: $\{V_\alpha, \text{PRES}_4\}_z$ $\{V_\alpha, \text{PAST}_5\}_w$

       Phonology: $/\ldots_\alpha\ldots/_z$ $/\ldots_\alpha\, t_5\ldots/_w$

So far this is straightforward. However, one complication in the weak paradigm bears mention. The suffixes for present 3rd singular and present 2nd plural, as well as those for past tense, begin with /t/; the suffix for present 2nd singular begins with /s/. When a verb stem that ends in an alveolar stop (/t/ or /d/) is followed by one of these affixes, an epenthetic schwa appears between them. Examples are *wartet* 'wait.PRES.3.SG' rather than **wart-t*, and *wartest* 'wait.PRES.2.SG' rather than **wart-st*.

This intrusion is clearly motivated by a phonotactic pressure to shun difficult clusters. But it cannot be purely automatic. Another solution could have been degemination to **/wart/*, which is what is found in the Dutch cognate: *hij wacht/*wachtet* 'he waits'. Moreover, if the stem (in German) ends in /s/ and the affix begins with /s/, we *do* get degemination, e.g. *rast* 'race.PRES.2.SG' rather than **rasest*. Similarly, although regular verbs in English epenthesize, as in *waited*, the irregular verbs with zero past tenses such as *put* can be regarded as degemination. So the schwa epenthesis, where it is actually found, is far from inevitable: it has to be learned and recorded in memory.

We account for this schwa by introducing a codicil to template (32) that addresses this particular case. This stipulates a schwa between the verb stem and whatever collection of suffixes follow it, if it happens that the stem ends with a /t/ and the suffixes begin with /t/. The schwa is neither part of the stem nor part of the affix; it is a free-floating piece of phonology.[25]

---

[24] Should it be useful to express the syncretism among the various forms (for instance 1 PL, 3 PL, and INF are all *-en*), we can add relational links across their phonology, as we did with English past and past participle in (21).

[25] More detail in (35): Schwa epenthesis cares only about phonology; it does not care whether the phonology of the affix comes from a tense or a person-number schema. Accordingly, we have left the affixal parts of (35) without links between morphosyntax and phonology. In any particular situation, these links will be filled in by the schemas for the affixes in question.

(35)   *Schwa epenthesis in weak paradigm*
    Morphosyntax: $\{V_\alpha, T, \text{PERS}, \text{NUM}\}_v$
    Phonology: $/\ldots[\text{-cont},\text{+alv}]_\alpha \; \partial \; [\text{+alv}]\ldots/_v$

        Example: *war - t   -   e - st*

(35) is more specific than the general template (32); hence it takes precedence.[26]

To sum up this section, Relational Morphology encodes each cell of a traditional paradigm matrix as an interface link between a complete set of morphosyntactic features and its phonological realization. In (31) we have seen the structure of a particular inflected verb; (33) shows how each combination of features is encoded as a schema. (34) shows how the contribution of an individual morphosyntactic feature can be singled out in terms of a more general schema.

As in English, the inflected forms of any verb are tied together relationally by a common coindex on the verb, that is, they are a set of sisters (for instance coindex 11 for *machen*). The schemas too are tied together into a paradigm by their shared Greek letter coindex, in this case α. Hence if one can identify one of the forms of a verb, one can derive the others. We discuss this process in section 5.5.

5.4.3 Past tense in the German strong paradigm

The German strong verbs resemble the English ablaut verbs, with a few extra wrinkles.[27] Here is the paradigm for *singen* 'sing.'

(36)   *Sample strong paradigm*

PRESENT	SG	PL		**PAST**	SG	PL
1	sing-e	sing-en		1	sang	sang-en
2	sing-st	sing-t		2	sang-st	sang-t
3	sing-t	sing-en		3	sang	sang-en
INFINITIVE	sing-en					

In (36), the present tense is the same as that of the weak verbs in (29). However, this is not the case with all strong verbs; we return to this point in section 5.4.4. In the past tense, as with English ablaut verbs, there is no dedicated past tense affix; rather, the stem undergoes ablaut. However, unlike English, the past tense is also suffixed (except in 1st and 3rd singular).

---

[26] We note that a similar schema is responsible for the presence of schwa in English *trusted*. And a similar *family* of schemas is responsible for schwa in the morphosyntactically unrelated *horses* (plural), *chooses* (present 3rd singular), and *Charles's* (possessive). For a different case, one might view the plural possessive *the boys'* as a degemination of /bojz-z/. All of these cases need to make reference to particular affixes and are hence morphologically conditioned.
[27] Wiese (1996a) enumerates all the possible ablaut alternations of German strong verbs. The situation is similar to that in English, as enumerated in Table 5.1.

Let us put this into RM terms. Provisionally assuming that one stores a stem form for *singen*, its most likely phonological form is /zɪŋ/, as in (37a). As argued by Wiese (1996a), it is also necessary to store a form that reflects the past tense inflections and their relation to the stem. This is shown in (37b); one could think of it as a "past tense stem." In its morphosyntax, it carries relational coindex 21, linking it with the "plain" stem. Its phonology also is marked with relational coindex 21, reflecting the fact that it is pronounced the same as /zɪŋ/ except for the vowel.

(37)   a. *singen (stem)*   b. *"Past tense stem"*
    Morphosyntax: V_{21} $\{V_{21}, \text{PAST}\}_{22}$
    Phonology: $/z *ɪ* ŋ/_{21}$ $/z *a* ŋ/_{21,/22}$

(37) is much like (24), the entries for English stem and past tense *sing*. The main difference is that in German, (37b) is not a complete inflected word, for it still needs Person and Number features in order to satisfy the template for inflected verbs. Here are two of the six schemas that license these features. In (38a), none of the morphosyntactic features have independent phonological exponents; in (38b), 3rd person and plural combine in the usual way to form the *-en* suffix.

(38)   a. *Past 1 sg schema*   b. *Past 3 pl schema*
    Morphosyntax: $\{V_\beta, \text{PAST}, 1, \text{SG}\}_x$ $\{V_\beta, \text{PAST}, 3_3, \text{PL}_7\}_y$
    Phonology: $/.../_{\beta,x}$ $/..._\beta ən_{3,7}/_y$

Unifying (37b), the past stem of *singen*, with (38a) and (38b) yields the fully inflected forms *sang* and *sangen*.

It is necessary in (38) to designate all the members of the strong paradigm as sisters. Hence the V feature carries the coindex β, contrasting with the weak paradigm, whose schemas are coindexed α. Also, since the strong verbs have to be listed, the V feature is a nonproductive variable.

More generally, as in English, it is necessary for the grammar to license ablaut as a way to express past tense. The general schema for ablaut past tenses (39) is identical to that for English (25).

(39)   *Stem and past tense stem sister schemas for ablaut past* (= (25))
    Morphosyntax: a. V_β b. $\{V_\beta, \text{PAST}\}_x$
    Phonology: $/[_\sigma ... *\text{Nuc}* \text{Coda}]/_\beta$ $/[_\sigma ... *\text{Nuc}* \text{Coda}]/_{\beta,x}$

(39) leaves open exactly what vowels in the stem alternate; the correct form of the past has to be learned for each verb. Learning (39) involves generalizing over all the individual verb alternations.

As in English, some of the alternations have a sizeable number of members, which might be encoded as subschemas to (39). For instance, the e/a alternation in *sprechen/sprach* has fifteen instances, and hence might warrant a subschema like (40).[28]

---

[28] The verbs with this pattern are *bergen, bersten, brechen, erschrecken, gelten, helfen, nehmen, schelten, sprechen, stechen, sterben, treffen, verderben, werben, werfen* (list from www.deutschplus.net/pages/Tabelle_starker_Verben).

(40) *Stem and past tense stem sister schemas for ɛ/a ablaut past*

Morphosyntax: a. V_γ b. $\{V_\gamma, \text{PAST}\}_x$

Phonology: $/[_\sigma \ldots *\varepsilon* \text{ Coda}]/_\gamma$ $/[_\sigma \ldots *a* \text{ Coda}]/_{\gamma,x}$

Thus again as in English, we can regard the strong verbs as forming an umbrella inflectional class, codified as (39), with some families of items forming subclasses, plus some residual singletons such as *gehen/ging*, *liegen/lag*, and *stehen/stand*.

5.4.4 A second vowel alternation

As mentioned a moment ago, some of the strong verbs have an additional vowel alternation in the present tense 2nd and 3rd singular, for example *sprechen* 'speak,' whose paradigm appears in (41).

(41) *Strong paradigm with vowel alternation in PRES 2/3 SG*

PRESENT	SG	PL		PAST	SG	PL
1	sprech-e	sprech-en			sprach	sprach-en
2	sprich-st	sprech-t			sprach-st	sprach-t
3	sprich-t	sprech-en			sprach	sprach-en
INFINITIVE	sprech-en					

Like *singen*, *sprechen* has a starred vowel /ɛ/ in its stem, which alternates with /a/ in the past tense, as seen in (42) (again setting semantics aside).[29]

(42)   a. *sprechen (stem)*   b. *sprach (past tense stem)*

Morphosyntax: V_{31} $\{V_{31}, \text{PAST}\}_{32}$

Phonology: $/\int pr *\varepsilon* x/_{31}$ $/\int pr *a* x/_{31,32}$

But in addition to the stored past stem, *sprechen* also needs a special schema for the errant vowel in the present tense. Here is the lexical entry for *spricht*.

(43)   *spricht (PRES 3 SG)*

Morphosyntax: $\{V_{31}, \text{PRES}_4, 3_3, \text{SG}_6\}_{33}$

Phonology: $/ /\int pr *I* x/_{31} t_{3,6} /_{33}$

The present tense ablaut in *sprechen* applies fairly broadly across German strong verbs, with the five patterns of alternation illustrated in (44).[30]

---

[29] We also set aside the phonetic realization of /x/ as [ç] after front vowels; see section 6.3.

[30] Or possibly more. (44a) and (44b) actually have two variants. In (44a), tense *e* alternates with tense *i* (*geben/gibt*, *treten/tritt*), and lax *e* with lax *i* (*sprechen/spricht*, *helfen/hilft*). Similarly, in (44b), lax *a* alternates with lax *ä* (*halten/hält*) and tense *a* with tense *ä* (*schlafen/schläft*). However, the difference may be predictable from the phonology of the stem.

(44)   a.   ɛ/e ~ ɪ/i   sprechen/spricht, helfen/hilft, geben/gibt (26 instances)

   b.   a ~ ɛ/æ   halten/hält, schlafen/schläft (18 instances)

   c.   e ~ i   lesen/liest, sehen/sieht (6 instances)

   d.   aʊ ~ ɔɪ   laufen/läuft (2 instances)

   e.   o ~ ø   stossen/stösst (only instance)

(45) is a pair of sister schemas that states the relation in the most general fashion possible: any vowel alternation satisfies it.[31]

(45)   a. *Default stem form*   b. *Special stem in* PRES 2/3 SG
   Morphosyntax: V_δ $\{V_\delta, \text{PRES}, 2_2/3_3, \text{SG}\}_\gamma$
   Phonology: $/\dots\text{*Nuc* Coda}/_\beta$ $//\dots\text{*Nuc* Coda}/_\beta \dots_{2/3}/_\gamma$

   (45) captures what has been called in the literature a *morphomic* pattern (Aronoff 1994): a regularity over a certain part of the paradigm, which holds irrespective of the phonology that realizes it. The cells of the paradigm it applies to (here, 2nd and 3rd singular, present tense) do not form a natural class and need to be stipulated.

   The formulation in (45) is probably too general, given the limited number of actual cases that it covers. Perhaps these alternations are best captured with a phonologically restricted schema for the /e/~/ɪ/ family (46) and another for the /a/~/ɛ/ family (not shown). The remaining cases in (44) may be treated as outliers that are close but not entirely faithful instances of these two.

(46)   /ɛ/ ~ /ɪ/ *family*
   Morphosyntax: V_δ $\{V_\delta, \text{PRES } 2_2/3_3, \text{SG}\}_z$
   Phonology: $/\dots\text{*ɛ* Coda}/_\delta$ $//\dots\text{*ɪ* Coda}/_\delta \dots_{2/3}/_z$

The verb shared between these schemas has its own Greek coindex δ, so the instances of the schemas form a small inflectional class, a subclass of the strong verbs.

5.4.5 Past participles

German past participles such as *ge-sag-t* 'say.PTCP' raise two issues, which we discuss in turn. First, the participles of strong verbs have their own ablaut patterns. Second, past participles have an apparent circumfix *ge…t*, which we will show is better treated as multiple exponence.

   The past participle of weak verbs is built directly on the stem; for instance *ge-mach-t* 'made.PTCP'. However, strong verbs display a wide range of vowel alternations in the participle. With some verbs, the vowel differs from that in both the present and past tense (47a); with some, it is the same as that of the present (47b); and with others it is

---

[31] For the fastidious: In order to combine 2nd and 3rd persons in (45b), we have used a variable to express their differing phonology, letting the regular realizations of person/number fill in the correct variant, /st/ or /t/. Alternatively, one could write separate schemas for the two cases and fill in the phonology completely in each one.

the same as that of the past (47c). (Coincidentally, the English glosses parallel the German, thanks to their historical connection.)

(47)   PRESENT.1.SG   PAST.1.SG   Past participle
    a. sing-e   'sing'   sang 'sang'   ge-sung-en   'sung'
    b. geb-e   'give'   gab 'gave'   ge-geb-en   'given'
    c. frier-e 'freeze'   fror 'froze'   ge-fror-en   'frozen'

To allow for the range of possibilities, we return to (39), the sister schemas for the stem and past tense stem for strong verbs, and add a third sister (48) for the past participle. As always, we are not regarding the participle as derived from the other forms; it is an equal sister in this trio.[32]

(48)   a. *Stem*   b. *Past tense stem*   c. *Past participle*
Morphosyntax: V_β $\{V_\beta, \text{PAST}\}_x$ $\{V_\beta, \text{PTCP}\}_y$
Phonology: $/[_\sigma \ldots \text{*Nuc* Coda}]/_\beta$ $/[_\sigma \ldots \text{*Nuc* Coda}]/_{\beta,x}$ $/\text{gə}/[_\sigma \ldots \text{*Nuc* Coda}]/_\beta \text{ən}/_y$

In order to capture the range of possibilities for the vowel in the past participle, we resort to what may or may not be a trick in the interpretation of *Nuc* in (48). As we have interpreted the star notation so far, it says that the starred constituents are different. In (48), this would imply that the present, past, and participle all have different vowels. This accounts for cases such as (47a). As for the remaining cases, suppose the stars indicate only the *potential* for contrast. This would allow the possibility of two of the starred nuclei being the same. Under this interpretation, (48) can also accommodate cases in which the participle is based on the present form, like (47b), and cases in which the participle is based on the past stem, like (47c).

(48) is the most general case: it does not specify what vowel alternates with what. For some of the patterns with relatively large numbers of members, e.g. the *singen/ sang/gesungen* family, with eighteen members,[33] again we can envision subschemas that specify their properties in fuller detail, including whether or not the vowel of the participle is shared with one or the other of its sisters.[34]

Turning to the affixes involved in the participle, the prefix and suffix are subject to different conditions: (a) the prefix *ge-* appears if and only if the stem begins with a stressed syllable; (b) the suffix is *-t* with weak verbs but *-en* with strong verbs. Hence among the weak verbs we find *ge-mácht* 'made' and *ge-ántwortet* 'answered,' with both the prefix and the *-t* suffix, but *rèservíert* 'reserved,' with the suffix but no prefix.

---

[32] Clahsen et al. (2002) (cited in Clahsen 2016) present experimental evidence that speakers give a certain primacy to the "basic" stem form. This leaves open the question of whether the primacy is due to specific lexical marking of the basic stem, or whether it is simply a product of frequency.

[33] The verbs in this class: *binden, dingen, dringen, finden, gelingen, klingen, ringen, schlingen, schwinden, schwingen, singen, sinken, springen, stinken, trinken, winden, wringen, zwingen*. Note the phonological parallel to the cognate class in English: all the stems end in nasals, mostly followed by velars.

[34] Ablaut occurs still more prolifically in German. For instance, *sprechen* has not only the past participle *gesprochen*, but also derivationally related nominals such as *Sprache* 'language,' *Sprichwort* 'proverb,' *Gespräch* 'conversation,' and *Widerspruch* 'contradiction.' Thus among the allomorphs of the stem *sprech-*, six different vowels occupy the "except" position. All these disparate forms are united through sharing structure with the same V and (almost) the same phonology.

Likewise, in the strong verbs, we find *ge-spróchen* 'spoken,' with both the prefix and the *-en* suffix, and *verspróchen* 'promised,' with the suffix but no *ge-* prefix. Hence we need separate schemas for the prefix and the two suffixes.

The schema licensing the prefix *ge-* is shown in (49); it is entirely productive.

(49)   *Past participle* ge- *prefix schema*
       Morphosyntax: $\{V_\alpha, \text{PTCP}_9\}_y$
       Phonology: $/g\partial_9 \acute{o}\dots_\alpha/_y$

           Examples: *ge - mach - t*
                        ge - sung - en
                        ge - antwort - et

The schemas licensing the suffix are differentiated by verb class: for weak verbs, productive V_α; for strong verbs, nonproductive V_β. (The ellipsis at the beginning of the phonology is there to allow room for *ge-*.)

(50)   a. *Weak participle suffix*   b. *Strong participle suffix*
        Morphosyntax: $\{V_\alpha, \text{PTCP}_{10}\}_z$ $\{V_\beta, \text{PTCP}_{11}\}_w$
        Phonology: $/\dots \dots_\alpha t_{10}/_z$ $/\dots \dots_\beta \partial n_{11}/_w$

          Examples: *ge-mach-t*   *ge-sung-en*

The upshot is that a single past participle form such as *gesungen* (51) inherits structure from four independent converging sources: its stem (coindex 21), the prefix schema (49) (coindex 9), the suffix schema (50) (coindex 11), and the schema for the *singen/sang/gesungen* family, contributing the choice of vowel. In particular, the single morphosyntactic feature PTCP corresponds to two pieces of phonology. We take it to be a virtue of our approach that all these factors can be brought to bear simultaneously.

(51)   Morphosyntax: $\{V_{21}, \text{PTCP}_{9,11}\}_{27}$
       Phonology: $/g\partial_9 /z*\upsilon*\eta/_{21} \partial n_{11}/_{27}$

The treatment of English participles is much the same as German, minus the *ge-* prefix. For instance, the vowel patterns of the English glosses in (47) parallel those of the German verbs, and many strong verbs have a participle with *-en* instead of *-d*, e.g. *know/knew/known*. Dutch is more complex because it has an additional combination, namely weak verbs with an *-en* participle (e.g. *gelachen* 'laughed'). Such words, then, both participate in productive schemas, namely the regular 'weak' inflection for the past tense, and at the same time are listed members of a nonproductive schema, namely that of the *-en* participle.

This completes our survey of verb inflection in English and German and their treatment in Relational Morphology. To be sure, these patterns are hardly of the complexity displayed by many languages of the world. We hope, however, that our analysis lays the groundwork for treating more elaborate systems in RM terms. We now turn to a larger issue that constantly arises in our approach: the interplay of storage and computation.

5.5 How are verbs stored? How are novel inflectional forms constructed?

In the last two sections, we have conveniently assumed that the lexical entry of a German verb is stored minimally: an uninflected stem form such as *mach-* (30), plus (for strong verbs) a past tense stem such as *sang-* (37b), a 2nd/3rd present such as *spricht* (43), and a past participle such as *gesungen* (51). It is now time to revisit this assumption and return to one of the fundamental questions of the Parallel Architecture and Relational Morphology: What forms of a paradigm are actually stored in the lexicon?

One possibility, widespread in the literature, is that the lexicon is nonredundant, and it specifies only the minimum that is necessary for constructing all the forms of the paradigm on demand. This might amount to storing just a stem in the lexicon. In addition, the grammar must contain the realization rules that specify how the stem is manipulated in order to produce the full paradigm. In the present approach, of course, the counterpart of the realization rules is the set of inflectional schemas, stored in the lexicon along with the words of the language.

For reasons detailed in Chapters 2 and 3, such an analysis in terms of nonredundant (or "impoverished") entries does not comport with the psycholinguistic view of grammar adopted here. Our sense is that the brain has no stake in reducing stored information to a minimum, at the expense of more computation. Rather, the brain thrives on opportunistic redundancy, which makes memory and processing more robust.

The psycholinguistic perspective raises more pointed issues as well. For instance, consider the process of acquiring an inflectional paradigm. The evidence in the input for a paradigm is some collection of fully inflected forms, which must be stored long enough to allow the learner to construct the relevant set of sister schemas (or realization rules). So, as in section 3.3, the question arises: when a schema eventually comes into play, what happens to these stored forms? Some part of their structure is now redundant, predicted by the schema. If the lexicon is supposed to be in principle nonredundant, then all the predictable information in these entries has to be stripped off. This strikes us as a pointless step: why should the brain delete potentially useful information? Similarly, when a novel inflected form is constructed, based on a stem and a schema, a nonredundant lexicon demands that it is immediately discarded after use. Again, why should the brain do this, if the newly computed form might be useful later on?

The diametric opposite of this approach is that the lexicon contains full paradigms of all inflectable words. But from a psycholinguistic perspective, this too is suspicious. It implies that in a massively inflected language like Turkish (Hankamer 1989), Archi (Kibrik 1998), or Dalabon (Evans, Brown, and Corbett 2001; Evans 2017), one stores thousands, perhaps even millions, of forms for every verb. Moreover, the question arises of how all these forms got there. If what one stores is entire paradigms, then at the first encounter with a single inflected form of a novel verb, one must generate all the other forms on the spot—possibly hundreds or thousands of them—to be squirreled away just in case one might encounter them someday. This too seems improbable.

A sort of compromise between these extremes posits that the lexicon contains some minimal set of forms, the "principal parts," that together are maximally informative about the rest of the paradigm (e.g. Blevins 2016). This is essentially what we have assumed above for the German verb. Couched in terms of storage, it is more realistic than the previous two approaches. Yet it still raises questions about acquisition. Does one wait to store a novel word until one has encountered all its principal parts? Moreover, how does the learner know in advance which are the lucky forms that are to serve as principal parts? Does one store a wider range of forms, and then, having determined which of them are principal parts, delete all the rest?

As made clear in previous chapters, our position is that storage is opportunistic: one provisionally stores whatever inflected forms one encounters, and one constructs schemas as the evidence comes in. (This appears to be also the position of Blevins 2016: 93.) As will be discussed in more detail in Chapter 7, regular inflected and derived forms are retained in memory to the extent that they are useful in processing, in particular if it is faster to retrieve them as a whole than to reconstruct them using the schema. Thus frequent forms, which are retrieved relatively often, tend to be retained, while infrequent forms, which are retrieved more rarely, will tend to decay in memory. Forms intermediate in frequency may be processed both in terms of storage and computation.

An important feature of our analysis is the dual roles of schemas. If a schema is used to construct a novel form online, it is fulfilling its generative function. But if the result is stored, the schema continues to motivate it through its relational function. For instance, as discussed in section 2.6, the same plural schema both generates the novel word *wugs* and motivates the stored collocation *shake hands*. This means that it is not of great theoretical importance whether or not any particular form is stored or constructed on demand: the schema takes responsibility for it either way.

Of course, a schema alone cannot generate a novel form: its variables must be instantiated by something already stored in the lexicon or already constructed online. So the question arises of what serves as this other ingredient. The simplest solution from a formal point of view invokes the traditional notion of a stem: for instance, the form *machst* 'make.PRES.2.SG' is constructed by adding the inflection -*st* to the stem *mach-*. But again, a psycholinguistic perspective leads us to question this as the exclusive mechanism. A stem form such as *mach-* never appears in isolation in the input, so to store it requires a certain amount of abstraction from the input. On the other hand, maybe abstraction isn't so bad, since we certainly need it in order to posit schemas.

We remain agnostic about whether the lexicon contains stems, or whether some words have stored stems and others do not.[35] In order to allow for the possibility of extending a paradigm without storing the stem, we need a mechanism that can generate a novel inflected form from an already known inflected form, without a stored stem from which they are both derived. For instance, if one knows the present 1st singular *mache* and wishes to construct the past 3rd plural, how does one do this? (52) illustrates the problem.

[35] A few verbs are stored *only* in a particular form. Well-known cases are *born* and *rumored*, which are stored as passive participles. Less familiar is *go* in the construction *go VP*, as in *go buy a car*. This can be used only in contexts that select the phonological form *go*: imperative (*Go buy a car!*), infinitive (*I should/need to go buy a car*), and conditional present (*whenever I go buy a car*)—but not **he goes buy(s) a car, *he's going buy(ing) a car, *he went buy/bought a car*, or **he has gone buy/bought a car*. Oddly, all forms are acceptable in the synonymous construction *go and VP*. The same is true of *come VP* versus *come and VP*.

(52)   Morphosyntax: $\{V_{11}, \text{PRES}, 1_1, \text{SG}_6\}_{12}$ $\{V_{11}, \text{PAST}, 3, \text{PL}\}_{13}$
       Phonology: $/\text{max}_{11} \, \partial_{1,6} /_{12}$ ⟷ $/ \text{ ??? } /_{13}$

Intuitively, the desired form is constructed "by analogy." We wish to dig a little deeper and see more precisely what "analogy" means here. A more articulated account of analogical derivation might say that it consists of a sequence of two operations: first the inflections are stripped off *mache*, and then the inflections for the past 3rd plural are added. The first of these operations, "stripping off the inflections," is a procedure we have not encountered before. In order to strip the inflections off *mache*, one must *identify* the inflections, in morphosyntax and phonology (as well as semantics, if relevant). In the morphosyntax, the inflections are of course the features PRES, 1, and SG; in the phonology, the inflections are the parts coindexed to the morphosyntactic inflections, hence in this case $/\partial/$. The result of removing these pieces in fact the form we have previously attributed to the stem, (53). Let us call this the "virtual stem."

(53)   Morphosyntax: $\{V_{11}\}$
       Phonology: $/\text{max}/_{11}$

The second step in the process is to add the inflections appropriate for the desired form. This can be accomplished by a procedure we already know: unifying the virtual stem with the schema for the desired inflection, in this case the past 3rd plural (54a) (= 33b)). The result is (54b), the desired form.[36]

(54)   a. *PAST 3 PL schema*   b. *machten*
Morphosyntax: $\{V_\alpha, \text{PAST}_5, 3_3, \text{PL}_7\}_y$ $\{V_{11}, \text{PAST}_5, 3_3, \text{PL}_7\}_{13}$
Phonology: $/\ldots_\alpha \, t_5 \, \partial n_{3,7} /_y$ $/\text{max}_{11} \, t_5 \, \partial n_{3,7} /_{13}$

The upshot is that it is in principle possible to derive one fully inflected form directly from another, with a virtual stem as an intermediate step.[37] If the stem is stored, of course, the first step of the process is unnecessary. And a virtual stem may come to be stored if it is computed frequently enough in the course of this sort of derivation. We leave the issue open; it probably is a matter for psycholinguistics and/or computational modeling rather than linguistic theory per se.[38]

---

[36] One little discrepancy: the desired form (54b) has a constant interface coindex 13 where the schema has a variable *y*. We are not going to work out the details.

[37] A hedge: We have not worked this out for cases in which ablaut comes into play.

[38] Lest this procedure seem baroque, we note that it is essentially a deconstruction of what has to happen in any use of analogy. Moreover, it is formally not unlike the process involved in resolving ellipsis, which is also often called analogical. For instance, consider the interpretation of (i).

(i) Fred likes fish, and Louise does too.

In order to interpret the second clause, one has to strip off the contrasting part of the meaning of the first clause to derive 'X likes fish'—the counterpart of our virtual stem—and then unify this with the elliptical clause to produce the meaning 'Louise likes fish too.' This basic mechanism appears in standard accounts of the semantics of focus and ellipsis (e.g. Merchant 2001), based in turn on the earlier approaches of Kraak (1967), Chomsky (1972), Jackendoff (1972), and Akmajian (1973), and developed formally by, for example, Rooth (1992). The account of Culicover and Jackendoff (2012), in the Simpler Syntax framework, grounds the approach in the same-except relation, introduced here in section 3.7.

In this context, we can ask the question that motivates the notion of principal parts. Suppose a language has multiple inflectional classes, and their phonology overlaps in certain cells of the paradigm. These particular cells offer no evidence as to which inflectional class a given form belongs to. For instance, suppose one knows only the present 1st singular *spreche* and wants to form the past 3rd plural. It is impossible to tell if the desired form will be *sprachen* or **sprechten*, or for that matter, some other ablaut possibility (perhaps aided and abetted by similar phonology in other verbs). In order to decide which form is correct, it is necessary to acquire a past tense form—but any past tense form will do, as they all have the same vowel.

Moreover, even if one has determined that the desired past tense form is *sprachen*, it is still impossible to know whether the present 3rd singular is *spricht* or **sprecht*. To determine this, it is necessary to hear either the actual form itself or the present 2nd singular, which has the same vowel. Finally, for the past participle, nothing in the paradigm of *sprechen* other than the participle itself can determine that the right vowel is /ɔ/, *gesprochen*.

Hence for strong verbs, one needs a collection of learned forms in order to fill out the paradigm by analogical derivation. In this particular case, the collection includes any present tense other than 2nd and 3rd singular, any past tense, a present tense 2nd or 3rd singular, and the participle. In contrast, to fill out a weak verb's paradigm, one needs only a single past tense form; this form distinguishes the weak verb class from the strong class; there are no further subdivisions within the weak class.

In short, the principal parts analysis of paradigms has a counterpart in Relational Morphology. The forms that distinguish inflectional classes must be learned and stored; but that does not preclude the storage of other forms as well. Moreover, there is no reason that different individuals cannot store different collections of forms, as long as the fully inflected forms come out the same in spoken language.

5.6 The Same Verb Problem

Section 3.6 mentioned a widely noticed issue in the analysis of inflectional paradigms (e.g. Beard 1988; Aronoff 1994: 28; Spencer 2013; Harley 2014), which we called the Same Verb Problem: many verbs with irregular paradigms cannot be identified with a particular meaning. For instance:

- *Take* has the past tense *took* regardless of whether it is a main verb, a part of an idiom (*took part, took a chance, took off*), a light verb (*took a walk*), or part of a morphologically complex verb (*undertook, partook*).
- *Do* has the past tense *did*, regardless of whether it is a light verb (*did a dance*), part of an anaphoric element (*I did too*), part of an idiomatic construction (*We did London, We did the dishes*), part of a morphologically complex verb (*undid*), or even a meaningless auxiliary (*He didn't win*).
- The past tense of main verb *go* is *went*, and it is also *went* in the past tense of idioms like *went nuts/bananas* and *went for broke*.

- The past tense of main verb *be* is *was/were*, and so is the past of auxiliary *be*.
- Spencer (2013) notes that *draw* as in *draw a picture* has the same past tense, *drew*, as *draw* in *draw blood* and *draw a cart*, as well as in the collocation *draw a conclusion*.
- Dutch *staan* 'stand' has the past tense *stond* and the past participle *gestaan*; the prefixed *bestaan* 'exist' has parallel past *bestond* and participle *bestaan*. Likewise for German *stehen/stand/gestanden* 'stand' and *verstehen/verstand/verstanden* 'understand.'
- These issues are not restricted to verbs. Nominalizations of prefixed or particle verbs match the nominalization pattern of their base, even when the complex verbs are semantically non-transparent: Dutch *vallen* 'to fall' nominalizes as *val* '(a) fall'; the particle verb *aanvallen* 'to attack' has the parallel nominal form *aanval* '(an) attack'; German *stehen* nominalizes as *Stand*, *verstehen* as *Verstand*.

In each of these cases, the differences in meaning require different lexical entries, and yet in some sense they all involve the same verb. So the question is: How is the structure of the inflectional paradigm shared among this range of lexical entries?

More is involved here than phonological similarity. There also exist homophonous verbs that inflect differently: *ring* a bell (*rang*), *wring* out a towel (*wrung*), and *ring* a city with highways (*ringed*). For a case in Dutch, the verb *zeggen* 'say' has the irregular past *zei*. But the verbs *toezeggen* 'agree, promise' and *afzeggen* 'cancel' often appear in the regular past tense forms *zegde toe* and *zegde af* rather than the expected irregular ?*zei toe* and ?*zei af*—that is, the *zeg* in these cases is *not* same verb as irregular *zeg*. These cases show that the lexicon somehow has to mark explicitly whether homophonous items share their inflectional paradigm and therefore are in a sense the "same verb" (e.g. the various *take*s and *do*s), or whether instead they have different paradigms and therefore are to be treated as different verbs (e.g. the various *(w)ring*s and *zeg*s).

How does the lexicon mark the sharing of an irregular paradigm? Since the verbs in question have multiple meanings—and in its auxiliary use, *do* has *no* meaning—we cannot identify the "same verb" by means of its semantics. And since shared phonology (e.g. *ring/wring*) is not enough to guarantee "same verb" status either, we are left with only morphosyntax as the possible locus of "same-verbness."

Stump (2001), Spencer (2013), Harley (2014), and Blevins (2016) propose to individuate lexical entries by assigning to each lexical item a "lexical index" that differentiates this item from all others. For instance, on Spencer's account, the various readings of *draw* receive lexical indices *draw*[1], *draw*[2], etc. He then sets up an equation between the inflectional forms associated with the various *draw*s. This equation is his version of an explicit link between the lexical entries.

We have three (perhaps minor) issues with this account. First, it is not clear how it extends to idioms. For instance, does the *take* in the idiom *take part* receive its own lexical index? It is not a lexical item, but only part of one. Second, it seems profligate to assign a lexical index to every item, regardless of whether it happens to participate in irregular inflection. Third, we find it hard to come up with an appropriate mentalistic construal for a unique index.

The Relational Morphology formalism can be extended in such a way as to have an effect similar to Spencer's account, while evading these issues. The point of Spencer's equation between lexical indices is to mark which items count as the same. This is precisely what is expressed by our relational coindices, which represent the ends of association lines between lexical entries or between shared parts of lexical entries. Words that do not take part in any morphological relations have no need for relational coindices.

In preceding sections, we used morphosyntactic coindices to express relations among the members of irregular paradigms. For the most extreme case, we linked *go* and *went* by coindexing the V feature in morphosyntax; similarly, *sprechen* and *gesprochen* count as versions of the same verb (or lexeme) by virtue of their bases being linked in phonology, morphosyntax and semantics. We can now use the same machinery to link different uses of the "same verb." The idea is that the link between morphosyntax and phonology is shared among these uses, but the link between morphosyntax and semantics is not shared, or, in the case of auxiliary *do*, there is no semantics for morphosyntax to link to. We have already seen the essence of this solution in our treatment of idioms in section 4.2, the relevant parts of which are repeated here.[39] (In the interest of sightliness, we include only relevant coindices.)

(55)   a. *chew* (stem)   b. *chew the fat*
    Semantics: $[\text{CHEW} (X,Y)]_1$ $[\text{CONVERSE} (X)]_2$
    Syntax: V_1 $[_{VP} V_1 [_{NP} \text{Det N}]]_2$
    Phonology: $/t\int uw_1/$ $/t\int uw_1 \eth \partial \ fæt /_2$

The verb is marked as morphosyntactically and phonologically the same (coindex 1) in both the "literal" verb *chew* (55a) and the idiom *chew the fat* (55b). However, the verb in (55b) has no interface link to the semantics—and neither do *the* and *fat*. Still, when it comes to morphosyntax and its connection to phonology, everything is shared. Unifying past tense with (55a,b) gives us (56a,b), in which the phonology of *chewed* is the same in the two cases.

(56)   a. *chewed*   b. *chewed the fat*
    Semantics: $[\text{PAST} [\text{CHEW} (X,Y)]_1]_3$ $[\text{PAST} [\text{CONVERSE} (X)]_2]_4$
    Syntax: $\{V_1, \text{PAST}_5 \}_3$ $[_{VP} \{V_1, \text{PAST}_5 \}_3 [_{NP} \text{Det N}]]_4$
    Phonology: $/ t\int uw_1 d_5 /_3$ $/ /t\int uw_1 d_5 /_3 \eth \partial \ fæt /_4$

Next consider what happens when the verb is irregular. (57) shows main verb *take*: (57a) is the stem (the present tense form would do equally well), and (57b) is the stored irregular past *took*.

(57)   a. *take* (stem)   b. *took*
    Semantics: $[\text{TAKE} (X, Y)]_6$ $[\text{PAST} ([\text{TAKE} (X, Y)]_6)]_7$
    Morphosyntax: V_6 $\{V_6, \text{PAST}\}_7$
    Phonology: $/t\ *ej*\ k/_6$ $/t\ *\upsilon*\ k/_{6,7}$

---

[39] Recently, some linguists have started to use the term ***flexeme*** to refer to a set of lexical items with identical inflectional behavior but different semantics, essentially what we are calling the "same verb" here (Fradin and Kerleroux 2003; Thornton 2018).

When *take* is part of an idiom such as *take part in NP*, the morphosyntax and phonology retain the coindex 6. But the semantics TAKE is no longer present, and only the entire syntactic configuration and the final NP are linked to the semantics, as shown in the stem (58).

(58)   *take part in* (stem)
 Semantics: [PARTICIPATE (X, Y_y)]$_8$
 Syntax: [$_{VP}$ V$_6$ N [$_{PP}$ P NP$_y$]]$_8$
 Phonology: / /t *ej* k/$_6$ part ɪn...$_y$ /$_8$

Unifying (58) with morphosyntactic past tense yields the configuration {V$_6$, PAST} in morphosyntax. This links to the morphosyntax and the phonology of (57b) (coindex 7)—just not to the semantics. Thus the outcome is (59), as desired.

(59)   *took part in*
 Semantics: [PAST [PARTICIPATE (X, Y_y)]$_8$]$_{10}$
 Syntax: [$_{VP}$ {V$_6$, PAST}$_7$ N [$_{PP}$ P NP$_y$]]$_{10}$
 Phonology: / /t *ʊ* k/$_{6,7}$ part ɪn...$_y$ /$_{10}$

Next consider Spencer's (2013) case of homonymous verbs that share irregular inflection, such as *draw* 'create a picture' and *draw* 'elicit' (as in *draw praise/jeers*), both of which have the past tense *drew* and the participle *drawn*. There is no sense that one of these is derived from the other (at least synchronically). So there need to be two distinct semantic structures attached to the same complex of morphosyntax and morphophonology.

A way to do this is give each of the two *draw*s its own link between semantics and morphosyntax, but to have them converge on the same morphosyntactic and phonological structure. (60) illustrates. (60a) is the entry for the stem of the 'draw a picture' reading;[40] (60b) for the 'elicit' reading. Each word has the standard interface links, here coindices 21 for (60a) and 22 for (60b). But crucially, there is an additional relational coindex 23 that marks the morphosyntax and phonology explicitly as the same in the two words. This coindex is absent in the semantics, which is what keeps the two words distinct.

(60)   a. *draw (a picture)*   b. *draw (praise)*
 Semantics   [CREATE (X, [PICTURE])]$_{21}$ [ELICIT (X, Y)]$_{22}$
 Morphosyntax: V$_{21,23}$ V$_{22,23}$
 Phonology: /dr *ɔə*/$_{21,23}$ /dr *ɔə*/$_{22,23}$

The past tense of the two verbs retains relational link 23, which stipulates that the two items are the same. The rest of the structure is exactly like other irregular verbs.

(61)   a. *drew (a picture)*   b. *drew (praise)*
 Semantics: [PAST [CREATE (X, [PICTURE])]$_{21}$]$_{24}$ [PAST [ELICIT (X, Y)]$_{22}$]$_{25}$
 Morphosyntax: {V$_{21,23}$, PAST}$_{24}$ {V$_{22,23}$, PAST}$_{25}$
 Phonology: /dr *uw* /$_{21,23,24}$ /dr *uw* /$_{22,23,25}$

---

[40] This reading of *draw* actually has two semantic argument structure frames: one where the direct object is a visual representation, as in *draw a picture/diagram/stripe*, and one where the direct object is what one is creating a visual representation *of*, as in *draw a horse/Einstein*. (60a) represents the former.

This treatment extends readily to prefixed verbs such as *withstand* ~ *withstood* and particle verbs such as *blow up* ~ *blew up* (both types are numerous in Dutch and German as well as English). Here are *withdraw* and *withdrew*. The morphosyntax and phonology now reflect that the verb is built from a preposition or particle plus a verbal stem, while the stem is linked with the other manifestations of *draw* in (60)-(61) (coindex 23).

(62)   a. *withdraw*   b. *withdrew*

	a. *withdraw*	b. *withdrew*
Semantics:	$[\text{RETREAT (X)}]_{26}$	$[\text{PAST } [\text{RETREAT (X)}]_{26}\,]_{28}$
Morphosyntax:	$[_V\, P_{27}\, V_{23}\,]_{26}$	$\{[_V\, P_{27}\, V_{23}\,]_{26}\,,\ \text{PAST}\,\}_{28}$
Phonology:	$/\text{wɪθ}_{27}\ \text{dr }{*}\text{ɔə}{*}_{23}\,/_{26}$	$/\text{wɪθ}_{27}\ \text{dr }{*}\text{uw}{*}_{23}\,/_{28}$

To sum up these cases, the "same verb" phenomenon arises when two items share structure in morphosyntax and phonology but not semantics. In the case of *take/took part* and *draw/withdraw*, the morphosyntax and phonology of one item are completely contained in the other item, but the semantics is unrelated. In the case of the two *draws*, the items are sisters that differ only in their semantics.

This analysis extends easily to cases of full suppletion, such as *go*, which has a huge variety of semantic functions, all of which carry over to the past tense *went*. In this case, the relational links in the phonology are absent as well, and only morphosyntax is shared.

5.7 The polysemy of morphosyntactic tense

The semantics of tenses presents a further case in which multiple meanings converge on a common morphology. As mentioned in section 5.1, the English present tense is used to express not only present time but a variety of other semantic functions.

(63)   a. Amy loves Olive.   [present time (with stative verb)]
       b. Cows eat grass.   [generic]
       c. If we go,...   [conditional]
       d. We leave on Tuesday.   [scheduled future]
       e. And then she says to me,... [informal narrative past/historic present]
       f. Stock Market Crashes!   ["hot news"]

Similarly, past tense can be used to express not just past time but also hypothetical future (*If we left tomorrow,...*) and past generic (*Back in those days, cows ate grass*).[41] But the morphology is preserved: irregular verbs are irregular in the past tense, regardless of what past tense happens to mean in any particular context. So we would like to say that morphological present and past are polysemous, just like *draw*. In other words, there is a many-to-many relation between meanings of a morphosyntactic tense and its possible phonological realizations, as sketched in Figure 5.1. We might call this the Same Tense Problem (though it may crop up with other features as well).

---

[41] Some of these readings may be determined constructionally. For instance, the hypothetical reading of past tense seems to occur only in the protasis of an *if-then* construction.

Semantics: PAST   HYPOTHETICAL   GENERIC-PAST

Morphosyntax: PAST

Phonology   /-d/   zero   ablaut   went   did

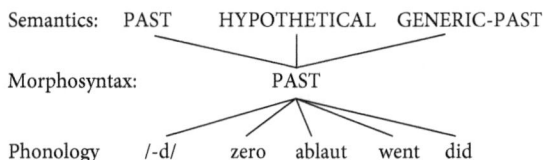

Figure 5.1 Taxonomy of meanings and forms of PAST

This situation could be accommodated by creating a schema for each possible combination of meaning and phonological realization. In the case of PAST, this would result in fifteen (= 3 × 5) separate schemas. (64) shows two of the fifteen: the highly frequent use of the regular past to express past time, and the more oddball use of the zero past to express a hypothetical.

(64)

a. *Past of weak verb,*   b. *Past of zero-past verb,*
   meaning past   *meaning hypothetical*

Semantics: $[\text{PAST} ([\text{F} (\ldots)]_x]_y$ $[\text{HYP} ([\text{F} (\ldots)]_z)]_w$

Morphosyntax: $\{V_x, \text{PAST}_7\}_y$ $\{V_z, \text{PAST}\}_w$

Phonology: $/\ldots_x d_7 /_y$ $/\ldots [\text{+alv, -cont}] /_{z,w}$

One might mitigate the clumsiness of this solution by connecting the fifteen schemas with relational links—one set linking those with similar semantics, and another, cross-cutting set linking those with parallel phonology. However, this still treats it as a coincidence that the cross-cutting is entirely uniform.

A different way to describe the situation, without multiplying every past tense schema by three and every present tense schema by five, is to separate the links between semantics and morphosyntax—the upper links in Figure 5.1—from those between morphosyntax and phonology—the lower links. The schemas in (65) isolate the upper links, between semantics and PAST, with no reference to the phonological realization. The three schemas are sisters by virtue of sharing the PAST feature and the variable that encodes the verb (coindex α). (A similar account, in a Construction Morphology framework, appears in Booij and Audring (2017); earlier antecedents include Beard's (1988) Separation Hypothesis and Jackendoff (1975).)

(65)

a. PAST *means past*   b. PAST *means hyp*   c. PAST *means generic past*

Semantics: $[\text{PAST} ([\text{F} (\ldots)]_\alpha)]_x$ $[\text{HYP} ([\text{F} (\ldots)]_\alpha)]_y$ $[\text{PAST-GEN} ([\text{F} (\ldots)]_\alpha)]_z$

Morphosyntax: $\{V_\alpha, \text{PAST}\}_x$ $\{V_\alpha, \text{PAST}\}_y$ $\{V_\alpha, \text{PAST}\}_z$

The schemas in (66) isolate three of the five lower links in Figure 5.1. Each of these schemas connects PAST to a different inflectional class, identified by the Greek letters.

(66)

a. *Regular past*   b. *Ablaut past*   c. *Zero past*

Morphosyntax: $\{V_\alpha, \text{PAST}_7\}_w$ $\{V_\gamma, \text{PAST}\}_v$ $\{V_\delta, \text{PAST}\}_u$

Phonology: $/\ldots_\alpha d_7 /_w$ $/\ldots *\text{Nuc}* \text{Coda}/_{\gamma,v}$ $/\ldots [\text{+alv, -cont}]/_{\delta,u}$

The upshot of all these schemas is that the structure of a particular verb in a particular context is motivated by a collection of lexical items. For instance, the verb *drew* in the sense of hypothetically creating a picture has the structure (67).

(67)   Semantics: $[\text{HYP } [\text{CREATE } (X, \underline{\text{PICTURE}})]_{21}]_{29}$
         Morphosyntax: $\{V_{21}, \text{PAST}\}_{23,29}$
         Phonology: $/\text{dr *uw*}/_{21, 23, 29}$

The contribution of the stem, coindexed 21, comes from (60a). The connection between HYP and PAST is inherited from/motivated by (65b). The connection between PAST and the choice of vowel is partially inherited from/motivated by (66b); the particular choice of vowel comes from (61a). The relational coindex 23, as before, connects the morphosyntax and phonology of this sense of *draw* to that of the other senses of the word. Thus all parts of the word are motivated.

We therefore have two possible accounts of the many-to-many relations that fall under the English past tense: encoding combinations of meanings and inflectional forms (64), or splitting off the relations between meaning and morphosyntax (65) from the relations between morphosyntax and phonology (66). Which one is correct? In particular, which one better represents what a speaker stores? In the spirit of what we have seen for inflectional paradigms, our inclination is to say both may be correct, though the choice may depend on frequency. For the highly frequent use of the regular past tense to express past time, it might be more efficient to store the three-level schema (64a). For less frequent combinations, say hypothetical meaning expressed with a rare zero-past verb such as *befit*, the combination of (65b) and (66c) might be more effective. We leave the issue open.

To sum up the last two sections: every theory has to contend with the Same Verb and the Same Tense Problems. We hope to have shown that the Relational Morphology formalism offers relatively natural accounts of them. What makes these accounts possible is the Parallel Architecture's strict separation of linguistic structure into three levels, connected by interface links. In each of the cases we have looked at in the last two sections, morphosyntax serves as a "pivot" to which phonology and semantics link individually.

5.8 Summary

This chapter has shown how the tools of Relational Morphology can be applied to patterns of inflectional morphology. First, the paradigm—the dimensions of the inflectional feature set—has to be defined, as motivated by syntactic function and phonological distinctiveness. In particular, phrasal syntax determines which morphosyntactically inflected forms are to be used in which syntactic positions. This much is shared by all approaches, in one way or another. What is more distinctive in the present approach is that the phonology associated with each combination of stem and morphosyntactic features is determined not by a "realization rule" or "spell-out," but by a nondirectional interface link between morphosyntax and phonology.

The members of a word's (or lexeme's) paradigm are tied together by relational links that connect the inflected forms to a common stem. These links are notated by numerical coindices. The paradigm for an inflectional class as a whole is a set of sister schemas, one for each cell in the morphosyntactic paradigm. It is tied together by relational links between the variables that stand for the stem in each schema, notated by Greek letter coindices. Different inflectional classes have different variables, and thus afford different phonological realization.

As seen in sections 5.6 and 5.7, similar machinery accounts for the identical inflections of homonymous verbs, such as the varied meanings of *take* and *draw*, and even for the many-to-many relations between meaning and phonology conveyed by morphosyntactic tense. These cases too are encoded by means of relational links in morphosyntax and phonology which result in their displaying the same phonological alternations.

Looking to broader issues, the "competence" theory—the theory of possible representations—leaves open which forms in a paradigm are stored in the brain, and which forms are built on demand. In particular, it is formally possible to build a novel form either from a stem (should stems be stored) or from another stored inflected form. The "performance" theory, which puts the representations to use, features opportunistic processing, biased toward storing high-frequency forms and building low-frequency forms on the fly. Whether stored or constructed, inflected forms are supported by schemas—in their relational function for stored items, and in their generative function for computed items.

6

Morphologically conditioned
phonological alternations

A major issue for morphological theory is how morphology interacts with phonology. The preceding two chapters have already discussed cases like infixation, which rips open the sequence of segments in the base, and ablaut, which replaces a vowel of the base. We now take up some phonologically more complex patterns. For example, the pair *decide/decision* (/dəsajd/ vs. /dəsɪʒən/) displays an alternation in both the second vowel and the third consonant; and the triplet *harmony* (/hárməni/) vs. *harmonic* (/harmánɪk/) vs. *harmonious* (/harmóʊniəs/) involves alternations in both vowel quality and stress placement. These alternations are conditioned by the presence of particular suffixes, and the question is how the grammar enables the suffixes to have these effects.

In order to tackle this question from the outlook of Relational Morphology, we first sketch how phonology fits into the Parallel Architecture, in sections 6.1 through 6.3. The rest of the chapter formalizes some standard morphophonological phenomena in Dutch, German, and English.

6.1 Phonology in the Parallel Architecture

As stressed in Chapter 1, a large-scale goal of the Parallel Architecture is to develop an integrated linguistic theory in which all the components fit together naturally. Phonology, like syntax and morphology, has traditionally been formulated in terms of rules that operate on representations or systems of interacting constraints. However, as has been stressed throughout the present work, the PA encourages a different conception:

> The rules of grammar are pieces of linguistic structure, stored in the lexicon, that both (a) capture generalizations about the structure of stored items and, (b) if productive, serve as templates available for the online construction of novel forms.

The challenge is to extend this outlook to phonology. Alas, it is incompatible with either of the major schools of thought in phonological theory.[1]

---

[1] Many of the points made in this section and the next appear in Mohanan (1986: Chapter 6), Ladd (2014), and Liberman (2018); we draw freely on their discussion.

The Texture of the Lexicon. First edition. Ray Jackendoff and Jenny Audring © Ray Jackendoff and Jenny Audring 2020. First published in 2020 by Oxford University Press. DOI: 10.1093/oso/9780198827900.001.0001

Consider first phonology in the style of *Sound Pattern of English* (SPE: Chomsky and Halle 1968) and its descendants, including for instance Lexical Phonology (Kiparsky 1982; Mohanan 1986, 1995). This approach maintains the traditional dichotomy of lexicon and grammar. The lexicon contains the "underlying forms" of words and/or morphemes; the grammar is made up of procedural rules, e.g. "voice a consonant that falls between two vowels." The rules apply in sequence (and in various versions, in cycles and/or blocks) to convert underlying forms into surface forms.

Such an approach to phonology cannot be incorporated into the Parallel Architecture, whose principles are stated as declarative schemas rather than as ordered procedural rules, and in which the schemas are in the same format as lexical items. And given that the PA does not countenance "underlying forms" in syntax (Culicover and Jackendoff 2005) and morphology (Chapters 4 and 5), ideally it should not allow them in phonology either.

A second major school of thought in phonology is Optimality Theory (OT: Prince and Smolensky 2004). Here, the "input" is a lexical form or a concatenation of forms, e.g. /kæt^z/. A very general function GEN creates a set of candidate realizations. Phonological principles are stated as violable constraints over these candidate realizations, applied simultaneously according to a language-particular ranking. The constraints can be understood either procedurally—"avoid forming clusters of obstruents that differ in voicing" or declaratively—"a cluster of obstruents that differ in voicing is (preferably) ungrammatical." The "output" is a surface form that maximally satisfies the ranked constraints. OT is somewhat closer in conception to the PA, in its declarative conception and in its simultaneously applied constraints. Another point of consilience is that PA, like OT, admits the possibility of violable constraints, for instance when a more specific item or schema overrides a more general one, i.e. in morphological blocking. (See Jackendoff (1983: Chapter 8) on violable constraints in semantics.)

There are however differences. First, OT still retains the strong distinction between lexicon and grammar. They are in entirely different formats: a constraint is not a word, and a word is not a constraint or a collection of them. Second, OT still has an "input" and an "output," even if, unlike SPE phonology, they are separated by only two steps, namely the generation of candidate realizations and the selection of a highest ranking candidate. Third (and this may or may not be only a matter of taste), the constraints of OT tend to be prohibitions—structures to be avoided, things you can't say or prefer not to say. In contrast, the words and schemas of PA are pieces of language at your disposal, affordances for things you *can* say (a point to which we return here and there).

At first blush, both SPE-style and OT-style phonology may feel fairly natural in terms of production: a speaker selects pieces out of the lexicon and then runs them through the grammar to determine the surface form. However, in the case of SPE, the lexical representation of a word can be quite distant from its surface form. One might therefore wonder why the surface form isn't stored in the first place, sparing the processor the trouble of regenerating it on every occasion the word is to be used.

Moreover, the mechanism for deriving surface forms is highly implausible as a model of processing. An SPE-style derivation would require a dozen or more steps performed in sequence, taking place faster than the speed of light if one is going to be able to speak at a normal rate.

In OT, by contrast, the "faithfulness constraints" create a pressure on lexical representations to resemble the surface form as closely as possible. Still, an OT-style derivation requires one to generate all possible outputs—no matter how far-fetched—then apply ranked constraints to winnow them down to the form chosen for production. And even if one can accept either SPE- or OT-style derivations as accounts of speech production, it is not clear how to turn their versions of grammar around to use them in speech perception.

Proponents of either style of phonology may protest that the theory is not intended as a model of processing: it is meant only to characterize linguistic competence in the abstract, and it leaves open the connection between competence and performance. Our response is that the PA has larger ambitions: it at least aspires to make such a connection explicit (Chapter 7; Jackendoff 2002, 2007a). We think it is a mistake to abandon this goal on the grounds that it is not compatible with the formalism; we prefer to question the choice of formalism, regardless of whether it is enshrined by tradition. Our goal therefore is to account for the sorts of phenomena addressed by these procedural approaches, but in schema-theoretic terms.

6.2 The status of phonetics

A further problem with both SPE and OT is their treatment of phonetics, which they take to be the output of phonology, or at least homomorphic to the output of phonology. The difficulty is that the usual repertoire of phonological distinctive features is not expressive enough to specify phonetic detail. As pointed out by Ladefoged (1980) and Port and Leary (2005), standard distinctive features cannot capture the exact value (or distribution of values) of vowels across different speech communities, such as the difference between the Chicago, Boston, and London pronunciations of *board*; nor can they capture the exact range of voice onset times for stops (e.g. Dutch vs. English and German: Simon and Leuschner 2010), or the exact range of pitches for intonation contours.

In addition, phonetics has to be integrated somehow with speed of speech, which has no connection with phonological distinctive features per se. And in speech perception, phonetics has to be partialed out from the acoustics of the speaker's voice and the speaker's affect (or emotional tone—joy, anger, sarcasm, and so on). Ladd (2014: 190), discussing these latter aspects of meaning, which he calls "indexical," puts it like this: "It is as if the signal is processed in different ways for different purposes: in effect, the brain considers the propositional and the indexical separately."

With some trepidation, we adopt an architecture advocated by Levelt, Roelofs, and Meyer (1999) and Ladd (2014): phonetic form is not the output of a phonological derivation. Rather, phonology and phonetics are independent but linked levels of rep-resentation. The forms of words are stored phonologically—though, as observed in section 3.4.3, nothing stands in the way of storing their phonetics as well. Following tradition, we will treat phonological structure as an algebraic level of representation, with discrete segments that are decomposed into distinctive features and that are con-catenated into units such as syllables, feet, and phonological words. A discrete metrical (or stress) tier interfaces with syllabic structure and also connects to an intonation tier that incorporates discrete H and L pitch accents (Pierrehumbert 1980; Pierrehumbert and Beckman 1988). Tone languages will have a tone tier as well. We differ from traditional accounts in that we wish to characterize this level declaratively rather than procedurally, and we wish not to appeal to underlying levels of phono-logical structure.[2]

Phonetics contrasts with these discrete phonological structures: it is its own dis-tinct level of representation, with a gradient (or analog) encoding of speech. In the spirit of the PA, phonetics is linked to phonology by an interface, which plays the role of what are sometimes called "rules of phonetic implementation" (e.g. Booij 2009). Such rules are usually thought of as unidirectional, mapping from phonology to phonetics. Following the PA, though, we wish to treat them as non-directional: they implement a correspondence between two levels rather than a derivation from one to the other. Hence in a model of performance, the linkage can be used both in production, going from phonology to phonetics, and in com-prehension, going in the opposite direction. In a sense, then, phonology can be thought of as the *digitization of phonetics*, recoding phonetics in discrete terms (Pisoni and Luce 1987; Jackendoff 2002).

In what terms is phonetics coded? One possibility is articulatory, along the lines of Browman and Goldstein's (1986, 1989) "gestural score," specifying target vocal tract positions, and with continuous analog movements of articulators. Another possibility is acoustic, perhaps along the lines of an internalized spectrogram, but normalized across speakers and across affect, with analog pitch and formant contours. A third possibility, which we favor, is that both sorts of representation are present: vocal tract configurations and timing are tightly aligned with idealized (or normalized) acoustic traces (this is also proposed by Pisoni and Luce 1987).

Such a link between acoustic traces and vocal tract gestures enables a speaker to map from vocal gesture to anticipated sound: "what it will sound like when you do such-and-such with your vocal tract." One can also map from desired sound to vocal gesture: "what to do with your vocal tract in order to make it sound like *this*." Such

---

[2] A somewhat similar proposal for abandoning a derivational approach to phonology appears in Goldsmith's (1993) and Lakoff's (1993) Harmonic Phonology, which posits three declarative levels linked by (in our terms) nondirectional interfaces. Their "M-level" might correspond roughly to our lexical listing; the "W-level" to the phonological effects due to sequencing lexical items; and the "P-level" to our phonetics. This approach seems to have been overwhelmed by the contemporaneous tsunami of Optimality Theory (but see also van der Hulst and Ritter 2000).

connections would be invaluable for vocal imitation, a crucial aspect of language acquisition (Fitch 2010).[3]

In turn, the acoustic and articulatory tiers of phonetic representation have interfaces with audition and motor control respectively, which are likewise gradient. The latter might be programs of muscle activations that actually move the vocal tract to desired positions. This arrangement of components is sketched in Figure 6.1.

Notice that voice recognition and affect recognition are outside phonetics and are not linked to phonology. This reflects the fact that one can recognize the voices and affect of speakers without knowing a word of the language they are speaking. Notice also that one's own affect also contributes to motor control, creating modulation in the output that a perceiver can detect.

Some evidence for such a dichotomy between phonology and phonetics comes from neuroscience. Myers (2007) and Myers et al. (2009) find a region in the left inferior frontal sulcus that shows sensitivity specifically to competition between phonological /d/ and /t/, defined more or less categorically. In contrast, left superior temporal regions show graded sensitivity to acoustic differences that differentiate phonetic instances of [da] and [ta] along a continuous spectrum of voice onset times (VOTs)—crucially, including VOTs outside the range of normal speech and therefore never heard. In other words, phonology and phonetics differ in what brain areas are sensitive to them.

The architecture in Figure 6.1 helps explain a well-known phenomenon in language acquisition (Werker and Tees 1984; Jusczyk 1997; Kuhl et al. 2005). Early in life, infants are sensitive to all sorts of phonetic distinctions, including distinctions not present in the language(s) in their environment. But at some point late in their first year, around eight to twelve months, they are said to lose the ability to make phonetic distinctions, and to be able to distinguish only among phonemes of the language they are about to learn. This phenomenon is often described as a loss of ability on the infants' part.

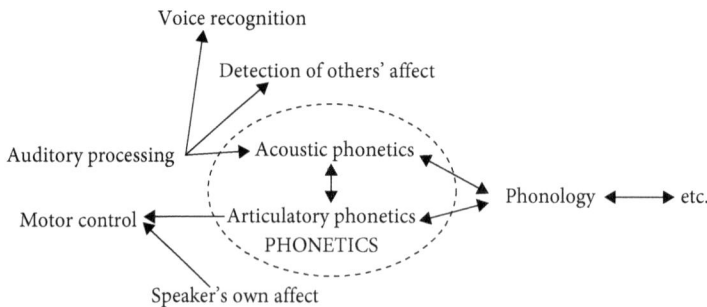

Figure 6.1 Architecture of phonology and phonetics

---

[3] A similar tight linkage between motor and acoustic representations is required for singing and for playing a musical instrument—though in the latter case it clearly involves a far greater degree of *conscious* learning. More generally, such linkages are necessary to integrate perception and action.

But consider it from the present perspective. Infants' input is acoustic or phonetic, that is, more or less raw perception. At the outset, phonetics is the only basis they have for distinguishing speech sounds, and they are busy trying to construct a phonological system for the ambient language, as well as the mapping between this system and phonetics—a nontrivial task. When they do manage to develop a phonological system and an interface to phonetics, these impose a partitioning on phonetic space. With this partitioning in place, hearing phonologically rather than phonetically becomes almost a reflex, as it is for adults who are not phoneticians. Hence only phonologically relevant distinctions are noticeable (except perhaps when listening to an unfamiliar accent). Infants have not *lost* anything, they have *gained* a very important ability for structuring their experience. (This argument appears also in Dresher 2014.)

This leads to the question of exactly what infants have learned. The traditional stance on phonological distinctive features (Jakobson, Fant, and Halle 1951; Chomsky and Halle 1968) is that they are universal, innate, and binary; languages differ only in how they make use of the features to construct a phonological repertoire. This position is challenged, more or less independently, by Anderson (1981), Port and Leary (2005), Ladefoged (2007), and Mielke (2008). They argue that there cannot be a universal set of phonological distinctive features, for at least three reasons. First, as observed above, distinctive features cannot capture the gradient phonetic distinctions necessary to characterize speech sounds crosslinguistically, such as the difference in voice onset time between Dutch, German, and English stops. Second, binary distinctive features do not lend themselves to making fine differences within a single language, such as in a language that has unusually numerous distinctions of vowel height or place of articulation. Third, it is difficult for binary features to characterize speech sounds that involve multiple points of articulation, such as labiovelars and clicks. More generally, the question arises of whether it makes sense to characterize as universal a repertoire that makes provision for every crazy phonological system.

Port and Leary and Ladefoged advocate abandoning feature-based phonological representations altogether in favor of purely phonetic systems. We propose an alternative, closer to Mielke's position: there is still an innate component to phonology, but it is not an innate feature space. Rather, what is present in the "language-ready brain" is the inclination and ability to categorize phonetic input in the ambient language in terms of a discrete phonological feature space. What results is a feature system that is tailored to the language being acquired. Once in place, this feature system maps to regions of phonetic space, in much the same way that color words map to regions in color space in a language-specific fashion, with central instances and with fuzziness or competition along the borders. For example, children learning a language with a five-vowel system would create (or "discover") only enough phonological features to distinguish among the five; learning a nine-vowel system would result in a richer repertoire of features. (See Dresher (2014) for a proposal as to how this comes about.)

This position also helps make sense of sign language phonology. One of the earliest and most robust results in sign language linguistics (Stokoe 1960; Klima and Bellugi 1979) is the analysis of signs in terms of a distinctive feature system, in which, for instance, handshape, motion, and the hand's location in signing space can vary independently, just like voicing, manner of articulation, and place of articulation in spoken languages. Where do these features come from? It is hard to imagine that humans are innately blessed with a repertoire of gestural distinctive features that are only of use just in case the individual happens to be deaf. But suppose that what they *are* blessed with is an inclination to parse communicative input into a systematic feature space. Then it needn't matter whether the input is vocal or gestural.

Driving this point home, it has been argued that the emerging sign language Al-Sayyid Bedouin Sign Language lacks a fully systematic use of phonological features (Sandler et al. 2011). The same also seems to be true of another such language, Central Taurus Sign Language (Caselli et al. 2014). So evidently a system of phonological features takes a while to develop in new sign language communities, because the input is not yet systematic enough for learners to construct a coherent system from scratch. The equivalent of phonetics—conventionalized but unsystematic gestures—is clearly present early on. But apparently learners can also nudge their internal encoding of the input toward greater phonological systematicity, leading to the gradual appearance of fully-fledged phonological structure over a few generations.

6.3 The status of phonotactics

An overall issue that arises in fleshing out the architecture in Figure 6.1 is the same as we have encountered with all the other components of the Parallel Architecture: what is the balance of power among the various components? Given a particular phenomenon, is it best described in terms of phonological structure, phonetic structure, the interface between them, or some combination? This section and the next explore a number of relatively clear cases; subsequent sections turn to more controversial situations.

First of all, a language's repertoire of available phonemes is discrete, so it belongs squarely in phonology. Similarly, phonotactics concerns the repertoire of combinations of speech sounds—the possible syllabic onsets, nuclei, and codas. This too is discrete, so it also belongs in phonology. For instance, a strict CV language would have the schema (1a) in its lexicon; more complex possibilities might include those in (1b,c).

(1) a. [$_\sigma$ CV]
     b. [$_\sigma$ CV(C)]
     c. [$_\sigma$ (C)CV(C)]

Likewise, the "syllabary" of Levelt (1989)—a stored inventory of a language's most common syllables—can also be easily stated in terms of phonological schemas in the lexicon. At the same time, the space of possible phonotactic patterns is constrained by considerations of "naturalness," which arise through the linkage to the gestural score. For instance, a language is more likely to have /bl/ onsets, which conform to the sonority hierarchy, than /lb/ onsets, which do not (Zhao and Berent 2017).[4]

Phonotactic principles are often stated as constraints. For instance, the absence of syllable-initial /ŋ/ in English might be stated as (2).

(2)   */ [$_\sigma$ ŋ ...] /

However, as we have stressed, we find it more desirable to state grammatical principles in terms of affordances—specifying what you *can* say rather than what you *cannot* say. An affordance can be acquired on the basis of forms that have been heard in the input. In contrast, acquiring a *constraint* requires first positing an overly general template and then noticing that some predicted form is not occurring, i.e. making use of negative evidence.

As an affordance, the distribution of /ŋ/ is to be accounted for by means of the positive schema (3), arrived at by having heard words like *sing, sink, sang,* and *sank.* There simply is no schema licensing /ŋ/ in an onset, because it has never been heard, and so a suitably conservative learner will never generalize to this context. (It is of course a tricky problem to work out what "suitably conservative" means! See section 7.8 for some discussion.)

(3)   /[$_\sigma$ ... [V, -tense] ŋ <k>]/

(3) stipulates that /ŋ/ appears only after lax vowels. For instance, */sejŋ/ and */siŋ/, with the tense vowels /ej/ and /i/, are not possible English words. This is of course quite eccentric. Syllable-final nasals other than /ŋ/ can be preceded by a tense vowel, as in *sane* and *seem,* and other syllable-final velars can as well, as in *lake* and *league.* In contrast, with /ŋ/, which is both nasal and velar, template (3) is about as general as it can be.[5]

Of course, phonotactic patterns interact intimately with word and syllable boundaries, as seen already in (3), so the grouping of phonemes into syllables must be marked in phonological structure. Furthermore, stress typically correlates with distinctions such as light vs. heavy syllables, so principles of stress too need to make reference to phonological structure. On the other hand, the realization of stress in terms of duration, amplitude, and pitch has to be encoded phonetically, so the interface has to mediate between discrete phonological stress and analog phonetic stress.

---

[4] The sonority hierarchy: Roughly, syllable onset clusters should increase in sonority, leading up to a maximally sonorous syllabic nucleus; coda clusters should decline in sonority (Juliette Blevins 1995).

[5] A bit of further detail: In *singer,* the affix is non-cohering, i.e. it leaves the syllabification and stress of its base intact. Hence /ŋ/ does not syllabify with it and remains a Coda: [$_\sigma$sɪŋ] [$_\sigma$r]. In *finger,* by comparison, the /g/ is the onset of the second syllable: [$_\sigma$fɪŋ] [$_\sigma$gr].

6.4 The phonology-phonetics interface

Let's look at the phonology-phonetics interface in a little more detail. The default mapping is one-to-one, or homomorphic, along the lines of (4). Each phoneme links to its own characteristic region of phonetic space.[6]

(4)   *Default phonology-phonetics linking (sample)*
       Phonology: $/m/_1$ Phonology: $/i/_2$
       Phonetics: $[m]_1$ Phonetics: $[i]_2$

As in the previous section, the phonology level of these correspondences is to be understood as a feature matrix, while the phonetic level is to be thought of as a gradient vocal tract gesture and the corresponding normalized acoustics. The subscripts, as usual, denote interface links between the two levels.

Decomposing (4) into features (at least for a first approximation): [+voice] in phonology corresponds to laryngeal vibration in phonetics; [+nasal] in phonology corresponds to velar lowering in phonetics; phonological [-continuant] corresponds to closure in an articulator, and so on. The default mapping divides phonetic space into regions that correspond to the discrete segments of the phonological space. Following standard findings in categorical perception, the phonetic regions have somewhat fuzzy boundaries, in that speakers' judgments of boundary cases are conflicted (Liberman and Studdert-Kennedy 1977; Myers et al. 2009).

However, different languages or dialects can map the same phonological segment to different regions in phonetic space (though still one-to-one within a particular language). For instance:

- English and Dutch differ in voice onset time of stops; hence, for instance, the value of phonetic [t] is different in the two languages. This difference is encoded in the acoustic phonetics and the gestural score, but the value of phonological /t/ is the same: unvoiced alveolar stop.
- Depending on the language (or dialect), phonological /r/ is realized phonetically as a retroflex liquid (English), an apical trill or tap (Spanish), or a uvular approximant (German).
- In some dialects of American English, phonological /æ/ maps essentially to phonetic [æ]; in others, it maps to something like [eə].
- English speakers typically enhance /ʃ/ with lip-rounding, whereas Chinese speakers do not (Keyser and Stevens 2006). This makes no difference in

---

[6] Unfortunately, the notations [m] and [i] in (4) look discrete, and more like phonology than is intended. But for present purposes, they are the best we can do without actually notating acoustic and gestural scores. From time to time we will use other notations where convenient. We beg the reader's indulgence.

We set aside an important complication: The acoustic form of most phonetic segments is conditioned in part by surrounding segments. The same issue arises on the motor side: it requires different muscle activations to get, say, from [p] to [a] than from [d] to [a]. Hence the default mapping must actually involve bigrams or even trigrams of segments. This is where a precompiled syllabary in the sense of Levelt (1989) might be useful.

phonology, but it has to be specified in the mapping between phonology and phonetics.

- Languages can differ in whether they treat a particular piece of gestural score as one phonological segment (Hebrew *etz* 'tree'– phonological $\widehat{/ts/}$[7]), or as two (English *rats* – phonological /ts/). A single language can even have it both ways, for instance German *Zeit* 'time' ($\widehat{/ts}$ajt/) vs. *ratsam* 'advisable' (/ratsam/). (See also Anderson 1981: 498–501 on the status of labiovelars.)
- Beckman and Pierrehumbert (1986) argue that languages can differ in the intonation patterns (phonetic) that are associated with pitch accents (phonological).

The Parallel Architecture opens the further possibility of noncanonical mappings between phonology and phonetics. For instance, aspiration of syllable-initial voiceless stops in English and German (but not Dutch) is usually ascribed to a so-called "low-level" phonological rule such as (5a). In the present approach, it can be attributed instead to the phonology-phonetics interface, using an interface schema along the lines of (5b). (5b) says that syllable-initial unvoiced stops in phonology have a late VOT in their phonetic realization. The result is that phonological unvoiced stops have aspirated and unaspirated allophones. (Again the phonetic notation is an approximation.)

(5)   a. *Aspiration as a procedural rule*
       [-cont, -voice] → [+asp] / [$_\sigma$ ____
      b. *Aspiration as an interface schema*
       Phonology: /[$_\sigma$ [-cont, -voice]$_x$...]/
       Phonetics: [late VOT]$_x$

The schema notation in (5b) invokes the same conditions as the rule notation in (5a). The condition [-cont, -voice], which appears as the "input" of (5a), appears in (5b) as the part of the phonology in (5b) that is coindexed with phonetics. The "output" of (5a), [+asp], appears in (5b) as the phonetic specification [late VOT]. The environment for (5a), namely syllable initial position, appears as the unindexed portion of the phonology in schema (5b), which likewise specifies the context. Thus in these respects, (5b) is a notational variant of (5a). The difference between the two is that the schema encodes not a *change* but a *correspondence*.

A further consideration is that (5b) is in competition with the default mapping, which would not aspirate a syllable-initial voiceless stop. For instance, (5b) links /tæp/ to [t'æp], while the default mapping would link it to [tæp]. However, (5b) is more specific than the default mapping, as it specifies the position of the segment in the syllable. So we can appeal to the Elsewhere Condition to block the default mapping, which gives (5b) the same effect as the traditional obligatory rule (5a). This approach

---

[7] Hebrew $\widehat{/ts/}$ is arguably a single segment because it can serve as one segment of a triliteral root. For instance, /ts-d-k/ appears in diverse morphological guises such as /tsɛdɛk/ 'justice', /tsədaka/ 'charity', /tsadik/ 'righteous'.

keeps phonology comparatively simple: stops do not have to be marked for aspiration in phonological structure. But this comes at the expense of extra complexity in the interface, namely (5b).

Alternatively, one could posit pairs of distinct phonemes, e.g. /t/ and /tʼ/, each confined to particular phonological contexts. This would enable the interface to maintain a one-to-one mapping, but at the expense of adding an extra phonological feature of aspiration, plus a specification of the contexts where it appears. For this case, the collective wisdom of the field says that there are not two distinct (underlying) phonemes, and hence (in terms of the present theory) the complexity belongs in the interface. (By contrast, in other languages, the best-known being Hindi, the feature of aspiration is phonologically distinctive, so there the complexity in fact does belong in phonology.)

Place assimilation can be similarly stated in terms of correspondence between phonology and phonetics. (6) is a schema for postvocalic palatalization of /x/ in German, capturing the phonetic distinction between the velar consonant in *ach* (phonetic [x]) and the palatal in *ich* (phonetic [ç]), both phonologically /x/. The outcome is a simplification of the gestural score, though at the expense of adding complexity to the interface.

(6)   Phonology: /[V, -back] x_3 /
      Phonetics: $[ç]_3$

This correspondence is language-specific. Yiddish, despite its close relation to German, realizes phonological /x/ via the default mapping [x], even in this context. In other words, Yiddish makes the opposite choice from German, keeping the interface simple at the expense of a more difficult gestural score.

Likewise, co-articulation can be treated as a matter of gestural timing in phonetics. For instance, in the gestural score, nasalization of a pre-nasal vowel amounts to opening the velum prior to closing the oral cavity with the lips or tongue. The effect of this simplification of the gestural score is a different phonetic vowel (Ladd 2014: 46). Prenasalization may or may not play a role in phonology, depending on the language. If it does not play a role (as in English and Dutch), vowel nasality is not encoded in phonology, but phonological vowels have phonetically unnasalized and nasalized allophones.

For another case of co-articulation, the normal pronunciations of *truck* and *draw* (in RJ's speech) are something like [tʃɹʌk] and [dʒɹɔ], where the phonological /t/ and /d/ are palatalized in the gestural score, but (presumably) not in the phonology. The upshot once again is that the interface becomes more complex to compensate for simplification of the gestural score.

In all these cases, a phonological segment has multiple phonetic realizations in different contexts. The opposite also occurs: a phonological distinction can be neutralized phonetically. A well-known old example is intervocalic flapping of /t/ and /d/ in American English, as in *writer* and *rider* (both [raɾɾər]). The conditions on this alternation can be stated as schema (7).

(7) Phonology: /...[V,+stress] [C, -cont, +alv]$_x$ [V,-stress].../
Phonetics: [ɾ]$_x$

Again, the interface adds a bit of complexity in the service of simplifying the gestural score.

For a different sort of case, consider fast (or casual) speech effects, such as phonetic [ðɪʃɪːr] for *this year*. This is clearly driven by gestural convenience. But the hearer ultimately has to recover the individual words. This could happen in either of two ways. First, the interface could license a mismatch, as in (8), where the phonological sequence /sj/ corresponds to phonetic [ʃ] (we omit contextual factors).

(8) *Fast speech*
Phonology: /sj/$_4$
Phonetics: [ʃ]$_4$

Alternatively, one might restore the simplicity of the interface by making [ðɪʃɪːr] into its own lexical item. This is possible because (in the present theory) the lexicon contains not just words but all sorts of idioms and collocations. The complexity of the collocation *this year* then resurfaces in phonology: [ðɪʃɪːr] comes to be treated as a phonological blend related to the constituent words, along the lines of *spork* and *Spanglish* in section 4.9.

Section 4.9 extended the coindexation notation so as to be suitable for blending and overlap. Instead of simply marking related phonological strings with a right-hand subscript, we marked the beginning of a string as well. (9) illustrates for the present case. The /ʃ/ in (9c) corresponds to the /s/ in (9a), so it has coindex 5 on its right-hand side. But the /ʃ/ also corresponds to the /j/ in (9b), so it gets a left-hand coindex 6 to mark the beginning of this link. This case is more complex than *spork*, because the /ʃ/ in (9c) is distinct from both /s/ and /j/. The same-except relation and the star notation of Chapters 4 and 5 come to the rescue: /ðɪʃ/ is the same as /ðɪs/ (coindex 5) except for the /ʃ/ (starred), and /ʃɪːr/ is the same as /jɪːr / (coindex 6) except for the /ʃ/ (again starred).

(9)   a. *this*   b. *year*   c. *this year*
Semantics: [THIS]$_5$ [YEAR]$_6$ [YEAR$_6$; THIS$_5$]$_8$
Syntax: Det$_5$ N$_6$ [$_{NP}$ Det$_5$ N$_6$]$_8$
Phonology: /ðɪ *s* /$_5$ /*j* ɪːr /$_6$ / $_5$ðɪ *$_6$ʃ$_5$* ɪːr$_6$ /$_8$

The choice between the interface account in (8) and the phonological account in (9) might depend on frequency: if one hears or uses [ðɪʃɪːr] a lot, it might pay to list it in the lexicon as a "prefab." Similar considerations apply to blends like *doncha* ('don't you'), *whyncha* ('why don't you'), and *I dunno* ('I don't know') (Bybee 2010: 41). Especially good candidates for storage include *wanna* ('want to'), *hafta* ('have to'), and the ever-popular *gonna* ('going to'), whose unreduced alternants are vanishingly rare in speech. Still, even if (9c) is stored, the interface principle (8) might be retained in order to motivate other alternations, especially novel ones. We return to blends in section 6.8.[8]

[8] Ernestus (2014) discusses several theoretical accounts of such phonetic reduction, as well as a body of experimental evidence. She concludes that a proper model has to include both storage of phonetic variants (here, possibly phonological variants as well) and more general principles for mapping phonetically reduced *(Continued)*

6.5 A test case: Final devoicing

The challenge for the PA conception of phonology as sketched so far is for it to account insightfully for a wide range of phonological phenomena without appeal to underlying forms—using only schemas with variables, interface links, relational links, the Elsewhere Principle, and the same-except relation. We can only be suggestive here, mostly just getting our feet wet and hoping to inspire some discussion.

As a first test case, we consider final devoicing in Dutch (Booij 1995) and German.[9] At first blush, it is a purely phonotactic phenomenon: obstruents in syllable-final position are always voiceless. However, this has ramifications for morphology, as it causes some stems ending in an obstruent to appear in two different forms, one with a voiceless and one with a voiced obstruent. For instance, Dutch singular *paard* [pa:rt] 'horse' corresponds to plural *paarden* [pa:rdən] 'horses'. This contrasts with non-alternating *kaart* [ka:rt] vs. *kaarten* [ka:rtən] 'cards'. The alternation occurs not just in the plural, but with any type of inflected or derived form, such as those in (10).[10]

(10)   a. Dutch:

pa:rt 'horse'	pa:rdən 'horses'
ma:nt 'month'	ma:ndələks 'monthly'
ra:t 'guess.PRES.1.SG'	ra:dən 'guess.PRES.1.PL'

b. German:

lie[p] 'dear'	lie[b]e 'love.PRES.1SG'
lie[p]ling 'darling'	lie[b]er 'sweet.M.SG'
lie[p]lich 'lovely'	
lie[p]ster 'dearest.M.SG'	

How do the tools of RM describe this alternation? Is it a matter of morphology, phonology, phonetics, and/or the interfaces among them?

The conventional way to account for final devoicing is to say that *paard* is stored as an underlying form, /pa:rd/, but it is modified by rule (11), resulting in /pa:rt/, which in turn maps homomorphically into phonetic [pa:rt].

(11)   *Final devoicing as a traditional procedural rule*
        [-son] → [-voice]/ ___ $_σ$]

On the other hand, if *paard* is followed by a vowel-initial cohering suffix such as /ən/, the /d/ resyllabifies as an onset, so it is not subject to (11), and the word is realized as /pa:rdən/.

---

variants to stored unreduced forms—here, the phonology-phonetics interface schemas. At least for a first approximation, the account here is consistent with her conclusions. We leave a more detailed comparison for future research.

[9] Liberman's (2018) discussion of reduction/deletion of final /s/ in Spanish makes many of the same points as we do here.

[10] The Maximal Onset Principle could in principle group the [p]'s in *Liebling* and *lieblich* into an onset cluster with the following [l]. However, they are in fact syllable-final, because *-ling* and *-lich* are "non-cohering" or "Level 2" suffixes, which leave the syllabification of their bases intact. See section 6.7, especially note 17.

The closest translation of (11) into RM notation is to treat it as a phonology-phonetics interface schema, along the lines of (12).

(12) *Final devoicing as a phonology-phonetics interface rule*
Phonology: /[...[-son]$_{x\sigma}$] /
Phonetics: [spread glottis]$_x$ (= phonetically unvoiced)

Instead of a mapping from underlying to surface phonology, this is a nondirectional correspondence between phonology and phonetics: any syllable-final obstruent in phonology, voiceless or not, corresponds to a voiceless segment in phonetics. This keeps the phonological relation simple: for instance, *paard* and *paarden* both have phonological /d/; the complexity is in the interface to phonetics. This captures the intuition that final devoicing is automatic and gestural, in other words, a phonetic effect not unlike aspiration (5b).

(12) has a possible advantage over (11). With careful measurement, it turns out that unvoiced obstruents with voicing alternations, such as in [pa:rt], are found to be slightly more voiced than those that do not alternate, such as in [ka:rt] (Hay and Baayen 2005; Port and Leary 2005; van Oostendorp 2008). That is, final devoicing is a (somewhat) gradient notion, which is what might be expected if phonetics is involved. The slight voicing in [pa:rt] can thus be seen as a result of pressure from faithfulness to underlying lexical form. For another such case, Port and Leary (2005) report parallel differences in the voicing of the D-flaps in *writer* vs. *rider* (7).

A disadvantage of both these treatments is that they assume phonological "underlying forms" such as Dutch /pa:rd/ and German /li:b/, which appear unaltered only in the company of vowel-initial suffixes, never as free forms. RM discourages such lexical entries. While we acknowledge that the theory might eventually have to admit them (for instance as stems, as in Chapter 5), we wish to explore other possibilities as well.

An alternative approach builds on the intuition that final devoicing is motivated by phonotactics. Syllable-initially, the phonotactics of Dutch and German license both voiced and voiceless obstruents, but syllable-finally they license only voiceless obstruents. This is the case whether or not the obstruents in question participate in a voicing alternation. Final devoicing in words like *paard* might therefore be thought of as an accommodation—a repair strategy that allows syllable-initial voiced obstruents to have morphological counterparts that are voiceless.[11]

To work out this approach, we first need to consider the phonotactic pattern for syllable-final obstruents. One way to state it is as a constraint: "No voiced obstruents in syllable-final position." Alternatively, it could be a positive but limited affordance: "Syllable-final position may be occupied by unvoiced obstruents." In line with the general philosophy of treating phonotactics as affordances rather than constraints, we choose the latter. This is stated in (13), following the example of (3), the

---

[11] This situation thus resembles the treatment in section 5.4.2 of schwa epenthesis as a repair in e.g. German *wartet*.

eccentric phonotactic pattern for English /ŋ/. We might think of (13) then not as final *devoicing*, with its procedural overtones, but as final *non*-voicing, a declarative affordance.[12]

(13) *Final non-voicing*
      Phonology: /[...[-son, -voice]$_\sigma$]/

The effect of (13) is to license unvoiced obstruents in final position. Since there is no corresponding schema for syllable-final voiced obstruents, such structures cannot occur. Booij (1995: 59) observes that even loanwords that do not alternate obey the template. For instance, the name *Sidney* is pronounced in Dutch as [sɪtni], and *advies* 'advice' as [atfis]. (In contrast, of course, English does have a schema that licenses syllable-final voiced obstruents.)

   This phonotactic pattern—the absence of syllable-final voiced obstruents from the phonotactic repertoire—appears to be a widespread tendency crosslinguistically (see Iverson and Salmons (2011) for a thorough discussion, with examples from a wide variety of languages). And although there are plenty of languages that, like English, allow syllable-final obstruents to be either voiced or unvoiced, we have encountered no citations of languages that require final *voicing* of obstruents.[13]

   This asymmetry has phonetic motivation: evidently syllable-final voiced obstruents are more difficult to produce than their voiceless counterparts (Keating 1985, 1988). This difficulty shows up in acquisition as well: Clark and Bowerman (1986) document children who have mastered word-final voiceless stops, e.g. [bɪt], but who either omit voiced stops e.g. [bɪ] for *big*, or substitute voiceless stops ([bɪk] for *big*) or nasals with optional voiceless stops ([pɪŋ(k)] for *pig*).[14]

   With the phonotactics in place, we now have to account for the morphological alternation illustrated in (10). (12) accounted for it with an interface schema between phonology and phonetics. Now we wish to state it as a relation between two phonological forms that share the same base. (14) shows the structures of *paard* and *paarden* on this account, including the syllabification. They are linked by the same-except relation: /paːrt/ in *paard* is the same as /paːrd/ in *paarden* (coindex 1), except for the voicing and syllabic position of the starred segments. Crucially, of course, the syllable boundary in *paard* falls at the end of the word, while the syllable boundary in *paarden* precedes the /d/, breaking up the base prosodically.

(14)

	a. *paard*	b. *paarden*
Semantics:	HORSE$_{1,2}$	[PLUR (HORSE$_1$)]$_3$
Morphosyntax:	[N$_1$, SG]$_2$	[N$_1$, PL$_4$]$_3$
Phonology:	/[paːr *t* $_\sigma$]/$_{1,2}$	/ /[$_\sigma$ paːr] [$_\sigma$*d*/$_1$ ən$_4$]/$_3$

---

[12] Final devoicing actually includes not just final obstruents but final clusters. We set this elaboration aside.
[13] The asymmetry here would lead an OT account to say that syllable-final voiceless obstruents are unmarked. The /paːrt/-/paːrdən/ alternation would then be the result of markedness considerations outranking faithfulness to the underlying /d/. English would then have the reverse ranking, favoring faithfulness over markedness.
[14] Thanks to Claartje Levelt for alerting us to these phenomena.

Unlike the interface formulation in (12), the phonology-to-phonetics interface this time is one-to-one: phonological /d/ and /t/ correspond to phonetic [d] and [t] respectively.

More generally, the relation between (14a) and (14b) can be motivated by the pair of morphophonological sister schemas in (15).

(15)   a. *Syllable-final unvoiced*
    Morphosyntax: $X_\alpha <\text{aff}_x>]_y$
    Phonology: $/... [... [\text{-son}, *\text{-voice}*] *_\sigma]* <..._x> /_y$

    b. *Syllable-initial voiced*
    Morphosyntax: $[X_\alpha \text{ aff}_z]_w$
    Phonology: $/...*[_\sigma* [\text{-son}, *\text{+voice}*]..._z] /_w$

This says that the base in the two sisters is the same (coindex α), except for the syllabi-fication and the voicing feature. The phonology in (15a) is a special case of the phono-tactic schema (13), and (15a) is productive and applies across the board. In contrast, (15b) is nonproductive: the items that begin with a voiced obstruent have to be listed.

What does this approach have to say about the form of storage? The non-alternating form *kaart* can be stored as such, and its plural can be either stored or generated online. The interest lies in the free form *paard*, which by assumption has to be stored as (14a). The plural also has to be stored, in the form (14b). Coindex 1 says that the two forms count as the same, except for the starred portions. However, the obstruents in question are an instance of the relation in (15), which motivates the difference between them. In addition, the plural affix is independently motivated by the Dutch plural schema (not shown). Hence the two entries are as fully motivated as possible; their marginal cost together (in the sense of Chapter 3) is (nearly) the same as that of either one alone.

This treatment may feel a little like overkill. It seems redundant to have both the phonotactic constraint (13) *and* the sister schemas (15) that together specify the alter-nation. Nevertheless, some evidence from language acquisition suggests that this is the right solution. Jusczyk et al. (1993) show that infants as young as nine months show some appreciation of language-specific phonotactics. But Buckler (2014) and Buckler and Fikkert (2016) show that even as late as age seven, Dutch children have not mastered the alternation of *d* and *t*. For instance, if they are given a singular such as *bed* [bɛt] 'bed,' and are asked to produce the plural, they have a strong tendency to produce a plural with an unvoiced obstruent such as [bɛtən], rather than the correct [bɛdən]—even when they know the word! In other words, the phonotactic constraint is learned well before the alternation, which argues that both play a role in the gram-mar. Hence a theory that calls for both phonotactics and schema (15) need not be in error just because the two are partially redundant.[15]

---

[15] Buckler also shows that Dutch children are much slower to get the alternation right than German children, and argues that this is because the cues in Dutch are sparser and to some extent confounded by other alternations.

We conclude that the PA conception of phonology affords at least two viable accounts of final devoicing: either a phonology-phonetics interface schema like (12), or phonotactics like (13) plus phonological sister schemas like (15). The latter is more complex, but there is some virtue in separating the phonotactics from the phonological alternation.

6.6 English vowel shift: A more clearly phonological phenomenon

For a somewhat more intricate case, we venture into the bit of English grammar whereby a suffix can affect the stress and vowel quality of its base, as in *harm*[ə]*ny* ~ *harm*[a]*nic* ~ *harm*[oʊ]*nious*. This section examines the alternations in vowel quality, and the next section looks at how suffixes wreak their changes on the base.

Table 6.1 gives a sample of the alternations. The relevant vowels are in bold and underlined. The orthography identifies them as variants of *a*, *e*, *i*, and *o* (*u* is less systematic and we omit it here). Each comes in three alternants. The tense (or "long") variants and the lax (or "short") variants both occur in stressed positions; the reduced alternants, all pronounced as schwa, occur only in unstressed positions. (In addition, there are tense unstressed variants in word-final position that do not participate in these alternations, e.g. *pretty*, *alumni*, *yellow*.)

Whatever the historical reasons behind the alternations in Table 6.1, the synchronic relation between the tense and lax alternants is phonologically and phonetically absurd. How can [aj] count as the same as [ɪ], and how can [oʊ] count as the same as [a]? And how does the grammar state the generalization?

SPE (Chomsky and Halle 1968) identifies the alternants as the same by giving them a common underlying form, which then undergoes a dizzying sequence of deformations to derive the surface forms. Attempts to account for the alternation in OT (e.g. McMahon 2007, Fulcrand 2015 and references therein) have invariably required unusual constraints and/or constraint interactions.

A difficulty for approaches that assume underlying forms (in SPE) or input forms (in OT) is that phonological and morphological derivations don't always align. For some cases, such as *adv*[æ]*ntage* ~ *adv*[ə]*ntageous*, the vowel in the morphological base is full and the vowel in the derived form is reduced, so it is easy to state a process of vowel reduction that accompanies the addition of the affix. However, *curiosity* is morphologically based on *curious*, but the reduced vowel in *curious* has to be based on the full vowel in *curiosity*. To derive a form like this, one has to assume an underlying form /kjʊriɑs/ that undergoes vowel reduction just in case it is *not* affixed. Such an underlying form may be perfectly all right within the ethos of SPE, but the more surface-oriented approach of RM encourages us to avoid it.[16]

---

[16] This situation parallels the discussion in section 3.4–3.5 of pairs such as *assassin* and *assassinate*. In that case, the morphology treats the latter as based on (and in procedural theories, derived from) the former. But semantically, an assassin is someone who assassinates people, so *assassin* has to be based on *assassinate*. In other words, the "direction of derivation" is conflicted. The present case shows a similar mismatch.

Table 6.1 Some English vowel alternations

	tense, stressed vowel	lax, stressed vowel	reduced vowel
a	[ej] prof**a**ne cap**a**cious advant**a**geous spont**a**neous cour**a**geous desper**a**tion	[æ] prof**a**nity cap**a**city adv**a**ntage democr**a**t	[ə] advant**a**ge spont**a**neity cour**a**ge desp**e**rate adv**a**ntageous democr**a**cy
e	[i] ser**e**ne homog**e**neous	[ɛ] ser**e**nity presid**e**ntial d**e**mocrat mom**e**ntous	[ə] homog**e**neity presid**e**nt d**e**mocracy mom**e**nt
i	[aj] contr**i**te critic**i**ze div**i**ne dec**i**de	[ɪ] contr**i**tion critic**i**sm div**i**nity dec**i**sion ac**i**dity mus**i**cian	[ə] or [ɪ] ac**i**d mus**i**c (not schwa)
o	[oʊ] atr**o**cious fer**o**cious verb**o**se c**o**ne harm**o**nious Newt**o**nian	[a] atr**o**city fer**o**city verb**o**sity c**o**nic harm**o**nic dem**o**cracy curi**o**sity	[ə] harm**o**ny Newt**o**n dem**o**crat curi**ou**s

A further problem is that some pairs in Table 6.1 involve morphological sister relations rather than mother/daughter relations, for instance *capacious ~ capacity*, *atrocious ~ atrocity*, *ferocious ~ ferocity*. There is no fact of the matter as to which one of these displays the underlying form of the vowel, and which one should be derived from the other. For an even more pointed case, should the second vowel of *harmony* be an underlying /a/, to go with *harmonic*, or should it be an underlying /oʊ/, to go with *harmonious*?

Relational Morphology does not view any of the words in Table 6.1 as synchronically "derived" from any of the others. They are surely all stored. In the RM framework, relations among them are to be motivated by nonproductive schemas. The issue, then, is how to construct schemas that relate them to each other. That is what we will attempt to work out here.

As with final devoicing, there are two main alternatives. The first is to localize the alternations in the phonology-phonetics interface. For instance, a schema like (16) could link phonological /i/ with phonetic [aj].

(16)   *Vowel shift as a phonology-phonetics interface schema*
   Phonology: /[V, +high, -back, -round, +tense, +stress]/$_1$ (= /i/)
   Phonetics: [aj]$_1$

On this account, the corresponding tense and lax vowels, such as in *divine* and *divinity*, would be close in phonology: /i/ vs. /ɪ/. But the interface would link phonological /i/ to phonetic [aj]—a major deviation from the default one-to-one mapping that governs the unmarked cases.

A disadvantage of this approach is that it commits us to saying that *divine* is stored in the phonological form /dəvin/. Such a treatment may be diachronically and orthographically attractive, but phonologically it is just weird. It is parallel to (but more extreme than) the unnaturalness of storing [pa:rt] as /pa:rd/ and [kjʊriəs] as /kjʊrias/. Moreover, this correspondence has to be confined to listed instances, so that, for instance, phonological *sheep* is not pronounced [ʃajp].

The other alternative is to encode the alternation within phonology itself, using a set of sister schemas. In the case of these alternations, we are talking about wholesale suppletion of phonological features (as bad as *go/went* in morphology). (17) states the /aj/ ~ /ɪ/ alternation: two phonological strings count as the same (coindex α), except that one has /aj/ and the other has /ɪ/, which count as the same (coindex 1), covarying with tenseness. (We omit the decomposition of the vowel space into further features, and we treat /aj/ as a syllabic nucleus consisting of a vowel plus a glide.)

(17)   *Vowel shift as a pair of phonological sister schemas*

Phonology: a. /...[*aj*, *+tense*, +stress]$_1$.../$_α$ b. /...[*ɪ*, *-tense*, +stress]/$_1$.../$_α$

This allows us to link *divine* and *divinity* as in (18). Coindex 11 in (18) corresponds to coindex α in (17), marking the two phonological strings that are (almost) the same. Coindex 1 says that the differences between them are licensed by (17). (Coindex 35 links the suffix to the *-ity* schema, not shown here.)

(18)   a. *divine*   b. *divinity*
       Phonology: /dəv *aj$_1$* n/$_{11}$ / /dəv *ɪ$_1$* n/$_{11}$ əti$_{35}$ /$_{12}$

This account leaves the phonology-phonetics interface simple; the complexity is localized in the phonology. The weirdness of the alternation is reflected in the fact that so much is starred. As is common for sister schemas, this pattern is not productive and is confined to listed instances of strings that instantiate the variable α.

The other tense/lax alternations have the same character. In these, the alternating vowels (I ~ ɛ; ej ~ æ; oʊ ~ a) share more features, so the excepts are not quite so radical.

(19) *Vowel shift as pairs of phonological sister schemas (continued)*

Phonology: a. /...[*i*, *+tense*, +stress]$_2$.../$_\beta$ /...[*ɛ*, *-tense*, +stress]$_2$.../$_\beta$
Phonology: b. /...[*ej*, *+tense*, +stress]$_3$.../$_\gamma$ /...[*æ*, *-tense*, +stress]]$_3$.../$_\gamma$
Phonology: c. /...[*oʊ*, *+tense*, +stress]$_4$.../$_\delta$ /...[*a*, *-tense*, +stress]]$_4$.../$_\delta$

Vowel reduction to schwa lends itself to the same two possible solutions as vowel shift. On one hand, it may be a matter of the phonology-phonetics interface, as in (20): every lax unstressed vowel in phonology is realized phonetically as schwa.

(20) *Vowel reduction as a phonology-phonetics interface rule*
      Phonology: /[V, -tense, -stress]$_z$/
      Phonetics: [ə]$_z$

Alternatively, vowel reduction may be a third sister to the schemas in (17) and (19), as in (21). The difference from (17) and (19) is that schwa can alternate with each of the other vowels, so it is multiply coindexed.

(21) *Vowel reduction via phonological sister schemas*
      Phonology: /...[*ə*, *-tense*, *-stress*]$_{1,2,3,4}$.../$_{\alpha,\beta,\gamma,\delta}$

Again, these two treatments make different commitments about what is stored. Consider the pair *harmonic/harmony*. In the interface account in (20), the phonological difference between the two underlined vowels is minimal. *Harmonic* is stored (or derived) as /harm[a, +stress]nɪk/; *harmony* is stored as /harm[a, -stress]ni/, and the phonological /a/ maps into phonetic schwa. However, in the phonological account in (21), *harmony* is stored as /harməni/, keeping the interface to phonetics simple; and the relation of schwa in *harmony* to /a/ in *harmonic* is mediated by the relation between schema (21) and the right-hand schema in (19c).

How do we choose between these alternatives? Theory-internally, the phonological sister schemas in (17), (19), and (21) are preferable, in that they do not commit us to storage of items in a form that never appears on the surface, such as /dəvin/ and /harmani/. But there is also some evidence from acquisition. Moskowitz (1973) and Jaeger (1986) show that children learn the vowel-shift alternations rather late, toward age ten. Moreover, appreciation of the alternations seems to be associated with the acquisition of English orthography, during which children are taught about "long" vowels ([aj], [ej], etc.) vs. "short" vowels ([ɪ], [æ], etc.). Jaeger in particular argues that words displaying the alternations are stored in surface form, and that the relations between them are captured by "lexical redundancy rules"—here, nonproductive schemas. We tentatively conclude that vowel shift, like final devoicing, is encoded in terms of phonological sister schemas. In this case, unlike final devoicing, there is no noticeable influence of phonetics, because each of the alternations involve such different vowels.

6.7 How affixes impose their will on the base

The next question is how the alternations in Table 6.1 are related to the presence of various affixes. For instance, as is well known, -*ity* is always preceded by a main stressed vowel, whatever the stress pattern of the related free form (e.g. *ácid* ~ *acídity*, *húman* ~ *humánity*); the same goes for -*ious* (*hármony* ~ *harmónious*, *lábor* ~ *labórious*). The vowel preceding -*ity* is almost invariably lax, whatever the features of the related free form (e.g. *serene* ~ *serenity*, *divine* ~ *divinity*). In contrast, the vowel preceding -*ious* is sometimes tense (*harmonious*, *courageous*) and sometimes lax (*rebellious*, *infectious*). How are these constraints imposed?

Before working out these cases, let us look at two simpler situations. In the first of these, the affix imposes no requirements at all on the phonology of its base; it is just tacked on. An example is -*ness*, which leaves its base unchanged, even when the result is a prosodically clumsy string of four consecutive unstressed vowels (e.g. *reasonable-ness*, *gravitylessness*). The schema for such suffixes is exactly the sort we have been writing all along, as in (22). (We omit semantics for convenience; index 36 links the suffix to all its instances.)

(22)   *Schema for* -ness
     Morphosyntax: $[_N A_x \, \text{aff}_{36}]_y$
     Phonology: $/\dots_x \, \text{nəs}_{36}/_y$

Such suffixes are called "Level 2" or "post-syntactic" in Lexical Phonology, and "non-cohering" in various other approaches.[17]

A second type of suffix places phonological restrictions on what it can be tacked onto. One such suffix is our friend $[_V \, A\text{-}en]$, which requires the base to be monosyllabic and to end with an obstruent, e.g. *harden*, *sweeten*, *blacken* but not **greenen*, **orangen* (see section 4.1). Another is the deverbal suffix -*al*, which attaches only to bases whose related verb has a stressed final syllable, such as *accrúal*, *acquíttal*, *deníal* but not **púrchasal*, **énvial* (Bauer, Lieber, and Plag 2013: 192; *búrial* is an exception).[18] As seen in Chapter 4, such constraints can be incorporated into a schema as a selectional restriction on the form of the base, as in (23). The variable stipulates the form of what may instantiate it—in (23), anything that ends with a stressed vowel plus an optional consonant.[19]

(23)   *Schema for deverbal* -al
     Morphosyntax: $[_N V_x \, \text{aff}_{37}]_y$
     Phonology: $//\dots[\text{V}, +\text{stress}] <\text{C}>/_x \, \text{əl}_{37}/_y$

---

[17] Non-cohering suffixes might also install a phonological word boundary around their base, for instance $/[\dots_{x \omega}] \, \text{nəs}_{36}/_y$ in (22). This would account for the preservation of the base's stress, as well as for the fact that the base does not resyllabify with a non-cohering affix (see e.g. section 6.3, note 5).

[18] This -*al* is not to be confused with the homophonous denominal -*al*, which does not require its base to end with a stressed syllable, for example *national* and *procedural*.

[19] Aronoff (1976: 80) points out some further detail beyond the optional consonant in (23).

Inkelas (2014: 41), following Poser (1984), calls these two sorts of affixation "recessive," and cites a number of such affixes in Japanese with various similar effects.

We now return to the case of -*ity*, which requires the preceding vowel to be main-stressed and lax. It differs from -*al* in that if a related free form doesn't match -*ity*'s template, -*ity* can still wrestle its base into the required shape. Four situations arise.

(24) a. If there is no related free form, the base ends with a main stressed lax vowel, as in *asperity, acuity, affinity, amenity, charity, debility,* and *fidelity*. This case shows us the basic template that -*ity* imposes on its base.

   b. If there is a related free form that has the required vowel and stress, such as *dense* and *complex*, the base preserves it intact: *density* and *complexity*.

   c. If the related free form has a final tense and stressed vowel, such as *profane* and *serene*, the base has the corresponding lax vowel in that position: *profanity* and *serenity*.

   d. If the related free form has a final unstressed vowel, as in *acid* and *human*, the base has a stressed lax vowel: *acidity* and *humanity*.

In other words, no matter what the related free form, -*ity* makes the base end with a stressed lax vowel.

Inkelas (2014: 42) cites a number of affixes like this in Japanese, with various effects on the base; some of them she calls "dominant," and some "dependent"; we will use the former term. Another way to characterize such a suffix is to call it "output-oriented": it is a requirement on the surface form, whatever the source. Output constraints are of course the fundamental tool of Optimality Theory (e.g. Burzio 1994; Prince and Smolensky 2004) but also appear as far afield as Construction Morphology (Booij 2010: 252) and the Network Model (Bybee 2010).[20]

The simplest of the four situations in (24) is when an -*ity* word lacks a related free form, as in (24a). In this case, even if the base is not related to a word, its final vowel has to be stressed and tense. Here is the schema (we omit semantics).

(25) *Schema for* -ity *words without related free form*

   Morphosyntax: $[_N - aff_{38}]_y$

   Phonology: $/ \ldots [\text{V}, -\text{tense}, +\text{stress}] <\text{C}> \text{əti}_{38} /_y$

   Example: *fid - e - l - ity*

---

[20] Bauer, Lieber, and Plag (2013: 184–93) discuss such differences in stress in terms of whether the affix in question induces stress shift or not. In the present case, the issue is not whether stress is shifted: the "shift" occurs exactly when the related free form does not correspond to the template. They later (193) acknowledge that output restrictions of the sort adopted here are probably the right solution.

The literature, going back to SPE, calls this shift in vowel quality Trisyllabic Laxing: the antepenultimate is a lax vowel. But, as SPE notices, -*ic* also requires a main-stressed lax vowel before it, as in *syllabic, iambic*—but here the requirements are applied to the penult. SPE artificially maintains the generality of Trisyllabic Laxing by positing that –*ic* is derived from –*ic*+*al*, providing an unheard extra syllable. Similarly, in order to maintain Trisyllabic Laxing, words like *vicious* need an extra underlying syllable, perhaps /visios/, so that the base *vice* can be antepenultimate. And Trisyllabic Laxing makes the wrong prediction about words like *harmonious, spontaneous,* and *congruity*, which have a tense vowel in the critical position. These difficulties arise from the fact that the alternations in question are morphologically rather than phonologically conditioned, a possibility not acknowledged in SPE.

In order to extend this to the situations in (24b,c,d), we need to introduce a sister schema for the related free form, and then specify the ways that the base can deviate from it. We do this by means of the star notation, as in (26).

(26) *Sister schemas for -ity words in general*

Morphosyntax: a. A_α b. $[_N <A_\alpha> aff_{38}]_\gamma$

Phonology: $/.../_\alpha$ $//... [V, *\text{-tense}, +stress*] <C> /_{<\alpha>} əti_{38}/_\gamma$

Example: *human*   *hum - a - n - ity*

Let's see how this works.

- For situation (24a), where there is no adjectival free form (i.e. if the A in angle brackets, coindexed as α, is not present), (26b) is identical to (25) and therefore accounts for the *-ity* words without a related free form, such as *fidelity*.
- If there is a related free form, (26a) says it must be an adjective, and it must be phonologically identical to the base (coindex α), except for possible differences in tenseness and stress on the final vowel, marked by the stars. This leads to the three possible situations (24b,c,d).
- In situation (24b), the base is identical to the free form, as in *dense ~ density* (27a). The base then corresponds to the pattern [V, -tense, +stress] automatically.
- In situation (24c), the vowel in the base differs in tenseness from that in the free form, as in *profane ~ profanity* (27b).
- In situation (24d), the two vowels differ in both stress and vowel quality, as in *human ~ humanity* (27c).
- The relationships among the vowels in (27c,d) are mediated by the vowel shift schemas in (17) and (19) and by the vowel reduction schema in (21). Therefore the starred vowels are linked by coindex 3.[21]

(27) a.   *dense*   *density*

Morphosyntax: A_{40} $[_N A_{40} aff_{38}]_{41}$

Phonology: $/dɛns/_{40}$ $//dɛns/_{40} əti_{38}/_{41}$

b.   *profane*   *profanity*

Morphosyntax: A_{42} $[_N A_{42} aff_{38}]_{43}$

Phonology: $/prəf *ej_3* n/_{42}$ $//prəf *æ_3* n/_{42} əti_{38}/_{43}$

c.   *human*   *humanity*

Morphosyntax: A_{44} $[_N A_{44} aff_{38}]_{45}$

Phonology: $/hjum *ə_3* n/_{44}$ $//hjum *æ_3* n/_{44} əti_{38}/_{45}$

To sum up this section: there is a simple basic difference between "recessive" affixes like *-ness* and *-al* on one hand and "dominant" affixes like *-ity* and *-ious* on the other.

---

[21] Of course there are often other differences between the stress of the base and that of the related word. An extreme case from Table 6.1 is *democrat/democracy*, in which all three vowels change their stress. For the moment, we assume that these further differences are due to other schemas for stress patterns, applied simultaneously. We set this issue aside for further research, no doubt at our peril.

A recessive affix may place constraints on the form of its base, as *-al* does in (23), and a related free form must conform to these constraints. A dominant affix likewise places constraints on its base; but in contrast, a related free form need not conform to them, because the constraints are marked as excepts, as in (26)-(27). Thus this difference need not be encoded as some sort of special feature on the affix: it follows directly from the affordances of our formalism. We take this to be a nice result.[22]

6.8 The microtexture of the lexicon: Blends with derivational affixes

Section 4.9.2 proposed treating the word *flattery* as a blend of the verb *flatter* and the suffix *-ery* found in *mockery* and *forgery*. Many more possible examples of blends arise with other affixes. This section describes some of them and extends the formalism suggested in section 4.9.2. We will show that these cases look more natural in terms of relational links than in terms of traditional derivation. At the same time, we show how intricately these small details of the lexicon are structured.

6.8.1 Evidence for blending

For a first case, we return to the suffix *-ous*. It has an allomorph *-ious*; the two are shown in (28).

(28) a. "Plain" *-ous*: cavernous, clangorous, dangerous, hazardous, perilous, poisonous, rapturous, resinous, scandalous, traitorous
  b. *-ious*: bilious, gaseous, laborious, rebellious, uproarious

There is also a third allomorph, *-uous*, as in *contemptuous*, *incestuous*, and *sensuous*, with many of the same properties as *-ious*. We set it aside.

The allomorphs *-ous* and *-ious* have slightly different phonological properties. Plain *-ous* leaves the final consonant of the related free form intact, as seen in (29a). In contrast, when the related free form ends in an alveolar, the base of *-ious* ends with a palatal instead, as in (29b).

(29) a. Plain *-ous*: covet ~ covetous; hazard ~ hazardous
  b. *-ious*: infect ~ infectious; avarice ~ avaricious

Plain *-ous* tends to preserve the stress of its related free form.[23] However, *-ious* requires stress immediately before it, whatever the stress of the related free form.

---

[22] In a Construction Morphology framework, Davis and Tsujimura (2018) develop schemas for Arabic morphology that have the properties of our dominant affixes.

[23] Well, not quite. If the related free form has three or more syllables and initial stress, stress of the *-ous* word is coerced onto the antepenult, e.g. mónotone ~ *monótonous*, cárnivore ~ *carnívorous*.

(30)   a. -*ous*: vénomous, rígorous, calámitous
      b. -*ious*: lábor ~ labórious; rébel ~ rebéllious; úproar ~ upróarious

Both plain -*ous* and -*ious* like stress on the antepenult, and they both omit a final unstressed /i/ of the related free form (31a,b) in order to achieve this pattern.

(31)   a. -*ous*: bígamy ~ bígamous; calámity ~ calámitous
      b. -*ious*: hármony ~ harmónious; ínjury ~ injúrious

(31a) shows that /i/ is affected whether or not it is suffixal: in *bigamy*, -*y* is a suffix, while in *calamity*, it is only the final vowel of the suffix -*ity*.

    Now consider *piteous*, which might be parsed as (32a,b, or c).

(32)   a. *pity+ous*   [plain -*ous*]
      b. *pit+ious*   [truncation of *y* + -*ious*]
      c. *pity+ious*   [blending of *y* with -*ious*, along the lines of -*ery* in *flattery*]

In fact, though, only the parse in (32a) is possible. As seen in (29b), -*ious* always palatalizes base-final /t/. Therefore if the parsing were (32b) or (32c), it would have to be pronounced *[pɪʃəs]. We conclude that in this case the suffix is plain -*ous*, and no truncation or blending is involved. (Other such examples are *beauteous* and *bounteous*; note that retaining the /i/ in these cases achieves the required antepenultimate stress.)

    However, the proper analysis is not always so clear. For instance, where is the morpheme boundary in *harmonious*? The same three possibilities present themselves: (33a), with plain -*ous*; (33b), with a truncation of *y*; or (33c), with a blending of *y* and *i*.

(33)   a. harmony+ous   [plain -*ous*]
      b. harmon+ious   [truncation of *y* + -*ious*]
      c. harmony+ious   [blending of *y* with -*ious*]

(33a) is unlikely: as seen in (31a), plain -*ous* would normally truncate the final /i/, yielding *[hármənəs]. However, we are still left with a choice between (33b), with truncation, and (33c), with blending. We are left with no basis for settling on a single correct analysis. (Other such examples are *luxurious, injurious, mysterious, envious, furious*, and *glorious*.)

    A similar situation arises with the denominal suffix -*al* (34a) and its allomorph -*ial* (34b). Their properties are similar to plain -*ous* and to -*ious* respectively.[24]

(34)   a. -*al*: dialectal, parental, suicidal, infinitival
      b. -*ial*: adverbial, baronial, gerundial, professorial

---

[24] A difference is that, unlike -*ous*, -*al* is dominant and requires its base to end with main stress, e.g. *vénomous* but *paréntal*. Notice that this requirement is different from deverbal -*al* as in e.g. *arrival*, discussed above.

Now consider how these allomorphs combine with a small collection of words that end in -*ia*, such as *bacteria*, *inertia*, and *malaria*, forming adjectives such as *bacterial*, *inertial*, and *malarial*. The question arises of how they are parsed. Here are five (!) possibilities.

(35) a. bacteria+l   [-*al*, truncation of affix-initial /ə/]
      b. bacteri+al   [-*al*, truncation of base-final /ə/]
      c. bacter+ial   [-*ial*, truncation of base-final /iə/]
      d. bacteria+al   [-*al*, blending of adjacent schwas]
      e. bacteria+ial [-*ial*, blending of adjacent /iə/'s]

As with *flattery* and *harmonious*, there seems to be no evidence and no principle for deciding which of these is the proper parse.

Yet another situation like this is found in the -*ion* nominals. This suffix too has a collection of allomorphs, including most prominently -*tion* and -*ation*. Some -*ion* nominals, such as (36a), appear to be the affixation of -*ion* to the related free form (with palatalization of the base-final /t/, to which we return). Other examples, such as (36b), are clearly the affixation of the allomorph -*ation* to the free form.

(36) a. desert+ion, extort+ion, digest+ion
      b. alter+ation, condens+ation, improvis+ation

A third set, words like *alternation* and *termination*, have related free forms that end in -*ate*. Are they parsed as (37a), with the shorter allomorph, or as (37b), with truncation of -*ate*?

(37) a. alternat+ion   [*alternate* + -*ion* allomorph]
      b. altern+ation   [*alternate* + -*ation* allomorph]

(37a) might make more sense, in terms of transparency of the parse. But there is really no fact of the matter as to whether -*ate*- belongs to the base or the affix. An alternative is that again, like *flattery*, these words are blends, and -*ate*- is motivated simultaneously by the base and the affix.

These three cases—*harmonious*, *bacterial*, and *alternation*—have in common a possible analysis in terms of blending: they all involve suffixes whose beginning is identical to the end of the base. Blending makes sense in the context of unification, the primary combinatorial operation of Relational Morphology. Recall that the result of unifying two items ABCD and CDEF is ABCDEF, with an overlap or blend between the two inputs, so that there is only one copy of the shared material. As a result, the overlapping material in the composed item is motivated by the schemas for both allomorphs, an advantage in storing and accessing it (see Chapter 3).

In contrast, a traditional derivational theory has to combine the two items into ABCDCDEF, then delete one of the CDs. Such an analysis appears in Aronoff (1976), for instance: *alternation* is derived from underlying *alternate+ation*, from which the first -*ate* truncates. However, an -*ate*-deletion rule misses two important facts. First, the choice of deleting the first or second -*ate*- is arbitrary. Second, the deletion is in the context of an adjacent identical stretch of phonology, not only in the case of *alternation* but also with *flattery*, *harmonious*, and *bacterial*. Unification explains these generalizations: the overlapping stretch of phonology belongs to neighbors on both sides.

From the point of view of a traditional treatment in terms of derivational word-formation rules, these ambiguous analyses are a problem: a word should have one and only one derivation, not, say, five, as in (34). From the point of view of Relational Morphology, though, it is not at all troublesome. There is no reason that multiple schemas cannot converge on a common form, which is multiply (or promiscuously, or redundantly) motivated. Various cases like this have been noticed in Audring, Booij, and Jackendoff (2017) and (for compounds) Jackendoff (2010). We take this to be another way in which a schema-theoretic approach is superior to a rule-based grammar.

6.8.2 Formalizing overlap

Section 6.4 proposed a notation for the lexicalized blending found in the casual pronunciation of *this year* as [ðɪʃiːr]. In that case we were dealing with an idiosyncratic item. Section 4.9.2 discussed a more systematic overlap, where the suffix -*ery* overlaps with its base in *flattery* and *discovery*, rather than **flatterery* and **discoverery*. The overlap (and haplology) is specific to this particular suffix: agentive -*er* gives us the nouns *flatterer* and *discoverer*, not **flatter*$_N$ and **discover*$_N$, and comparative -*er* gives *cleverer*, not **clever*$_{comparative}$. We conclude that an affix's capability for overlap has to be somehow built into its schema. This subsection formalizes two of the overlaps discussed in the previous subsection, involving the -*ious* suffix.

We begin as usual by working out the structure of individual instances, and then we extract schemas. (38) shows the structure of *envious* and its link to *envy*. As in section 4.9.2 and 6.4, we notate the overlap by coindexing both the left-hand and right-hand edges of the components. For instance, in (38b), the right-hand index of *envy* (coindex 1) falls to the right of the left-hand index of -*ious* (coindex 3), with the result that the region in between, namely /i/, belongs to both constituents.

(38) Morphosyntax: a. N_1 b. $[_A N_1 aff_3]_2$
       Phonology: /ɛnvi$_1$/   /$_1$ɛnv$_3$i$_1$ əs$_3$/$_2$

The use of -*ious* therefore has two options (so far—a third in a moment). In the first, the free form is simply concatenated with the affix, as in *laborious*; the schema is (39b). In the second option, if the affix can overlap with the related free form, it must do so, as in *envious*. The schema for this option is (39c). As the two schemas are nearly identical, they can be linked by coindex δ, making them sisters (i.e. allomorphs). The difference between them is in the form and position of the end of the base: in (39b), the base is simply con-catenated with the suffix; in (39c), the base ends in /i/ and overlaps with the beginning of the suffix. The Elsewhere Condition guarantees that the more specific option, i.e. overlap, applies whenever possible.[25] Hence *envious* overlaps but *laborious* does not. (We omit the specification that the suffix must be immediately preceded by main stress.)

(39) *Sister schemas for* -ious   *No overlap*   *Overlap*

      Morphosyntax: a. N_α b. $[_A N_\alpha \text{aff}_3]_\delta$ c. $[_A N_\alpha \text{aff}_3]_\delta$
      Phonology: $/_\alpha \cdots _\alpha/$ $/_\alpha \cdots_{\alpha 3} i \ \text{əs}_3]_\delta$ $/_\alpha \cdots _3 i_\alpha \text{əs}_3]_\delta$

      Examples: *labor/envy*   *labor - i - ous*   *env-i -ous*

But there is more to the treatment of *-ious*. Normally this suffix is pronounced /-iəs/ or /-jəs/, as in *envious*, *laborious*, and *rebellious*. However, if the free form ends with /t/ or /s/, these are replaced in the derived form with /ʃ/, and the /i/ of the suffix disappears (though not in the spelling!), as in *infect ~ infectious* and *avarice ~ avaricious*. Following the treatment of casual *this year* as [ðɪʃiːr], we propose that the /ʃ/ in *infectious* is a blend of /t/ or /s/ with /i/. (40) shows how this looks in *infect* and *infectious*. Again, the coin-dices mark the beginning as well as the end of the phonological spans in question.

(40) Morphosyntax: a. V_4 b. $[_A V_4 \text{aff}_3]_5$
      Phonology: $/_4 \text{ɪnfɛk} *t*_4/$ $/_4 \text{ɪnfɛk}_3 *ʃ*_4 \text{əs}_3/_5$

The /ʃ/ in (40b) belongs to both the base and the affix, falling within the spans of both coindex 3 and coindex 4. It is starred to show that it differs from the starred /t/ in *infect* (40a). But the stars around /ʃ/ also mark that it differs from the /i/ in the usual version of the suffix. In other words, /ʃ/ in (40b) counts as a variant of /ti/—a single segment in place of two–without having to decide which of the two it is derived from and how the other is deleted.[26]

To account for this allomorph of *-ious*, we need to supplement (39b,c) with a third sister schema, shown in (41). It is linked to (39b,c) by coindex δ. (For convenience, we use /T/ for the features shared by /t/ and /s/.)

(41) *Sister schemas for* -tious, *with overlap and palatalization*

      Morphosyntax: a. V_γ b. $[_A V_\gamma \text{aff}_3]_\delta$
      Phonology: $/_\gamma \cdots *T*_\gamma/$ $/_\gamma \cdots_3 *ʃ*_\gamma \text{əs}_3/_\delta$

      Example: *infec- t*   *infec - ti - ous*

The difference between (41b) and the basic form (39b) lies in the additional starred segments: /i/ appears in (39b) but not in (41b); /ʃ/ appears in its place. At the same

---

[25] To be a little careful: It is not clear that the overlapped version is more specific than the non-overlapped one. However, it is more highly marked, or less canonical, and perhaps that is the appropriate criterion for apply-ing the Elsewhere Condition here.

[26] In an SPE-style treatment of this pattern, of course, the /i/ would cause the /t/ to palatalize, and then it would delete. The present treatment avoids the need for rule ordering.

time, /ʃ/ also takes the place of the /T/ in (41a)—that is, it stands in for both part of the related free form and part of the suffix, the same sort of blend found in *this year*.

At this point, our formalism begins to fail us. We have used the star notation to mark excepts, where two otherwise identical pieces of structure differ. In the present case, /ʃ/ is exceptional with respect *both* to the base (41a) and to the unblended suffix schema (39b). In other words, for these more complex cases, excepts have to be coindexed to what they are exceptions to. Rather than confront the reader (and ourselves!) with such complexity, we stop here. Nevertheless, we have gone far enough to show how even a single affix can fragment into a complex family of allomorphs. To our knowledge, comparable complexity shows up in every approach to these phenomena.

We emphasize again that although the overlaps discussed in this section, especially the palatalization, are motivated by phonetic fluency, their details have to be localized in the interface between morphosyntax and phonology, not in the phonetics or the phonology-phonetics interface. Different affixes allow different possible blends. For instance, consider what happens to /d/ at the end of a free form, when followed by various affixes, all of which palatalize /t/ and /s/ to /ʃ/ or /tʃ/.

(42)   a. In the context of *-ious*, /d/ remains alveolar [d], for instance in *studious*, *insidious*, *odious*, and *tedious*.

   b. In the context of *-uous* and *-ual*, it can be either [d] or [dʒ], as in *ar[dju]ous* or *ar[dʒ]ous, gra[dju]al* or *gra[dʒu]al*.

   c. Preceding *-ion*, it surfaces sometimes as /ʒ/, for instance in *persuade ~ persuasion, explode ~ explosion*, and *divide ~ division*; sometimes as /ʃ/, as in *concede ~ concession*.

   d. If preceded by /n/, it comes out as /tʃ/, as in *intend ~ intention, suspend ~ suspension, apprehend ~ apprehension*.

These tiny morphophonological details are part of one's knowledge of English, and have to be encoded in the schemas for the affixes in question. In particular, each of these palatalization schemas represents a conventionalized way to simplify the gestural score, but each one is a little different. (See Halle (2005) for similar remarks on velar softening (*electri[k] ~ electri[s]ity*, crosslinguistically.) As usual, there may be good historical reasons for these differences, but if one is not a philologist, they are not part of one's knowledge of English.

Of course we have only scratched the surface here (see for instance Aronoff's (1976) and Bochner's (1993) extensive discussion of allomorphs of *-ation*, or for that matter SPE). However, we hope to have shown that these complex alternations can be stated fairly readily in terms of nonproductive schemas, whose structure is a distillation of their instances. In particular, we believe that the treatment of morphophonological overlaps in constructional/relational terms offers a novel and in some respects more intuitive approach than has been possible within other approaches to phonology.

6.9 Conclusion

More generally, this chapter is intended as a proof of concept for applying the Parallel Architecture and Relational Morphology to phonological alternations, including some moderately intricate phenomena. A crucial aspect of the approach is that many phonological alternations are not pure phonology, but rather are tied to specific morphological constructions (as argued also by Booij and Audring 2017). Obviously, it remains to be seen how this approach fares with the abundant phonological and phonetic issues in the literature. In particular, it remains to be seen if the treatment of phonological phenomena in terms of affordances—what you *can* say, rather than constraints—what you want to *avoid*, can be carried through consistently. It is also important to determine to what degree affordances can conflict with one another and therefore need to interact in violable fashion, parallel to OT violable constraints and/or the Elsewhere Condition.

Looking more broadly at Part II of the present book, we have shown how the theory developed in Part I can account for a wide and (we hope) representative range of morphological and phonological phenomena, using a relatively lean collection of theoretical machinery. What we find especially attractive about the present approach is that it begins to make good on the promise of a common architecture across semantics, syntax, morphology, phonology, and phonetics—in other words, a unified linguistic theory.

PART III

BEYOND MORPHOLOGICAL THEORY

7

Language processing and language acquisition through the lens of Relational Morphology

7.1 Introduction

Chapter 1 expressed our desire for the Parallel Architecture and Relational Morphology to make contact with language processing and language acquisition. This concern has played a role here and there in our exposition; the present chapter addresses it more systematically. The basic question is: What is happening to the linguistic representations stored in memory when they are being used in language production and comprehension, and how do these representations come to be formed as language is being learned? We cannot pretend to account for all the experimental results reported in a vast and often conflicted literature. Rather, more modestly, we wish to show how experimental findings can be brought to bear on RM and on linguistic theory in general, and reciprocally, how RM can help sharpen issues in processing and acquisition, by giving them a firmer grounding in the character of the representations.

We will not have much to say about neural computation or brain localization. We are more interested here in *what* the brain is doing than in *how* and *where* it does it. In the terms of David Marr's (1982) levels of inquiry in cognitive science, our approach is "algorithmic" rather than "implementational": it focuses on the steps in processing linguistic information rather than on the relation between the informational "software" and the neural "hardware." Nevertheless, an algorithmic theory sets boundary conditions on what the neurons have to be able to do, and in that respect we hope to make a contribution to the implementational level as well—if only to pose challenges.

The first part of the chapter (sections 7.2–7.5) deals with language processing, the second part (sections 7.6–7.9) with acquisition. The two parts are not independent, given that what the language learner ultimately has to acquire is not just "knowledge of language" but the ability to *produce* and *comprehend* language in real time.

7.2 Theory of processing: Basic assumptions

The psycholinguistic literature demonstrates that morphological structure plays a role in language processing (see e.g. Nooteboom, Weerman, and Wijnen 2002; Baayen and Schreuder 2003; Zwitserlood 2004, 2018; Amenta and Crepaldi 2012; Clahsen 2016). We wish to show here how morphological effects could arise as a consequence of the

The Texture of the Lexicon. First edition. Ray Jackendoff and Jenny Audring © Ray Jackendoff and Jenny Audring 2020.
First published in 2020 by Oxford University Press. DOI: 10.1093/oso/9780198827900.001.0001

structures posited by Relational Morphology. In order to do so, we first must briefly set out our basic assumptions about language processing, building on the treatment in Jackendoff (1987, 2002, 2007a).

7.2.1 Long-term memory and working memory

A processor for language requires at least two distinct components: long-term memory and working memory. Long-term memory (LTM) contains the lexicon, which now includes all facets of "knowledge of language": pieces of linguistic structure, with or without variables, connected by interface links and relational links. Stored structures in LTM are activated in production by a speaker's desire to say something, and in comprehension by incoming linguistic input. Once activated, the structures become available to a limited-capacity working memory (WM), which transiently assembles the activated pieces from LTM into larger structures, either to create an utterance (in production), or to analyze and parse the input (in comprehension). In other words, WM is where productive schemas perform their generative function, either in creating things to say or in reconstructing what an interlocutor is saying.[1]

This distinction is not present in every theory of processing. Many approaches, especially those based on neural networks, conceive of working memory as merely the subset of the long-term network that is currently activated. However, a pure network architecture of this sort cannot on its own assemble structures in the course of producing or understanding a novel sentence. Here are two arguments why not (for more arguments, see Marcus 1998, 2001; Jackendoff 2002; and Gallistel and King 2009).

First, suppose one has heard the sentence *Ozzie kissed Harriet*. If one simply activates the lexical entries for *Ozzie*, *kissed*, and *Harriet*, it is impossible to tell who did the kissing: the linear order, syntactic structure, and meaning of the sentence as a whole are lost. In particular, a transient connection has to be established between the argument structure of *kissed* and the two nouns: *Ozzie* has to be bound to the role Agent and *Harriet* has to be bound to the role Patient, on the basis of their word order. This requires a mechanism that can encode the word order of arbitrary pairs or groups of words, and that can encode agentivity of arbitrary words in relation to arbitrary predicates. As argued by Marcus (1998, 2001), such a mechanism goes beyond the capability of a pure network architecture.

---

[1] LTM corresponds roughly to the "memory" component in Hagoort's (2005, 2013) MUC ("memory, unification, control") approach; WM corresponds roughly to his "unification" component (though we are not necessarily committed to his account of the localization of these components).

Baddeley's (1986) notion of working memory is inadequate for our purposes. He conceives of WM as a place where material is temporarily stored and rehearsed. In contrast, we see it as a place where structures are *built* online, more or less along the lines of a so-called "blackboard" architecture (Reddy et al. 1973). Readers committed to Baddeley's use of the term "working memory" should feel free to substitute another name for what we have in mind.

Eriksson et al. (2015) reviews much current thinking on WM, with considerable discussion of brain localization. However, there is little attention to the main function of WM that concerns us here, namely the assembly of stored units into larger transient structures.

Second, suppose one has heard the sentence *The little cat bit the big cat*. Simply activating the *cat* node in a network is not sufficient to encode two distinct cats, one characterized as *little* and one as *big*. Stronger activation of the *cat* node will not do the trick: that would just lead to a stronger or more robust cat that is both little and big. Alternatively, one might claim that the *cat* node ceases to be activated after the first occurrence of the word and is reactivated on the second occurrence. But this too is inadequate: in order to understand the sentence, both cats have to be activated at once. Jackendoff (2002) calls this the "Problem of 2," and shows that it occurs not only in language, but in other cognitive domains as well.

A working memory that is separate from LTM provides a facility where such transient binding and assembly can take place. For instance, the entries of *Ozzie* and *Harriet* can be unified with the grammatical and thematic roles of *kissed*—on this particular occasion. Furthermore, WM can contain two separate tokens of *cat*, each independently linked to the single lexical entry for *cat* in LTM, and each with its own role in the meaning of the sentence.

Such an architecture, however, presents deep challenges to a theory of neural implementation. For one thing, it is unknown how neurons encode something as simple as a speech sound in memory—how they distinguish a /p/ from a /t/. So much the worse for elaborate hierarchical linguistic structures such as the idiom *cut the mustard*: how do the neurons distinguish it from, say, the collocation *cut the cake*? Moreover, it is unknown how material can in effect be "copied" (or "coindexed") from LTM into WM, and how WM can unify these retrieved pieces by instantiating variables. And finally, the process of learning new words or phrases involves creating novel structures in WM and copying them into LTM, in effect adding new nodes and links to the LTM network. Such a notion of "copying" seems like an idea held over from classical AI, not brainlike at all. We are not aware of any proposals about neural computation that can fulfill these functions—that specify how the neurons do what they do. (Smolensky and Legendre 2006, Martin and Doumas 2017, and Baggio 2018 are possible exceptions; see Dehaene et al. 2015 for an assessment of what is known). We take it that one of the Big Questions for cognitive neuroscience is how to reconcile these apparently incompatible demands from the representational theory and the theory of neural implementation.

7.2.2 Promiscuous processing

Following much contemporary thought, we assume that lexical access is "promiscuous."[2] By this, we mean that in language comprehension, every item in LTM that is sufficiently similar to the current input is activated and (if sufficiently active) retrieved into WM.

---

[2] This idea goes back to Swinney (1979); Tanenhaus, Leiman, and Seidenberg (1979); the TRACE model (McClelland and Elman 1986); and cohort theory and its descendants (Marslen-Wilson and Tyler 1980; Marslen-Wilson 1987; Marslen-Wilson and Zwitserlood 1989). See also, for instance, McQueen, Dahan, and Cutler (2003).

There it serves as a candidate for "what is being heard," in competition with other candidates, each seeking to inhibit the others. The strength of each competitor in WM depends on a number of factors, including its current level of activation in LTM (i.e. its resting activation plus priming), the relative strength of its competitors, and how well it integrates with the input and the current context.

The competition among candidate analyses need not be resolved immediately. Consider the minimal pair in (1).

(1)   a. That's not *a parent*; it's actually <u>a teacher</u>.
      b. That's not *apparent*; it's actually <u>pretty obscure</u>.

If spoken casually, without special intonation, an ambiguity arises at the italicized words. The two interpretations differ in their word boundaries—what phonological and syntactic units one is hearing. But the ambiguity cannot be resolved until the semantic processing of the underlined words, three words downstream and in a different prosodic unit. Yet there is no intuitive sense of garden pathing or other difficulty in processing. We take from this that both of the possible structures are maintained and updated in WM until the point where one of them can be extinguished. Moreover, the resolution of the competition depends on semantics—here, the fact that *parent* is contrastive with *teacher*, while *apparent* is contrastive with *obscure*.[3]

A parallel situation arises in examples like (2). Here the ambiguity is between *the* as a determiner or as the marker of the "comparative correlative" construction (Culicover and Jackendoff 2005). The ambiguity cannot be resolved until six words downstream, but again there is no sensation of a garden path, at least intuitively.

(2)   a. *The* more attractive and intuitively plausible <u>theory</u> isn't always right.
         [*the* = determiner]
      b. *The* more attractive and intuitively plausible <u>a theory</u> is, the better a chance it
         has of becoming popular. [*the* = mark of comparative correlative construction]

Experimental evidence for multiple syntactic parses appears in, for instance, Tanenhaus et al. (1995), Ferreira and Patson (2007), Coppock (2009). (However, we know of no experiments testing the particular situations in (1) and (2).)[4]

---

[3] Gow and Gordon (1995) find that hearing *two lips* primes *tulips*, despite the differences in word boundary and prosody. Likewise, Tabossi, Burani, and Scott (1995) find that in Italian, responses to an associate of *visite* 'visits' are faster after *visi tediati* 'bored faces' than in a control condition. Again the priming violates a word boundary. The situation in (1), however, not only involves an ambiguous word boundary, it shows how long a resolution of the ambiguity can be postponed.

[4] The time course of eliminating competing candidates may depend on the disparity of their strengths. For instance, in the notorious garden path example *The horse raced past the barn fell*, the past tense interpretation of *raced* is hugely dominant over the relatively rare passive participle. A third candidate, rarely mentioned, is the lexical item *horse race*, which likely reinforces the interpretation of *the horse* as Agent rather than Patient. The upshot is that the Agent reading of *horse* is so powerful that it eliminates the correct candidate before the crucial evidence arrives. As is well known, if the example is manipulated so as to reduce the disparity, both candidates survive long enough to mitigate the garden path effect, so that (ia) and (ib) are about equally acceptable. Note in particular that the sequence *horse pull* is not a lexical item, so it cannot influence the interpretation the way *horse race* does.

   (i) a. The horse pulled past the barn fell.
      b. The horse pulled past the barn a heavy wagon loaded with crates.

7.2.3 The lexicon as a network; spreading activation

As in many approaches, we envisage the lexicon as a network in LTM consisting of linked nodes. Our working hypothesis is that the representation of lexical knowledge in the network directly mirrors RM's representation of morphologically and syntactically complex lexical items. In particular, the layers of the network are to be identified with the PA's semantic, (morpho)syntactic, and phonological structure, and the connections between layers are to be identified with the PA's interface links among levels.

We differ from many network models (including neural networks) in that we do not regard nodes in the network as simple monads. Rather, they are structures, as in Levelt, Roelofs, and Meyer (1999), Booij (2010), and Bybee (2010). For instance, the lexical entry for *harden* comprises semantic, morphosyntactic, and phonological nodes, each with internal structure; the three nodes are connected by interface links, as in (3). In other words, the network has no independent level of "lexical nodes." Rather, a "lexical node" is a complex of semantic, morphosyntactic, and phonological nodes, each with its own structure, the three connected by interface links.[5]

(3) Semantics: $[\text{BECOME} (X, \text{HARD}_1)]_2$
     Morphosyntax: $[_V A_1 \text{ aff}_3]_2$
     Phonology: $/ \text{hard}_1 \text{ ən}_3 /_2$

The relations among words in the network are not encoded as simple links between nodes. Rather, relational links pinpoint the regions of similarity among structures. For instance, the relation between *harden* and *whiten* is a connection not between putative *harden* and *whiten* nodes, but rather between their shared *-en* suffixes, the shared parts of their meanings, and their shared morphosyntax (they are both verbs with an adjectival base).

Yet another difference from traditional networks, again following the representational theory, is that the network includes not only all the words and all the stored multi-word units but also all the rules, in the form of schemas. These too are lexical items, with all the privileges and responsibilities thereof.

We conceive of the lexicon as supporting spreading activation, in much the sense of standard approaches going back at least to Collins and Loftus (1975). However, again we propose an important refinement arising from the representational theory: since nodes are connected by interface and relational links, these links form the pathways for spreading activation.

First consider the role of interface links. In language comprehension, an input signal necessarily activates the phonological layer first. The interface links then permit

---

[5] The "lemma level" of Levelt (1989) and others corresponds to our semantic and morphosyntactic levels and the links between them. The "lexeme" or "word form" level corresponds to our phonological level, or to our phonological and morphosyntactic levels and the links between *them*. (This is a different notion of lexeme than is prevalent in morphological theory.) In the model of Levelt, Roelofs, and Meyer (1999), lexical semantics is encoded at an independent conceptual level; the lemma level codes syntactic information, while the lexeme level codes morphological and phonological information.

this activation to be passed on to syntax and semantics. Once these higher levels are activated, the encoding of context and priming by syntax and semantics can show their effects. From that point, the semantics can feed activation or inhibition back down the interface links to phonology, as is necessary, for instance, in assigning word boundaries in (1a,b). Similarly, in language production, the semantic (or "message") layer is activated first, and it passes activation through the interface links to syntax and phonology. But phonological self-monitoring ("Did I say what I meant to?") suggests that phonological activation can influence semantic activation as well. This aspect of spreading activation is, we think, uncontroversial.[6]

Of more interest to us here is spreading activation along relational links. We propose that the strength of such spreading activation can be modulated in part by how extensive the linkage is. For instance, *piggish* activates both *pig* and the [N-*ish*] schema to some degree, and the semantics of *pig* activates the semantics of *cow* to some degree. Thus the question arises: If two nodes n_1 and n_2 are relationally linked to each other, how strongly (and/or how quickly) does activation of n_1 spread to n_2? We conjecture that three and possibly four factors are involved.

- First, the extent to which n_2 is activated (and/or how quickly it is activated) should be proportional to the degree to which n_1 is activated.
- Second, the activation of n_2 should also be proportional to how much structure is shared between n_1 and n_2, that is, how much of each of them is coindexed with the other, on all levels of representation.[7] For instance, we might expect *walked* to spread more activation to *walk* than *malicious* spreads to *malice*, because of the greater phonological and semantic differences in the latter pair. (Some experimental evidence that this is the case is discussed by Zwitserlood 2018.)
- Third, perhaps the amount of activation that n_1 spreads to n_2 depends on the number of items that n_1 is linked to: n_1 only has so much activation to spread around. So if n_1 has more neighbors, each one gets less activation spread to it. This would lead to effects of neighborhood size on spreading activation. (This factor is suggested by Collins and Loftus; see also Kapatsinski 2007.)
- Finally, it is possible that a relational link has its own intrinsic strength, based not only on how frequently and strongly n_1 activates n_2, but also on how frequently and strongly n_2 activates n_1.

Do items to which activation has spread then pass the gift on, activating *their* neighbors—what we might call second-order activation? Our hunch is that there should be no way to prevent this. However, a second round of spreading activation has to occur later than the first, perhaps too late to have an effect on current

---

[6] It is a matter of debate whether syntax is necessarily activated before semantics in comprehension, and before phonology in production. We take no position on this question.

[7] This factor is sometimes coded as Levenshtein distance—though usually only in terms of how many orthographic differences separate the two items.

processing. In addition, by the time activation moves outward in this second iteration, it may be so attenuated that it can be disregarded.

A further question along similar lines: If n_1 spreads activation to n_2, does n_2 then spread activation back to n_1, creating a resonance between them? If so, it is a special case of second-order activation, and the same factors of attenuation and timing come into play—whatever those factors may be.

7.3 Lexical access

Having laid out basic properties of WM and LTM, we now look more closely at what happens to them in the course of lexical access.

7.3.1 Speed of access

Probably the most thoroughly investigated feature of lexical access is the correlation between, on one hand, the speed of lexical access in various comprehension and production tasks (e.g. lexical decision and picture naming), and on the other hand, the frequency of the word being identified, where frequency of the word in an individual's experience is approximated by counting the word's occurrences in a corpus (Oldfield and Wingfield 1965). What brain mechanism is responsible for this correlation?

We can imagine four possibilities: First, a strong exemplar theory would claim that the brain stores every single instance of a word's use, building up a "mental corpus" for which the written corpus is a proxy (Taylor 2012).[8] The idea then is that more frequent words produce more mental tokens, which then combine forces to strengthen or speed up response. However section 3.4.1 posed objections to exemplar theory as a model of lexical storage. We also find it implausible as a model of processing. For one thing, it is not clear how to apply this approach to language production: how does a speaker construct an output based on a cloud of exemplars? And in either production or comprehension, are all the exemplars activated? It would seem to take *more* work rather than *less* to activate thousands or tens of thousands of stored instances.

A second possible account of the speed-frequency correlation (now probably obsolete) is that each lexical item is associated with a counter that keeps track of the number of times the item has been encountered. Besides the fact that the brain likely doesn't count, it is not clear what sort of mechanism could translate higher numbers into faster reaction times.

A third possibility (Forster 1976; Yang 2016) is that lexical items are ranked by frequency, and lexical access goes through the list serially, starting with the most frequent items, hence finding less frequent items later. Such a mechanism implausibly

---

[8] Similarly, Pierrehumbert (2001) proposes a "cloud" of stored phonetic exemplars rather than a unified phonological representation.

requires a pass through a lexicon of tens of thousands of items within a few hundred milliseconds. It also presumes that the brain creates the ranking in the first place, perhaps by counting instances. Hence it inherits the disadvantages of the previous account.

The account that we prefer treats the relation between speed and frequency as the product of two correlations. First, reaction time correlates with resting activation in LTM: the higher an item's level of resting activation, the faster and/or more strongly it responds (Bybee 1995 and Baayen, Dijkstra, and Schreuder 1997 use the term "lexical strength"; Pinker 1999 calls it "memory strength"; see also Plag 2003). Second, as in practically every theory of lexical acquisition (e.g. McClelland and Elman 1986; Norris et al. 2000), we assume that an item's level of resting activation is incrementally driven up by repeated use, along familiar lines of Hebbian learning. On this account, then, the brain has no direct representation of frequency as such (as it does in the previous two accounts). Rather, frequency in a written corpus stands proxy for a typical individual's frequency of use, which affects resting activation—which in turn affects reaction time. This hardly seems controversial in the literature.

We can add several possible refinements. First, as suggested by Bybee (1995), new occurrences of high-frequency items may not have much effect on resting activation, which is already high, while new occurrences of low-frequency items may have a comparatively greater effect. For instance, hearing the word *tomorrow* has far less effect on resting activation than hearing, say, *sarsaparilla*. One way to think about this is that as an item's resting activation gets higher, it takes less effort to activate the item for use in an utterance, but more effort to increment its resting activation per se. (We leave open whether resting activation approaches a ceiling asymptotically as frequency increases, or whether, alternatively, resting activation is potentially unbounded but grows more slowly as frequency increases.[9])

Second, resting activation of an item might depend on its "newsworthiness"—its ability to attract attention. For instance, an instance of the vivid *-fie* suffix in Dutch, such as *fietsfie* 'photo of oneself on a bike' (see section 2.9), might have a higher resting activation than a relatively humdrum combination such as *insipidly*, all else being equal.

Third, a crucial part of our story is Relational Morphology's hypothesis that schemas are lexical items right alongside words. Hence in processing they should behave like words. In particular, a schema should have a resting activation level that is correlated with its frequency. In turn, its frequency is the sum of the frequencies of its instances. Thus a schema with a substantial number of instances is liable to have a relatively high resting activation, possibly even at ceiling. Moreover, it should be able to be primed by related lexical items or schemas, raising its activation above resting level.[10]

---

[9] In the former of these scenarios, the resting activation might be proportional to a function such as $(1 - 1/n)$ or $(1 - 1/\log n)$, where n is the number of encounters with the word in question; this function asymptotes at 1. In the latter scenario, resting activation might be proportional to a function such as $\log n$; this has no upper bound but grows more slowly as n increases.

[10] O'Donnell (2015), working in a traditional framework with procedural word formation rules, speaks of "rule weights" based on a rule's frequency of application. In the present approach, the weight of a rule can be recast as the lexical strength of a schema, which is no different in character from the lexical strength of words.

Fourth, we suspect that so-called "resting activation"—in fact *any* "level of activation"—is actually stochastic, varying over time, rendering neural computation inherently noisy. This view seems to be common currency among neuroscientists who study brain dynamics, e.g. Huk and Hart (2019). One consequence of this noisiness is that performance is always at least a bit variable. This is why people make speech errors, why psychological experiments require some extravagant number of subjects and experimental stimuli in order to obtain a statistically reliable result, and why even an expert basketball player can't sink a free throw every time. As Dinstein, Heeger, and Behrmann (2015) put it: "Neural variability is likely maladaptive for optimizing performance accuracy on single trials, but it seems to be important for enabling exploration, plasticity, and learning."[11]

Fifth, there is likely a "decay function" or "forgetting function" that slowly decrements resting activation of weak items (Langacker 1987; Hofstadter and Mitchell 1995; Kapatsinski 2007). As a result, a rarely used item that is not especially attention-worthy may decay into the noise before another instance is encountered. In contrast, for a frequent item, another instance is liable to come along in time to bump the item's resting activation up. Questions that arise include: What is the time course of decay? What factors might affect this time course?

On this scenario, "extinguishing" an item's resting activation need not be a matter of reducing it to zero or some other arbitrary threshold. Rather, when its activation is low enough to get swallowed up in the ambient noise, it is no longer detectable and can have no effects. (Although, being stochastic, it may occasionally happen to be strong enough to "peek out," for instance when recalling or recognizing a word or a phrase or a tune one has not heard in thirty years or more.)

7.3.2 Priming

Activation of a node in the LTM network can be raised temporarily above resting level through a number of familiar types of priming. These can be spelled out explicitly in terms of the constructs of Relational Morphology.

First, after an item in LTM is activated, we assume, following the consensus in the literature, that it takes a little while to settle back down to resting activation. This provides an account of *identity* (or *repetition*) *priming*: if the item recurs in the input soon enough, its level in LTM is still above resting activation, and thus it is easier to summon it into WM, resulting in more rapid identification. (This factor is shared with every approach to priming.)

Second, if an item is activated in LTM, activation spreads to lexical items connected to it by relational links, along lines suggested in section 7.2.3. We thus have an account

---

[11] Note that this notion of noise is internal to the processing mechanism itself. It differs from "noisy channel" models of processing (Gibson, Bergen, and Piantadosi 2013), which address the processor's means of coping with noise in the incoming signal.

of *neighbor priming*: activating a node n_1 spreads activation to its neighbor n_2, which is therefore quicker to respond to a matching input. Following the discussion in section 7.2.3, the strength of spreading activation depends on the strength of the relational links involved, which in turn depends on the amount of shared structure. Since n_2 is not identical to n_1, they do not share all their structure. Therefore neighbor priming of n_2 by n_1 it is predicted to be less than n_1's own identity priming , as seems consistent with the experimental evidence (Baayen 2014; O'Donnell 2015: section 1.2.3). Kielar et al. (2008) (cited in O'Donnell 2015: section 4.3.4) further suggest that the strength of neighbor priming is proportional to the amount of shared structure, as our analysis would predict. Similarly, Pinker (1999) offers evidence that a regular stem is primed more strongly by its past tense than is an irregular stem—again, on our analysis, because the regular and its past share more structure, and therefore have stronger relational links.

In addition, recall that there are separate relational links for phonology, morphosyntax, and semantics. This makes it possible for priming effects to differ across phonological, morphological, and semantic neighbors, as has been found experimentally (Zwitserlood 2018 and references therein). In particular, there is evidence that morphological similarity supplements priming of phonology and semantics alone (Feldman 2000; Koester and Schiller 2008); Smolka, Preller, and Eulitz (2014) find that morphological priming for German prefixed verbs is more robust than either phonological or semantic priming.

Furthermore, O'Donnell (2015: section 1.2.3), citing de Vaan, Schreuder, and Baayen (2007) and Meunier and Segui (1999), reports that "higher-frequency items show smaller effects of priming by shared structures than lower-frequency items." This follows from the assumption in the previous section that as resting activation is higher, it takes comparatively more effort to raise it the same amount.

A particular case of neighbor priming is *semantic priming*, which involves shared conceptual structure. A word can be semantically primed if it shares some of its conceptual structure with a previous word or phrase in the discourse, or with the conceptual structure of some aspect of world knowledge, linguistic or nonlinguistic, that is active in the current situation. Here again we are in concurrence with the literature, adding only that relational links on the semantic/conceptual level provide the routes for spreading activation.

Finally, the continuity between words and rules in Relational Morphology's lexicon immediately yields an account of *syntactic* (or *structural*) *priming*. For instance, if one has heard a ditransitive dative structure (e.g. *Sam handed Kate a banana*), one is more likely to favor producing a ditransitive (e.g. *Anne sent Max a message*) over a prepositional dative (*Anne sent a message to Max*). If words and rules are entirely different mental entities, syntactic priming requires a separate mechanism from word priming, as noted by Bock and Loebell (1990) in an early description of the effect. On the present account, though, syntactic priming is not a surprise: it is another form of identity priming. The ditransitive dative construction is a lexical item in LTM, and in this case it has not entirely returned to resting activation, so at the moment it is easier to activate than usual (Ziegler, Snedeker, and Wittenberg 2018).

7.3.3 Competition in working memory

Section 7.2.2 proposed that the response to an input is "promiscuous." Each item in LTM that (sufficiently) matches the input is activated and linked to a copy in WM (or however LTM items are represented in WM); each of these candidates then attempts to unify with whatever structure is already present in WM. We now elaborate this scenario in light of section 7.3.2, looking this time at word identification. Our analysis, we think, reflects consensus in the literature; we go through it in some detail in order to lay the groundwork for addressing the role of schemas in processing in sections 7.4 and 7.5.

Candidates come to WM with differing strengths of activation, depending on their resting activation, the degree to which they have been primed, and the degree to which they match the input. In addition, parallel to Collins and Loftus's proposal for spreading activation mentioned above, the total activation in WM may be limited, so that the more candidates there are, the less each of them is activated. Thus the limited capacity of WM comes not just from the sheer number of items, but from the amount of activation available to maintain candidate analyses.[12] For instance, a common word-initial cluster such as /st/ in the input would activate many candidates, but not very much each. In contrast, a rare cluster such as /dw/ would activate fewer candidates, but to a greater degree (even if it has a lower resting activation itself). In turn, each candidate inhibits the others in proportion to its strength.

As subsequent input comes in, many candidates will be inconsistent with it and will therefore be discarded. For instance (as in cohort theory and its descendants), an initial /ʃi.../ will activate *she, sheep, sheet, sheath, shield, sheepish, sheepdog*, and so on, in proportion to their resting activation plus priming (if any). There are probably too many candidates for any single one to stand out against the background noise. But a continuation to /ʃip/ will weed out most of the candidates:[13] only *sheep, sheepish, sheep-dog*, and *sheepherding* are left standing in WM, and they compete with each other—even though, paradoxically, they simultaneously prime each other in LTM.

Normally, the candidate with highest activation will succeed in eliminating the others.[14] However, this takes some time, during which further input may reweight the candidates. For a trivial example, suppose the preceding part of the utterance were *baa baa black sh*.... This would activate the fixed expression whose continuation is *-eep*, thereby adding strength to *sheep* at the expense of *sheepish*. On the other hand, subsequent input can wipe out the dominant candidate: the utterance *could* after all turn out to be *baa baa black shoes*! Or suppose the preceding part of the utterance were *I bought a cow and a sh*.... Here the semantics of *cow* would prime the semantics of *sheep, pig, chicken*, and so on, and the syntactic frame would prime for a

---

[12] This feature of competition in WM is not confined to language. In a similar vein, Bays (2015) argues that the limited channel capacity of visual WM is a result of noise in neural computation: as the number of candidates increases, their variability increases, "until they can no longer be distinguished from random noise."

[13] Actually, the process of weeding out may start earlier, thanks to coarticulation cues in the /i/ vowel.

[14] Alternatively, the "winner" is an item whose activation exceeds some threshold, or whose activation is proportionately greater than other candidates.

noun; hence both factors would tend to favor *sheep* over *sheepish*. Still, the utterance could turn out to be *I bought a cow and a sheepish monkey*, reweighting the candidates, presumably at some cost in time and/or effort that could be detected by brain imaging techniques.

These examples have well-known parallels in the syntactic parsing literature, and we think the solutions are the same. For instance, *a cow and a sheepish monkey* parallels examples like Ferreira and Patson's (2007) *While Susan dressed the baby cried*. In this example, the dominant interpretation initially treats *the baby* as the direct object of *dress*, but subsequent input shifts dominance to the interpretation in which *the baby* is the subject of the embedded clause.

7.3.4 Probabilistic/predictive parsing

This conception of WM processing offers a connection with probabilistic/predictive approaches to syntactic parsing (e.g. Hale 2003, 2011; Levy 2008; Kuperberg and Jaeger 2016). The basic idea of these approaches is that at any particular moment, the processor is predicting what is to come in the input. Moreover, these predictions are not all-or-nothing, but probabilistic. As new input comes in, its surprisal—basically its deviation from prediction—affects processing time and electrophysiological measures of processing effort. The crucial notion, surprisal, is measured independently via corpus frequency and cloze probability. Continuations with low surprisal (*baa baa black…*sheep) are processed faster and elicit a lower processing cost than continuations with high surprisal (*baa baa black…*shoes).

To translate this approach into the terms of Relational Morphology, let's ask how a prediction is coded in WM. There are two cases. First, an item can be primed, raising its activation relative to other candidates. This can be uncontroversially interpreted as increasing its probability. The second case, however, is more interesting. A candidate structure in WM typically includes material that continues beyond the input: the hearer has activated some lexical item—a word, a fixed expression, a piece of syntactic structure, or even a semantic frame—but only the beginning of it has actually been heard. The part of this item that has *not* yet been heard can be considered a prediction of what is to come. For instance, as observed earlier, an initial /ʃi…/ activates *she, sheep, sheen, sheet*, and so on. Each of these activated items constitutes a prediction about the continuation. In other words, predictions amount to pieces of lexical structure in WM that anticipate future parts of the input.

The probability assigned to each prediction can be reframed as the relative strength of activation of the candidates in WM, which, as we have seen, varies with frequency, priming, and the number of alternative candidates. A low-surprisal continuation is one that conforms to a high-strength candidate, such as the continuation…*eep* after *baa baa black sh…*. A high-surprisal continuation is one that conforms to a low-strength candidate, such as the continuation…*oes* in the same context. A high-surprisal continuation has the effect of dethroning a leading candidate and elevating a lowly one; this seems a reasonable cause for increased processing effort, in proportion to the disparity in strength between the two competitors. We are not aware of any attempts to adapt the mathematics of the surprisal perspective to a framing in terms of competitive activation, but it should be possible.

A possible rationale for undertaking such a reframing is that probabilistic prediction does not extend very comfortably to an account of language production. Speakers are not *predicting* what word they are going to utter, they are *choosing* it. Probabilistic prediction makes little sense in this context. In contrast, the present approach to comprehension appears to lend itself to a complementary treatment of production, following lines proposed by Levelt (1989), in which words and structures are competing for eventual expressive output. In our view, the main difference between comprehension and production is that in the former, lexical access is looking for words that match a heard *phonology*, while in the latter, lexical access is trying to match a desired *semantics* (Jackendoff 1987, 2002; Momma and Phillips 2018).

7.4 Lookup versus (or alongside) computation

After this long excursus on processing in general, we return to the question of how morphological schemas play a role in processing.

Much of the literature on morphological processing is concerned with the question of lookup versus computation: When processing morphologically complex words, does one process them as whole words, or does one decompose them into constituents? Various positions have been proposed (for two recent surveys, see Zwitserlood 2018 and Gagné and Spalding 2019):

- All decomposition, a.k.a. full parsing, in which complex items are accessed entirely by composing their parts (Taft and Forster 1975; MacKay 1978; Taft 2004)
- All whole-word, a.k.a. full listing, in which all items are accessed as monadic units; internal structure plays no role (Butterworth 1983; and in a way Rumelhart and McClelland 1986)
- Some words (e.g. regulars) processed decompositionally, others (e.g. irregulars) as whole words (Clahsen 1999; Yang 2016; O'Donnell 2015 makes the choice probabilistic)
- Simultaneous decomposition and whole-word retrieval, in competition, a.k.a. Race model (Frauenfelder and Schreuder 1992; Baayen, Dijkstra, and Schreuder 1997; Pinker 1999; Reifegerste, Meyer, and Zwitserlood 2017)
- Simultaneous decomposition and whole-word retrieval, potentially either competing or reinforcing each other (Kuperman et al. 2009).

Given the non-compositional semantics of many morphologically complex words, and given the hordes of morphologically complex words without a lexical base (e.g. *tedious*), we can immediately reject the all-decomposition theory: such words cannot be derived from independent stored parts. And given speakers' ability to understand novel morphologically complex words—particularly in languages with exuberantly productive morphological systems, such as Turkish (Hankamer 1979)—we can also immediately reject a purely whole-word theory. The next option categorically divides the morphologically complex words into those that are stored and those that are composed online (for example Yang's (2016) serial traversal of a list of exceptions). This seems to require an advance decision whether or not to attempt decomposition. We prefer an approach in the same spirit as promiscuous lexical access: the brain tries both routes at once and lets the chips fall where they may.

The choice thus comes down to the last two theories. Of these two, we favor the latter. On one hand, when the decompositional and whole-word strategies result in incompatible candidates, they compete. But on the other hand, when they result in compatible candidates, they reinforce each other (a situation that physicists call *constructive interference*), and their redundancy creates a more robust outcome and potentially a faster reaction time. We will see this in action in the next section.

7.5 Schemas in the processing of four kinds of words

We now return to the question posed at the beginning of this chapter: What is happening to morphological representations in memory during their use in language processing? In particular, what role do schemas play? To begin to answer these questions, we rather obsessively deconstruct the steps involved in lexical access from the perspective developed in sections 7.2–7.4. We address words of four kinds: (a) a monomorphemic word (*hurricane*); (b) a novel bimorphemic word (*purpleness*); (c) a stored word with a legitimate suffix but a nonce base (*scrumptious*); and (d) a stored bimorphemic word (*sheepish*).

We idealize to the situation where the word is being heard in isolation. External factors such as priming and syntactic or semantic context will affect all four cases comparably. For instance, if previous context has set up a syntactic expectation of an adjective, say *the extremely…*, this bias will facilitate the activation of the adjectives *scrumptious* and *sheepish*, and it will inhibit the activation of the nouns *hurricane* and *purpleness*.[15] We add that visually presented words will have a different time course, because they can be perceived all at once rather than sequentially.

The monomorphemic word *hurricane* sets the background for the other three cases.

- By the time /hr̩ık/ is heard, the processor has reached the uniqueness point—the point where all candidates but one have been discarded. The only viable candidate remaining is indeed *hurricane*.

---

[15] Slightly more precisely, *extremely* activates the syntactic frame [$_{AP}$ Adv A] and unifies with its Adv position. The open Adjective slot that remains is receptive to *scrumptious* and *sheepish* but not to *hurricane* and *purpleness*.

- Hence the continuation of the input is predicted to be /ejn/, and when that comes, the prediction is confirmed.
- The resting activation of *hurricane* is bumped up.

Next consider a novel word with a lexical base, say *purpleness*. This word is altogether plausible, given *blackness*, *whiteness*, and *redness*, but it is not a stored lexical item (at least it wasn't for the authors, before they made it up as an example).[16]

- By the time /pṛpl/ is heard, the cohort has been reduced to *purple*, whose semantics primes that of other color words to some extent.
- But there is no hint that *purpleness* is coming, since (by assumption) there is no such word in the lexicon that could be activated.
- When /nəs/ is heard, the lexical item *purple* is now incompatible with the input ("This input isn't a word I know") and so *purple* may start to decay in WM.[17]
- However, /nəs/ activates the [$_N$ A-*ness*] schema, whose variable prompts the processor to look for a preceding adjective.
- *Purple*, still (somewhat) active, satisfies the variable. It becomes reactivated, and it unifies with the [$_N$ A-*ness*] schema, in conformance with the input.

This is a pure case of what the literature calls decomposition or computation, as opposed to full-word lookup. However, processing doesn't end here. Things continue to reverberate in the lexical network.

- Since [$_N$ A-*ness*] is still active in LTM, it can't help but prime all the -*ness* words— but only a little each, because there are so many of them. This effect amounts to morphological priming: if another -*ness* word shows up in the input, its processing will be enhanced, though only a little. (Duñabeitia, Perea, and Carreiras (2008) find masked priming by suffixes in visual word recognition, though Giraudo and Grainger (2003) do not.)
- The resting activation of *purple* and that of [$_N$ A-*ness*] are bumped up.
- *Purpleness* is tentatively entered in the lexicon. That is, the hearer might be on the way to learning a new word.

The third case is *scrumptious*. This has the common suffix -*ous*, but it is attached to a nonce base *scrum(p)(t)* that lacks a related free form. As stressed in previous chapters, such items are ubiquitous in English morphology. To our knowledge, psycholinguistic research has not had much to say about them (Hay 2001 is an exception). Our intuition is that such items ought to take less effort to identify than comparably long

---

[16] Others may well have independently made it up, in which case it may well be found in a corpus. Indeed, COCA has 7 instances, but this should be compared to 683 for *redness* and 2365 for *blackness*. And the BNC appears to have no instances at all.

[17] If the word were not heard in isolation, the syllable /nəs/ might be part of a following word, say, *purple nasturtium*, leading to further hypotheses in competition.

and frequent monomorphemic words, say (for purpose of argument) *crocodile* and *hurricane*. Let's walk through the processing of *scrumptious*.

- Unlike the case of *purpleness*, when /skrʌmptʃ/ is heard, there is no free form in the lexicon that can be activated. Rather, the cohort in WM is reduced to the single word *scrumptious*; in effect, there is a strong prediction that the next segment of the input will be *-ous* (just as /hɹɪk/ predicted /ejn/ above).
- The predicted word *scrumptious* activates its "mother schema" in LTM, the $[_A - ous]$ schema.
- When the whole word /skrʌmptʃəs/ has been heard, the predicted lexical item *scrumptious* is already present in WM and satisfies the input.
- The $[_A - ous]$ schema also satisfies part of the input, redundantly.
- The resting activation of *scrumptious* and that of $[_A - ous]$ are bumped up.

We conjecture that the activation of the affix schema should add strength, robustness, and/or speed to the identification of the input, compared to a monomorphemic word, which does not get the extra boost. In addition:

- To some small degree, *scrumptious* and the schema may also activate other *-ous* words such as *joyous* and *glamorous*. But these words are not compatible with the input, whereas the schema is. So the sister words have little effect on this case of processing. Still, the influence of the schema, such as it is, is another instance of morphological priming.[18]

Finally, we turn to *sheepish*, which combines the conditions of the previous two cases: the whole word is a lexical item, *and* the base has a related free form.

- At the point where /ʃip/ has been heard, it activates the lexical items *sheep*, *sheepish*, *sheepherding*, *sheepskin*, and so on, in proportion to their resting activation. The input cannot yet be definitively identified.
- However, once the whole word /ʃipɪʃ/ has been heard, the lexical items *sheep*, *sheepherding*, and so on are incompatible with the input and start to decay; on the other hand, *sheepish* becomes activated even more, and satisfies the input.
- But now /ɪʃ/ in the input also activates $[_A N\text{-}ish]$.
- $[_A N\text{-}ish]$ partly satisfies the input, redundantly supporting the affix of *sheepish* (just like *-ous* in *scrumptious*).
- In addition, the variable of $[_A N\text{-}ish]$ can be unified with *sheep*, which is still present (even if attenuated) in WM. The resulting composed structure is compatible with the input, just as the whole word is. Hence the identification of the input as

---

[18] This case differs from one discussed more frequently in the literature, in which a masked prime such as *corner* facilitates *corn* (Rastle, Davis, and New 2004). In such a case, something that looks like a suffix but is not is stripped off to reveal a real but unrelated word. In the present case, what looks like a suffix really *is* a suffix, but if it is stripped off, the result is a nonword.

the word *sheepish* is supported by both the lexical item *sheepish* and the assembly of the lexical items *sheep* and [$_A$ N-*ish*].

- The resting activation of *sheepish*, *sheep*, and [$_A$ N-*ish*] are all bumped up.

Again, given the success of both whole-word and compositional routes in processing, we expect *sheepish* to be identified more robustly and faster than are monomorphemic *hurricane*, purely compositional *purpleness*, and partially compositional *scrumptious*, all else being equal. We are not aware of experimental research that compares this full ensemble of situations. (However, Schreuder and Baayen (1995) argue that redundancy speeds up processing in a different set of cases.)

The compositional route takes more steps than the whole-word route: the base and the affix schema have to be retrieved, and the base has to be unified with the affix. Each of these steps takes time; in particular, the base and the affix schema cannot be unified until they are both retrieved. So the contribution of the whole word will tend to be dominant in determining the speed of processing. However, if the whole word is infrequent, hence relatively slow, but the base and the affix are both frequent, hence relatively fast, the compositional route may be faster and/or stronger. This is in accord with Baayen and Lieber (1991), who show that the compositional route takes precedence if the affix in question has a large number of low-frequency instances (and hence is itself high frequency), and particularly if the base is of relatively high frequency compared to the derived word.[19]

Hay (2001) and Hay and Baayen (2005) discuss such gradient results and conclude that the compositionality of morphologically complex items is not discrete but graded: words are divided into morphemes *to such-and-such a degree*. We suggest that the gradient they observe is not graded compositionality per se; it is rather a result of the relative strength and/or speed of whole-word access vs. compositional access. Translating their analysis into our terms, the relative difficulty of the compositional route depends on: (a) the resting activation of the affix schema (which depends on how numerous and how frequent its instances are); (b) how much the rest of the word is shared with a related free form (in *sheepish*, a lot; in *malicious*, less, because of the phonological differences from *malice*; in *scrumptious*, not at all—see Zwitserlood 2018); and (c) the resting activation of the related free form, if there is one. Similarly, Hay and Baayen speak of the role of "paradigmatic analogy" in conditioning neighborhood effects; in the present account this corresponds to the strength of relational links.[20]

To sum up this section: We have tried to show that relational links and schemas, even if only used relationally, can do some useful work in speeding up processing and

---

[19] There may be individual differences in this balance. Reifegerste, Meyer, and Zwitserlood (2017) show that older speakers tend to rely on storage to a greater extent than younger speakers, who make more use of composition. See also Dąbrowska (2018).

[20] Hay and Baayen argue for degrees of morphological compositionality rather than an account like ours, on the grounds that gradience also appears in speech production. However, we see no reason why speech production should not also be subject to competition and/or resonance among multiple routes of processing, one of the themes of Levelt (1989), for instance.

making it more robust. This conclusion rests on a large number of premises that we have tried to lay out here.

- Words and rules (now schemas) are stated in the same format, namely as pieces of linguistic structure connected by interface links.
- Words and schemas are stored together in a network of lexical relations, formalized as relational links.
- Schemas are stored in memory with a resting activation related to their frequency, just like words.
- Schemas unify in WM with their bases, in exactly the same way as verbs unify with their arguments.

A larger conclusion is that Relational Morphology's theory of representations can serve as a foundation for a processing theory that brings the theories of competence and performance into more intimate contact. We hope this approach offers an incentive to revisit the theoretical underpinnings of the experimental literature and to design new experiments, for instance to study the processing of words like *scrumptious*, which turn out to be far more numerous than has generally been recognized. We also hope that this approach might lead to computational modeling that allows one to fine-tune the theory's many parameters such as activation strength, the relative timing of the many events going on in lexical access, and the balance among them, in such a way as to best reflect the experimental results.

7.6 Acquisition of words

We now switch gears and turn from the transient processing of morphology to the more gradual process of acquiring morphological structure and morphological relations. We cannot pretend to address all the formidable problems of word and grammar learning. We limit ourselves to observing where the main issues of acquisition research intersect with Relational Morphology. We hope to show how a formulation in RM terms can lead to a more graceful integration of linguistic theory with the theory of acquisition.

The problem of grammar acquisition is traditionally stated in terms of how a language learner acquires productive procedural rules of grammar such as "to form the past tense of a verb in English, add -*d*." Reframed in the terms of Relational Morphology, the question is how a language learner acquires productive schemas such as (4).

(4)   Semantics: $[PAST (SITUATION_x)]_y$
       Morphosyntax: $\{V_x, PAST_1\}_y$
       Phonology: $/..._x d_1/_y$

The rest of this chapter works out some of the issues involved in answering this question.

An obvious first consideration is that one cannot infer a general rule or schema without first collecting some evidence for it, in the form of words that motivate and are motivated by it. In this sense, our approach is "usage-based" (e.g. Culicover and Nowak 2003; Tomasello 2003; Goldberg 2006; Ambridge and Lieven 2011). Therefore, before tackling the acquisition of schemas, we need to sketch the acquisition of words. As always, RM regards a word as a linkage of a piece of semantic structure, a piece of morphosyntactic structure, and a piece of phonological structure. Hence learning a word requires building these structures and establishing the interface links between them, thereby adding nodes and links to the lexical network.

It is not necessary for all the parts of a lexical item to be acquired at once. A learner can arrive at a concept first and link it to phonology later, for instance by asking "What's *this* called?" Or a learner may encounter a novel phonological word and figure out the concept linked to it, for instance by asking "What's a *fendle*?" Alternatively, the learner may attempt to guess the concept associated with a novel word, using any available contextual cues. The bulk of the word learning literature is concerned with the last of these situations, in which the child hears a novel word and is trying to figure out what it refers to—more often than not, unconsciously.

In filling out the structure of a newly encountered word, the learner may use knowledge already in place. For instance, suppose the learner already commands some aspects of syntactic structure. Then canonical interface links between syntax and semantics can help fill out a new word's lexical entry: words for objects are always nouns, and words for activities are frequently verbs (though, for instance, *bath* and *nap* are not). Thus if the learner has determined that a word refers to an object, the canonical linkage suggests that it is a noun; this is "semantic bootstrapping" in the sense of Pinker (1989). The influence can also go in the other direction. For instance, "syntactic bootstrapping" in the sense of Landau and Gleitman (1985) involves using syntactic argument structure as a strong (albeit not entirely reliable) cue for semantic argument structure. But regardless of whether acquisition of a new word begins with phonology, with syntax, or with semantics, the result is new nodes and new interface links in the lexical network.

Given the opportunistic nature of processing, we are inclined toward a theory of word learning that is similarly opportunistic, along the lines of the "Propose but Verify" model of Trueswell et al. (2013), an elaboration on so-called fast mapping (e.g. Bloom 2000). Basically, the learner creates a "proposed" lexical entry for a (phonological) word when it is used in a situation conducive to determining its meaning, for instance shared attention (Tomasello 2003) and/or a sufficiently rich linguistic context. This hypothesized meaning is retained in long-term memory as a tentative lexical item, until another encounter with the same phonological word. If the new context is consistent with the hypothesized meaning, the lexical entry is "verified"—given legitimate status; if not, the hypothesis is discarded.[21] In other words, in the ideal case, only two encounters

---

[21] The procedure as described here fails with homonyms. Stevens et al. (2017) tweak the procedure in order to escape this problem. We will not address these details here.

(of the right sort) are necessary to create a lexical item. This comports with experimental evidence for one-trial learning (e.g. Carey 1978; de Vaan, Schreuder, and Baayen 2007). It also is consistent with the popular experimental paradigm that tests children's generalization of novel words after one presentation ("This is a dax" [showing the child a nonsense object]. Now, is *this* a dax?" [showing some other, different object]: Macnamara 1982; Landau, Smith, and Jones 1988;Waxman and Klibanoff 2000; etc.).[22]

On the other hand, an item encountered and stored just once is liable to be extinguished by the decay or "forgetting" function in LTM. As a result, an infrequent and/or unverified item disappears into the background noise. Then, as far as the brain is concerned, the next encounter with this item is effectively the first time.

While we acknowledge that two encounters with a word may not always result in a fully specified lexical entry or even a lasting one, we part company with approaches in which the learner collects a large corpus of uses and runs statistics on cooccurrences, as in cross-situational learning models (e.g. Smith, Smith, and Blythe 2011; O'Donnell 2015; Yang 2016). We find it unlikely that one saves up a corpus of unanalyzed instances until such time as one can run statistics on it. How do you know when you have enough evidence? Why not start working out word meanings right away? The assumptions of the statistical approach seem to us rather reminiscent of Chomsky's (1965) idealization of instantaneous learning in choosing a grammar, ignoring the incrementality of language acquisition.

As outlined in section 7.3, we assume that a word has a resting activation in LTM. So we must also ask: What determines (or influences) the initial level of resting activation for a newly encountered word? For the sake of concreteness, we'll suppose that any new word is supplied with some baseline level of resting activation (parallel to the "entrance fee" for lexical storage in section 3.8). This level can be augmented by enhanced attention to the word or to its context, by "newsworthiness" or novelty (i.e. unexpected structure), or by emotional impact. The result is a higher initial resting activation, in effect making the word more memorable. In the Propose but Verify scenario, another possible factor is one's confidence in a hypothesized word meaning: higher confidence results in higher resting activation.[23]

Note that frequency cannot boost activation at this first encounter. To be sure, the first encounter must be stored, because if it is not, the word can't be recognized the next time. But, as a matter of logic (and as pointed out by Bybee (2010) and Goldberg (2019)), a learner can't know in advance whether the word is going to be frequent or not. It can't signal "You're hearing me for the first time, but make sure and notice me: I'm

---

[22] The semantics initially assigned to a word can be relatively coarse or vague, to be sharpened later. Ozturk and Papafragou (2008) show that Turkish-speaking children use evidential morphology in a grammatically correct fashion long before they get the semantics right. Similarly, one of RJ's daughters at around 2;5 would answer the question "What color is *this*?" with a legitimate color word, but hardly ever the right one. She had evidently learned that the color names form a semantic space labeled *color*, but she had not yet linked this space to a perceptual space. Indeed, linking to semantics is not always necessary. Young children learn phonological sequences that (for them at that moment) have no meaning, for instance the alphabet song and the number sequence.

[23] Stevens et al. (2017) treat this as the probability of the hypothesis. Our interpretation in terms of confidence is endorsed by Lila Gleitman (p.c.).

really frequent!" High frequency just bumps up the item's resting activation more quickly, thanks to more frequent subsequent encounters.

We should also ask what role existing relational links and schemas play in word learning. Our intuition is that if relational links can be formed between a new word and items already in the lexicon, this should make it more memorable. To flesh this intuition out, consider what occurs in encountering a novel word in the input. As usual in processing, the input activates candidate matches in LTM. However, in this case, no matches appear. Suppose the new word is monomorphemic, say *tarpaulin*. Then it gets no help from the lexicon and it must be processed and entered into the lexicon as a whole, with a certain amount of effort. On the other hand, suppose it's a word like *purpleness*, whose parts are existing lexical items that can be activated independently, as in section 7.5. In that case, the parse of the word is at least in part precompiled, requiring less effort and resulting in greater confidence. In turn, greater confidence results in higher resting activation. In short, the more a new word can be motivated by existing lexical items (including schemas), the higher its initial resting activation and therefore the better chance it will survive in the lexicon.

7.7 How are relational links acquired?

The question of how candidates are proposed and verified (or alternatively, discarded) is not restricted to word learning. The acquisition of schemas raises parallel questions: First, what leads a learner to posit a candidate schema? Second, when does a learner have sufficient evidence to judge a candidate schema as a "fact" rather than a "hypothesis"? Is the difference marked by some sort of diacritic? Or is the difference a matter of gradient commitment or gradient confidence? And third, when does a learner decide that there is insufficient evidence to support a candidate schema, and therefore decide to throw it out? Or is this too a matter of gradient commitment? We explore these questions in the next sections.

Our eventual goal, along with all approaches to acquisition of grammar (as opposed to acquisition of words), is to describe how learners acquire rules of grammar—in our terms, productive schemas. We can identify three necessary components to this process. Each raises its own problems.

- It is first necessary to recognize similarities among words, and to install hypothesized relational links among them, making them sisters.
- Based on families of sisters, hypothesized schemas have to be constructed and added to the lexicon.
- It must then be determined whether a hypothesized schema is productive or nonproductive.

Consider first the establishment of relational links. Initially, a relational link between two words has to be posited on the basis of what is observable, namely shared phonology.

However, phonological similarity is obviously not enough. For instance, *van* and *vanish* are related phonologically, but unlike *pig* and *piggish*, they are not related morphologically. But the acquisition process can't know this in advance! It therefore must guess that if there is phonological relatedness, there is also morphological relatedness. The guesses take the form of putative relational links at the morphosyntactic and semantic levels.[24]

Suppose the learner already knows the free form *pig*, and now encounters *piggish*. By virtue of its phonological similarity to *pig*, the acquisition process can divide it into two segments, the first of which can be linked to the free form, semantically as well as phonologically. The other segment, *-ish*, does not correspond to a free form. But suppose that other items such as *foolish* and *childish* are already known. Then the acquisition process can detect the similarity of *piggish* to these other items: not just phonological similarity, but parallel morphosyntactic categories for the base (noun) and the whole word (adjective), plus semantic parallelism (LIKE (X)). Hence provisional morphosyntactic and semantic links can be posited not only between *pig* and *piggish*, but also between *piggish*, *foolish*, and *childish*.

Now consider *vanish*. It exhibits phonological similarity to *van* and to *foolish*. But there is no meaning relation between *van* and *vanish*, and there is neither a morphosyntactic nor a semantic relation between the *-ish* in *vanish* and the *-ish* in *foolish*. In particular, *vanish* is a verb and *foolish* is an adjective. So in this case the acquisition process rejects the hypothesis of a morphological relation.[25]

There is an important caveat, though. The learner may not yet know enough relevant words to set up a relational link, especially in the case of affixes. For instance, there might not be enough *-ish* words in the learner's lexicon, complete with structured meanings, to apply these criteria correctly to *piggish* and *vanish*. Yet the process of establishing relational links must start somewhere. How does the mind decide when to start trying to form links? Again, there is no way to know in advance if it is on the right track.

In the spirit of promiscuity in processing, we conjecture that the acquisition process does not wait for sufficient evidence to come in. Rather, it may start positing candidate links as soon as there are as few as *two* comparable items, say *van* and *vanish* (though it may require more, of course).[26] Such candidate links are perhaps marked with low confidence, but they are there, awaiting verification. Most of them are doomed to failure,

---

[24] Notice that in order to guess that two items are morphologically related, learners have to come to the task with the assumption that there *is* such a thing as morphological relatedness, and they have to be biased to look for it. This bias has to be one component of the "language-ready brain."

[25] Nevertheless, the phonological relation may remain and affect processing. Rastle, Davis, and New (2004), in the visual masked priming paradigm mentioned in note 18, show that *-er* is tentatively identified as an affix in *corner* and *brother*, and the remainders prime *corn* and *broth* respectively. In contrast, the *-el* in *brothel*, which (orthographically) does not resemble an English affix, has no effect on *broth*. This suggests that *corner* and *brother* retain phonological links to the *-er* schema.

We should add that there could of course be a word *vannish*, as in *Your car is so big that it's kind of vannish*. Here the meanings and morphosyntactic features are related in the proper way, and so relational links are legitimate.

[26] We can't resist two anecdotal instances of a learner positing a one-off morphological relation based on shared phonology. First, at about 3;0, RJ's grandson responded to someone's remark about Saturday, saying "it makes you sad." Second, at about 4;11, and more sophisticated, he joked, "You know what coffee sounds like? It makes you cough!" In both cases, he has used phonological relations between known words to posit novel morphological and semantic links, in both instances a causative semantic relation. Clark (1993: 40–1) documents a large number of such analyses made by another child between 2;4 and 3;5, some accurate, some far from it.

either when outright counterevidence rolls in (say the actual meaning of *vanish*), or when confirming evidence fails to appear after some time, and the link decays into the noise. But some candidates will be confirmed by later evidence, raising their resting activation and/or their confidence level, and these are the ones that will survive.

An important reason for the acquisition process to be relatively liberal is that it had better not insist on canonical morphological structure, in which all parts of a new word have relational links to other lexical items. There are numerous cases in which the similarities are less than perfect, yet relational links are desirable. Chapter 4 discussed many of these, for example:

- Words whose bases are not linked to free forms, yet the remainder is a legitimate affix. Among such cases are the *-ous* words, some of which have lexical bases (*hazardous, incestuous*) but others do not (*scrumptious, fastidious*). Recall also the *-id* words (*vivid, fetid, valid*), none of which has a lexical base. In these cases, the items can be linked through the morphosyntax as well as the phonology of the suffix, but the base cannot be linked to anything.
- Words whose affix has (near-)unique phonology (*laughter, hatred, comparison*). These examples have strong relational links to the related free form, in phonology, morphosyntax, and semantics. In particular, these examples feature the same semantic relation to their respective bases as more common affixes such as *-tion*. So their relational links are strong, aside from the phonology of the affix.
- Words whose phonological similarity to their base is less than perfect, because of umlaut, ablaut, blending, truncation, or more extensive deviations in vowel quality and stress (*democrat ~ democracy*). In these cases, much more depends on strong morphosyntactic and semantic links in order to make up for the weaker phonological connection.

In short, the acquisition process cannot predict what sort of evidence will arrive when, so it has to posit candidate sister links based on the information it has at the moment, and then let subsequent experience determine which candidates live and which die. If confirming evidence arrives, the candidate's resting activation and confidence level are boosted. If conflicting evidence arrives, the candidate is dropped (as in Propose but Verify). If no further evidence arrives, the candidate gradually decays into the noise.

7.8 Scaling up to schemas

7.8.1 Using Structural Intersection to construct schemas

So far, we have established sister relations among lexical items, by adding relational links to the network. We have not yet isolated the affix *-ish* with its own entry, namely a schema for *-ish* words. So next comes the step of creating schemas and adding them to the lexicon. The intuition behind this procedure is simple. *Piggish, childish, sluggish,* *foolish*, and so on are linked as sisters, as in (5), and so the acquisition process can construct a tentative schema that expresses what they have in common.[27]

(5)   Semantics: a. $[\text{LIKE}(\text{PIG}_1)]_2$ b. $[\text{LIKE}(\text{CHILD}_3)]_4$ c. $[\text{LIKE}(\text{SLUG}_5)]_6$
      Morphosyntax: $[_A \, N_1 \, \text{aff}_7]_2$ $[_A \, N_3 \, \text{aff}_7]_4$ $[_A \, N_5 \, \text{aff}_7]_6$
      Phonology: $/\text{pɪg}_1 \, \text{ɪʃ}_7/_2$ $/\text{tʃajld}_3 \, \text{ɪʃ}_7/_4$ $/\text{slʌg}_5 \, \text{ɪʃ}_7/_6$

Again, stressing the declarative nature of schemas, the acquisition process does not posit a *rule* that *generates* these words. That would be pointless, because the words are already there in the lexicon. Rather, the procedure has to construct a schema that captures the similarities among the instances encountered so far, and which contains variables where the instances differ.

We propose thinking of this procedure in terms of an operation we will call **Structural Intersection (SI)**. This operation can be thought of as like Boolean intersection, except that it is defined over structures rather than sets. The input to SI is two or more structures; its output is a structure that preserves the parts of the input structures that are the same, and which leaves unspecified (or variable) the parts where the input structures do not correspond. For a simple case, the Structural Intersection of ABCD and ABCE would be ABCx.[28]

Applying Structural Intersection to *piggish*, *childish*, and *sluggish* in (5), four things are the same: the semantic function [LIKE (X)], the morphosyntax $[_A \, N \, \text{aff}]$, the phonology /ɪʃ/, and the geometry of their interface links. However, the bases are different, so they are replaced by variables. What also drops out is the item-specific interface links (coindices 1-6), which are replaced by links with variable coindices. The result is the schema (6), which is added to the lexicon.

(6) $(5a) \cap (5b) \cap (5c) =$ Semantics: $[\text{LIKE}(\text{X}_x)]_y$
      Morphosyntax: $[_A \, N_x \, \text{aff}_7]_y$
      Phonology: $/\ldots_x \, \text{ɪʃ}_7/_y$

Once a putative schema is in place, a newly encountered sister (say *foolish*) can undergo Structural Intersection with it. Since the schema represents the maximum that the sisters have in common, this application of Structural Intersection will simply yield the schema again (with an exception to be discussed in a moment), thereby strengthening the schema's resting activation.

At this point, the usual question arises: how many instances does it take to motivate a schema? Just as with relational links, it obviously takes at least two sisters over whose similarities a generalization can be drawn. After hearing two instances, there is no way of knowing whether another instance is going to come along. So, in line with the opportunistic nature of language processing, and in particular Propose but Verify, it might make sense to posit that as soon as a pair can be related as sisters, a tentative

---

[27] To keep things simple, we abstract away from the other *-ish* suffix, which attaches to adjectives and means 'somewhat X', e.g. *warmish* and *lateish*.
[28] SI might be thought of as a "dual" of the operation of unification, which, recalling section 2.2, is a sort of Boolean union over structures. It is intended to have an effect similar to Albright and Hayes's (2003) Minimum Generalization Learner, and Yang's (2005, 2016) invocation of the Yip/Sussman (1997) learning model.

schema is "proposed," which in principle can be "verified" by a third instance. Again, as with words, if it takes a long time for the next instance to come along, we may suppose that the resting activation of the tentative schema gradually decays into the noise. And three instances may not even be enough to save the putative schema from oblivion: as we have remarked at several points, it is not clear when a pattern among sisters is strong enough to warrant a schema. (One possibility is that a schema survives if it can form a relational "hub" in the sense of section 3.8, such that the links of instances to the schema are fewer and stronger than the links among all the individual sisters.)

7.8.2 Establishing the generality of a schema

The process of Structural Intersection has a useful consequence. Applying it to two lexical items yields the narrowest generalization consistent with both of them. For instance, recall the restriction on the $[_V$ A-*en*] schema (*harden, whiten*, etc.): the base must be monosyllabic and end in an obstruent. This comes automatically from applying Structural Intersection to A-*en* words, which all observe the restriction. There is no need to posit a more general rule and then pare it down. At the same time, all idiosyncratic features of individual instances, such as SLOPPY in the semantics of *piggish*, will be excluded from the schema.

Similarly, simplifying to a toy example, suppose the learner derives a schema from encountering *piggish* and *owlish*. Both bases denote animals, so the schema will include the feature ANIMAL in the semantics, and it will support new instances such as *wolfish*. In general, this is a good thing, because it keeps the learner conservative.

But now suppose the learner encounters *childish*, whose base is not an animal. What happens then? First, *childish* will still be detected as a sister of *piggish* and *owlish*. It shares with them the phonology of the affix, the morphosyntax, and the meaning LIKE(X), plus the mildly pejorative affect. However, its relation to the previous instances will be slightly more distant: it only shares ANIMATE with them rather than the narrower ANIMAL. Hence, when *childish* undergoes Structural Intersection with *piggish*, *owlish*, and the existing schema, the outcome will be a new tentative schema, with ANIMATE instead of ANIMAL as the restriction on the semantic variable.

Now what happens? There are two possibilities: (a) the original schema with the narrower variable is discarded; or (b) both schemas are entertained side by side and they fight it out. We favor the second option, because it leaves open various possible outcomes that seem to actually occur. Let us work through some of them.

We first notice that *childish* is an instance only of the ANIMATE -*ish* schema, so activation of *childish* will spread to this schema but not (or not as much) to the ANIMAL -*ish* schema. If more items turn up that satisfy the broader schema but not the narrower one (e.g. *boyish, clownish, ghoulish, devilish*), the ANIMATE -*ish* schema will be strengthened in relation to the narrower ANIMAL schema.

But suppose the learner also encounters more animal -*ish* words such as *bearish* and *mulish*. These will spread activation to both the ANIMAL and the ANIMATE -*ish* schemas. However, they will spread it more to the ANIMAL schema, because they are more like the ANIMAL schema—they have a richer relational link. Hence, if the narrower schema receives enough motivation from relatively numerous instances, it can survive in the face of competition with the broader schema. This is the case where the narrower schema yields what Albright and Hayes (2003) call an "island of reliability."[29]

Next suppose that the learner goes on to encounter *-ish* words like *bookish* or *feverish*, whose bases are not even animate. Then Structural Intersection will create a still broader schema, with fewer semantic restrictions on the base. However, as there are few instances of *-ish* adjectives with inanimate bases,[30] this broader schema might remain weak in comparison to the far more populated ANIMATE *-ish* schema.

Finally, suppose that, having formed an ANIMATE and an ANIMAL *-ish* schema, the learner comes to encounter a lot more *-ish* words with human bases, say *thuggish*, *foolish*, *girlish*, *amateurish*, and so on. Given what we've proposed so far, these would simply be assimilated into the ANIMATE class. This strikes us as wrong. Why should the learner not also recognize a subclass of HUMAN *-ish* words, with its own schema? That is, how can a narrower schema be created when a broader schema is already in place?

Such a schema can be created if we take seriously the promiscuity of processing. So far, we have not said how the acquisition process decides what items Structural Intersection applies to. We have assumed that once a schema is formed, new instances undergo Structural Intersection with it. But there is no reason to restrict it this way. Let us suppose instead that new instances undergo SI not just with the schema but with its instances as well, promiscuously. What will happen? Let us suppose the learner's lexicon at the moment contains *piggish*, *childish*, the ANIMAL *-ish* schema, and the ANIMATE *-ish* schema, and that the learner now encounters *boyish*.

- If *boyish* intersects with *piggish*, the result is the ANIMATE schema.
- If *boyish* intersects with the ANIMATE schema, the result is again the ANIMATE schema.
- If it intersects with the ANIMAL schema, the result is yet again the ANIMATE schema.
- But if it intersects with *childish*, the result is a new schema, a putative HUMAN *-ish* schema.

If enough human cases come along, this schema will acquire sufficient strength to survive in the lexicon.[31]

Figure 7.1 shows the resulting taxonomy of *-ish* schemas (excluding [A-*ish*], e.g. *warmish*).

---

[29] Langacker (1999: 106) similarly recognizes the advantage of lower-level schemas because of their greater degree of overlap with the input.

[30] A CELEX search yields only about a dozen instances of *-ish* words with inanimate bases: *bookish*, *faddish*, *feverish*, *hellish*, *huffish*, *liverish*, *modish*, *nightmarish*, *novelettish*, and *stylish*, plus *pettish*, with a now obscure base. *Lumpish* and *cloddish* are ambiguous. Some of these have the standard [LIKE(X)] semantics, others have more distant semantic connections to their bases.

[31] CELEX yields around forty-five *-ish* words with human bases, and twenty with animals as bases (exact numbers depend on whether speakers are aware of the meaning of the base, some of which are obscure). We presume this is sufficient for both schemas.

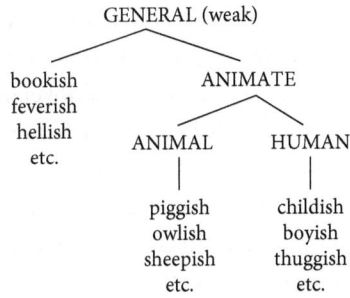

Figure 7.1 Taxonomy of [$_A$ N-ish]

We have described the construction of the taxonomy in Figure 7.1 as if it occurs in the order ANIMAL first, then ANIMATE, GENERAL, and HUMAN in that order. The first three were "bottom-up," in the sense that relatively narrow schemas give rise to broader ones; the last was "top-down," constructing a narrower schema inside a broader one. But given the promiscuity of Structural Intersection and the number and frequency of the various -*ish* words, the order of presentation should not matter in the long run.

Another example of narrow subschemas within broader ones can be drawn from the strong verbs of English, as discussed in Chapter 5. The most general sister schemas for ablaut capture the fact that the present and past tenses of an English verb may be the same except for the vowel. This schema pertains to the entire panoply of possible vowel changes, including singletons like *run ~ ran*. But there likely are also some narrower sister schemas within the ablaut verbs, such as the alternation *sting ~ stung*, with about thirteen instances. Such a hierarchy of schemas and subschemas is possible only if the acquisition process can discover multiple layers of generalization. (And this is essentially the result arrived at by Albright and Hayes's (2003) model of verb acquisition, albeit in a rule-theoretic framework.)

A further such case might be the English zero denominal verbs (section 4.3). The broad schema characterizes the possibility of denominal verbs whose meaning is some function of the base noun. But within this broad schema fall a variety of narrower schemas with a stipulated function, such as 'put N on y' (*butter, paint, saddle*), 'fasten y with N' (*glue, button, nail*), and so on. Some of these, such as the fasteners, are productive within their limited semantic range: when the fastener *velcro* arrived on the scene, the verb *velcro* entered the language with no fuss whatsoever. (Section 2.9 mentioned some similar phenomena in Dutch.) In addition, there are irregular singletons, such as the colloquial verb *door (a cyclist)*, 'open a car door in front of an oncoming cyclist, resulting in a collision' which do not fall under any of the subschemas.

On the other hand, consider the (nonproductive) voicing of final /f/ in English plurals, e.g. *halves, wolves*, and so on (section 4.10). This extends to voicing of /s/ only in the word *houses* (we think). On our story, a learner encountering *houses* will construct a broader schema that includes /s/ as well as /f/. But aside from *houses*, no instances of the schema with /s/ ever turn up, and the instances with /f/ are better supported by the original schema, so the broader schema withers and leaves *houses* as an outlier that differs from the original schema in place of articulation.

We conclude that when the learner encounters a novel item that *almost* conforms to an existing schema (tentative or established), the schema is not automatically broadened to fit. Rather, a new, broader tentative schema is constructed, existing alongside the narrower schema, and the two interact dynamically: sometimes one or the other disappears into the noise, but under certain circumstances both can survive. Conversely, a narrower schema can be constructed within a broad one, and if reliable enough, it can survive as a subschema.

7.9 Scaling up to productive schemas

The learning procedure so far produces tentative schemas on the basis of two or more sister items in the lexicon. It does not yet determine whether the schema in question is productive or not. For this, we return in part to discussion in sections 2.8.2 and 2.9, concerning productivity and the learning of productive schemas.

First, recall that in Relational Morphology, the distinction between a productive and a nonproductive schema is not a difference between two kinds of rules, one "in the grammar" and one "in the lexicon." Rather, the distinction is marked by a diacritic on the schema's variables. So the acquisition procedure is formally simple: it has to set the value of the diacritic.

How does this procedure work? There are (at least) two basic questions. First, given a newly minted schema, does the learner initially assume that it is productive, or that it is nonproductive? Second, what are the criteria for relinquishing that initial assumption?

As suggested in section 2.8.2, we are inclined to think that the initial step is nonproductivity, and productivity is an "upgrade." To push this point further: suppose the learner were to begin by assuming the new schema is productive. Then a nonproductive schema would have to result from a "downgrade." But this would require negative evidence: the absence of a wide range of predicted instances. Given that in many languages (e.g. the Germanic languages), the majority of derivational schemas are nonproductive, it would take a formidable amount of negative evidence to arrive at the correct grammar.

An additional consideration: It is generally accepted in the literature that when learners start overgeneralizing a regular pattern (e.g. **throwed* instead of *threw*), they have constructed a productive rule/schema (in this case, the English regular past tense). This schema is temporarily stronger than the irregular forms it displaces, yielding the famous U-shaped curve of acquisition: children at first get irregulars right, then erroneously assimilate them to regulars, then slowly recover the correct irregular forms. Now suppose that *all* morphological schemas were initially assumed productive. In that case, we would expect far more overgeneralization than the small amount that actually occurs (Pinker 1999: 87). In particular, we would expect overgeneralization of all sorts of morphological patterns, which as far as we know has not been observed.

Suppose, alternatively, that learners initially assume that a newly constructed schema is *non*productive. Since the schema has been constructed on the basis of existing instances in the lexicon, and is linked to them, it already functions relationally. Following the Relational Hypothesis of Chapter 2, a schema is productive if it also can be used generatively. So the learner's task is to seek evidence for the schema being used generatively. If there is no such evidence, the schema fails to be productive. But it still does its relational work, easing processing of its existing instances and easing acquisition of new ones. In morphology, at least in the languages we have looked at here, relatively few schemas achieve fully productive status. This is in line with what Tomasello (2003) and others in child language acquisition refer to as item-based knowledge.

Our hope, then, is that the decision to go productive can be based on positive evidence, and the question is what that evidence might be. The difficulty is that the learner can never encounter the unlimited number of instances that a productive schema affords, and so the evidence must be in some sense indirect—it must be some property of the distribution of instances that the learner *does* encounter. As discussed in section 2.9, a large number of transparent instances helps (Clark 1993); a broad-range variable helps (Goldberg 1996; Pinker 1999); a large number of low-frequency instances helps (Baayen and Lieber 1991; O'Donnell 2015); and a relatively small number of exceptions helps (Yang 2005, 2016).[32] All of these point to a schema being judged productive if it is especially strong, frequent, and general.

Yet we have doubts that this is enough. For instance, the *(all) X-d out* construction, mentioned in section 2.9 (see also Hugou 2013), is completely productive and has a broad-range variable: any noun and any agentive intransitive verb can fill the variable (with perhaps some prosodic preferences). Yet this construction is highly infrequent. So we are led to ask: How long does one have to store instances of this construction before hearing enough of them to justify a schema? And how many more instances— and how long—does it take in order to decide that the schema is productive?

Yang (2005, 2016) addresses these sorts of questions in terms of a criterion for productivity, the Tolerance Principle. He proposes that the acquisition process constructs and retains a putative word formation rule (in present terms, a schema) if the number of exceptions is sufficiently small compared to the number N of bases in the lexicon that fall under the pattern, where "sufficiently small" is defined as "less than $N/\ln N$." He tests this hypothesis with a computational model.

Yang may be right about basing a criterion for productivity of a rule on the relative proportion of its exceptions. But we find many aspects of his proposed mechanism implausible: first, that in lexical access the brain performs a serial search over the lexicon, second, that the brain constructs and regularly updates a ranked list of exceptions

---

[32] —where for Yang, an exception is an item that does not undergo the rule—in our terms, a word that could serve as the base of a schema, but doesn't. He does not address the case of complex forms that lack a related free form, which presumably should count as exceptions as well.

(potential bases that do not undergo the rule), and third, that it performs a numerical calculation over the size of the lists of instances and exceptions.

Yang's mechanism also presumes that if a base can undergo the rule, the output is not listed in the lexicon (e.g. *walk* is stored but *walked* is not). Yet in order to motivate the rule in the first place, the output of at least some instances had to have been listed. Moreover, if the putative rule doesn't work out because it has too many exceptions, its putative outputs are now themselves exceptions and have to be listed. So outputs of the rule must be listed long enough to motivate the hypothesized rule, only to be thrown away when the rule is established. But then, if the rule turns out to be a failure, the entries have to be resurrected, a course of events that we find implausible.

Another proposal for deciding whether an affix is productive, also based on computational modeling, appears in O'Donnell (2015). The task O'Donnell sets for his model is to decide which words in a corpus should be stored in the lexicon and which should instead be generated by rule; in the latter case, the rules are productive. He tests five different mathematical models of how this decision is made, by training them on part of the corpus and testing them on the entire corpus. He shows that one of the models, Fragment Grammars, best fits linguistic and psycholinguistic criteria for productivity.[33] As with Yang's approach, O'Donnell's model does come up with a correct result about the relative productivity of various affixes. However, deriving this result involves computationally intensive statistical calculations that optimize the balance of storage vs. computation for the lexicon as a whole.

In short, it is not clear to us how the procedures employed by Yang and O'Donnell relate to what the brain does. We doubt that the brain counts frequencies and runs statistics over its contents. One might reply that these models are meant to be "computational" in Marr's sense: they are intended only to describe the function the brain is carrying out, without any commitment as to the brain mechanism involved. Having aspired here, insofar as possible, to connect our theory of representation to a theory of processing, we find such a response unsatisfying. However, we acknowledge that such measures may well stand proxy for something that more directly corresponds to neural storage and computation.

We do not ourselves have a theory of what makes a schema go productive. We have however made some progress. It is no longer necessary for the process of acquisition to make such a sharp dichotomy between the storage of lexical items and the computation of items by means of generative rules. We have softened the dichotomy by: (a) treating productive rules as schemas, in the same format as words; and (b) providing the intermediate steps of sister relations and nonproductive schemas on the way

---

[33] As mentioned in note 10, O'Donnell's exposition is based on a *Syntactic Structures*-like formalism for rules, augmented by probabilities assigned to individual rules. This is readily translated into our schema-theoretic formulation, in which relative lexical strength of schemas replaces probability of application of a rule. O'Donnell treats the internal structure of the words and the repertoire of candidate rules as given; this parallels our proposal that the decision for or against productivity is based on the prior existence of nonproductive schemas that motivate and are motivated by a set of sisters.

between full idiosyncrasy and full productivity. We hope to have shown that these are steps in the right direction.

7.10 Conclusions

This chapter has shown that the theoretical constructs of Relational Morphology offer a relatively detailed way of talking about what happens to the mental representations involved in language processing and language acquisition. To sum up, the features of RM that have played a role in our story are:

- Schemas taking the place of rules as the mechanism of combinatoriality
- The unity of words and schemas, which share a common format in the lexicon
- The presence of explicit relational links between lexical items, forming sister relations and rendering the lexicon a richly interconnected network
- The existence of nonproductive schemas
- The unity of productive and nonproductive schemas, depending only on a diacritic on the variable that specifies its (degree of) openness

In addition, we have adopted the following overall positions on processing:

- Lexical entries are encoded in long-term memory as complexes of structured nodes, connected by interface and relational links, following the representational theory.
- Working memory, where transient structures are built online, is a distinct mental faculty from long-term memory, where knowledge of language is stored.
- Processing is opportunistic, using whatever pieces of structure are currently available.
- Within the limits of its capacity, WM can entertain multiple analyses at once, either competing or reinforcing each other.
- "Lexical strength" is a function of resting activation in LTM; its level is raised by repeated experience and possibly lowered by forgetting. (And frequency in a corpus is a proxy for lexical strength.)
- Incoming input and spreading activation in LTM both create transient activation of items above their resting level.

From these premises, we have been able to develop the following points concerning processing:

- Spreading activation is a function of relational links, not just coarse "association." The intensity of spreading activation from one item to another is in part determined by the amount of structure they share, as marked explicitly by relational links.

- "Lexical access" (i.e. retrieving words) is the same process as (the understudied) "rule access" (i.e. retrieving schemas).
- "Cohort" processes in phonology and anticipatory parsing ("prediction") in morphology and syntax are essentially the same process.
- Lexical and structural priming are the same process (though possibly with different strengths and time-courses).
- Nonproductive schemas reinforce the activation of their instances during processing.

And we have developed the following conception of acquisition:

- Acquisition of a word amounts to adding pieces of phonology, syntax, and semantics to the lexical network, and connecting them with interface links.
- Discovering sister relations between a new lexical item and items already in LTM amounts to adding relational links between them.
- Acquisition of a rule amounts to adding a schema to the lexical network—pieces of phonology, syntax, and/or semantics, connected by interface links. In other words, the process of introducing a new rule is formally similar to introducing a new word. There are not separate "modules" or "components" for word learning and rule learning.
- Acquisition of a schema is based on first discovering sister relations among some set of existing items; the schema is created by performing Structural Intersection on the sisters.
- "Propose but Verify" (or some variant thereof) applies equally to word learning and to schema learning. In word learning, it minimally requires one instance to propose and one to verify; in schema learning, it minimally requires two instances to propose a sister relationship and a third to verify it. (More instances are always helpful, though.)
- A schema becomes productive not by moving to a different formal domain, but by adjusting the diacritic on its variable.
- Stored items are not automatically erased from the lexicon when they fall under a productive schema. They are still motivated by the schema in its relational role.

Many of these points are reinterpretations or extensions of well-known positions in the literature. What we hope to have contributed is a strong and direct connection between Relational Morphology's theory of linguistic representations and the theories of language processing and acquisition. We take this to be progress toward our goal of developing a thoroughly integrated theory of language.

8

Applying the tools to other domains

This chapter further pursues the goal of integrating linguistic theory both internally and with theories of other mental faculties. We show how the theoretical constructs of the Parallel Architecture and Relational Morphology can be applied rather naturally to a number of domains outside morphology. Sections 8.1 and 8.2 extend RM's nonproductive schemas and sister schemas to phrasal syntax, highlighting the continuity between word grammar and phrasal grammar. We then turn to other linguistic phenomena that lend themselves to analysis in terms of additional levels of representation, linked by interface components: register, bilingualism, and dialect (section 8.3); orthography (section 8.4); and metrical structure in poetry (section 8.5). Finally, we venture out of language entirely: section 8.6 summarizes general properties of Relational Morphology's lexicon, and suggests that a similar profile can be found for long-term memory in four nonlinguistic cognitive domains.

These discussions are intended as no more than promising sketches. Each of them no doubt deserves at least a book of its own. We bring them up here as an invitation for future research.

8.1 Nonproductive schemas in syntax

Recall the Relational Hypothesis from Chapter 2:

- All schemas can function relationally, capturing and motivating patterns within the lexicon.
- A subset of schemas, the productive ones, can also function generatively, to create novel structures, the "discrete infinity" that is characteristic of natural language. Their instances may but need not be listed in the lexicon.
- The remaining schemas are nonproductive, and all their instances must be listed in the lexicon.

The Parallel Architecture instantiates the principles of both morphology and phrasal syntax as schemas. We therefore might conjecture that the Relational Hypothesis applies not only to morphology but also to phrasal syntax. Section 2.6 addressed part of this conjecture, arguing that phrase structure rules function both generatively and relationally. For instance, the transitive VP schema (1) in its generative function

The Texture of the Lexicon. First edition. Ray Jackendoff and Jenny Audring © Ray Jackendoff and Jenny Audring 2020.
First published in 2020 by Oxford University Press. DOI: 10.1093/oso/9780198827900.001.0001

makes it possible to create novel VPs such as *insult the captain, protect the crocodiles,* and *drink the ink.*

(1)   [$_{\text{VP}}$ V – NP]

But it also functions relationally, motivating transitive VP idioms stored in the lexicon such as *chew the fat, call the shots,* and *shoot the breeze.* In fact, as pointed out in section 2.6, the vast majority of idioms conform to standard phrase structure schemas and are motivated by standard phrase structure rules, functioning relationally. Without the relational function, there is no way both for idioms to be stored and for their syntactic regularity to be captured by canonical phrase structure rules.

The Relational Hypothesis further claims that there exist *non*productive schemas, which support items stored in the lexicon but which cannot be (readily) extended to new cases. However, the idea of nonproductive syntactic rules is more or less anathema to standard syntactic theory, which sees syntax exclusively as what gives language its unbounded creativity.

But this objection makes a logical error. In order to give language its unbounded creativity, it only needs *some* productive patterns. That doesn't mean that *all* syntactic patterns have to be productive. In fact, although syntax tends to be far more reliably productive than morphology, one can find pockets of syntax here and there that are genuinely nonproductive. Here are a number of them (for more, see Culicover 1999, Culicover and Jackendoff 2005 (especially section 1.5), and Kay 2013).

8.1.1 Vulgarities

We saw in section 2.7 that idioms like *drive someone crazy/bananas/*etc. and German *jemandem auf die Nerven/den Sack/*etc. *gehen,* 'getting on someone's nerves', can be characterized in terms of nonproductive schemas. Another case of this sort is the family of intensifiers that can follow any wh-word in a question.

(2)   {who/what/when/where/how} {the hell/the heck/the fuck/the devil/the dickens/in the world/in God's name/etc.}…

This family overlaps with but does not coincide with the family of intensifiers available in the two constructions illustrated in (3) (Hoeksema and Napoli 2008).

(3)   a. beat the hell/heck/crap/piss/*fuck out of NP
       b. get the hell/heck/fuck/*crap/*piss out of here

These distributions suggest that, although these patterns have some degree of generality, individual instances are learned one by one, with occasional improvisation.[1]

---

[1] In his 2016 morphology course, RJ cited *what the piss* as ungrammatical, whereupon a majority of students in the class assured him that they would say it. Language change in progress!

8.1.2 Predicative clichés: *A as an N*

English has a substantial family of clichés (at least 100) with the structure *A as (the/ an) N*. Some make literal sense (4a), some don't (4b). A few, such as those in (4c), are minor elaborations on the structure.[2]

(4) a. black as coal, fat as a pig, gentle as a lamb, light as a feather, pretty as a picture, quick as a wink, red as a beet, rich as Croesus, silent as the grave
  b. clean as a whistle, cool as a moose, fit as a fiddle, loose as a goose, neat as a pin, easy as pie, pleased as punch, right as rain, ugly as sin
  c. bright as a new penny, cold as a witch's tit, honest as the day is long, plain as the nose on your face, scarce as hen's teeth, snug as a bug in a rug

These clichés permit the omission of the first *as* (5a). This is dispreferred with the productive *as*-comparative (5b,c).

(5) a. She's (as) pretty as a picture.   [cliché]
  b. She's as pretty as my Aunt Shirley.   [*as*-comparative]
  c. ?She's pretty as my Aunt Shirley.

Speakers know (some substantial subset of) these clichés—otherwise they couldn't be clichés. But in addition, one's knowledge of English must recognize the pattern that they all exemplify. In present terms, then, this pattern is encoded as a nonproductive schema. It shares structure with the normal productive *as*-comparative schema, including the comparative's semantics.

8.1.3 Place names again

Consider again the two syntactic schemas for place names in (6) (= Chapter 2, (18c,d)). As in Chapter 2, double underlines indicate productive (open) variables, and single underlines designate nonproductive (closed) variables.

(6) a. Syntax: $[_{NP} \text{Det}_6 [_N \underline{\underline{N}}_y \underline{N}_x]]_z$ [e.g. *the Lehigh River*]
  Phonology: $/\eth\vartheta_6 \underline{\underline{\ldots}}_y \underline{\ldots}_x /_z$

  b. Syntax: $[_{NP} \text{Det}_6 \underline{N}_x [_{PP} P_7 [_{NP} \underline{\underline{N}}_y]]]$ [e.g. *the Gulf of Mexico*]
  Phonology: $/\eth\vartheta_6 \underline{\ldots}_x \vartheta v_7 \underline{\underline{\ldots}}_y /_z$

As observed in section 2.7, note 13, these are genuinely syntactic patterns, since they admit adjectival modification after the determiner: *the polluted and over-romanticized Hudson River*, *the shark-infested Bay of Fundy*. Nevertheless, the geographic feature name is not open: an open variable would predict that we could say **the Morris Mountain* (like *the Hudson River*) or **the River of Halle* (like *the Bay of Fundy*).

---

[2] We thank Hildy Dvorak and Linda Taylor for creative assistance in collecting these examples.

Therefore these are syntactic patterns, one of whose variables is closed, hence nonproductive.

8.1.4 Unusual determiners: *What a discovery!*

A curious corner of the English determiner system contains complex determiners of the form *X a*. The pattern has the instances illustrated in (7); there is no fully productive principle behind the list.

(7) *Simple "predeterminer"+ a*
    a. such a tree
    b. what a tree
    c. quite a tree
    d. many a tree
    e. hardly a tree
    f. nary a tree

    Degree word + adjective + a
    g. that beautiful a tree
    h. how tall a tree
    i. as beautiful a tree (as I've ever seen)
    j. *more beautiful a tree
    k. *twenty feet tall a tree
    l. *very/quite tall a tree

The overall pattern is nonproductive, with the six instances in (7a-f)—the last of which is archaic and occurs only in this construction—plus a sub-pattern containing an adjective phrase. Within the adjective phrase, the choice of degree word is closed, restricted to *this, that, so, too, how,* and *as.* But the choice of adjective is fully productive: we can say things like *how tantalizing an idea* or *as ridiculous a movie as I've ever seen.*[3] Figure 8.1 shows the taxonomy under which these forms fall.

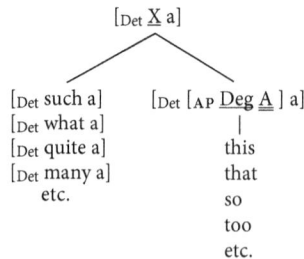

Figure 8.1 Taxonomy of [$_{Det}$ $\underline{X}$ a]

---

[3] The form with an AP is often supplanted in colloquial American English by *how big of a ....* Plurals show further eccentricity, for instance:

(i) a. such/what/*quite/many/*hardly/*nary trees
    b. *that beautiful trees (cf. *trees that beautiful*)
    c. *how beautiful trees (cf. **trees how beautiful*)

So again we have a syntactic pattern with a mixture of productive and nonproductive variables.

8.1.5 Sluice-stranding

Consider next the construction Sluice-stranding (Culicover 1999; Culicover and Jackendoff 2005). In ordinary Sluicing, which is fully productive, a *wh*-phrase appears in place of a full indirect question (8a), and this *wh*-phrase can include a pied-piped preposition (8b). In Sluice-stranding, however, a preposition appears *after* the *wh*-phrase, as if it has been left over from the elided clause (8c).

(8) a. John left the meeting, but I don't know when.   [Sluicing]
    b. John left the meeting, but I don't know with whom.   [Sluicing with pied-piped P]
    c. John left the meeting, but I don't know who with.   [Sluice-stranding]

In ordinary Sluicing with pied-piping, any combination of *wh*-word and pied-pipeable preposition is possible, consistent with the semantics; the combinations need not be stored. However, in Sluice-stranding, it turns out that only certain *wh*-words are possible, and each one permits a different collection of prepositions.

(9) but I don't know
    a. who with/to/from/for/*on/*next to/*about/*beside
    b. what with/for/from/of/on/in/about/at/*before/*into/*near/*beside
    c. how much for/*by/*with [*note also* *how many for]
    d. where to/from/?at/*near
    e. *which (book) with/to/on/in/from/next to/about/beside

Culicover and Jackendoff conclude that both the *wh*-variable and the preposition variable in this construction are closed, and so Sluice-stranding is nonproductive. In other words, there is indeed a surface pattern that can be captured with a general schema [*wh*-word P], but acceptable cases of Sluice-stranding must still be learned individually and listed.

8.1.6 The NPN construction

Our last case of a nonproductive construction is the NPN construction (mentioned in section 3.2; details in Jackendoff 2008). This structure appears in a number of idioms such as *hand over fist*, *hand in glove*, *tongue in cheek*, and *tit for tat*. For five prepositions, the choice of noun is broader, but each preposition has its own semantic and syntactic idiosyncrasies. All of them, however, require the two nouns to be identical.

(10) a. day by day, paragraph by paragraph, country by country
     b. dollar for dollar, student for student, point for point
     c. term paper after term paper, picture after picture
     d. book upon book, argument upon argument
     e. face to face, bumper to bumper

By, for, after, and *(u)pon* are fully open as to the choice of noun, within the semantic constraints of the construction. But one sense of N *to* N, the sense that denotes juxtaposition of parts of two objects, is nonproductive and idiosyncratic. Two people can stand *back to back* but not *front to front*—instead they are *face to face*. *Hand to hand* mostly occurs only in the context of combat; *cheek to cheek* in the context of dancing; *eye to eye* in the context of *seeing eye to eye*. The juxtaposition meaning of *side to side* is usually expressed instead by the idiomatic *side by side*; and, unexpectedly, *side to side* can also denote oscillatory motion, parallel to *back and forth, up and down,* and *round and round.*

In short, the NPN construction as a whole is nonproductive: it has as instances a list of idioms plus the five subconstructions illustrated in (10). In turn, four of the five subconstructions are fully productive, but the one with *to* is nonproductive. Figure 8.2 is the inheritance hierarchy for the construction. (We set aside the question of how to require the two nouns to be identical; something akin to our account of reduplication in Chapter 4 might be appropriate.)

To sum up this section, both productive and nonproductive schemas are found in phrasal syntax as well as morphosyntax. Both sorts of schemas can be encoded in the same form: expressions consisting of some combination of variables and constants. It is not schemas per se that are open or closed; it is the variables in the schemas. Schemas containing open variables are different only in that an indefinite number of further instances can be created online without any effort or sense of "coining," and therefore need not be stored in memory.

In turn, this result supports our proposal to treat word grammar and phrasal grammar as uniformly as possible. Limited productivity is not specific to morphology; it extends across the entire lexicon, including syntax. By marking variables closed vs. open, it is simple to make the distinction between partially and fully productive patterns. In contrast, it is uncomfortable at best to generate patterns such as those illustrated here with standard syntactic rules.

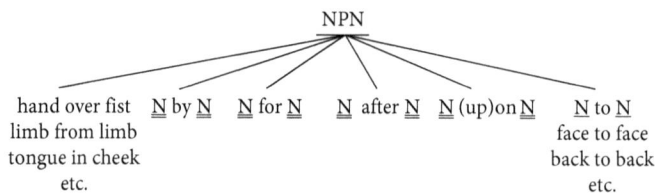

Figure 8.2 Taxonomy of the NPN construction

8.2 Sister schemas in syntax

Another important construct of Relational Morphology is *sister schemas* (Construction Morphology's *second-order schemas*). These are pairs (or n-tuples) of schemas that share structure; however (a) neither is contained in the other, and (b) there is no evidence for a more abstract "mother" schema from which they inherit their shared structure. We have invoked sister schemas for a wide variety of phenomena, including for instance the *-ism/-ist* alternation (section 4.8.2), inflectional paradigms (Chapter 5), and English vowel alternations (section 6.6). Continuing the theme of the previous section, we are led to ask whether there could be sister schemas in phrasal syntax as well—closely related constructions, connected by relational links, neither of which is derived from (or a special case of) the other.

Ideas along these lines have begun to emerge, especially in Construction Grammar. Typically, CxG's constructions are characterized in terms of inheritance: more specialized constructions inherit structure from more general ones, as described in Chapter 3. But a number of researchers (e.g. Cappelle 2006; Booij 2010; Norde 2014; Van de Velde 2014; Booij and Masini 2015; Zehentner 2016; Traugott 2018; Zehentner and Traugott, forthcoming) have noticed the utility of "horizontal" connections between constructions, in addition to standard "vertical" inheritance. The RM formalism invites us to state such "horizontal" connections in terms of sister schemas.

8.2.1 Verb-particle alternations

One candidate pair of constructions comes from Cappelle (2006). He proposes to relate the two possible positions of English particles (*pick up the book* vs. *pick the book up*) in terms of two "allostructions" that are both daughters of a more abstract construction that allows the particle in either position, as in (11). This basically packs the information from both forms into the superconstruction.

(11) (after Cappelle 2006: 18)

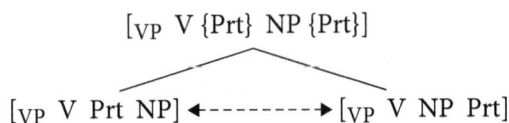

$$[_{VP} \ V \ \{Prt\} \ NP \ \{Prt\}]$$

$$[_{VP} \ V \ Prt \ NP] \longleftarrow \!\!-\!\!-\!\!-\!\!-\!\!-\!\!-\!\!-\!\! \longrightarrow [_{VP} \ V \ NP \ Prt]$$

Stepping back a little, Cappelle's account parallels a morphological analysis that we rejected in sections 3.4 and 3.5, in which *ambition* and *ambitious* were to be related through an abstract "mother" *ambit-*. We proposed instead to treat them as sisters without a lexical base that they could both inherit from. As in that case, if we can relate the two daughter schemas in (11) directly, the abstract mother node does no further work. In fact, in order to learn the more abstract schema, one would first have to acquire the sister schemas and establish their relation.

Here is what a simple version of the particle alternation looks like, couched as a sister relation.

(12) *Particle alternation*

Semantics: a. $[X]_{x,\delta}$ b. $[X]_{y,\delta}$

Syntax: $[_{VP} V_\alpha \, Prt_\beta \, NP_\gamma \,]_x$ $[_{VP} V_\alpha \, NP_\gamma \, Prt_\beta \,]_y$

Coindex x links the unspecified semantics $[X]$ to a syntactic structure with a postverbal particle. Coindex y links the same semantics, $[X]$, to a syntactic structure with a post-object particle. The two meanings are the same, as indicated by the relational coindex δ. In the syntax, the verb, the particle, and the NP are shared by the two constructions (coindices α, β, γ). But the NP and the particle are in opposite order in the two sisters. The overall effect is that if one encounters a particular verb and a particular particle in one of these constructions, one can expect to find them in the other. There is no need for an abstract superconstruction to relate them.

As in Cappelle's account, formulating the particle alternation in terms of sister schemas allows the two configurations to have their own idiosyncrasies. For instance, a post-object particle allows a specifier (underlined in (13a)), and if it is a spatial particle, it alternates with spatial PPs (13b). Both of these options are impossible with postverbal particles (13c,d).

(13) a. I'll look the answer <u>right</u> up. Please carry that box <u>back</u> up.
      b. Please carry that box <u>up the stairs</u>.
      c. I'll look (*right) up the answer.
      d. Please carry up (*the stairs) that box.

This suggests that while the postverbal particle is a simple bare item (Toivonen 2006), the post-object particle is the head of an intransitive PP. In that case, the syntax of schema (12b) might be restated as (14).

(14) Syntax: $[_{VP} V_\alpha \, NP_\gamma \, [_{PP} Prt_\beta] \,]_y$

What is new in this analysis is that the sister schemas involve difference of *position* rather than (or in addition to) difference of content. Difference of position is found only very rarely in morphology (see section 1.6), but of course it is endemic in syntax. Despite all the parallelisms we have observed between morphology and syntax, this difference between the two stands out as an important reason to keep them partly distinct.

8.2.2 The dative alternation

A more complex case is the dative alternation—the relation between the two VPs in (15).

(15) a. give a book to Bill   *(prepositional dative)*
      b. give Bill a book   *(ditransitive dative)*

In early transformational grammar, the relation between these two was routinely described in terms of a derivation along the lines of (16).

(16) $V\ NP_1\ to\ NP_2 \Rightarrow V\ NP_2\ NP_1$

However, it soon became clear (e.g. Oehrle 1976; Erteschik-Shir 1979) that a purely syntactic derivation along the lines of (16) doesn't work, for several reasons.

- There are plenty of verbs that have a prepositional dative but lack a ditransitive dative, for instance *donate, provide, deliver*. Most of these are polysyllabic, but *say* is not.

(17)   a.   present/provide/deliver a book to Bill
            say a few words to Bill
       b.   *present/provide/deliver Bill a book
            *say Bill a few words

- There are plenty of ditransitive verbs without a to-dative counterpart. Many of these are verbs of creation and have a for-dative counterpart instead (18a), but there are also outliers such as *ask* and *cost* (18b).

(18)   a.   bake Bill a cake; fix Bill a drink
            bake a cake for/*to Bill; fix a drink for/*to Bill
       b.   ask Bill a question; [the ticket] cost Bill $5
            ask a question *for/*to/of Bill; *cost $5 to/for Bill

- The indirect object in the ditransitive dative must be an animate Recipient or Beneficiary (19a),[4] and need not be a spatial Goal (19b). Animacy is not necessary in the prepositional dative (19c).

(19)   a.   send Bill/*New York the book [* unless *New York* denotes 'people in New York']
       b.   sell Bill the house [house doesn't move in space]
       c.   send the book to Bill/to New York

In response to the constraint illustrated in (19), many researchers (e.g. Pinker 1989; Goldberg 1995; Larson 2017) take the position that the two dative constructions have different meanings: the prepositional dative denotes caused motion, while the ditransitive dative denotes change of possession. This is incorrect. *Donate* and *bequeath*, for instance, denote change of possession, not caused motion, yet they occur only in the prepositional dative; and *sell the house to Bill* likewise denotes change of possession, not of position. Moreover, *Joe threw Bill the ball* says that Bill came to have the ball

---

[4] Or so it is often asserted. But there are cases where the Recipient is inanimate, for instance *give my car new tires, give the wall a coat of paint* but *give new tires to my car, *give a coat of paint to the wall.*

(i.e. change of possession),[5] but it also entails that the ball arrived at Bill by virtue of caused motion. The correct generalization seems to be that the prepositional dative expresses either change of possession, caused motion, or both; while the ditransitive dative expresses change of possession, plus optional caused motion as the means of change of possession. (See Jackendoff 1990, section 9.5; Rappaport Hovav and Levin 2008.)

The upshot is that the two constructions share a great deal of structure in both syntax and semantics, but neither construction can be based on the other. Nor is there an obvious abstract "mother" schema from which they both inherit—except perhaps at the semantic level. Zehentner and Traugott (forthcoming) suggest that these constructions display a "horizontal" relation. In present terms, they display the symptoms of a pair of sister schemas, along the lines of (20).

(20) a. *Prepositional dative*

        Semantics: $[\text{CAUSE}\,(\text{Agent: }\underline{X},\,[\text{GO}_{\text{poss}}\,(\text{Theme: }\underline{Y}_{\beta},\,\text{TO Recipient: }\underline{Z}_{\gamma})])]_{z,\delta}$

        Syntax: $[_{\text{VP}}\,\underline{V}_{\alpha}\,\underline{\text{NP}}_{\beta}\,[_{\text{PP}}\,P_1\,\underline{\text{NP}}_{\gamma}\,]\,]_z$

        Phonology: $/\ldots\text{tuw}_1\ldots/_z$

    b. *Ditransitive dative*

        Semantics: $[\text{CAUSE}\,(\text{Agent: }\underline{X},\,[\text{GO}_{\text{poss}}\,(\text{Theme: }\underline{Y}_{\beta},\,\text{TO Recipient: }\underline{Z}_{\gamma})])]_{w,\delta}$

        Syntax: $[_{\text{VP}}\,\underline{V}_{\alpha}\,\underline{\text{NP}}_{\gamma}\,\underline{\text{NP}}_{\beta}\,]_w$

        Phonology: $/\ldots/_w$

Taking this apart:

- The semantics, syntax, and phonology of the prepositional dative are linked by interface coindex z; those of the ditransitive are linked by coindex w.
- In the semantics, (20a) and (20b) both denote a caused change of possession (linked by relational coindex δ). If the verb itself also contributes caused motion (e.g. *send, deliver, throw*), the two semantic functions coexist in tandem, as in *Joe threw Bill the ball.*
- In the syntax, the two VPs share a verb (coindex α) and two NP arguments (coindices β and γ), linked to the Theme and Recipient respectively. However, the arguments are in opposite order in the VP, and (20a) embeds the second NP within a PP. The choice of arguments is free, but the verb variable is closed: the verbs that participate in the dative alternation have to be listed.[6]

---

[5] Actually, all that is necessary in some cases is that the Agent *intends* for the Recipient to come to have the Theme, as seen in (i)–(ii).

(i) Susan threw Bill the ball, but he didn't catch it.
(ii) Amy wrote Joe a letter, but she never sent it.

[6] Although only a restricted class of verbs appears in the ditransitive, it is possible that any verb that appears in the ditransitive with the proper meaning (e.g. excluding *envy*, which is not transfer of possession) can also be used in the prepositional dative (as suggested by Bresnan and Nikitina 2009, citing corpus data). If this proves to be the case, the V in the ditransitive schema (20b) can be upgraded to productive.

- Finally, in phonology, the preposition in (20a) is pronounced *to* (coindex 1). The rest of the phonology is filled in by the particular verb and the NPs.

In short, neither of the schemas in (20) is a special case of the other; nor is there a more abstract schema from which they both inherit their shared properties. Thus the dative alternation is a prime candidate for sister schemas in syntax: if one finds a verb that falls under one of the schemas, it is possible that it will fall under the other as well.[7]

8.2.3 Alternations with symmetric predicates

Another possible candidate for sister schemas is the characteristic alternation of symmetric predicates, illustrated in (21).

(21) a. John and Harry are similar. This shoe and that shoe match. *(Conjoined structure)*
    b. John is similar to Harry.   This shoe matches that shoe.   *(Nonconjoined structure)*

Many predicates participate in this alternation, for instance the verbs *collide, coincide,* and *match,* the adjectives *similar, parallel, congruent, homologous,* and *simultaneous,* and even nouns such as *friends, colleagues,* and *cousins.* Early work (e.g. Gleitman 1965; Lakoff and Peters 1966; McCawley 1971) attempted to derive one of these from the other, with questionable success. For one thing, a syntactic derivation from one to the other is ugly under anyone's theory. But in addition, the conjoined structure cannot be consistently derived from the non-conjoined structure, because the conjoined subject can be replaced by a plural NP such as in (22), which has no nonconjoined counterpart.

(22) These boys are similar. These shoes match.

Nor can the nonconjoined structure be derived straightforwardly from the conjoined structure, because there are variants on how the postverbal NP is realized, depending on the choice of predicate.

(23) a. X and Y intersect.   X intersects Y.
    b. X and Y rhyme.   X rhymes **with** Y.
    c. X and Y are identical. X is identical **to** Y.
    d. X and Y are cousins.   X is a cousin **of** Y.

---

[7] We set aside many further details of the dative alternation, such as the for-dative (Jackendoff 1990), the dative alternation in light verb constructions (*give Bill a kiss/give a kiss to Bill*) (Bresnan and Nikitina 2003; Wittenberg and Snedeker 2014), and prosodic and information structure constraints (Arnold et al. 2000; Wasow 2002). In particular, the interaction of argument structure alternations with prosodic and information structure effects presents an important challenge to construction-based approaches, including ours.

In other words, neither the conjoined structure (21a) or the nonconjoined structure (21b) can be derived from the other. Nor do we think it possible to posit an abstract construction from which they both inherit. The best approach (we think) is to treat them as sister constructions with a great deal of shared structure, such that if a predicate denotes the proper sort of semantic relation and appears in one of these syntactic frames, it almost certainly appears in the other. (An exception is *resemble*, which only occurs in the nonconjoined form.)

It might be argued (as with the dative alternation) that the two constructions differ in meaning, so there is no need to relate them. For instance, Tversky (1977) argues that (21a) and (21b) are actually not synonymous: (21a) is symmetrical but (21b) is not. His evidence is that experimental subjects judge sentences like (24a) to differ in meaning from sentences like (24b), whereas (24c,d) are synonymous.

(24) a. North Korea is similar to Red China.
      b. Red China is similar to North Korea.
      c. North Korea and Red China are similar.
      d. Red China and North Korea are similar.

However, even if the meanings of the two constructions are slightly different, the grammar should still be able to express the general relation between them, factoring out the differences in the usual fashion. (After all, *-ism* and *-ist* words don't mean the same, but they are still in a sister relation.)

Furthermore, Gleitman et al. (1996) demonstrate that these predicates are themselves inherently symmetrical. In the conjoined structure, the symmetry emerges in its pure form, according the participants equal status. The difference in meaning in (26a,b) arises from the semantic prominence associated with subject position: the subject is understood to be the distinguished or "figural" member of the pair, in the sense of Talmy (1985)—the individual to whom attention is being drawn. That is, even though the sentences differ in meaning, the predicate *similar* is itself still symmetrical.

Within this sister relation, individual predicates specify whether they require a preposition, and if so, which one. On the other hand, the choice of preposition is limited to *with, to, from* (as in *differ from*), *of*, and perhaps a few others, suggesting that there might be some subschemas for particular common choices. We leave the question open.

Formalizing this sister relation presents a challenge both in the semantics and the syntax, and we will not attempt it here. Crucially, the relation must be stated in a sufficiently general fashion to include verbs such as *match*, adjectives such as *similar*, and nouns such as *cousin*. Moreover, as McCawley (1971) points out, the same alternation can also be found inside complex nominals.

(25) a. John('s) and Harry's resemblance   *(Conjoined structure)*
         the resemblance between John and Harry
         John('s) and Harry's collaboration
         a collaboration between John and Harry

b. John's resemblance to Harry   *(Nonconjoined structure)*
   John's collaboration with Harry

In addition, certain verbs display a similar alternation in object position.

(26) a. Pat mixed/combined the green paint and the blue paint.   *(Conjoined)*
      b. Pat mixed/combined the green paint with the blue paint.   *(Nonconjoined)*

In short, in a full statement of the sister schemas for symmetrical predicates, the syntax has to be general enough to encompass all these possibilities. We leave open how this is accomplished.

8.2.4 Nominals of particle verbs

For a further case where constructions are clearly related, but it is impossible to state a mother that is neutral between them, consider the nominals of particle verbs. This relation is pointed out for Dutch by Booij and Masini (2015), and the same relation obtains in English.

(27) X blows up ~ blowup
      X picks Y up ~ pickup
      X throws Y away ~ throw-away
      X knocks Y out ~ knockout

The nouns are semantically related to the particle verbs in more or less the usual way that nominals are related to verbs: a blowup is an event of something blowing up; a pickup is something or someone that is picked up, or the action of picking something or someone up; a throw-away is something that's thrown away, and so on. However, there is no way to state a common syntactic form shared between them, and they share only parts of their semantics. So the case for an abstract mother is slim. Moreover, following the venerable arguments of Chomsky (1970) for the Lexicalist Hypothesis, there is no way to derive one from the other or to derive both from a common underlying form.

   However, we can again treat the alternation in terms of sister schemas, like (28) (we omit the semantics).

(28) a. Syntax: $[_{VP}\,V_\alpha\,Prt_\beta\,<NP>]$ b. Morphosyntax: $[_N\,V_\alpha\,Prt_\beta]$

The verb and the particle are shared, but the optional object in the phrasal construction is not. What is interesting here is that there is a sister relation between a syntactic phrase on one hand and a morphological compound on the other—that is, the sister relation cuts across components of the grammar.

   In all four of these cases, we find a pair of syntactic patterns that intuitively should be related by the grammar, and that do not lend themselves to deriving one pattern from the other or to positing a mother schema under which they can both fall. We have shown that sister schemas offer an insightful way of encoding them. Looking more broadly, these analyses invite the question of whether this is an attractive way to capture argument structure alternations in general, and if so, what the syntactic world looks like from such a perspective. We cannot hope to answer this question here. What we hope to have shown, though, is that there is at least a useful place for sister schemas in syntax as well as in morphology.

Surprisingly, this description of syntactic alternations in terms of related constructions evokes an honorable precedent, namely Zellig Harris's (1957) notion of transformations. Unlike the transformations of his student Chomsky, which rewrote one syntactic structure as another through movement, insertion, or deletion, Harris's transformations were conceived as relationships between constructions, motivated by shared co-occurrence restrictions—in our terms, shared variables. Harris (1957) covers many of the same phenomena as early Chomskyan generative grammar (e.g. Chomsky 1957; Lees 1960), with many parallel analyses, for instance the idea of a simply structured kernel sentence and the treatment of the passive auxiliary as a discontinuous *be+en*. Could Harris have been right about how to account for these phenomena?[8]

8.3 Speech register, bilingualism, and dialect

8.3.1 Register

We next turn to extensions of the Parallel Architecture that involve adding further levels of representation and further interfaces to the standard levels of phonology, syntax, and semantics. For a first case, let us see how the PA might handle the issue of *register*. Every speaker has command of various registers keyed to various social situations. In a traditional view of the lexicon, it is easy to see how to mark *words* for register: a register attribute can be added to a word's lexical entry. In the PA, this amounts to adding a further tier or level of representation linked to a word's phonology, (morpho)syntax, and semantics.[9] For instance, (29a,b) are possible lexical entries for *surely* and *asshole*, one (relatively) formal (or even pompous) and one casual and vulgar. On the other hand, many words, perhaps most, are unmarked for register, for instance *giraffe* (29c).

(29)

	a.	b.	c.
Semantics:	[ONE CAN BE SURE]$_1$	[DESPICABLE PERSON]$_2$	[GIRAFFE]$_3$
Syntax:	Adv$_1$	N$_2$	N$_3$
Phonology:	/ʃʊrli/$_1$	/æʃowl/$_2$	/dʒəræf/$_3$
Register:	formal$_1$	casual/vulgar$_2$	–

---

[8] It should go without saying—but we will say it anyway—that these parallels do not sway us toward Harris's anti- (or a-)mentalism, nor toward his belief that all of grammar can be discovered through sufficiently thorough examination of privileges of co-occurrence, without appeal to meaning.

[9] Höder (2014) and others regard this register attribute as belonging to pragmatics.

This "register tier" is pretty simple. Its possibilities amount to an enumeration of the possible registers; there doesn't seem to be any need for hierarchical structure (at least not in English). Nevertheless, it is a dimension along which lexical items can vary, one that is independent of (or orthogonal to) the standard levels of phonology, syntax, and semantics.

The register feature is not just for language. It is actually an abstraction over social situations, playing a role in social relations between interlocutors, in principles of social interaction (i.e. manners), and even in determining what it is appropriate to wear on what social occasions. We leave it to sociolinguistics to characterize the range of possible registers in language and their culture-dependence. However, an independent question is how register interacts with grammar, and how to capture that interaction *within* a theory of grammar. This is the issue we are concerned with here.

The basic principle is that register should harmonize across the utterance (and with the social situation). By "harmonize," we mean that the register features of individual items in an utterance (or conversation) should not clash, while items that are unmarked for register are compatible with any register. So, for instance, (30a,b) do not clash, but (30c) does. (Exclamation points annotate register clash.)

(30) a.   Surely, Bill bought a giraffe.
            [formal]
      b.   That asshole bought a giraffe.
                [casual]
      c.   !!Surely, that asshole bought a giraffe.
            [formal]   [casual]

In other words, different registers do not require entirely separate lexicons. Rather, certain items in the lexicon are appropriate in one register and inappropriate in others, and the remainder are indifferent to register.

Grammatical constructions also can be marked for register. For instance, wh-phrases with pied-piped prepositions (31a) belong to a formal register, and paratactic conditionals (31b) are informal or casual.

(31) a. With whom are you talking?
         The person with whom I'm talking is a doctor.
      b. That guy shows up here again, I'm outta here.
         You break my chair, I break your arm.

In traditional generative grammar, the register of a grammatical construction has to be associated with the application of a rewrite rule—either a phrase structure rule or a transformation. For instance, the operation of pied-piping with wh-movement somehow has to be marked as formal, and a putative rule of *if-then* deletion for (31b) has to be marked as informal. (This is the way Labov (1969) built variable rules into the grammar in the early days; see also Cedergren and Sankoff (1974).) In other words, the standard framework requires two entirely different mechanisms to code register in the grammar—one for words and one for rules; and it is not clear how they interact with each other.

The Parallel Architecture eliminates this problem, because it encodes rules of grammar as pieces of structure stored in the lexicon. For instance, a pied-piped preposition is formalized as a partial treelet that can be associated with wh-questions and relative clauses, as in (32a); and the paratactic conditional is formalized as a meaningful construction along the lines in (32b). Since these are lexical entries, they can be coded with a register feature, exactly like words.

(32) a. Syntax: $[_{S/CP} [_{PP} P [_{NP} +wh]] \ldots]_x$
         Register: $formal_x$
      b. Semantics: $[IF \ X_y \ THEN \ Y_z]_w$
         Syntax: $[S_y, S_z]_w$
         Register: $casual_w$

The register features of syntactic/semantic constructions, just like those of words, have to harmonize with the rest of the utterance. A clash occurs when a formal item, *either* a word *or* a construction, co-occurs with a casual item, again either a word or construction. Here are some combinations.

(33) a.   *Casual conditional construction + formal word*
           You so much as mention politics, (!!surely) Bill gets mad.
           (cf. *You so much as mention politics, I'm tellin' ya, Bill gets mad*)

      b.   *Casual conditional construction + formal wh-construction*
           !!You so much as mention politics, the people to whom you're talking get mad.
           (cf. *. . . the people you're talking to get mad*)

      c.   *Formal wh-construction + casual conjunction construction + casual word*
           !!The person to whom me and Bill were talking is an asshole.
           (cf. *The guy me and Bill were talking to . . .*)

In other words, by adding a register tier to lexical entries, the Parallel Architecture offers a simple unified description of register harmony for words and grammatical constructions alike. And since the register feature is also keyed to features of the social situation, the use of appropriate register in appropriate situations falls out naturally too.

An important part of the account is that we do not need multiple "grammars," one for each register. Rather, there is one grammar/lexicon, and register differences are confined to just those lexical items where it makes a difference. The rest of the grammar/lexicon is neutral and harmonizes with items from any register.

8.3.2 Bilingualism

This approach to register also lends itself to encoding the knowledge of an individual who speaks two or more languages. This is obviously important to linguistic theory as well as to sociolinguistics, given the significant proportion of bi- and multilingual speakers across the world. Here we abstract away from important issues such as the speaker's relative command of L1 and L2 and the age at which L2 has been acquired. We focus on how knowledge of L1 and of L2 is segregated, so that the speaker does not mix words and grammatical constructions indiscriminately.

Various proposals, including some that adopt a Parallel Architecture framework (e.g. Francis 2012; Sharwood Smith and Truscott 2014), in effect claim that each language has its own segregated "bin" (or module) of words and rules of grammar (or parameter settings, as in Yang (2002), for instance). Language use at any particular moment is confined to one bin, though possibly with influences from other bins. Alternatively, in some semantic network models of the lexicon, L1 and L2 each have a so-called "language node" in memory, and every word is linked to one or the other of them (e.g. Grainger, Midgley, and Holcomb 2010). When one of the language nodes is "turned on," the speaker is biased to speak and understand that language.

Each of these proposals requires a way to identify which language each word belongs to. The "bin" theory does this by listing which words are in each bin. The "language node" theory does it by establishing a link between each word and one of the language nodes. We propose to do the same thing in a more direct way: added to each word is a "language feature" whose value is L1 or L2 (or as many languages as the speaker commands), in direct parallel to the register feature just proposed. De Bot, Lowie, and Verspoor (2005), Höder (2012), Breuer (2015), and Archibald and Libben (2019) propose a similar language feature.

This language feature is in effect a further level of representation, extrinsic to phonology, syntax, and semantics—and like register, formally very simple. In fact, the language feature actually aligns a great deal with the register feature, since choice of language in multilinguals is often keyed to particular social situations—certainly who one is talking to, but also issues of ingroupness, prestige, and so on. So there is a reason beyond pure linguistic formalism for treating them the same way. (De Bot et al. and Breuer also extend the language feature to register.)

(34) illustrates with the lexical entries for a pair of translation equivalents in an English-German bilingual. Notice that the relational link is on the semantic level only (coindex 3); this is what marks the two words as translation equivalents.

(34) Semantics: a. $DOG_{1,3}$ b. $DOG_{2,3}$
      Morphosyntax: N_1 $[N, \text{MASC}]_2$
      Phonology: $/dɔg/_1$ $/hʊnt/_2$
      Language: $L1_1$ $L2_2$

An alternative would be to have just one semantic structure $DOG_{1,2}$ that is linked to both sets of syntactic and phonological structures. (Höder (2012: 248) adopts this solution and calls the shared semantics a "lexical diaconcept.") We prefer the treatment in (34), because it allows for differences in shades of meaning between nearly synonymous items, as is common.

Again, in the Parallel Architecture, not just the words but also the rules of grammar are lexical items—pieces of stored structure in the lexicon. So they too can be assigned a language feature. (35) shows lexical items for an English-German bilingual:

approximations of the respective phrase structure rules for main clauses, annotated with language features. Here, unlike (34), there is no associated semantics or phonology; these are just pieces of syntax associated with language features.

(35) Syntax: a. $[_S \text{ NP-Aux-VP}]_4$ b. $[_{\text{Smain}} \text{ XP-VP}_{\text{main}}]_5$
       Language: L1_4 L2_5

As argued in Chapter 6, the lexicon also contains phonotactic schemas, as well as the interface schemas that relate phonology to precise phonetic realization. These too differ from language to language, and the language feature can be attached to them as well.

What keeps a speaker from mixing languages indiscriminately, then, is the need (or desire) for the language feature to remain constant across the utterance (or conversation), in parallel to harmony in register. Unlike register, though, there are not a lot of neutral items: nearly everything in the lexicon has to be marked for which language it belongs to (unless the languages are very close relatives, say Dutch and Frisian).

Of course bilingual speakers do not always harmonize completely: they may borrow and code-switch. So the principle of language harmony is not absolute. This is not the venue to try to work out the grammar of borrowing and codeswitching. However, in the present terms, the basic formal question for borrowing and codeswitching is not how to jump from one entire grammar to another, but the more localized issue of how the grammar negotiates disharmony at particular points in the syntax.

Given representations like (34) and (35) and the sort of promiscuous processing described in Chapter 7, one might expect a bilingual brain to spread activation of both words and schemas across languages, especially on the semantic level. Psycholinguistic research bears this expectation out. According to Kroll et al. 2015:

> ...both languages are always active when bilinguals listen to speech, read words in either language, and plan speech in each of the two languages .... [N]ot only does the native language influence the L2, but the L2 comes to influence the L1 once bilinguals are adequately proficient in the L2,... The parallel activation of the two languages imposes the requirement that bilinguals learn to regulate the resulting cross-language competition.

Moreover, bilinguals apparently accomplish this regulation in a way that affects domain-general processes of resolving competition among candidates (Bialystok 2015). These results are just about what the PA's view of the lexicon and processing predicts.

8.3.3 Dialect

Somewhere between register and choice of language is the command of two or more dialects of the same language. In this case, there will not be two distinct sets of words and schemas with different language features. Rather, as with register, many words and many grammatical schemas will be neutral as to dialect. But there also will be many dialect-marked words, dialect-marked grammatical constructions, and dialect-marked phonetic realizations of the phonological system. Again the principle is to require harmony on the dialect feature, where the neutral items are acceptable with either choice.[10]

A welcome implication of this approach is that linguistic theory does not have to make a sharp distinction between "languages" and "dialects." According to the present treatment, if two systems have a relative preponderance of neutral items, suitable for either system, we are inclined to call them dialects of each other. If they have a relative preponderance of language-marked items, we are inclined to call them different languages. For in-between cases, we are not forced to make a decision, at least on linguistic grounds. This strikes us as the correct conclusion. (To be sure, there may well be political reasons to distinguish two closely related languages, as in Francis (2016); we recall Max Weinreich's storied characterization of a language as "a dialect with an army and a navy.")

We wish to stress that we intend our analysis only to be suggestive, showing that a class of intensely studied phenomena, typically lying outside of standard issues of formal grammar, can be recast in terms of the Parallel Architecture. However, two important points have emerged. First, the continuity between words and rules in the PA allows a unified account of how consistency of register, language, and dialect are maintained, instead of requiring separate accounts for the lexicon and for the grammar. Second, distinctions among registers and among dialects do not require separate whole grammars; rather, the differences are localized in the actual items and constructions that are different. We take this to be a nice result.[11]

8.4 Orthography

Next let us consider orthography. It is fairly obvious that an alphabetic or syllabic writing system must consist of a mapping between visible letter forms and phonological structure. Depending on the writing system, the mapping may involve morphosyntactic and/or semantic structure as well. In a writing system of any complexity, the mapping is many-to-many, not one-to-one. This makes it impossible to state a set of fully productive rules that derive orthographic form from phonology or vice versa.

---

[10] This is actually overly simplistic. Suppose an individual speaks two dialects of a language, say standard German and Berlin German, plus an unrelated language, say Japanese. It will not do to leave the elements common to the two German dialects neutral for language, because that would imply that such items would be usable in Japanese as well. This situation requires a more ramified treatment of the language feature. We will not pursue it here.

[11] Notice that the "bin" theory of bilingual memory has to account for items that are language or dialect neutral by placing them in both bins, somehow connected to each other; and the "language node" theory has to connect neutral items to both language nodes. In other words, both approaches say that neutral items encode more information than monolingual items. The present approach, in which neutral items are unmarked, says that neutral items require *less* information. We think this is an advantage for the present approach, but don't have strong arguments.

Rather, the relation between them has much more the flavor of the Parallel Architecture: two independent levels of structure linked by a set of interface schemas, some general and some very specific. Different writing systems employ different repertoires of orthographic forms and different interfaces to phonology (or in the case of logographic systems, to morphosyntax and/or semantics; see Coulmas (2003) for a survey, and Breuer (2015) for a proposal similar to ours).

Looking a little more closely, it makes sense to divide this interface between phonology and vision in two, by inserting between phonology and letter forms an intermediate level of representation that we might call **orthographic structure**. The rationale behind this extra complexity is that writing systems present two independent dimensions of variation. The first dimension is the "rules of spelling," which define a repertoire of **graphemes** (loosely, an alphabet), and stipulate the relation of grapheme sequences to linguistic structure. The second dimension is the realization of graphemes in visible form. The rules of spelling do not care at all about how graphemes are written in different fonts or about the choice of printing vs. cursive. For example, the visible form "s" in one font and the quite dissimilar "*ƨ*" in another both count as the grapheme <s>. For that matter, braille and sign language finger-spelling conform to the rules of spelling; they just offer alternative mappings from graphemes to letter forms. We thus arrive at an architecture along the lines of Figure 8.3. (For the moment, we ignore the contributions of morphosyntax and semantics.)

The level of orthographic structure is therefore an abstraction. When we talk about the spelling of a word, we are actually referring to its orthographic structure, not precisely how it looks. As is customary, we will notate orthographic structure with angle brackets.

One of the primitive relations in the orthographic level is '<x> precedes <y>', usually corresponding to phonological order. The letter form level realizes this relation spatially (except in finger-spelling!), and different writing systems realize it differently: left to right, right to left, or top to bottom. This choice is therefore part of the grapheme-to-letter form interface.[12]

Turning more specifically to the orthographic level: In an alphabetic writing system, the basic orthographic units are the letters of an alphabet (for convenience, we set aside non-alphabetic systems). In a system that distinguishes upper and lower case, this distinction matters for spelling, so it is a feature of graphemes. The orthographic inventory also contains numerals, special signs like <&> and <$>, and punctuation marks like <.> and <?>. Diacritics such as apostrophe, umlaut, cedilla, and accents might be considered orthographic "bound forms," because they have to be attached to another grapheme. The inventory also has to contain space, < >, so that a writing system can specify whether it uses spaces between words or not (early Greek

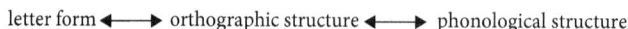

letter form ◄───► orthographic structure ◄───► phonological structure

Figure 8.3 Architecture of writing systems

---

[12] Some configurations are exceptions to the normal correspondence of orthographic and phonological order, for instance <$5>, pronounced *five dollars*, and German <29>, pronounced *neunundzwanzig* 'nine-and-twenty.'

and Latin did not: Coulmas 2003), or whether compounds are spelled with spaces (in English, sometimes) or not (in German).

For our purposes, the real interest is in the interfaces between the orthographic level and linguistic structures. Not all the conditions are purely phonological, for example:

- The conventions for capitalization depend on (morpho)syntax: upper case is assigned to the first grapheme of a sentence, to the first grapheme of a proper name, and, in German, to the first grapheme of a noun.
- The use of spaces (or not) in compounds depends on recognizing compounds in morphosyntax.
- The use of spaces in general is associated with delimiting words, and sometimes serves as an intuitive criterion for wordhood (see Haspelmath 2011 for discussion).
- Spelling sometimes depends on recognizing particular morphosyntactic affixes. For instance, phonological /əs/ at the end of a word is spelled <ous> if it is linked to the affix of the $[_A - ous]$ schema. But the same phonological /əs/ is spelled <ess> when it is linked to the end of the $[_N$ A-*ness*] schema. (See also Berg and Aronoff 2017.)

Let's write some interface schemas. A simple spelling rule for German is that /ə/ as a syllabic nucleus is invariably spelled <e>, e.g. /mɪt:ə/ = <Mitte>.[13] We can encode this by writing a schema that links the orthographic tier with phonological structure, as in (36).

(36)   Phonology: $/ə_1/$
       Orthography: $<e_1>$

However, <e> does not always spell /ə/, e.g. <Bett> = /bɛt/; so the regularity only goes in one direction, from schwa to <e>. In order to formalize this one-way entailment, we adapt the underlining notation for productivity from Chapter 2. There, a double underline signified a productive variable, and a single underline signified a nonproductive variable. In the present case, we wish to say that the mapping from /ə/ to <e> is productive—every /ə/ is spelled <e>; but the mapping in the other direction is nonproductive—only some <e>'s are pronounced /ə/. We notate this by doubly underlining /ə/ and singly underlining <e> in the schema, as in (37).

(37)   Phonology: $/\underline{\underline{ə}}_1/$
       Orthography: $<\underline{e}_1>$
       "/ə/ is always spelled <e>; <e> is sometimes pronounced /ə/."

Hence if one encounters a new spoken word whose pronunciation contains schwa, it will be spelled <e>, but an <e> in a new written word will not necessarily be pronounced schwa.[14]

---

[13] Schwa can also appear as an offglide in a diphthong, in which case it may be spelled <r>, as in /ʃtɛən/ = <Stern>.

[14] For sticklers: The underline notation here has a slightly different interpretation than in morphology. There, the underlining pertains to the productivity of variables, whereas here it is treated as a property of constants. A more compatible notation for orthography might be (i). If desired, one can think of (37) as an abbreviation for (i), paralleling the treatment of English vowel shift in section 6.6.

(i)   Phonology: $/\underline{...}_x\, \underline{\underline{ə}}_1\, \underline{...}_y/_z$
      Orthography: $<\underline{...}_x\, e_1\, \underline{...}_y>_z$

We can borrow the Elsewhere Condition from morphology. Consider for instance the treatment of /ʃ/ in German. Normally this is spelled as the trigraph <sch>, as in (38).

(38)   Phonology: /ʃ$_2$/
        Orthography: <sch$_2$>

"<sch> is always pronounced /ʃ/; /ʃ/ is sometimes spelled <sch>."
e.g. <Schnee> = /ʃneː/ 'snow'; <schauen> = /ʃawən/ 'look'; <Fisch> = /fɪʃ/ 'fish'

However, in one circumstance, /ʃ/ is spelled <s>, namely syllable-initially before /p/ and /t/, i.e. obstruents. (39) shows the schema. (/p/ and /t/ are the only obstruents that can appear in an onset cluster in German.)

(39)   Phonology: /[$_\sigma$ ʃ$_3$ [-son].../
        Orthography: <s$_3$>

"Syllable-initial /ʃ/ before an obstruent is always spelled <s>; <s> is sometimes pronounced /ʃ/."
e.g. <sprechen> = /ʃprɛxən/ 'speak'; <stehen> = /ʃteːən/ 'stand'

The phonological context in (39) is more specific than that in (38), so, by the Elsewhere Condition, (39) blocks (38) in this particular context. Thus (38) can be considered completely productive, aside from being blocked by (39).

Next, consider the pronunciation of the grapheme <s>, which maps to several pronunciations beside that in (39). Syllable-initially before vowels it is pronounced /z/. This can be notated as (40).

(40)   Phonology: /[$_\sigma$ z$_4$ V.../
        Orthography: <s$_4$>

"Syllable-initial /z/ followed by a vowel is always spelled <s>; <s> is sometimes pronounced /z/."
e.g. <sein> = /zajn/ 'be'; <suchen> = /zuxən/ 'seek'

In all other circumstances, <s> is pronounced /s/. This appears to be the productive default, blocked by both (39) and (40).

(41)   Phonology: /s$_5$/
        Orthography: <s$_5$>

"<s> is always pronounced /s/; /s/ is sometimes spelled <s>." (Blocked by (39)-(40))
e.g. <Preis> = /pʁaɪs/ 'prize'; <das> = /das/ 'the.NEUT.SG.NOM/ACC'

Other ways of spelling /s/, which also block (41), include <ss> and <ß>. (42) gives an overview of this fragment of German spelling rules; the numbered interface links correspond to schemas (38)-(41).

(42)   Phonology: /ʃ/   /z/   /s/

            (38)   (40) (41)
                 (39)

        Orthography: <sch>   <s>   <ss>   <ß>

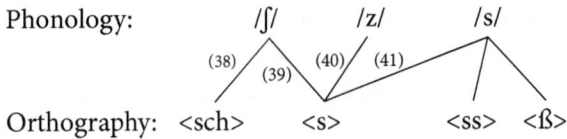

Next we look at the rule for capitalizing German nouns. The default value of the case feature on graphemes is lower case, as stated in (43a). The more specific schema in (43b) blocks (43a) by the Elsewhere Condition. For these schemas, we need a variable that ranges over graphemes; we enlist the symbol λ (as in "letter") for this purpose.

(43)   a. *Default lower case grapheme*
           Orthography: < [λ, lower case] >
        b. *Capitalization of German nouns*
           Morphosyntax: $\underline{\underline{N}}_x$
           Orthography: < [λ, upper case] ...>$_x$

(43b) says that the first grapheme of a sequence that spells a noun is upper case. (43b) is productive in mapping from noun to upper case (N is double-underlined), but there are other contexts such as sentence-initially that also require upper case, so the mapping in the other direction is not absolute.

More marginal patterns can also be accommodated. For example:

- The English trigraph <igh> has only about twenty instances, such as <high>, <sigh>, <fight>, <light>, which are all monosyllabic and end in either /aj/ or /ajt/. It is invariably pronounced /aj/. Its schema appears in (44).

(44)   Phonology: /$_\omega$ [$_\sigma$...$\underline{aj}$(t_9)] /$_x$
        Orthography: <...$\underline{\underline{igh}}$($t_9$)>$_x$

        "<igh(t)> is always pronounced /aj(t)/ word-finally; word-final aj(t) is sometimes spelled <igh(t)>."

- The sequence <eigh>, with only about ten instances (e.g. <weigh>, <sleigh>, <eight>, <freight>) has similar conditions[15] and is invariably pronounced /ej/, with one outlier, <height> = /hajt/. Its schema is (45).

(45)   Phonology: /$_\omega$ [$_\sigma$...$\underline{ej}$(t_9)] /$_y$
        Orthography: <...$\underline{\underline{eigh}}$($t_9$)>$_y$

        "<eigh(t)> is always pronounced /ej(t)/word-finally; word-final /ej(t)/ is sometimes spelled <eigh(t)>."

- The sequence <ough>, with about twenty examples, is notoriously variable, with <bough> = /baʊ/, <though> = /ðoʊ/, <through> = /θruw/, <fought> = /fɔt/, <cough> = /kɔf/, and <rough> = /rʌf/. There might be a somewhat loose schema

---

[15] Except for *eighteen*, *eighty*, and *neighbor*, where it is neither in a monosyllable nor at the end of a word.

along the lines of (46), but the particular pronunciation has to be specified word by word. This parallels the situations in morphology where the proper affix must be specified on a word-by-word basis, e.g. *refusal* and *confusion* rather than **refusion* and **confusal*.

(46)   Phonology: $/_\omega [_\sigma \ldots [\underline{V, +back}](\underline{f,t}_9)]/_z$
        Orthography: $<\ldots\underline{ough(t}_9)>_z$

"<ough(t)> is always pronounced with a back vowel (plus /f/ or /t/) word-finally; words ending with a back vowel (plus /f/ or /t/) are sometimes spelled with <ough(t)>."

Of course, individual words can always specify idiosyncratic parts of their spelling, for instance /wʌn/ = <one> and /wɪmən/ = <women>—just as words can specify idiosyncratic parts of their morphology such as the -*red* in *hatred*. Borrowings often retain the spelling from their source language, in defiance of the spelling rules of the target language. For instance, <chauffeur> is perfectly regular in French orthography but quite idiosyncratic in both English and German. And there are orthographic truncations such as /vr̩səs/ = <vs.> and, in the morphosyntactic context of titles, /daktr̩/ = <Dr.>—not to mention the outrageous correspondence /paʊnd/ = <lb.>.

Pursuing the parallel with morphology, let's think for a moment about how knowledge of orthography is stored. As in morphology and syntax, we have been able to treat rules of spelling as schemas for interface links, here between orthographic structure and phonological (and sometimes morphosyntactic) structure. So again, rules can be considered part of the lexicon. Moreover, the rules of spelling, like morphophonology, run the gamut from productive to idiosyncratic, with all manner of cases in between.

Exactly what does one store? A counterpart of the Impoverished Entry theory of Chapter 3 would say that one stores only the parts of the spelling of words that are not predictable from their phonology. For instance, <sprechen> is fully predictable from its phonology plus schema (39) and schemas for the other letters, so it needn't be stored at all. Similarly, the only part of <women> that has to be stored would be the <o> = /ɪ/ mismatch, perhaps like this:

(47)   Phonology: $/ w ɪ_{12} mən/_{13}$
        Orthography: $<\ldots o_{12}\ldots>_{13}$

But as with morphology, we ask whether this emphasis on minimizing storage is realistic. To be sure, one has to store both the regularities and the idiosyncrasies of spelling. But this does not preclude storing the orthography of words whose spelling is perfectly regular, in parallel to the full entry theory of Chapter 3.

In particular, imagine what happens in reading: one is matching a sequence of perceived letter forms to phonological words. If orthography is stored with minimal redundancy, this basically amounts to sounding every word out, using the sometimes arcane "spelling rules" in reverse to reconstruct the intended phonology. The only part of the spelling that would not need to be reconstructed from more general principles would be the word-particular idiosyncrasies such as the <o> in (47).

This procedure sounds rather like the strategy of beginning readers who have to laboriously sound out every word, letter by letter. In contrast, skilled readers are capable of picking up whole orthographic words at a glance, often as fast as they can identify individual letters. Adams (1990: 105) therefore argues for a "dual-route" theory of word reading:

> The emerging view is that skillful word recognition involves both direct visual processing [accessing the word as a whole – RJ/JA] and phonological translation [by individual graphemes]. However, these two routes stand, not as independent alternatives to one another, but as synergistic parts of the same process.

This implies that the orthographic form of (at least) many words is stored explicitly (though independently of font: see experiments cited in Adams 1990: 97). Notice how this is parallel to our position on morphological processing in sections 7.4 and 7.5, where we proposed that the decompositional route and the whole-word route can reinforce each other.

The upshot is that for skilled readers, a full entry theory is more appropriate: the full spelling of a familiar word is (more often than not) stored as a unit linked to the phonology. The function of "rules of spelling" such as (36)-(46) is primarily relational, motivating the spelling of existing words and making their processing more efficient. These are the "spelling patterns" that children acquire as they learn to read, that enable them to decode and spell more efficiently and reliably (Adams 1990 again; Wolf 2007; Neijt, Peters, and Zuidema 2012; Zuidema and Neijt 2017). Moreover, if a whole word is stored orthographically, it can be coindexed directly with syntactic and semantic units as well as phonology, again speeding up processing.[16]

To sum up, the constructs of Parallel Architecture and Relational Morphology are well suited to describing orthography and its relation to speech.

8.5 Generative metrics

Another appealing extension of the PA/RM machinery is to generative metrics—the study of poetic meters and their realizations in lines of poetry (e.g. Halle and Keyser 1971; Kiparsky and Youmans 1989; Lerdahl 2001; Fabb and Halle 2008; Hayes 2010; Hayes, Wilson, and Shisko 2012). A Parallel Architecture treatment is in fact implicit in most versions of generative metrics: the goal is to delineate acceptable correspondences between a *metrical grid*, which defines the poetic meter, and the phonology of the text, especially its stress contour.[17] Framed in the terms of the Parallel Architecture, the metrical grid is a separate level of representation, and the problem is to specify both it and its interface with phonology. Here we will not attempt to adjudicate among the

---

[16] There is also an introspective observation that supports stored full forms. Sometimes, when hesitating about the spelling of a word, a writer will write down both/all candidates and check which one 'looks better,' i.e. matches the representation that is stored in memory, but too weakly to be recoverable without outside support.

[17] An exception is Fabb and Halle (2008), who generate the metrical grid from the phonology of the text rather than establishing a match between the two.

various approaches in the literature; we confine ourselves to showing how some rela-tively simple phenomena in generative metrics can be recast in Parallel Architecture format.

Example (48) is an illustration of one of the simplest situations. The subscripts here designate the usual interface links, extended now to the metrical grid. (For convenience, we notate both stress contour and metrical grid in terms of the rudimentary distinction S 'strong' vs. W 'weak.')

(48) Segmental phonology: $\text{the}_1 \ \text{cur}_2 \ \text{few}_3 \ \text{tolls}_4 \ \text{the}_5 \ \text{knell}_6 \ \text{of}_7 \ \text{par}_8 \ \text{ting}_9 \ \text{day}_{10}$
      Stress tier: $W_1 \ S_2 \ W_3 \ S_4 \ W_5 \ S_6 \ W_7 \ S_8 \ W_9 \ S_{10}$
      Metrical grid: $W_1 \ S_2 \ W_3 \ S_4 \ W_5 \ S_6 \ W_7 \ S_8 \ W_9 \ S_{10}$

Gray, "Elegy Written in a Country Churchyard,"
from Halle and Keyser (1971: 165)

The metrical grid here defines ten positions, alternating weak and strong. The text has ten syllables with alternating stress, so its repeated weak-strong contour perfectly matches the metrical grid, as indicated by the coindices.

This is a canonical one-to-one match. However, as we have seen with every other interface, a one-to-one correspondence is only the simplest, most stereotypical case. There are many deviations from this match, to some extent differing from one poetic tradition to the next, or even from one poet or one poem to the next. So the leading questions of generative metrical theory are:

• What is the metrical grid for this particular poem, poet, or poetic tradition?
• What is the range of possibilities for metrical grids in general?
• What is the meter-phonology interface for this particular poem, poet, or poetic tradition?
• What is the range of possibilities for the meter-phonology interface in general?

The metrical grid typically consists of a regular repeated pattern of strong and weak positions (or, in syllable-counting genres such as haiku, just a sequence of positions not differentiated by strength).[18] In many treatments, the positions are grouped into feet, reflecting the repeated pattern. Some weak positions, especially at the edges of the line, can be optional. (49a) is a version of the grid for iambic pentameter, with an optional initial position and an optional extrametrical final weak position. Other meters have different arrays of elements; for instance (49b) is trochaic tetrameter, and (49c) is a meter that simply counts syllables without regard to stress contour. (*X* notates a grid position that may be either strong or weak.)

---

[18] Lerdahl (2001) suggests that the regularity of the metrical grid arises from borrowing properties from the metrical grid in music, which likewise consists of regular repeated patterns of strong and weak beats. Hence, he proposes, metrical poetry in a sense treats language as though it were music.

(49)   a. *Iambic pentameter*
       Metrical grid: $[_{Line} [_{Foot} (W) S] [_{Foot} W S] [_{Foot} W S] [_{Foot} W S] [_{Foot} W S](W)]$

       b. *Trochaic tetrameter*
       Metrical grid: $[_{Line} [_{Foot} S W] [_{Foot} S W] [_{Foot} S W] [_{Foot} S (W)]]$

       c. *Syllable-counting meter*
       Metrical grid: $[_{Line} X X X X X]$

Most of the interest, however, is in the interface between the grid and phonological stress. A basic condition (in some genres) is that every syllable of the text, whether strong or weak, corresponds to a metrical position, whether strong or weak, and vice versa, as in (50).

(50)   *Syllables correspond to metrical positions*
       Segmental phonology: σ_x
       Metrical grid: X_x

Hayes, Wilson, and Shisko (2012) state a constraint so obvious that it is usually overlooked: a line cannot end in the middle of a word.[19] They state this principle as a constraint on the interface, as something that is forbidden. In keeping with the strong preference in PA/RM for stating principles in positive terms, what one *can* do, we restate this constraint as schema (51), which stipulates that a Line corresponds to a sequence of phonological words. (* denotes the "Kleene star," i.e. an unspecified number of ω's.

(51)   *Lines begin and end with complete words*
       Segmental phonology: $/ \omega* /_y$
       Metrical grid: $[_{Line} \ldots]_y$

For a stress-based meter, more detail is necessary. In the simplest version of the interface, phonological S always corresponds to metrical S, and phonological W corresponds to metrical W.

(52)   *Simple stress-based meter*
       Stress tier: a. $\ldots S_x \ldots$ b. $\ldots W_z \ldots$
       Metrical grid: $\ldots S_x \ldots$ $\ldots W_z \ldots$

This suffices for the stereotypical line in (48), but in general it is too rigid.

More interesting are the schemas that weaken the rigidity of the interface. For instance, Halle and Keyser (1971) point out an exception to (50): there are lines in which a word-final vowel is immediately followed by another vowel, and both vowels link to the same metrical position. (53) is such a line, and (54) is the schema that licenses

---

[19] This constraint is violated by Tom Lehrer as a metrical joke:
    And you may have thought it tragic,
    Not to mention other adjec-
    -Tives, to think of all the weeping they will do.
        "We Will All Go Together When We Go"
        <www.youtube.com/watch?v=TIoBrob3bjI>

this possibility. (The coindexation in (53) is self-evident, so we dispense with notating it; the relevant positions are marked in bold italic.)

(53)   Segmental phonology: Yet dear *ly* *I* love *you* *and* would be lov ed fain
       Stress tier: W   S   *W W*   S   *W*   *W*   S   W   S   W   S
       Metrical grid: W   S   *W*   S   *W*   S   W   S   W   S

Donne, "Holy Sonnet 14," from Halle and Keyser (1971: 171)

(54)   *Two adjacent vowels in one metrical position*
       Segmental phonology: $/\ldots V_{x\,\omega}]\,[_\omega V_y \ldots/$
       Metrical grid: $X_{x,y}$

(54) says that if a word ending with a vowel (coindex *x*) is followed by a word that begins with a vowel (coindex *y*), the two may correspond to a single metrical position. Fabb and Halle (2008) find a similar possibility in various genres of Romance poetry, but they treat the word-final vowel as unlinked to a metrical position, a different sort of exception to (50).

Another way of making the meter more flexible is to weaken the requirements in (52), such that only certain stressed syllables are required to fall in strong metrical positions, and/or only certain unstressed syllables are required to fall in weak metrical position. Halle and Keyser (1971: 169) propose such a weakening: a stressed syllable that is surrounded by unstressed syllables—a so-called stress maximum—has to correspond to a strong metrical position, and everything else is free. Halle and Keyser state it like this:

> DEFINITION:…a fully stressed syllable…between two unstressed syllables in the same syntactic constituent within a line of verse…is…a "stress maximum."…Stress maxima occur in S positions only, but not in all S positions.

Bringing this a little up to date, "syntactic constituent" probably ought to be replaced by "Intonational Phrase" (IP) (there was no theory of prosodic constituents in 1971). With this emendation, we can translate Halle and Keyser's hypothesis into present terms as (55).[20]

(55)   *Stress maximum schema*
       Stress tier: $[_{IP} \ldots W_x\, S_y\, W_z \ldots]$
       Metrical grid: $[_{Line} \ldots W_x\, S_y\, W_z \ldots]$

---

[20] We note that the definition of stress maximum varies from one source to another, and that its usefulness as a theoretical construct has been called into question by Hayes, Wilson, and Shisko (2012), among others. This is not the place to decide among the alternatives; the analysis here is meant simply as an illustration of how metrical theory translates into PA-style analysis.

(55) is meant to replace the overly rigid (52). Its stress tier spells out the criteria for a stress maximum: a stressed syllable surrounded by less- or unstressed syllables within an Intonational Phrase. The links to the metrical grid stipulate that these three syllables all fall somewhere within the same Line. The stressed syllable is linked to a strong position in the grid; the two other syllables are linked to weak positions. Where the configuration in (55) is not met, the correspondence is governed by (50), which maps syllables of any weight into any metrical position.

Let's see how (55) applies to some noncanonical lines. In (56), the syllables *leaves*, *world*, and *dark-* each fall in the center of a W-S-W stress contour, so they count as stress maxima, and they link to strong metrical positions.

(56) Segmental phonology: And leaves the world to darkness and to me
Stress tier: W S W S W S W W W W
Metrical grid: W S W S W S W S W S

> Gray, "Elegy Written in a Country Churchyard,"
> from Halle and Keyser (1971: 165)

However, aside from these W-S-W configurations, the correspondence of syllables to meter is free. Hence the unstressed syllable *and* can fall in a strong position, as can *me* (which might or might not be stressed).

Consider next (57). It has only one W-S-W configuration, *-son'd God for*, whose central syllable indeed corresponds to a metrical S.

(57) Segmental phonology: Batter my heart, three-person'd God, for you
Stress tier: S W W S   S S W S W W
Metrical grid: W S W S   W S W S W S

> Donne, "Holy Sonnet 14,"
> from Halle and Keyser (1971: 170)

What about the rest of the line? Notice that a line-initial stressed syllable, such as *Bat-*, is not surrounded by unstressed syllables in the same line, so it does not count as a stress maximum. Hence it can be linked to a weak metrical position. Moreover, like *and* in (56), *-ter* is an unstressed syllable in a strong position. The effect is of a line-initial trochee. Furthermore, none of the remaining stressed syllables in (57)—*heart*, *three*, and *per-*—counts as a stress maximum, because they are not surrounded by unstressed syllables. Hence *three* can be tolerated in a weak metrical position. All in all, given all these deviations from rigid meter, it may even be hard to tell that the line is iambic pentameter, at least out of the context of other, more canonical lines.

In short, the stress maximum schema (55) opens up a significant range of possibilities for licensing lines of iambic pentameter; this is what gives the meter its rich flexibility.

However, the meter does have its limits. Consider (58), from a Keats sonnet (cited in Halle and Keyser 1971: 171).

(58) Segmental phonology: How many bards gild the lapses of time
   Stress tier: S S W S S W S W W S
   Metrical grid: W S W S W S W S W S

The only W-S-W configuration in the phonology of (58) is the string *the lapses*. Alas, its central syllable corresponds to a W position, in violation of the stress maximum schema. Does that mean that the schema is formulated incorrectly? Halle and Keyser argue that it is not. Rather, they say (171), "it seems quite clear that the poet is purposely moving outside of the meter in order to caricature metrically the sense of the line. The line is literally what it speaks of figuratively, a 'lapse of time.' This metrical joke requires that the line be treated as unmetrical."

It of course remains to be seen if the analyses of various other approaches to generative metrics can be recast in Parallel Architecture format.[21]

The literature on generative metrics has primarily focused on the acceptability of individual lines. But the schemas of the Parallel Architecture can also be readily deployed for other poetic phenomena. For instance, it is necessary to characterize rhymes, independent of their use in poetry. Two words (or phrases) rhyme if they are phonologically the same from their principal stress onwards, and are preferably different before. (59) is a pair of sister schemas with a relational link between the parts that rhyme. (ρ in the segmental phonology stands for the rhyme of a syllable; σ^* stands for zero or more further syllables; S in the stress tier stands for main stress, and W* stands for any number of weak or unstressed syllables.)

(59) *X rhymes with Y*
   Segmental phonology: $/\ldots/\rho_\alpha\,\sigma^*/_\beta/_x$ $/\ldots/\rho_\alpha\,\sigma^*/_\beta/_y$
   Stress tier: $[S_\alpha\,W^*]_\beta$ $[S_\alpha\,W^*]_\beta$

This says that given two words or phrases, linked to different (morpho)syntax and semantics (coindices x and y), they rhyme if the stretch starting with the rhyme of the last stressed syllable (coindex α) is the same in both (coindex β)—regardless of what precedes the stress. The unlimited number of syllables following the strong stress is included in order to encompass rhymes as elaborate as Ira Gershwin's *embraceable you/irreplaceable you* and *tipsy in me/gypsy in me*.

Schemas can also be used to characterize poetic forms larger than a line, such as limericks and sonnets. A text is judged to be a limerick if it conforms to a particular metrical pattern and a particular rhyme scheme; moreover, a large class of limericks begin with the text *There once was a X from Y, who....* For an anonymous example:

---

[21] A theory-internal question in our analysis is how the various schemas interact with each other. For example, how does the loose interface schema (50) come to be blocked by the stress maximum schema? We assume this is accomplished by some version of the Elsewhere Condition, but limitations of space and patience prevent us from being more precise here.

More generally, there is an issue as to whether metricality should be treated as categorical—a line is metrical or not, regardless of its complexity—or whether it should be a gradient notion. Halle and Keyser and Fabb and Halle favor a categorical analysis; Hayes, Wilson, and Shisko go for gradience. In a way this resembles our question in section 2.9 about the productivity of schemas: Is productivity gradient, or are productive schemas a different animal from nonproductive ones?

(60)   There once was a young lady named Bright
        Whose speed was much faster than light
        She set out one day
        In a relative way
        And returned on the previous night.

The stipulations on number of syllables and rhyme scheme can be encoded as the schema in Figure 8.4. Like morphological and syntactic schemas, this schema can be used relationally, to motivate learned limericks, and generatively, to appreciate novel ones.

The basic meter is anapestic (two Ws preceding an S). Each line has different phonological content overall (coindices x, y, z, w, and v, linked to syntax and semantics). Lines 1, 2, and 5 each have three strong stresses, and they rhyme (coindex β); lines 3 and 4 have two strong stresses, and *they* rhyme (coindex γ). In addition, not shown is the semantic tier of line 5, which should be designated as a punch line, however one does that.

Figure 8.4 is highly redundant, in three respects. First, the relation between the stress tier and the metrical grid is at its most stringent, in that phonological stress always corresponds to metrical S, and phonological nonstress corresponds to metrical W, as stipulated in schema (52). Second, the formula for rhyming at the end of each line is a special case of the general rhyme formula (59). A third redundancy is that the metrical grids for lines 1, 2, and 5 are identical, and so are those for lines 3 and 4. This is expressed by relational links ϕ and η between the identical lines in the grid.

It would be impossible for the lexicon to eliminate all this redundancy from the schema, and especially from a memorized limerick such as (60). For instance, the last word of lines 2 and 5 rhyme with the last word of line 1 and are hence partially predictable. But what would be left after the predictable parts were removed would be

Line 1: Segmental phonology: $/ . . . \qquad /\rho_\alpha(\sigma)/_\beta /_x$
     Stress tier: $\quad /(W)\ W\ S\ W\ W\ S\ W\ W\ S_\alpha(W) /_x$
     Metrical grid: $\quad [_{Line} (W)\ W\ S\ W\ W\ S\ W\ W\ S_\alpha(W)]_\phi$

Line 2: Segmental phonology: $/ . . . \qquad /\rho_\alpha(\sigma)/_\beta /_y$
     Stress tier: $\quad /(W)\ W\ S\ W\ W\ S\ W\ W\ S_\alpha(W) /_y$
     Metrical grid: $\quad [_{Line} (W)\ W\ S\ W\ W\ S\ W\ W\ S_\alpha(W)]_\phi$

Line 3: Segmental phonology: $/ . . . \qquad /\rho_\gamma/ /_z$
     Stress tier: $\quad /(W)\ W\ S\ W\ W\ S_\gamma /_z$
     Metrical grid: $\quad [_{Line} (W)\ W\ S\ W\ W\ S_\gamma]_\eta$

Line 4: Segmental phonology: $/ . . . \qquad /\rho_\gamma/ /_w$
     Stress tier: $\quad /(W)\ W\ S\ W\ W\ S_\gamma /_w$
     Metrical grid: $\quad [_{Line} (W)\ W\ S\ W\ W\ S_\gamma]_\eta$

Line 5: Segmental phonology: $/ . . . \qquad /\rho_\alpha(\sigma)/_\beta /_v$
     Stress tier: $\quad /(W)\ W\ S\ W\ W\ S\ W\ W\ S_\alpha(W) /_v$
     Metrical grid: $\quad [_{Line} (W)\ W\ S\ W\ W\ S\ W\ W\ S_\alpha(W)]_\phi$

Figure 8.4 The limerick schema

phonological tatters. The only way that makes sense to store a known limerick is to store it in its entirety but to mark relevant parts as the same, i.e. again a full entry theory of storage. (This parallels the argument about the color of Peanut's paws in Chapter 3.)

Schemas like Figure 8.4 can be constructed for other sorts of extended formulaic utterances. Consider the genre of knock-knock jokes, which have roughly the two-person schema (61).

(61)   A: Knock knock.
      B: Who's there?
      A: X
      B: X who?
      A: X Y [Semantics: punch line]

Both participants have to know the schema in order to perform the joke properly.

Again, we conclude that the basic premises and theoretical constructs of the Parallel Architecture permit the approach to be extended beyond the canonical levels of phonology, morphology, syntax, and semantics. As with the other phenomena explored in this chapter, this moves the theory further toward an integrated account of knowledge of language in all its facets.

8.6 Beyond language: Extension of the RM lexicon to memory in other faculties

Throughout our exposition, we have stressed the importance of thinking of "knowledge of language" in terms of what is stored in long-term memory. Taking on a broader perspective, we might consider Relational Morphology, complete with its structured lexical entries, interface links, relational links, and schemas, to be a theory of one department of long-term memory. A natural question then is whether this theory scales up beyond language, to other cognitive capacities.

A working hypothesis that we find attractive is that memory is memory is memory: pretty much the same organization is to be found in memory for every cognitive domain. The differences among them lie in the units out of which the domain is constructed, their affordances for combination, and their interfaces to other domains. Language differs from other faculties, then, because it deals in syntactic, morphosyntactic, and phonological units, and because it interfaces with conceptual structure (meaning) on one end and with auditory (or in the case of signed languages, visual) perception and motor control on the other—and because it is used for conventionalized communication. (For the wider context of this hypothesis, see Jackendoff 1987, 2007b; similar ideas are proposed by Bod 2006 and by Hauser and Watumull 2016.)

This hypothesis invites us to seek similarities between linguistic memory and memory in other domains. Abstracting away from the content and function of linguistic memory to see its overall organization, we find general properties such as these:

- A vast lexicon, with tens of thousands of items, accessible nearly instantaneously
- Lexical items that involve multiple levels of representation, coordinated by interface links, plus links to nonlinguistic levels as well (e.g. to voice quality, identity of speaker, and affect on the phonological end and to spatial structure on the semantic end)
- Hierarchical constituent structure within items, on all three levels
- Both free items (e.g. *pig*), which can occur independently, and bound items (e.g. *-ish*), which occur only attached to other material
- Relational links among items that pick out shared structure
- Regularities across items that are picked out by schemas
- Schemas that both motivate structure within stored items (their relational role) and create novel structured items, in either production or perception (their generative role)

Very speculatively, let us see if these properties can plausibly be shared with other domains. Here are some promising candidates.[22]

8.6.1 Knowledge of music

- Vast lexicon: Yes! One can recognize hundreds if not thousands of popular songs, folk songs, nursery rhymes, and, for some people, 45-minute symphonies and the like—to the extent that one can identify them immediately on hearing just a few random seconds of music (say, when turning on the radio).
- Lexical items that involve multiple levels of representation: Yes! Following Lerdahl and Jackendoff (1983), Jackendoff and Lerdahl (2006), music cognition involves independent levels of grouping structure, metrical structure, and tonal hierarchy (or "prolongational reduction"), linked by a rich system of interface principles, abstracted away from timbre (pure sound quality).
- Hierarchical constituent structure within items: Yes! Music stored in memory has hierarchical structure on all of its levels.
- Free vs. bound items: It is hard to identify a musical counterpart of affixes. In Western tonal music, one possibility is the dominant harmony in a dominant-tonic cadence, whose function is to relax into the tonic. Another is the appoggiatura, a particular kind of transient dissonance that has to be resolved.
- Relational links among items that pick out shared structure: Here music might be a bit different from language: we might want to posit relational links *inside* a melody, picking out repetitions and variations of motives, using the same-except relation. For instance, one recognizes that the second phrase of *Happy Birthday* is the same as the first, except that the last two notes are a step higher. This sort of internal relational link does not appear prominently in morphology or syntax,

[22] Miller and Johnson-Laird (1976: 150–2) discuss the need for a variety of memory fields, including our domains of geographical and person memory.

though it does occur in reduplication and in rhetorical speech registers with heightened affect such as poetry, preaching, and political speeches.

- Regularities across items picked out by schemas: Yes! The well-formedness rules and preference rules of Lerdahl and Jackendoff can be recast as schemas. Schemas are also an attractive way to characterize conventionalized forms such as 32-bar popular song form, 12-bar blues, and classical sonata and minuet form. Like the limerick schema in the previous section, these have to be specified in terms of abstract skeletons of meter and harmony, to be fleshed out by the creator's choice of notes conforming to the schema.
- Schemas both motivate structure within stored items and assign structure to novel items: Yes! There is no reason to believe that the structures of known music and newly experienced music are different in character. Well-known music may be represented more richly in memory, but according to the same principles.

8.6.2 Understanding of physical objects

- Vast lexicon: Yes! One can recognize thousands of objects and object types—without the necessary use of linguistic labels. (This includes animate objects such as pigs and people.)
- Multiple linked levels of representation: Yes! Following section 1.2, one's knowledge of an object comprises not just how it looks, but may also include how it feels (haptic representation), what sounds it makes, and how one uses it (action representations).
- Hierarchical constituent structure within items: Yes! Following Marr (1982), objects can be understood as having a hierarchical decomposition. A chair has legs, a seat, and a back; the back may have decorations; the decorations may be segmented into various parts, and so on. A pig has legs, a tail, and a head with eyes, ears, nose, and mouth.
- Free items and bound items: A stripe is physically bound: there can't be a stripe without a surface. Holes, cracks, and dents are also possible bound items: there can't be a hole without a volume in which it is situated. A handle may be physically free (say, if it can be bought in the hardware store) but it is functionally bound (its proper function is to be a handle of something, used to pick that something up).
- Relational links among items that pick out shared structure: Yes? One can appreciate the similarity of structure between the seats of armchairs and wheelchairs, despite considerable visual difference. One can appreciate the similarity in function between radically different kinds of bottle openers or lamps or faucets.
- Regularities among items picked out by schemas: Yes! Any sort of prototype representation (e.g. a Marr 3D model) is in effect a schema. Schemas can pick out generalizations about the layout of parts: e.g. windows are normally placed in

walls, not floors. Rumelhart (1980) (in his pre-connectionist days) uses the term "schema" in precisely this sense, speaking for instance of a schema for a face, with subschemas for noses and eyebrows and so on.

- Schemas both motivate structure within stored items and assign structure to novel items: Again, there is no reason to think that when a representation of a novel object is committed to memory, the principles determining its structure should be any different.

8.6.3 Knowledge of geography and spatial layout

By this term we mean to encompass two different tasks that require similar sorts of knowledge: finding one's way from one place to another (Lynch 1960; Landau and Hoffman 2012), and knowing where to find particular objects. (These might however be separate domains.)

- Vast lexicon: Yes! How many places, streets, routes, does one know? How many associations of objects with places does one know? Where can the milk be found in the supermarket? Where does one keep the electrical tape? Where did I park my bike this morning? (And possibly: In which publication did Chomsky say such-and-such?) It's hard to know how to count, but we have huge amounts of such knowledge.
- Multiple linked levels of representation: Hard to know.
- Hierarchical constituent structure within items: Yes! Where is the supermarket? Where is the milk within the supermarket? My brother's house is on a particular street in a particular neighborhood of a particular city, in a particular part of a particular state.
- Free items and bound items: Hard to know.
- Relational links among items that pick out shared structure: Maybe. Similarities among airports or among fast-food joints?
- Regularities among items, picked out by schemas: Yes! What is one likely to find in an airport? in a bank? in a restaurant?
- Schemas both motivate structure within stored items and assign structure to novel items: Yes! One may use what one knows about supermarkets, based on supermarkets one has experienced, to make informed guesses about how a newly encountered supermarket is going to be organized. For instance, the paper napkins are likely to be near the paper towels.

8.6.4 Social knowledge

This encompasses a number of issues: people one knows and what one knows about them; conventionalized social actions; and issues of moral value (Jackendoff 2007b).

- Vast lexicon: Yes! One knows thousands of people to some degree or another, including not only how they look, but their personalities and their social ties such as kin, spouses, ethnicity, religion, and occupation. One knows lots of rules of proper behavior, though it's hard to know how to count them: the fork goes to the left of the plate, people go to church on Sundays, you should give kids birthday presents....

- Multiple linked levels of representation: Yes! A person is conceptualized as a linked physical instantiation (or body) and a social presence (or "soul") (Bloom 2004, Jackendoff 2007b). Social actions have a physical instantiation linked to a social or moral value. For instance, shaking hands is a physical action fulfilling various social functions, the most prominent of which are greeting and taking leave.

- Hierarchical constituent structure within items: Yes! Family structure, group structure (groups within groups within groups), authority (or rank) hierarchy.

- Free items and bound items: Moral values are not free-floating: They must be attached to some action.

- Relational links among items picking out shared structure: Yes? Shared rank (all sergeants), shared occupation (all psycholinguists), shared intellectual ancestry (all former students of Lila Gleitman, and *their* students). Similarities among games: what soccer (a.k.a. football) and hockey have in common, and how that is different from what pingpong and tennis have in common.

- Regularities picked out by schemas: Yes! All customs and rituals (formal and informal, including games) stipulate an abstract schema that specifies each participant's role. The actual participants on any particular occasion then satisfy the variables in the schema. This is basically the idea behind Schank's (1973) "scripts" (e.g. how a restaurant works), Minsky's (1975) "frames" (e.g. how a birthday party works), Rumelhart's (1980) schemas (how a buying/selling transaction works), Fillmore's (1982) "frame semantics," Goffman's (1974) much more elaborate "frames," and at a very general level, Fiske's (1991) four elementary forms of human relations.

- Schemas both motivate structure within stored items and assign structure to novel items: The stored items here would be particular occasions stored in episodic memory. They are presumably structured according to the same principles as one's assessment of ongoing events.

Our conclusion is that, at least at this impressionistic level, many general properties of linguistic knowledge are replicated in other domains of knowledge. People such as Lakoff (1987) and Rumelhart (1980) might say this shows there's nothing special about language. But that's too coarse a judgment. As observed at the beginning of this section, domains differ in what their structures are made of: phonological, morphological, and syntactic units in language; sequences of pitches with duration in music; visual/spatial units in object knowledge and geographical knowledge; persons, units of interpersonal behavior, and social/moral value in social knowledge. To a considerable extent, these domains intersect with Spelke's (2000) and Carey's (2009) "domains of core knowledge."

In order to develop this line of inquiry further, we need theories of representation in these other domains—theories that are comparable in sophistication with linguistic theory. Speculative though this last section has been, it is an intriguing step in integrating the language faculty with the rest of the mind. In turn, this reflects well on our linguistic theory: to the extent that it invites such integration, it encourages us to think we're on the right track.

9

Coda: What have we done?

9.1 The machinery of Relational Morphology

Let's step back and review what we've accomplished in the preceding chapters. First, in Parts I and II, we described a considerable range of morphological phenomena, using a limited and well-motivated set of theoretical constructs. Some of these are necessary in any theory of morphology:

- Semantic, morphosyntactic, and phonological structures. We have been careful to keep them distinct, in the spirit of the Parallel Architecture. We have also been careful not to introduce any nontraditional features or structures (except perhaps in the way we have distinguished inflection from derivation).
- *Interface links*, which tie together corresponding pieces of phonology, morphosyntax, and semantics. Any theory that considers language to be a sound-meaning mapping requires something with the same function. However, we have also extended the use of interface links to phonetics, orthography, and even to nonlinguistic representations such as spatial structure.

Relational Morphology shares further characteristics with constraint-based theories such as HPSG, LFG, Construction Grammar, and Construction Morphology. First, the lexicon does not just list words; nor is it just "a list of basic irregularities" or "a collection of the lawless." Rather, it contains full representations of words, including material that is predictable. In addition to words, the lexicon contains idioms, collocations, meaningful constructions, and entries for bound items such as affixes and perhaps stems.

Like the other constraint-based theories, RM's grammar is formulated in terms of declarative *schemas* rather than procedural derivational rules such as word formation rules or realization rules. As a result, RM does not have the computational power afforded by rules or rule blocks that apply one after another or at different points in a derivation. Instead, the central concept is the *relation* among lexical entries, which gives the theory its name.

As in CxG and CxM, schemas are in the same format as words and can therefore be considered lexical items (more discussion below). However, as we have pointed out several times, RM differs from CxG and HPSG in that it countenances lexical entries that lack a semantic component; that is, not all words and schemas are Saussurean signs. To be sure, this difference makes RM's schemas potentially more expressive and less constrained than CxG's constructions. But this extra expressiveness has been

The Texture of the Lexicon. First edition. Ray Jackendoff and Jenny Audring © Ray Jackendoff and Jenny Audring 2020.
First published in 2020 by Oxford University Press. DOI: 10.1093/oso/9780198827900.001.0001

justified by the use of schemas in phenomena as disparate as allomorphy, inflectional classes, orthography, and generative metrics, where meaning plays no role.

Pieces of structure are combined into larger novel configurations by **unification**, a procedural operation shared with the other constraint-based theories. Although it is more powerful than the traditional substitution of arguments for variables or the Minimalist Program's Merge, unification is arguably necessary not only for language but also for other cognitive capacities. Hence its use in linguistic theory has a deeper justification.

On the other hand, Relational Morphology features the following innovations:

- Schemas have two possible functions. First, in their *generative* function, they team up with unification to create more complex structures; in this fashion they function like traditional rules. Second, in their *relational* function, they codify patterns of similarity among items in the lexicon.

- In addition to interface links, the lexicon contains *relational links* that connect parts of one lexical entry to another, marking them as the same. Connections can be made between words, between a schema and its instances, or between schemas. A schema fulfills its relational function by virtue of the relational links to its instances.

- Relational links take the place of the inheritance links in HPSG, LFG, and CxG. They are more flexible than inheritance links, in that they allow for "horizontal" connections between items in addition to the "vertical" connections of inheritance. These connections have proven essential for such phenomena as "derived" forms without a lexical root, sister words that cannot be derived from each other, and complex words that are motivated by multiple schemas (for instance in blends).

- The connections established by relational links also take the place of relations created by *deriving* one form from another. Relational links are more powerful than derivational rules, in that they can establish a wider range of connections. But this power is necessary, in order to account for the rampant idiosyncrasy found throughout morphology.

- RM makes a distinction between *productive* and *nonproductive variables* in schemas. This replaces the strict distinction between "grammatical" and "lexical" rules found in many theories. Thus it allows for the possibility of a graceful gradient of productivity from marginal families (e.g. *horror ~ horrible ~ horrify* etc.), through nonproductive families with hundreds of members (X-*ous*), to fully productive patterns (X-*ness*).

- A final innovation is the *same-except relation*, which obtains between items connected by relational links. It allows items that are not strictly identical to still register as related. This relation too adds power to the descriptive apparatus, but it is arguably a domain-general component of cognition, and it helps relational links do more of the work usually attributed to derivational rules that change one form into another.

Crucially, productive schemas can be used not only in their traditional generative function of constructing novel structures, but also relationally, to support instances stored in the lexicon. Nonproductive schemas, by contrast, function only relationally. The overarching generalization is the **Relational Hypothesis**: All schemas can be used relationally, and a particular subset of them, the productive ones, can also be used generatively. From this follows the corollary which (we think) is the most unexpected result of this study: the generative property of language, the "infinite use of finite means," emerges from and rides on top of the system of lexical relations.

This calls for a major reassessment of the goals of linguistic theory. The theory can no longer concentrate just on the productive and creative aspects of language. It is as at least as important to investigate the structure of the lexicon, which contains a heterogeneous mixture of complete generality, total arbitrariness, and everything in between.

There is a further methodological conclusion. The traditional concentration on regularity has made it seem essential to wring every bit of systematicity out of every linguistic phenomenon. With the focus of inquiry more balanced between regularity and idiosyncrasy, there is no shame in concluding that some things in language are simply arbitrary. At the same time, this does not necessarily make them any less interesting.

9.2 Boundary issues

Section 1.1 promised a treatment of a number of boundary issues in linguistic theory—issues that concern basic distinctions the theory must make, and that therefore configure the overall architecture of the language faculty. Here is where things stand.

First, Relational Morphology eliminates the boundary between lexicon and grammar, following the lead of the Parallel Architecture and Construction Grammar. This is possible because schemas, the theory's counterpart of traditional rules, are in the same format as words. The difference between them is simply that schemas contain variables, while stereotypical words do not. The traditional distinction is further eroded by the fact that a word's subcategorization and selectional constraints can also be considered variables in the word's structure, and hence are schema-like.

This continuity between words and schemas leads to important generalizations. For instance, it permits sister relations among schemas (e.g. X-*ism* ~ X-*ist*) to be described in terms entirely parallel to sister relations among words (e.g. *optimism* ~ *optimist* and *assassin* ~ *assassinate*). This continuity affords a simple formalization of schema acquisition: a hypothesized schema is a tentative lexical item, constructed directly from the words that serve as evidence for it. This procedure contrasts with a traditional rule, which requires a leap from the format of words in the lexicon to the format of rules in the grammar.

Second, we promised to eliminate the putative boundary between core and peripheral phenomena, and with it the proposal that only the core needs to be regarded as central to linguistic theory. It follows from the Relational Hypothesis that so-called core phenomena are in fact based on the very same machinery necessary to account for the periphery. (This argument is a variant of Culicover (1999), who argues that any mechanism that can learn the periphery can also learn the core.)

A further consequence is that the distinction between productive (i.e. more "core") patterns and nonproductive ("peripheral") patterns is now not a matter of situating them in different parts of the grammar, or "in the grammar" versus "in the lexicon." Rather, they are both situated in the lexicon and encoded in the same format. The difference between them is localized in the nature of their variables, hence a relatively minor distinction. Moreover, their formal similarity explains why productive schemas can also function relationally, just like nonproductive schemas.

Some other boundaries have not been eliminated, but we have been able to clarify them. For instance, we have maintained the boundary between morphology and phrasal syntax. However, this does not mean that morphology is "computed in the lexicon" "before" syntax, or that it is computed "after" syntax, on the way to phonology. Rather, following the tenets of the Parallel Architecture, morphosyntax is its own component of grammar, governing the internal structure of words, with its own characteristic primitives and principles of combination, and with interfaces to phonology and semantics.

Morphosyntax shares structure with phrasal syntax at the level of maximal X^0s, in particular its syntactic category labels and inflectional features. A stored complex lexical item like *raining cats and dogs* partakes of both kinds of structure: its words are combined according to phrasal syntax; and the words themselves are structured according to the morphosyntax and morphophonology of the present participle and the plural. The only idiosyncrasy lies in the mapping to semantics. Certain items, such as *matter-of-factly* and *smoked pork shoulder boiled dinner*, show inversion of this typical configuration, with phrasal syntax inside of morphosyntax. In addition, the boundary is permeable enough that some cells of an inflectional paradigm may be expressed morphologically while others are expressed syntactically.

Another boundary we have addressed is that between derivational and inflectional morphology. Derivational morphology typically has morphosyntactic structure of the form $[_Y Z \text{ aff }]$, where Y and Z are X^0 syntactic categories that may or may not be the same, and aff is the morphosyntactic mark of a derivational relation. An important variant is the common configuration $[_Y - \text{ aff}]$, which lacks a lexical base. Aff stereotypically is expressed or realized as a phonological prefix or suffix; but it can also be phonologically realized by morphological devices such as umlaut, circumfixation, infixation, or reduplication.

Inflectional morphology is expressed by about the same range of phonological realizations as derivational morphology. The difference between them lies in morphosyntax, where inflection has two special properties. First, the grammar of a language specifies what syntactic categories are inflected and in what syntactic configurations, and it specifies the range of available values for each feature (tense, aspect, number, gender, case and so on), arranging them into paradigms. Second, inflections are formalized as features that form a set together with the syntactic category feature of the base. A typical configuration is something like {N, FEM, PL}, where N may have internal derivational structure.

A final boundary we have sketched here is that between phonology and phonetics. Instead of thinking of phonetic representations as the "output" of the phonological component, we have suggested that phonology and phonetics are separate components or modules, built from different units. Phonology is discrete and feature-based; phonetics is analog and deals in vocal gesture and the corresponding acoustic properties. The two are connected not by a derivation but by an interface, through which phonology carves out regions in phonetic space, and through which, reciprocally, phonetics puts pressure on phonology to conform to ease of articulation and acoustic discriminability. We have arrived at this configuration because the Parallel Architecture demands it. Treatments of phonological phenomena in terms of "inputs" and "outputs" mediated either by derivational rules or by OT constraint satisfaction are not within the PA's ambit. It remains a huge challenge to see whether more standard treatments of both phonology and phonetics can be reconciled with this framework.

9.3 What *can't* the theory describe?

In presentations of Relational Morphology, we have often been asked questions like:"What *can't* your theory do? Is it falsifiable? How is it constrained? What do you claim is an impossible human language?" We suspect that some readers will have similar issues, so it behooves us to try to address them.

Let's begin with falsifiability. To be sure, it is often possible to show that a particular analysis within a particular framework is incorrect. But that doesn't overthrow the framework! In fact, no overarching theory of any complexity (at least in linguistics) is falsifiable in the Popperian sense. Rather, when one discovers that the theory fails to describe something, there are two possible strategies. One way is to declare the phenomenon in question off limits, restricting the theory's scope to, say, inflection but only marginally to derivation, or to morphology but not syntax, or only to productive rules, or only to "core grammar" or "competence." PA/RM leaves the door open to a wider range of phenomena than most theories we are familiar with. But we too have our limits. For example, we have deliberately excluded issues of language change, on the grounds that we are interested in an individual's synchronic knowledge of language; and we have declared the neural implementation of language out of bounds, at least for the present.

Another way to deal with a local failure in the theory is to devise a fix, a patch, that takes care of the embarrassment. The questions raised by this practice are (or ought to be): How many such fixes are needed? How general or how narrow are they? How deeply do they undermine basic tenets of the theory? What assumptions or analyses do you have to throw out? The fixes keep the theory alive and perhaps even vigorous, but there may come a point when the theory collapses under their weight. (The classic case is of course Ptolemaic epicycles in describing celestial mechanics.) Opponents of the theory will judge the theory to have collapsed much sooner than its proponents, who will persist, lest their life's work be rendered pointless.

In the present study, we too have encountered situations in which the theory required fixes. For instance, the theory as it stood at the end of Part I was unable to express relations among schemas, such as the parallelism between the *pessimism/minimalism* pattern and the *pessimist/minimalist* pattern. The fix we introduced was the sister schema notation, based on the second-order schemas of Construction Morphology. This definitely made the theory more powerful, but we have shown that this additional power permits the theory to extend to a vast range of important generalizations, including inflectional paradigms, inflectional classes, stem and affix allomorphy, and reduplication. Moreover, the formalism we devised was a simple extension of that for sister *words*, so it not only conformed to the spirit of the theory, it strengthened it.

Another inadequacy of the original formalism in Part I was its inability to express umlaut and ablaut patterns. The fix we adopted was the same-except relation, formalized by means of the star notation. Again this added expressive power to the theory, as observed in section 9.1. But we defended its inclusion on the grounds of its ubiquity in other domains of cognition. There should be no reason to deny morphology a representational device that is free for the taking in the mind's computational resources. Moreover, like sister schemas, the same-except relation is of widespread utility in describing morphological phenomena. In particular, it does the work often attributed to analogy, of which it is an extremely constrained version.

In short, we confess to having extended the power of the theory with these additions to the machinery, but we maintain that they are the right sort of fixes—not simply stipulative, but of broad generality and in tune with the theory's basic tenets. Is it now *too* powerful? It's hard to say.

Next consider the question of how constrained RM is. This is actually two different questions. The first is how broad or narrow a repertoire of theoretical constructs the theory invokes. But this has to be evaluated in the context of how broad the theory's coverage is. We don't think we could make do with any less than the constructs enumerated in section 9.1 and still achieve the same generality of coverage. Moreover, each of these constructs either has counterparts in other theories or is arguably domain-general, so it is not clear to us that any other theory covers the same ground with fewer resources.

The second question concerning constraint is how broad or narrow a set of possible languages the theory describes. This question is tricky to answer, because this set had better include all existing languages. And every time you claim some pattern is impossible, someone comes up with a language with just that pattern. In fact, given the wild things that turn up in language after language, the challenge for the theory is usually to be rich *enough*. In Chapter 6, for instance, the complex allomorphy of well-studied English suffixes outstrips the ability of the formalism to describe it; and the English vowel alternations, though we have managed to describe them, are just weird. Similarly, the architecture of the interface between morphosyntax and phrasal syntax in sections 1.5 and 5.1 more or less constrains morphology to be syntax-free, aside from inflectional features. Yet we readily find violations such as those mentioned above, in which phrasal structure appears within words. In the face of such situations, over and over again, we are reluctant to insist that the theory declare anything absolutely off limits.

One way to constrain the class of possible languages is through psycholinguistic considerations. The classic example is Miller and Chomsky's (1963) argument that it is processing difficulty, not grammatical impossibility, that rules out recursively center-embedded sentences. Similarly, no linguistic theory that we know of explicitly rules out a language with 102 vowels, or a language in which all lexical items are pronounced the same.[1] Such languages would be unlearnable and useless for communication. They offer no reason to constrain the theory of representations itself. More generally, it can't be settled in advance how the constraints on possible languages are distributed among representational capacity, processing, functionality, and acquisition.

Above all, Relational Morphology is constrained at its most general level by its insistence on mentalism. We have taken care to show that the theoretical constructs listed in section 9.1 are psychologically plausible, not just "metaphorical" or "abstract" in some unclear sense. An important anchor for the theory has been the question of what is stored—both what *must* be stored and what *can* be stored. This question serves as a crucial bridge between the linguistic theory and psycholinguistic considerations.

9.4 The scope of the theory

One gauge of a theory's success is its ability to bring a wide range of phenomena under a unified set of constructs. What made Newton's theory of gravity great was that it explained not only apples falling on his head, but the tides! And planetary motion! We cannot hope to be that cosmic. However, we do think that Relational Morphology does help achieve a striking degree of integration and extension of scope for linguistic theory.

First, as already mentioned, the Relational Hypothesis now brings together the analysis of productive and nonproductive patterns under a single construct, the theory of schemas and relational links. No longer is it necessary to wall off idiosyncrasy as an aberration best ignored.

Second, the Parallel Architecture as developed in Jackendoff (2002) and Culicover and Jackendoff (2005) was justified primarily on its integration of syntax and semantics. Relational

---

[1] We are reminded of the trick sentence *Buffalo buffalo Buffalo buffalo buffalo buffalo Buffalo buffalo* (you can look it up!).

Morphology significantly sharpens the approach and extends it to morphology and (to a certain extent) phonology and phonetics. As a result:

- The architecture of language can now be seen as a collection of discrete levels of representation, each with its own characteristic primitives and principles of combination.
- The levels are connected by interface links, not by derivations. In the simplest cases, interface links create one-to-one mappings between aspects of the levels they tie together. But mismatches are ubiquitous and to be expected.
- Stored pieces of structure (i.e. lexical items) include not just fully specified constructs, but also schemas, which contain variables.
- Stored pieces of structure may involve a single level, such as in phrase structure rules and phonotactics. Alternatively, they may involve linked levels, the stereotypical case of which is a word. But stored structure may also involve any combination of levels.
- At each level of representation, stored pieces of structure can be connected by relational links, which encode patterns of redundancy. Alternations are encoded in terms of relational links between sister schemas.

The methodological problem that occurs with this conception of the architecture is to determine which components of grammar are responsible for any particular linguistic phenomenon—which levels of representation and which interfaces are involved. We think this is the right problem to have, in that it clarifies the extent to which the levels of representation are independent yet mutually constraining.

However, the advantage of Relational Morphology is not limited to internal integration of linguistic theory. Section 1.1 promised to reevaluate the boundary between competence, the theory of linguistic representations, and performance, the theory of language processing and acquisition. RM, following the Parallel Architecture, allows a more integrated treatment of the two. The representations posited by RM can be concretely incorporated into a model of performance with features such as promiscuous processing, spreading activation, frequency effects, neighborhood effects, prediction, and learning based on minimum exposure. We consider this an important argument for the approach, one that goes beyond its adequacy in describing morphological phenomena.

Finally, Relational Morphology addresses the relation between language and the rest of the mind. For one thing, language has interfaces with other mental capacities. Chapter 1 discussed the interface of semantics with the understanding of physical space; this interface is what gives us the essential ability to talk about what we see. Chapter 6 added the interface between phonology and the gestural score, a kind of representation dealing with action planning. Chapter 8 added interfaces connecting phonology and morphology to orthography, which in turn has interfaces to the visual system (and the motor system, if one is writing or typing). In addition to enriching the scope of linguistic theory, this basic architecture—representational systems connected by interfaces—confirms the choice of the PA as the proper way to think about language.

There is also a different respect in which Relational Morphology permits integration of language with the rest of the mind. As discussed in section 9.1, we have proposed that some constructs of RM are domain-general, especially unification and same-except. On a larger scale, Chapter 8 has sketched ways in which the structure of the lexicon—which now constitutes all of knowledge of language—is paralleled by the character of knowledge in other important cognitive domains. What distinguishes language from these other capacities is the character of its representations and the interfaces among them—and therefore its function in the larger mental ecology. We take it as a virtue that many of the tools of morphology can be applied to other subdomains of language, especially syntax, as well as to other cognitive domains. Morphology isn't its own island.

Of course, the theory presented here leaves a great deal for future research. In fact, given its scope, it raises many deep questions that could not have previously been envisioned. We think that this is a sign of progress. What we offer here is a product of a long and arduous evolution, with all these issues in mind. No doubt its evolution will continue.

References

Ackema, Peter, and Ad Neeleman (2004). *Beyond Morphology: Interface Conditions on Word Formation*. Oxford: Oxford University Press.

Ackerman, Farrell, and Gert Webelhuth (1999). *A Theory of Predicates*. Stanford: CSLI.

Adams, Marilyn Jager (1990). *Beginning to Read*. Cambridge, MA: MIT Press.

Akmajian, Adrian (1973). 'The role of focus in the interpretation of anaphoric expressions', in Stephen Anderson and Paul Kiparsky (eds.), *A Festschrift for Morris Halle*. New York: Holt, Rinehart, and Winston, 215–26.

Alber, Birgit, and Sabine Arndt-Lappe (2012). 'Templatic and subtractive truncation', in Jochen Trommer (ed.), *The Morphology and Phonology of Exponence*. Oxford: Oxford University Press, 289–325.

Albright, Adam, and Bruce Hayes (2003). 'Rules vs. analogy in English past tenses: A computational/experimental study', *Cognition* 90: 119–61.

Alegre, M., and Peter Gordon (1999). 'Frequency effects and the representational status of regular inflections', *Journal of Memory and Language* 40: 41–61.

Ambridge, Ben, and Elena Lieven (2011). *Child Language Acquisition: Contrasting Theoretical Approaches*. Cambridge: Cambridge University Press.

Amenta, Simona, and Davide Crepaldi (2012). 'Morphological processing as we know it: An analytical review of morphological effect in visual word identification', *Frontiers in Psychology* 3: Article 232. doi: 10.3389/fpsyg.2012.00232

Anderson, Stephen R. (1977). 'On the formal description of inflection', *Proceedings of the Chicago Linguistic Society* 13: 15–44.

Anderson, Stephen R. (1981). 'Why phonology isn't "natural"', *Linguistic Inquiry* 12: 493–540.

Anderson, Stephen R. (1982). 'Where's morphology?' *Linguistic Inquiry* 13: 571–612.

Anderson, Stephen R. (1992). *A-morphous Morphology*. Cambridge: Cambridge University Press.

Anderson, Stephen R. (2004). 'Towards a less "syntactic" morphology and a more "morphological" syntax', in Piet van Sterkenburg (ed.), *Linguistics Today: Facing a Greater Challenge*. Amsterdam: Benjamins, 31–45.

Archibald, John, and Gary Libben (2019). 'Morphological theory and second language acquisition', in Jenny Audring and Francesca Masini (eds.), *The Oxford Handbook of Morphological Theory*. Oxford: Oxford University Press, 522–40.

Arndt-Lappe, Sabine, and Ingo Plag (2013). 'The role of prosodic structure in the formation of English blends', *English Language and Linguistics* 17: 537–63.

Arnold, Jennifer E., Anthony Losongco, Thomas Wasow, and Ryan Ginstrom (2000). 'Heaviness vs. newness: The effects of structural complexity and discourse status on constituent ordering', *Language* 76: 28–55.

Aronoff, Mark (1976). *Word Formation in Generative Grammar*. Cambridge, MA: MIT Press.

Aronoff, Mark (1994). *Morphology By Itself: Stems and Inflectional Classes*. Cambridge, MA: MIT Press.

Aronoff, Mark (2016). 'A fox knows many things but a hedgehog one big thing', in Andrew Hippisley and Gregory Stump (eds.), *The Cambridge Handbook of Morphology*. Cambridge: Cambridge University Press, 186–205.

Aronoff, Mark, and Mark Lindsay (2014). 'Productivity, blocking, and lexicalization', in Rochelle Lieber and Pavol Štekauer (eds.), *The Oxford Handbook of Derivational Morphology*. Oxford: Oxford University Press, 67–83.

Aronoff, Mark, Irit Meir, and Wendy Sandler (2005). 'The paradox of sign language morphology', *Language* 81: 301–44.

Asudeh, Ash, and Ida Toivonen (2014). 'Lexical-Functional Grammar', in Bernd Heine and Heiko Narrog (eds.), *The Oxford Handbook of Linguistic Analysis*. Oxford: Oxford University Press, 373–406.

Audring, Jenny, Geert Booij, and Ray Jackendoff (2017). 'Menscheln, kibbelen, sparkle: Verbal diminutives between grammar and lexicon', Linguistics in the Netherlands 2017, 1-15. doi: 10.1075/avt.34.01.aud

Audring, Jenny, and Francesca Masini (eds.) (2019). The Oxford Handbook of Morphological Theory. Oxford: Oxford University Press.

Austin, Peter (1981). A Grammar of Diyari, South Australia. Cambridge: Cambridge University Press.

Baayen, Harald (1989). 'A Corpus-Based Approach to Morphological Productivity. Statistical Analysis and Psycholinguistic Interpretation', PhD thesis, Vrije Universiteit Amsterdam.

Baayen, Harald (1992). 'Quantitative aspects of morphological productivity', in Geert Booij and Jaap van Marle (eds.), Yearbook of Morphology 1991. Dordrecht: Foris, 109–50.

Baayen, Harald (1993). 'On frequency, transparency and productivity', in Geert Booij and Jaap van Marle (eds.), Yearbook of Morphology 1992. Dordrecht/Boston/London: Kluwer, 181–208.

Baayen, Harald (2007). 'Storage and computation in the mental lexicon', in Gonia Jarema and Gary Libben (eds.), The mental lexicon: Core perspectives. Amsterdam: Elsevier, 81–104.

Baayen, Harald (2014). 'Experimental and psycholinguistic approaches to studying derivation', in Rochelle Lieber and Pavol Stekauer (eds.), The Oxford Handbook of Derivational Morphology. Oxford: Oxford University Press, 95–117.

Baayen, Harald, Ton Dijkstra, and Robert Schreuder (1997). 'Singulars and plurals in Dutch: Evidence for a parallel dual-route model', Journal of Memory and Language 37: 94–117.

Baayen, Harald, and Rochelle Lieber (1991). 'Productivity and English derivation: A corpus-based study', Linguistics 29: 801–44.

Baayen, Harald, and Robert Schreuder (eds.) (2003). Morphological Structure in Language Processing. Berlin and New York: Mouton de Gruyter.

Baayen, Harald, Robert Schreuder, Nivja de Jong, and Andrea Krott (2002). 'Dutch inflection: The rules that prove the exception', in Sieb Nooteboom, Fred Weerman, and Frank Wijnen (eds.), Storage and Computation in the Language Faculty. Dordrecht: Kluwer, 61–92.

Bach, Emmon (1983). 'On the relation between word-grammar and phrase-grammar', Natural Language and Linguistic Theory 1: 65–90.

Bach, Emmon (2002). 'On the surface verb q'ay'ailqela', Linguistics and Philosophy 25, 531–44.

Baddeley, Alan (1986). Working Memory. Oxford: Clarendon Press.

Baerman, Matthew, Greville G. Corbett, and Dunstan Brown (eds.) (2011). Defective Paradigms: Missing Forms and What They Tell Us. Proceedings of the British Academy 163. Oxford: Oxford University Press and British Academy.

Baeskow, Heike (2004). Lexical Properties of Selected Non-native Morphemes of English. Tübingen: Gunter Narr Verlag.

Baggio, Giosuè (2018). Meaning in the Brain. Cambridge, MA: MIT Press.

Baker, Brett (2018). 'Super-complexity and the status of "word" in Gunwinyguan languages of Australia', in Geert Booij (ed.), The Construction of Words: Advances in Construction Morphology. Cham, Switzerland: Springer, 255–86.

Baker, Mark (1988). Incorporation: A Theory of Grammatical Function Changing. Chicago: University of Chicago Press.

Barðdal, Johanna (2008). Productivity: Evidence from Case and Argument Structure in Icelandic. Amsterdam: John Benjamins.

Bauer, Laurie (2001). Morphological Productivity. Cambridge: Cambridge University Press.

Bauer, Laurie (2002). 'What you can do with derivational morphology', in Sabrina Bendjaballah, Wolfgang U. Dressler, Oskar E. Pfeiffer, and Maria D. Voeikova (eds.), Morphology 2000: Selected papers from the 9th Morphology Meeting, Vienna, 24-28 February 2000. Amsterdam/Philadelphia: John Benjamins, 37–48.

Bauer, Laurie, Rochelle Lieber, and Ingo Plag (2013). The Oxford Reference Guide to English Morphology. Oxford: Oxford University Press.

Bays, Paul M. (2015). 'Spikes not slots: Noise in neural populations limits working memory', Trends in Cognitive Sciences 19 (8): 431–8. doi: https://doi.org/10.1016/j.tics.2015.06.004

Beard, Robert (1988). 'On the separation of derivation from morphology: Toward a lexeme/morpheme-based morphology', Quaderni di Semantica 9: 3–59.

Beckman, Mary, and Janet Pierrehumbert (1986). 'Intonational structure in Japanese and English', *Phonology Yearbook* 3: 255–309.

Berg, Kristian, and Mark Aronoff (2017). 'Self-organization in the spelling of English suffixes: The emergence of culture out of anarchy', *Language* 93: 37–64.

Berwick, Robert, and Noam Chomsky (2016). *Why Only Us?* Cambridge, MA: MIT Press.

Bialystok, Ellen (2015). 'The impact of bilingualism on cognition', in Robert Scott and Stephen Kosslyn (eds.) *Emerging Trends in the Social and Behavioral Sciences*. Hoboken, NJ: John Wiley & Sons, 1–12. doi: https://doi.org/10.1002/9781118900772.etrds0340

Bickel, Balthasar, Goma Banjade, Michael Vinding, Elena Lieven, Netra Prasad Paudyal, Ichchha Purna Rai, Monika Chauhan Rai, Novel Kishore Rai, and Sabine Stoll (2007). 'Free prefix ordering in Chintang', *Language* 83: 43–73.

Bickel, Balthasar, and Johanna Nichols (2007). 'Inflectional morphology', in Timothy Shopen (ed.), *Language Typology and Syntactic Description* (Revised second edition). Cambridge: Cambridge University Press, 169–240.

Blevins, James (2006). 'Word-based morphology', *Journal of Linguistics* 42: 531–73.

Blevins, James (2016). *Word and Paradigm Morphology*. Oxford: Oxford University Press.

Blevins, James, Farrell Ackerman, and Robert Malouf (2019). 'Word and Paradigm Morphology', in Jenny Audring and Francesca Masini (eds.), *The Oxford Handbook of Morphological Theory*. Oxford: Oxford University Press, 265–84.

Blevins, Juliette (1995). 'The syllable in phonological theory', in John Goldsmith (ed.), *The Handbook of Phonological Theory*. Oxford: Blackwell, 206–44.

Bloom, Paul (2000). *How Children Learn the Meanings of Words*. Cambridge, MA: MIT Press.

Bloom, Paul (2004). *Descartes's Baby: How the Science of Child Development Explains What Makes us Human*. New York: Basic Books.

Bloomfield, Leonard (1933). *Language*. New York: Holt, Rinehart, and Winston.

Boas, Hans, and Ivan Sag (eds.) (2012). *Sign-Based Construction Grammar*. Chicago: University of Chicago Press.

Bochner, Harry (1993). *Simplicity in Generative Morphology*. Berlin and New York: Mouton de Gruyter.

Bock, Kathryn, and Helga Loebell (1990). 'Framing sentences', *Cognition* 35: 1–39.

Bod, Rens (2006). 'Exemplar-based syntax: How to get productivity from examples', *The Linguistic Review* 23: 291–320.

Booij, Geert (1995). *The Phonology of Dutch*. Oxford: Clarendon Press.

Booij, Geert (1996). 'Inherent versus contextual inflection and the split morphology hypothesis', in Geert Booij and Jaap van Marle (eds.), *Yearbook of Morphology 1995*. Dordrecht: Kluwer, 1–16.

Booij, Geert (1997a). 'Allomorphy and the autonomy of morphology', *Folia Linguistica* 31: 25–56.

Booij, Geert (1997b). 'Autonomous morphology and paradigmatic relations', in Geert Booij and Jaap van Marle (eds.), *Yearbook of Morphology 1996*. Dordrecht: Kluwer, 35–53.

Booij, Geert (2009). 'Lexical storage and phonological change', in Kristen Hanson and Sharon Inkelas (eds.) *The Nature of the Word: Studies in Honor of Paul Kiparsky*. Cambridge, MA: MIT Press, 487–505.

Booij, Geert (2010). *Construction Morphology*. Oxford: Oxford University Press.

Booij, Geert (2012). *The Grammar of Words* (3rd edition). Oxford: Oxford University Press.

Booij, Geert (2017). 'Inheritance and motivation in Construction Morphology', in Nikolas Gisborne and Andrew Hippisley (eds.) *Defaults in Morphological Theory*. Oxford: Oxford University Press, 18–39.

Booij, Geert (ed.) (2018a). *The Construction of Words: Advances in Construction Morphology*. Cham, Switzerland: Springer.

Booij, Geert (2018b). 'The construction of words: Introduction and overview', in Geert Booij (ed.) *The Construction of Words: Advances in Construction Morphology*. Cham, Switzerland: Springer, 3–16.

Booij, Geert (2019). *The Morphology of Dutch* (2nd edition). Oxford: Oxford University Press.

Booij, Geert, and Jenny Audring (2017). 'Construction Morphology and the Parallel Architecture of grammar', *Cognitive Science* 41 (S2): 277–302. doi: 10.1111/cogs.12323

Booij, Geert, and Jenny Audring (2018a). 'Category change in Construction Morphology', in Kristel Van Goethem, Muriel Norde, Evie Coussé, and Gudrun Vanderbauwhede (eds.), *Category Change from a Constructional Perspective* (Constructional Approaches to Language). Amsterdam: John Benjamins, 209–28.

Booij, Geert, and Jenny Audring (2018b). 'Partial motivation, multiple motivation: The role of output schemas in morphology', in Geert Booij (ed.), *The Construction of Words: Advances in Construction Morphology*. Cham, Switzerland: Springer, 59–80.

Booij, Geert, and Francesca Masini (2015). 'The role of second order schemas in the construction of complex words', in Laurie Bauer, Livia Kőrtvélyessy, and Pavol Štekauer (eds.), *Semantics of Complex Words*. Cham, Switzerland: Springer, 47–66.

Botha, Rudolf (1968). *The Function of the Lexicon in Transformational-Generative Grammar*. The Hague: Mouton.

Botha, Rudolf (1981). 'A base rule theory of Afrikaans synthetic compounding', in Michael Moortgat, Harry van der Hulst, and Teun Hoekstra (eds.), *The Scope of Lexical Rules*. Dordrecht: Foris, 1–77.

Bresnan, Joan (ed.) (1982). *The Mental Representation of Grammatical Relations*. Cambridge, MA: MIT Press.

Bresnan, Joan (2001). *Lexical-Functional Syntax*. Oxford: Blackwell.

Bresnan, Joan, and Sam Mchombo (1995). 'The Lexical Integrity Principle: Evidence from Bantu', *Natural Language and Linguistic Theory* 13: 181–254.

Bresnan, Joan, and Tatiana Nikitina (2009). 'The Gradience of the Dative Alternation', in Linda Uyechi and Lian Hee Wee, (eds.) *Reality Exploration and Discovery: Pattern Interaction in Language and Life*. Stanford: CSLI Publications, 161–84.

Breuer, Esther (2015). *First Language versus Foreign Language*. Frankfurt am Main: Peter Lang.

Bromberger, Sylvain, and Morris Halle (1989). 'Why phonology is different', *Linguistic Inquiry* 20: 51–70.

Browman, Catherine P., and Louis Goldstein (1986). 'Towards an articulatory phonology', *Phonology Yearbook* 3: 219–52.

Browman, Catherine P., and Louis Goldstein (1989). 'Articulatory gestures as phonological units', *Phonology* 6: 201–51.

Brown, Dunstan (2019). 'Network Morphology', in Jenny Audring and Francesca Masini (eds.), *The Oxford Handbook of Morphological Theory*. Oxford: Oxford University Press, 305–26.

Brown, Dunstan, and Andrew Hippisley (2012). *Network Morphology: A Defaults-based Theory of Word Structure*. Cambridge: Cambridge University Press.

Bruening, Benjamin (2018). 'The Lexicalist Hypothesis: Both wrong and superfluous', *Language* 94: 1–42.

Buckler, Helen (2014). 'The Acquisition of Morphophonological Alternations across Languages', Ph.D. dissertation, Radboud University, Nijmegen. Ipskamp Drukkers.

Buckler, Helen and Paula Fikkert (2016). 'Using distributional statistics to acquire morphophonological alternations: Evidence from production and perception', *Frontiers in Psychology* 7: article 540, doi: http://dx.doi.org/10.3389/fpsyg.2016.00540

Burzio, Luigi (1994). *Principles of English Stress*. Cambridge: Cambridge University Press.

Busa, Federica (1997). 'Compositionality and the Semantics of Nominals', Ph.D. dissertation, Dept. Of Computer Science, Brandeis University.

Butterworth, Brian (1983). 'Lexical representation', in Brian Butterworth (ed.), *Language Production* (vol. 2). London: Academic Press, 257–94.

Bybee, Joan (1985). *Morphology: A Study of the Relation between Meaning and Form*. Amsterdam/ Philadelphia: John Benjamins.

Bybee, Joan (1995). 'Regular morphology and the lexicon', *Language and Cognitive Processes* 10: 425–55.

Bybee, Joan (2001). *Phonology and Language Use*. Cambridge: Cambridge University Press.

Bybee, Joan (2010). *Language, Usage and Cognition*. Cambridge: Cambridge University Press.

Bybee, Joan, and James McClelland (2005). 'Alternatives to the combinatorial paradigm of linguistic theory based on domain general principles of human cognition', *The Linguistic Review* 22: 381–410.

Bybee, Joan, and Carol Moder (1983). 'Morphological classes as natural categories', *Language* 59: 251–70.

Bybee, Joan, and Dan Slobin (1982). 'Rules and schemas in the development and use of the English past tense', *Language* 58: 265–89.

Cappelle, Bert (2006). 'Particle placement and the case for "allostructions"', *Constructions* online, SV1-7, 1–28.

Carey, Susan (1978). 'The child as word learner', in Morris Halle, Joan Bresnan, and George A. Miller (eds.), *Linguistic Theory and Psychological Reality*. Cambridge, MA: MIT Press, 264–93.

Carey, Susan (2009). *The Origin of Concepts*. Oxford: Oxford University Press.

Caselli, Naomi, Rabia Ergin, Ray Jackendoff, and Ariel Cohen-Goldberg (2014). 'The emergence of structure in Central Taurus Sign Language'. Talk presented at From Sound to Gesture, Padova, Italy.

Cedergren, Henrietta, and David Sankoff (1974). 'Variable rules: Performance as a statistical reflection of competence', *Language* 50: 333–55.

Chater, Nick, and Paul Vitányi (2003). 'Simplicity: A unifying principle in cognitive science?', *Trends in Cognitive Sciences* 7: 19–22.

Chomsky, Noam (1957). *Syntactic Structures*. The Hague: Mouton.

Chomsky, Noam (1959). Review of B. F. Skinner, *Verbal Behavior*, *Language* 35: 26–58.

Chomsky, Noam (1965). *Aspects of the Theory of Syntax*. Cambridge, MA: MIT Press.

Chomsky, Noam (1970). 'Remarks on nominalization', in Roderick Jacobs and Peter Rosenbaum (eds.), *Readings in English Transformational Grammar*. Waltham, MA: Ginn and Company, 184–221. Also in Chomsky, *Studies on Semantics in Generative Grammar*. The Hague: Mouton.

Chomsky, Noam (1972). 'Deep structure, surface structure, and semantic interpretation', in Danny Steinberg and Leon Jacobovits (eds.), *Semantics*. Cambridge: Cambridge University Press, 183–216. Also in Chomsky, *Studies on Semantics in Generative Grammar*. The Hague: Mouton.

Chomsky, Noam (1981). *Lectures on Government and Binding*. Dordrecht: Foris.

Chomsky, Noam (1986). *Knowledge of Language: Its Nature, Origin, and Use*. New York: Praeger.

Chomsky, Noam (1995). *The Minimalist Program*. Cambridge, MA: MIT Press.

Chomsky, Noam, and Morris Halle (1968). *The Sound Pattern of English*. New York: Harper and Row.

Christiansen, Morten, and Inbal Arnon (2017). 'More than words: The role of multiword sequences in language learning and use', *Topics in Cognitive Science* 9: 542–51.

Chumakina, Marina, and Greville G. Corbett (eds.) (2013). *Periphrasis: The Role of Syntax and Morphology in Paradigms*. Oxford: Published for the British Academy by Oxford University Press.

Clahsen, Harald (1999). 'Lexical entries and rules of language: A multidisciplinary study of German inflection', *Behavioral and Brain Sciences* 22: 991–1060.

Clahsen, Harald (2016). 'Experimental studies of morphology and morphological processing', in Andrew Hippisley and Gregory Stump (eds.), *The Cambridge Handbook of Morphology*. Cambridge: Cambridge University Press, 792–819.

Clahsen, Harald, Peter Prüfert, Sonja Eisenbeiss, and Joana Cholin (2002). 'Strong stems in the German mental lexicon: Evidence from child language acquisition and adult processing', in Ingrid Kaufmann and Barbara Stiebels (eds.), *More than Words: A Festschrift for Dieter Wunderlich*. Berlin: Akademie-Verlag, 91–112.

Clark, Eve (1993). *The Lexicon in Acquisition*. Cambridge: Cambridge University Press.

Clark, Eve, and Melissa Bowerman (1986). 'On the acquisition of final voiced stops', in Joshua A. Fishman et al. (eds.), *The Fergusonian Impact*, (Vol. 1). Berlin: Mouton de Gruyter, 52–68.

Clark, Eve, and Herbert Clark (1979). 'When nouns surface as verbs', *Language* 55: 767–811.

Collins, Allan, and Elizabeth Loftus (1975). 'A spreading activation theory of semantic processing', *Psychological Review* 82: 407–28.

Collins, Allan, and M. Ross Quillian (1969). 'Retrieval time from semantic memory', *Journal of Verbal Learning and Verbal Behavior* 9: 240–7.

Comrie, Bernard (1999). 'Grammatical gender systems: A linguist's assessment', *Journal of Psycholinguistic Research* 28(5): 457–66.

Coppock, Elizabeth (2009). 'Parallel grammatical encoding in sentence production: Evidence from syntactic blends', *Language and Cognitive Processes* 25: 38–49.

Corbett, Greville G. (1991). *Gender*. Cambridge: Cambridge University Press.

Corbett, Greville G. (2006). *Agreement*. Cambridge: Cambridge University Press.

Corbett, Greville G. (2007). 'Canonical typology, suppletion and possible words', *Language* 83: 8–42.

Corbett, Greville G., and Matthew Baerman (2006). 'Prolegomena to a typology of morphological features', *Morphology* 16: 231–46.

Corbett, Greville G., and Norman M. Fraser (2000). 'Default genders', in Barbara Unterbeck and Matti Rissanen (eds.), *Gender in Grammar and Cognition*. Berlin: Mouton de Gruyter, 55–98.

Coulmas, Florian (2003). *Writing Systems: An Introduction to their Linguistic Analysis*. Cambridge: Cambridge University Press.

Croft, William (2001). *Radical Construction Grammar*. Oxford: Oxford University Press.

Croft, William (2003). 'Lexical rules vs. constructions: A false dichotomy', in Hubert Cuyckens, Thomas Berg, René Dirven, and Klaus-Uwe Panther (eds.), *Motivation in Language: Studies in Honour of Günter Radden*. Amsterdam: John Benjamins, 49–68.

Crowhurst, Megan (1998). '*Um* infixation and prefixation in Toba Batak', *Language* 74: 590–604.

Culicover, Peter W. (1999). *Syntactic Nuts: Hard Cases in Syntax*. Oxford: Oxford University Press.

Culicover, Peter W. (in preparation). *The Origin of Languages*.

Culicover, Peter W., and Ray Jackendoff (2005). *Simpler Syntax*. Oxford: Oxford University Press.

Culicover, Peter W., and Ray Jackendoff (2012). 'Same-Except: A domain-general cognitive relation and how language expresses it', *Language* 88: 305–40.

Culicover, Peter W., Ray Jackendoff, and Jenny Audring (2017). 'Multiword constructions in the grammar', *Topics in Cognitive Science* 9: 552–568. doi: 10.1111/tops.12255

Culicover, Peter W., and Andrzey Nowak (2003). *Dynamical Grammar*. Oxford: Oxford University Press.

Dąbrowska, Ewa (2018). 'Experience, aptitude and individual differences in native language ultimate attainment', *Cognition* 178: 222–35.

Daelemans, Walter, and Koenraad De Smedt (1994). 'Default inheritance in an object-oriented representation of linguistic categories', *International Journal Human-Computer Studies* 41: 149–77.

Davis, Stuart, and Natsuko Tsujimura (2018). 'Arabic nonconcatenative morphology in Construction Morphology', in Geert Booij (ed.), *The Construction of Words: Advances in Construction Morphology*. Cham, Switzerland: Springer, 315–39.

De Bot, Kees, Wander Lowie, and Marjolijn Verspoor (2005). *Second Language Acquisition: An Advanced Resource Book*. New York: Routledge.

De Haas, Wim, and Mieke Trommelen (1993). *Morfologisch handboek van het Nederlands: een overzicht van de woordvorming*. 's-Gravenhage: SDU Uitgevers.

Dehaene, Stanislas, Florent Meyniel, Catherine Wacongne, Liping Wang, and Christophe Pallier (2015). 'The neural representation of sequences: From transition probabilities to algebraic patterns and linguistic trees', *Neuron* 88: 1–19. http://dx.doi.org/10.1016/j.neuron.2015.09.019

De Saussure, Ferdinand (1959). *Course in General Linguistics*. New York: Philosophical Library. (Translation of *Cours de linguistique générale*, 1915.)

De Vaan, Laura, Robert Schreuder, and R. Harald Baayen (2007). 'Regular morphologically complex neologisms leave detectable traces in the mental lexicon', *The Mental Lexicon* 2: 1–24.

Dinstein, Ilan, David J. Heeger, and Marlene Behrmann (2015). 'Neural variability: Friend or foe?', *Trends in Cognitive Sciences* 19: 322–8. doi: 10.1016/j.tics.2015.04.005

Di Sciullo, Anna Maria, and Edwin Williams (1987). *On the Definition of Word*. Cambridge, MA: MIT Press.

Downing, Pamela (1977). 'On the creation and use of English compound nouns', *Language* 53: 810–42.

Dowty, David (1991). 'Thematic proto-roles and argument selection', *Language* 67: 547–619.

Dresher, B. Elan (2014). 'The arch not the stones: Universal feature theory without universal features', *Nordlyd* 41: 165–81. Special issue on Features, Martin Krämer, Sandra Ronai, and Peter Svenonius (eds.).

Dressler, Wolfgang (2006). 'Compound types', in Gary Libben and Gonia Jarema (eds.), *The Representation and Processing of Compound Words*. Oxford: Oxford University Press, 23–44.

Duñabeitia, Jon Andoni, Manuel Perea, and Manuel Carreiras (2008). 'Does darkness lead to happiness? Masked suffix priming effects', *Language and Cognitive Processes* 23: 1002–20. doi: 10.1080/01690960802164242

Embick, David (2015). *The Morpheme: An Introduction*. Boston and Berlin: Mouton de Gruyter.

Embick, David, and Rolf Noyer (2007). 'Distributed Morphology and the syntax-morphology interface', in Gillian Ramchand and Charles Reiss (eds.), *The Oxford Handbook of Linguistic Interfaces*. Oxford: Oxford University Press, 289–324.

Enger, Hans-Olav (2009). 'The role of core and non-core semantic rules in gender assignment', *Lingua* 119: 1281–99.

Eriksson, Johan, Edward K. Vogel, Anders Lansner, Fredrik Bergström, and Lars Nyberg (2015). 'Neurocognitive architecture of working memory', *Neuron* 88: 33–46. https://doi.org/10.1016/j.neuron.2015.09.020

Ernestus, Mirjam (2014). 'Acoustic reduction and the roles of abstractions and exemplars in speech processing', *Lingua* 142: 27–41.

Erteschik-Shir, Nomi (1979). 'Discourse constraints on dative movement', in Talmy Givon (ed.), *Syntax and Semantics, 12: Discourse and syntax*. New York: Academic Press, 441–67.

Evans, Nicholas (2017). 'Polysynthesis in Dalabon', in Michael Fortescue, Marianne Mithun, and Nicholas Evans (eds.), *The Oxford Handbook of Polysynthesis*, 759–81. Oxford: Oxford University Press, 759–81. doi: 10.1093/oxfordhb/9780199683208.013.43

Evans, Nicholas, Dunstan Brown, and Greville G. Corbett (2001). 'Dalabon pronominal prefixes and the typology of syncretism: A Network Morphology analysis', in Geert Booij and Jaap van Marle (eds.), *Yearbook of Morphology 2000*. Dordrecht: Springer, 187–231.

Evans, Roger, and Gerald Gazdar (1996). 'DATR: A language for lexical knowledge representation', *Computational Linguistics* 22: 167–216.

Fabb, Nigel, and Morris Halle (2008). *Meter in Poetry: A New Theory*. Cambridge: Cambridge University Press.

Feldman, Laurie B. (2000). 'Are morphological effects distinguishable from the effects of shared meaning and shared form?', *Journal of Experimental Psychology: Learning, Memory, and Cognition* 26: 1431–44.

Fernández-Domínguez, Jesús (2016). 'The semantics of primary NN compounds: From form to meaning, and from meaning to form', in Pius ten Hacken (ed.), *The Semantics of Compounding*. Cambridge: Cambridge University Press, 129–49.

Ferreira, Fernanda, and Nikole Patson (2007). 'The "Good Enough" Approach to Language Comprehension', *Language and Linguistics Compass* 1: 71–83. doi: 10.1111/j.1749-818X.2007.00007

Fillmore, Charles (1982). 'Frame semantics', in The Linguistic Society of Korea (eds.), *Linguistics in the Morning Calm*. Seoul: Hanshin Publishing Company, 111–37.

Fillmore, Charles, Paul Kay, and Mary Catherine O'Connor (1988). 'Regularity and idiomaticity in grammatical constructions: The case of *let alone*', *Language* 64: 501–38.

Fiske, Alan P. (1991). *Structures of Social Life: The Four Elementary Forms of Human Relations*. New York: Free Press.

Fitch, W. Tecumseh (2010). *The Evolution of Language*. Cambridge: Cambridge University Press.

Fitch, W. Tecumseh, Marc Hauser, and Noam Chomsky (2005). 'The evolution of the language faculty: Clarifications and implications', *Cognition* 97: 179–210.

Fodor, Janet D. (1998). 'Learning to parse', in David Swinney (ed.), *Anniversary Issue of Journal of Psycholinguistic Research* 27: 285–318.

Forster, Kenneth I. (1976). 'Accessing the mental lexicon', in Roger J. Wales and Edward Walker (eds.), *New Approaches to Language Mechanisms*. Amsterdam: North-Holland, 257–87.

Fradin, Bernard, and Françoise Kerleroux (2003). Troubles with lexemes', in Geert Booij, Janet DeCesaris, Angela Ralli, and Sergio Scalise (eds.), *Selected Papers from the Third Mediterranean Morphology Meeting*. Barcelona: IULA – Universitat Pompeu Fabra, 177–96.

Francis, Norbert (2012). *Bilingual Development and Literacy Learning: East Asian and International Perspectives*. Hong Kong: City University of Hong Kong Press.

Francis, Norbert (2016). 'Language and dialect in China 2016', lingbuzz/003228.

Fraser, Bruce (1970). 'Idioms within a transformational grammar', *Foundations of Language* 6: 22–42.

Frauenfelder, Uli, and Robert Schreuder (1992). 'Constraining psycholinguistic models of morphological processing and representation: The role of productivity', in Geert Booij and Jaap van Marle (eds.), *Yearbook of Morphology 1991*. Dordrecht: Springer, 165–83.

Fulcrand, Julien (2015). 'A reanalysis of the great English vowel shift under contrast preservation theory', *Linguistic Research* 32: 533–71.

Gaeta, Livio (2008). 'Die deutsche Pluralbildung zwischen deskriptiver Angemessenheit und Sprachtheorie', *Zeitschrift für Germanistische Linguistik* 36(1): 74–108. doi: 10.1515/ZGL.2008.005

Gagné, Christine L. (2009). 'Psycholinguistic perspectives', in Rochelle Lieber and Pavol Stekauer (eds.), *The Oxford Handbook of Compounding*. Oxford: Oxford University Press, 255–71.

Gagné, Christine L., and Thomas L. Spalding (2019). 'Morphological theory and psycholinguistics', in Jenny Audring and Francesca Masini (eds.), *The Oxford Handbook of Morphological Theory*. Oxford: Oxford University Press, 541–53.

Gallistel, C. R., and Adam King (2009). *Memory and the Computational Brain*. Malden, MA: Wiley-Blackwell.

Gazdar, Gerald, Ewan Klein, Geoffrey Pullum, and Ivan Sag (1985). *Generalized Phrase Structure Grammar*. Cambridge, MA: Harvard University Press.

Gentner, Dedre, and Eyal Sagi (2006). 'Does "different" imply a difference? A comparison of two tasks', in Ron Sun and Naomi Miyake (eds.), *Proceedings of the 28th annual conference of the Cognitive Science Society*. London: Psychology Press, 261–6.

Ghomeshi, Jila (1997). 'Non-projecting nouns and the *ezafe* construction in Persian', *Natural Language and Linguistic Theory* 15: 729–88.

Ghomeshi, Jila, Ray Jackendoff, Nicole Rosen, and Kevin Russell (2004). 'Contrastive Focus Reduplication in English (The salad-salad paper)', *Natural Language and Linguistic Theory* 22: 307–57.

Gibbs, Raymond (1985). 'On the process of understanding idioms', *Journal of Psycholinguistic Research* 14: 465–72.

Gibson, Edward, Leon Bergen, and Steven Piantadosi (2013). 'Rational integration of noisy evidence and prior semantic expectations in sentence interpretation', *Proceedings of the National Academy of Sciences* 110 (20): 8051–6. https://doi.org/10.1073/pnas.1216438110

Giraudo, Hélène, and Jonathan Grainger (2003). 'On the role of derivational affixes in recognizing complex words: Evidence from masked priming', in Harald Baayen and Robert Schreuder (eds.), *Morphological Structure in Language Processing*. Berlin and New York: Mouton de Gruyter, 209–32.

Gisborne, Nikolas (2019). 'Word Grammar Morphology', in Jenny Audring and Francesca Masini (eds.), *The Oxford Handbook of Morphological Theory*. Oxford: Oxford University Press, 327–45.

Gleitman, Lila (1965). 'Coordinating conjunctions in English', *Language* 41: 260–93.

Gleitman, Lila, and Henry Gleitman (1970). *Phrase and Paraphrase*. New York: Norton.

Gleitman, Lila, Henry Gleitman, Carol Miller, and Ruth Ostrin (1996). 'Similar, and similar concepts', *Cognition* 58: 321–76.

Glucksberg, Sam (1993). 'Idiom meanings and allusional content', in Cristina Cacciari and Patricia Tabossi (eds.), *Idioms: Processing Structure, and Interpretation*. Hillsdale, NJ: Lawrence Erlbaum, 3–26.

Goffman, Erving (1974). *Frame Analysis: An Essay on the Organization of Experience*. Cambridge, MA: Harvard University Press.

Goldberg, Adele (1995). *Constructions: A Construction Grammar Approach to Argument Structure*. Chicago: University of Chicago Press.

Goldberg, Adele (2006). *Constructions at Work: The Nature of Generalization in Language*. Oxford: Oxford University Press.

Goldberg, Adele (2019). *Explain Me This*. Princeton: Princeton University Press.

Goldsmith, John (1979). *Autosegmental Phonology*. New York: Garland Press.

Goldsmith, John (1993). Harmonic Phonology', in John Goldsmith (ed.), *The Last Phonological Rule: Reflections on Constraints and Derivations*. Chicago: University of Chicago Press, 21–60.

Gow, David W., and Peter C. Gordon (1995). 'Lexical and prelexical influences on word segmentation: Evidence from priming', *Journal of Experimental Psychology: Human Perception and Performance* 21: 344–59.

Grainger, Jonathan, Katherine Midgley, and Phillip Holcomb (2010). 'Re-thinking the bilingual interactive-activation model from a developmental perspective (BIA-d)', in Michèle Kail and M. Hickmann (eds.), *Language Acquisition across Linguistic and Cognitive Systems*. Philadelphia: John Benjamins, 267–84.

Hagoort, Peter (2005). 'On Broca, brain, and binding: A new framework', *Trends in Cognitive Sciences* 9: 416–23.

Hagoort, Peter (2013). 'MUC (Memory, Unification, Control) and beyond', *Frontiers in Psychology* 4: article 416. doi: 10.3389/fpsyg.2013.00416

Hale, John (2003). 'The information conveyed by words in sentences', *Journal of Psycholinguistic Research* 32: 101–23.

Hale, John (2011). 'What a rational parser would do', *Cognitive Science* 35: 399–443.

Hale, Kenneth, and Samuel Jay Keyser (2002). *Prolegomenon to a Theory of Argument Structure*. Cambridge, MA: MIT Press.

Halle, Morris (1973). 'Prolegomena to a theory of word formation', *Linguistic Inquiry* 4: 3–16.

Halle, Morris (2005). 'Palatalization/velar softening: What it is and what it tells us about the nature of language', *Linguistic Inquiry* 36: 23–41.

Halle, Morris, and Samuel Jay Keyser (1971). *English Stress: Its Form, Its Growth, and its Role in Verse*. New York: Harper and Row.

Halle, Morris, and Alec Marantz (1993). 'Distributed Morphology and the pieces of inflection', in Kenneth Hale and Samuel Jay Keyser (eds.), *The View from Building 20*. Cambridge, MA: MIT Press, 111–76.

Hankamer, Jorge (1989). 'Morphological parsing and the lexicon', in William Marslen-Wilson (ed.), *Lexical Representation and Process*. Stanford, CA: CSLI, 392–408.

Harley, Heidi (2014). 'On the identity of roots', *Theoretical Linguistics* 40: 225–76.

Harris, Zellig S. (1957). 'Co-occurrence and transformation in linguistic structure', *Language* 33: 283–340.

Haspelmath, Martin (1996). 'Word-class-changing inflection and morphological theory', in Geert Booij and Jaap van Marle (eds.), *Yearbook of Morphology 1995*. Dordrecht: Springer, 43–66.

Haspelmath, Martin (2011). 'The indeterminacy of word segmentation and the nature of morphology and syntax', *Folia Linguistica* 45: 31–80.

Haspelmath, Martin, and Andrea Sims (2010). *Understanding Morphology* (2nd edition). London and New York: Routledge.

Hauser, Marc, Noam Chomsky, and W. Tecumseh Fitch (2002). 'The faculty of language: What is it, who has it, and how did it evolve?', *Science* 298: 1569–79.

Hauser, Marc, and Jeffrey Watumull (2016). 'The Universal Generative Faculty: The source of our expressive power in language, mathematics, morality, and music', *Journal of Neurolinguistics* 43 Part B: 78–94. doi: 10.1016/j.jneuroling.2016.10.005

Hay, Jennifer (2001). 'Lexical frequency in morphology: Is everything relative?', *Linguistics* 39: 1041–70.

Hay, Jennifer, and Harald Baayen (2005). 'Shifting paradigms: Gradient structure in morphology', *Trends in Cognitive Sciences* 9: 342–8.

Hayes, Bruce (1983). 'A grid-based theory of English meter', *Linguistic Inquiry* 14: 357–93.

Hayes, Bruce (2010). Review of Fabb and Halle 2008, *Lingua* 120: 2515–21.

Hayes, Bruce, Colin Wilson, and Anne Shisko (2012). 'Maxent grammars for the metrics of Shakespeare and Milton', *Language* 88: 691–731.

Heim, Irene, and Angelika Kratzer (1998). *Semantics in Generative Grammar*. Malden, MA: Blackwell.

Höder, Steffen (2012). 'Multilingual constructions: A diasystematic approach to common structures', in Kurt Braunmüller and Christoph Gabriel (eds.), *Multilingual Individuals and Multilingual Societies*, (Vol. 13). Amsterdam: John Benjamins, 241–58. doi: 10.1075/hsm.13.17hod

Höder, Steffen (2014). 'Phonological elements and Diasystematic Construction Grammar', *Constructions and Frames* 6: 202–31.

Hoeksema, Jack, and Donna Jo Napoli (2008). 'Just for the hell of it: A comparison of two taboo-term constructions', *Journal of Linguistics* 44: 347–78.

Hoffmann, Thomas, and Graeme Trousdale (eds.) (2013). *The Oxford Handbook of Construction Grammar*. Oxford: Oxford University Press.

Hofstadter, Douglas, and Melanie Mitchell (1995). 'The Copycat project: A model of mental fluidity and analogy-making', in Douglas Hofstadter and the Fluid Analogies Group (eds.), *Fluid Concepts and Creative Analogies*. New York: Basic Books, 205–67.

Horn, Laurence (1993). 'Economy and redundancy in a dualistic model of natural language', in Susanna Shore and Maria Vilkuna (eds.), *SKY 1993: 1993 Yearbook of the Linguistic Association of Finland*, 33–72.

Horn, Laurence (in preparation). 'The lexical clone: Pragmatics, prototypes, productivity', in Rita Finkbeiner and Ulrike Freywald (eds.), *Exact Repetition in Grammar and Discourse*. Berlin: De Gruyter.

Hornstein, Norbert (2018). 'The Minimalist Program after 25 years', *Annual Review of Linguistics* 4: 49–65.

Hugou, Vincent (2013). 'The *Xed out* construction: Between productivity and creativity', *Quaderns de Filologia. Estudis lingüístics. Vol. XVIII*: 83–95.

Huk, Alexander, and Eric Hart (2019). 'Parsing signal and noise in the brain', *Science* 364 (19 April 2019): 236–7.

Humboldt, Wilhelm von (1999 [1836]) *On the Diversity of Human Language Construction and its Influence on the Mental Development of the Human Species* (orig. *Über die Verschiedenheit des menschlichen Sprachbaus und seinen Einfluss auf die geistige Entwicklung des Menschengeschlechts*). Michael Losonsky (ed.), Cambridge: Cambridge University Press.

Hüning, Matthias (2009). 'Semantic niches and analogy in word formation: Evidence from contrastive linguistics', *Languages in Contrast* 9(2): 183–201. doi: 10.1075/lic.9.2.01hun

Hüning, Matthias (2010). 'Adjective + Noun constructions between syntax and word formation in Dutch and German', in Sascha Michel and Alexander Onysko (eds.), *Cognitive Approaches to Word Formation*. Berlin: De Gruyter Mouton, 195–218.

Hüning, Matthias (2018). 'Foreign word-formation in Construction Morphology: Verbs in -*ieren* in German', in Geert Booij (ed.), *The Construction of Words: Advances in Construction Morphology*. Cham, Switzerland: Springer, 341–98.

Inkelas, Sharon (2014). *The Interplay of Morphology and Phonology*. Oxford: Oxford University Press.

Inkelas, Sharon, and Cheryl Zoll (2005). *Reduplication: Doubling in Morphology*. Cambridge: Cambridge University Press.

Iverson, Gregory K., and Joseph C. Salmons (2011). 'Final devoicing and final laryngeal neutralization', in Marc Oostendorp, Colin J. Ewen, Elizabeth Hume, and Keren Rice (eds.), *The Blackwell Companion to Phonology*. Oxford: Blackwell. doi: 10.1002/9781444335262.wbctp0069

Jackendoff, Ray (1972). *Semantic Interpretation in Generative Grammar*. Cambridge, MA: MIT Press.

Jackendoff, Ray (1975). 'Morphological and semantic regularities in the lexicon', *Language* 51: 639–71.

Jackendoff, Ray (1983). *Semantics and Cognition*. Cambridge, MA: MIT Press.

Jackendoff, Ray (1987). *Consciousness and the Computational Mind*. Cambridge, MA: MIT Press.

Jackendoff, Ray (1990). *Semantic Structures*. Cambridge, MA: MIT Press.

Jackendoff, Ray (1996). 'The architecture of the linguistic-spatial interface', in Paul Bloom, Mary Peterson, Lynn Nadel, and Merrill F. Garrett (eds.), *Language and Space*. Cambridge, MA: MIT Press, 1–30.

Jackendoff, Ray (1997). *The Architecture of the Language Faculty*. Cambridge, MA: MIT Press.

Jackendoff, Ray (2002). *Foundations of Language*. Oxford: Oxford University Press.

Jackendoff, Ray (2007a). 'A Parallel Architecture Perspective on Language Processing', *Brain Research* 1146, 2–22. Revised version: 'A Parallel Architecture Model of Language Processing', in Kevin Ochsner and Stephen Kosslyn (eds.) *Oxford Handbook of Cognitive Neuroscience*, (Vol. 1), Oxford: Oxford University Press, 577–94.

Jackendoff, Ray (2007b). *Language, Consciousness, Culture*. Cambridge, MA: MIT Press.

Jackendoff, Ray (2008). '"Construction after construction" and its theoretical challenges', *Language* 84: 8–28.

Jackendoff, Ray (2010). 'The ecology of English noun-noun compounds', in Ray Jackendoff (ed.), *Meaning and the Lexicon*. Oxford: Oxford University Press, 413–51.

Jackendoff, Ray (2011). 'What is the human language faculty? Two views', *Language* 87: 586–624.

Jackendoff, Ray (2013). 'Constructions in the Parallel Architecture', in Thomas Hoffmann and Graeme Trousdale (eds.), *The Oxford Handbook of Construction Grammar*. Oxford: Oxford University Press, 70–92.

Jackendoff, Ray (2015). 'In defense of theory', *Cognitive Science* 41 S2: 185–212 (special issue in commemoration of RJ's Rumelhart prize) https://doi.org/10.1111/cogs.12324

Jackendoff, Ray, and Fred Lerdahl (2006). 'The Capacity for Music: What's Special about it?', *Cognition* 100: 33–72.

Jackendoff, Ray, and Steven Pinker (2005). 'The nature of the language faculty and its implications for the evolution of language (Reply to Fitch, Hauser, and Chomsky 2005)', *Cognition* 97: 211–25.

Jaeger, Jeri J. (1986). 'On the acquisition of the vowel shift rule', *Proceedings of the Twelfth Annual Meeting of the Berkeley Linguistics Society*, 159–71.

Jakobson, Roman, Gunnar Fant, and Morris Halle (1951). *Preliminaries to Speech Analysis.* Cambridge, MA: MIT Press.

James, William (1890). *The Principles of Psychology.* New York: Henry Holt and Co. Reprint: New York, Dover Books, 1950.

Joshi, Aravind (1987). 'An introduction to Tree-Adjoining Grammars', in Alexis Manaster-Ramer (ed.), *Mathematics of Language.* Amsterdam: John Benjamins, 87–114.

Jusczyk, Peter. 1997. *The Discovery of Spoken Language.* Cambridge, MA: MIT Press.

Jusczyk, Peter W., Angela Friederici, Jeanine Wessels, Vigdis Svenkerud, and Ann Marie Jusczyk (1993). 'Infants' sensitivity to the sound patterns of native language words', *Journal of Memory and Language* 32: 402–20. http://dx.doi.org/10.1006/jmla.1993.1022

Kapatsinski, Vsevolod (2007). 'Frequency, neighborhood density, age-of-acquisition, lexicon size, neighborhood density and speed of processing: Towards a domain-general, single-mechanism account', in Susan Buescher, Keri Holley, Evan Ashworth, Clay Beckner, Briony Jones, and Christopher Shank (eds.), *Proceedings of the 6th Annual High Desert Linguistics Society Conference.* Albuquerque, NM: High Desert Linguistics Society, 121–40.

Kay, Paul (2013). 'The limits of Construction Grammar', in Thomas Hoffmann and Graeme Trousdale (eds.), *The Oxford Handbook of Construction Grammar.* Oxford: Oxford University Press, 32–48.

Keating, Patricia (1985). 'Universal phonetics and the organization of grammars', in Victoria Fromkin (ed.), *Phonetic Linguistics: Essays in Honor of Peter Ladefoged.* New York: Academic Press, 115–32.

Keating, Patricia (1988). 'The phonology-phonetics interface', in Frederick J. Newmeyer (ed.), *Linguistics: The Cambridge Survey. I. Linguistic Theory: Foundations.* Cambridge: Cambridge University Press, 281–302.

Kemps, Rachèl J. J. K., Mirjam Ernestus, Robert Schreuder, and Harald Baayen (2005). 'Prosodic cues for morphological complexity: The case of Dutch plural nouns', *Memory and Cognition* 33(3): 430–46.

Keyser, Samuel Jay, and Kenneth Stevens (2006). 'Enhancement and overlap in the speech chain', *Language* 82: 33–63.

Kibrik, Aleksandr E. (1998). 'Archi', in Andrew Spencer and Arnold M. Zwicky (eds.) *The Handbook of Morphology.* Oxford: Blackwell, 455–76.

Kielar, Aneta, Marc F. Joanisse, and Mary L. Hare (2008). 'Priming English past tense verbs: Rules or statistics?', *Journal of Memory and Language* 58: 327–46.

Kim, Yuni (2010). 'Phonological and morphological conditions on affix order in Huave', *Morphology* 20: 133–63.

Kiparsky, Paul (1982). Word-formation and the lexicon', in Frances Ingemann (ed.), *Proceedings of the Mid-America Linguistics Conference.* Lawrence, Kansas.

Kiparsky, Paul, and Gilbert Youmans (eds.) (1989). *Phonetics and Phonology: Rhythm and Meter.* New York: Academic Press.

Klima, Edward, and Ursula Bellugi (1979). *The Signs of Language.* Cambridge, MA: Harvard University Press.

Koester, Dirk, and Niels O. Schiller (2008). 'Morphological priming in overt language production: Electrophysiological evidence from Dutch', *NeuroImage* 42: 1622–30. doi: 10.1016/j.neuroimage.2008.06.043

Köpcke, Klaus-Michael (1982). *Untersuchungen zum Genussystem der deutschen Gegenwartssprache.* Tübingen: Niemeyer.

Köpcke, Klaus-Michael (1998). 'The acquisition of plural marking in English and German revisited: Schemata versus rules', *Journal of Child Language* 25: 293–319.

Kraak, Albert (1967). 'Presuppositions and the analysis of adverbs', Cambridge, MA: MIT, ms.

Kroll, Judith F., Paola E. Dussias, Kinsey Bice, and Lauren Perrotti (2015). 'Bilingualism, Mind, and Brain', *Annual Review of Linguistics* 1: 7.1–7.18. doi: 10.1146/annurev-linguist-030514-124937

Kuhl, Patricia, Barbara Conboy, Denise Padden, Tobey Nelson, and Jessica Pruitt (2005). 'Early speech perception and later language development: Implications for the "critical period"', *Language Learning and Development* 1: 237–64.

Kuperberg, Gina R., and Florian T. Jaeger (2016). 'What do we mean by prediction in language comprehension?', *Language, Cognition and Neuroscience* 31: 32–59.

Kuperman, Victor, Robert Schreuder, Raymond Bertram, and Harald Baayen (2009). 'Reading polymorphemic Dutch compounds: Toward a multiple route model of lexical processing', *Journal of Experimental Psychology: Human Perception and Performance* 35: 876–95. http://dx.doi.org/10.1037/a0013484

Kwon, Nahyun, and Erich Round (2015). 'Phonaesthemes in morphological theory', *Morphology* 25: 1–27. doi: 10.1007/s11525-014-9250-z

Labov, William (1969). 'Contraction, deletion, and inherent variability of the English copula', *Language* 45: 715–62.

Ladd, D. Robert (2014). *Simultaneous Structure in Phonology*. Oxford: Oxford University Press.

Ladefoged, Peter (2007). 'Articulatory features for describing lexical distinctions', *Language* 83: 161–80.

Lakoff, George (1970). *Irregularity in Syntax*. New York: Holt, Rinehart, and Winston.

Lakoff, George (1987). *Women, Fire, and Dangerous Things*. Chicago: University of Chicago Press.

Lakoff, George (1993). 'Cognitive Phonology', in John Goldsmith (ed.), *The Last Phonological Rule: Reflections on Constraints and Derivations*. Chicago: University of Chicago Press, 117–45.

Lakoff, George, and Stanley Peters (1966). 'Phrasal conjunction and symmetric predicates', *Mathematical Linguistics and Automatic Translation* Report NSF-17. Cambridge, MA: Harvard University Computation Laboratory.

Lamb, Sydney (1966). *Outline of Stratificational Grammar*. Washington, DC: Georgetown University Press.

Landau, Barbara, and Lila Gleitman (1985). *Language and Experience: Evidence from the Blind Child*. Cambridge, MA: Harvard University Press.

Landau, Barbara, and Lila Gleitman (2015). 'Height matters', in Ida Toivonen, Piroska Csuri, and Emile van der Zee (eds.), *Structures in the Mind: Essays on Language, Music, and Cognition in Honor of Ray Jackendoff*. Cambridge, MA: MIT Press, 187–210.

Landau, Barbara, and James Hoffman (2012). *Spatial Representation: From Gene to Mind*. Oxford: Oxford University Press.

Landau, Barbara, and Ray Jackendoff (1993). '"What" and "where" in spatial language and spatial cognition', *Behavioral and Brain Sciences* 16: 217–38.

Landau, Barbara, Linda Smith, and Susan Jones (1988). 'The importance of shape in early lexical learning', *Cognitive Development* 3: 299–321.

Landauer, Thomas, and Susan Dumais (1997). 'A solution to Plato's problem: The latent semantic analysis theory of acquisition, induction, and representation of knowledge', *Psychological Review* 104: 211–40.

Langacker, Ronald (1987). *Foundations of Cognitive Grammar*, (Vol. 1). Stanford: Stanford University Press.

Langacker, Ronald (1999). *Grammar and Conceptualization*. Berlin and New York: Mouton de Gruyter.

Lappe, Sabine (2007). *English Prosodic Morphology*. Dordrecht: Springer.

Larson, Richard (2017). 'On "dative idioms" in English', *Linguistic Inquiry* 48: 389–426.

Lees, Robert (1960). *The Grammar of English Nominalizations*. The Hague: Mouton.

Lepic, Ryan, and Corrine Occhino (2018). 'A Construction Morphology approach to sign language analysis', in Geert Booij (ed.), *The Construction of Words: Advances in Construction Morphology*. Cham, Switzerland: Springer, 141–72.

Lerdahl, Fred (2001). 'The sounds of poetry viewed as music', *Annals of the New York Academy of Sciences* 930: 337–54. doi: 10.1093/acprof:oso/9780198525202.003.0027

Lerdahl, Fred, and Ray Jackendoff (1983). *A Generative Theory of Tonal Music*. Cambridge, MA: MIT Press.

Levelt, Willem J. M. (1989). *Speaking*. Cambridge, MA: MIT Press.

Levelt, Willem J. M., Ardi Roelofs, and Antje Meyer (1999). 'A theory of lexical access in speech production', *Behavioral and Brain Sciences* 22: 1–75.

Levy, Roger (2008). 'Expectation-based syntactic comprehension', *Cognition* 106: 1126–77.

Libben, Gary (2006). 'Why study compounds? An overview of the issues', in Gary Libben and Gonia Jarema (eds.), *The Representation and Processing of Compound Words*. Oxford: Oxford University Press, 1–21.

Liberman, Alvin, and Michael Studdert-Kennedy (1977). 'Phonetic perception', in Richard Held, Herschel Leibowitz, and Hans-Lukas Teuber (eds.), *Handbook of Sensory Physiology*, (Vol. viii), *Perception*. Heidelberg: Springer.

Liberman, Mark (2018). 'Towards progress in theories of language sound structure', in Diane Brentari and Jackson Lee (eds.), *Shaping Phonology*. Chicago: University of Chicago Press, 201–22.

Liberman, Mark, and Alan Prince (1977). 'On stress and linguistic rhythm', *Linguistic Inquiry* 8: 249–336.

Lidz, Jeffrey (2001). 'Echo reduplication in Kannada and the theory of word formation', *Linguistic Review* 18: 375–94.

Lieber, Rochelle (1992). *Deconstructing Morphology: Word Formation in Syntactic Theory*. Chicago: University of Chicago Press.

Lieber, Rochelle (2019). 'Theoretical issues in word formation', in Jenny Audring and Francesca Masini (eds.), *The Oxford Handbook of Morphological Theory*. Oxford: Oxford University Press, 34–55.

Lynch, Kevin (1960). *The Image of the City*. Cambridge, MA: MIT Press.

MacKay, Donald (1978). 'Derivational rules and the internal lexicon', *Journal of Verbal Learning and Verbal Behavior* 17: 61–71.

MacDonald, Maryellen, Neal J. Pearlmutter, and Mark Seidenberg (1994). 'Lexical nature of syntactic ambiguity resolution', *Psychological Review* 101: 676–703.

MacKay, Donald G. (1978). 'Derivational rules and the internal lexicon', *Journal of Verbal Learning and Verbal Behavior* 17: 61–71.

Macnamara, John (1982). *Names for Things*. Cambridge, MA: MIT Press.

Marantz, Alec (1982). 'Re reduplication', *Linguistic Inquiry* 13: 435–82.

Marantz, Alec (1997). 'No escape from syntax: Don't try morphological analysis in the privacy of your own lexicon', Philadelphia: University of Pennsylvania Working Papers in Linguistics 4/2, 201–25.

Marantz, Alec (2005). 'Generative linguistics within the cognitive neuroscience of language', *The Linguistic Review* 22: 429–46.

Marcus, Gary (1998). 'Rethinking eliminative connectionism', *Cognitive Psychology* 37: 243–82.

Marcus, Gary (2001). *The Algebraic Mind*. Cambridge, MA: MIT Press.

Marcus, Gary, Ursula Brinkmann, Harald Clahsen, Richard Wiese, and Steven Pinker (1995). 'German inflection: The exception that proves the rule', *Cognitive Psychology* 29: 189–256.

Marr, David (1982). *Vision*. San Francisco: Freeman.

Marslen-Wilson, William (1987). 'Functional parallelism in spoken word-recognition', *Cognition* 25: 71–102

Marslen-Wilson, William, and Lorraine Tyler (1980). 'The temporal structure of spoken language understanding', *Cognition* 8: 1–71

Marslen-Wilson, William, and Pienie Zwitserlood (1989). 'Accessing spoken words: The importance of word onsets', *Journal of Experimental Psychology: Human Perception and Performance* 15: 576–85.

Martin, Andrea E., and Leonidas A. A. Doumas (2017). 'A mechanism for the cortical computation of hierarchical linguistic structure', *PLoS Biology* 15(3): e2000663. doi: 10.1371/journal.pbio.2000663

Massam, Diane (2017). 'Incorporation and Pseudo-Incorporation in Syntax', *Oxford Research Encyclopedia of Linguistics*. doi: 10.1093/acrefore/9780199384655.013.190

McCarthy, John (1982). 'Prosodic structure and expletive infixation', *Language* 58: 574–90.

McCarthy, John, and Alan Prince (1995). 'Prosodic morphology', in John Goldsmith (ed.), *The Handbook of Phonological Theory*. Cambridge, MA: Blackwell, 318–66.

McCawley, James (under the pseudonym Quang Phuc Dong) (1971). 'A note on conjoined noun phrases', in Arnold Zwicky, Peter Salus, Robert Binnick, and Anthony Vanek (eds.) (1992), *Studies Out in Left Field: Defamatory Essays Presented to James D. McCawley on the Occasion of His 33rd or 34th Birthday*. Philadelphia and Amsterdam, John Benjamins, 11–18 (reprint of 1971 edition).

McClelland, James, and Jeffrey Elman (1986). 'The TRACE model of speech perception', *Cognitive Psychology* 18: 1–86.

McMahon, April (2007). 'Who's afraid of the vowel shift rule?', *Language Sciences* 29: 341–59.

McQueen, James M., Anne Cutler, and Dennis Norris (2006). 'Phonological abstraction in the mental lexicon', *Cognitive Science* 30: 1113–26.

McQueen, James M., Delphine Dahan, and Anne Cutler (2003). 'Continuity and gradedness in speech processing', in Niels O. Schiller and Antje S. Meyer (eds.), *Phonetics and Phonology in Language Comprehension and Production*. Berlin: Mouton de Gruyter, 39–78.

Meibauer, Jörg (2007). 'How marginal are phrasal compounds? Generalized insertion, expressivity, and I/Q interaction', *Morphology* 17: 233–59.

Merchant, Jason (2001). *The Syntax of Silence*. Oxford: Oxford University Press.

Merlan, Francesca (1982). *Mangarayi*. Lingua Descriptive Series. Amsterdam: North Holland.

Meunier, Fanny, and Juan Segui (1999). 'Morphological priming effect: The role of surface frequency', *Brain and Language* 68: 54–60.

Mielke, Jeff (2008). *The Emergence of Distinctive Features*. Oxford: Oxford University Press.

Miller, George, and Noam Chomsky (1963). 'Finitary models of language users', in R. Duncan Luce, Robert R. Bush, and Eugene Galanter (eds.), *Handbook of Mathematical Psychology*, (Vol. 2). New York: Wiley, 419–91.

Miller, George, and Philip Johnson-Laird (1976). *Language and Perception*. Cambridge, MA: Harvard University Press.

Millikan, Ruth (1984). *Language, Thought, and other Biological Categories*. Cambridge, MA: MIT Press.

Minsky, Marvin (1975). 'A framework for representing knowledge', in Patrick H. Winston (ed.), *The Psychology of Computer Vision*. New York: McGraw-Hill.

Mithun, Marianne (1986). 'On the nature of noun incorporation', *Language* 62: 32–7.

Mohanan, K. P. (1986). *The Theory of Lexical Phonology*. Dordrecht: Reidel.

Mohanan, K. P. (1995). 'The organization of the grammar', in John Goldsmith (ed.), *The Handbook of Phonological Theory*. Oxford: Blackwell, 24–69.

Momma, Shota, and Colin Phillips (2018). 'The relationship between parsing and generation', *Annual Review of Linguistics* 4: 233–54.

Moravcsik, Edith (1978). 'Reduplicative constructions', in Joseph H. Greenberg (ed.), *Universals of Human Language*, iii: *Word Structure*. Stanford: Stanford University Press, 297–334.

Moscoso del Prado Martín, Fermín, Aleksandar Kostić, and Harald Baayen (2004). 'Putting the bits together: An information theoretical perspective on morphological processing', *Cognition* 94: 1–18.

Moskowitz, Breyne (1973). 'On the status of vowel shift in English', in Timothy E. Moore (ed.), *Cognitive Development and the Acquisition of Language*. New York: Academic Press, 223–60.

Murphy, Gregory (2002). *The Big Book of Concepts*. Cambridge, MA: MIT Press.

Myers, Emily (2007). 'Dissociable effects of phonetic competition and category typicality in a phonetic categorization task: An fMRI investigation', *Neuropsychologia* 45: 1463–73.

Myers, Emily B., Sheila E. Blumstein, Edward Walsh, and James Eliassen (2009). 'Inferior frontal regions underlie the perception of phonetic category invariance', *Psychological Science* 20: 895–903.

Napoli, Donna Jo (2019). 'Morphological theory and sign languages', in Jenny Audring and Francesca Masini (eds.), *The Oxford Handbook of Morphological Theory*. Oxford: Oxford University Press, 594–613.

Nash, David (1980). 'Topics in Warlpiri Grammar', Ph.D. dissertation, MIT.

Nediger, Will A. (2017). 'Unifying Structure-Building in Human Language: The Minimalist Syntax of Idioms', Ph.D. dissertation, University of Michigan.

Neijt, Anneke, Mijntje Peters, and Johan Zuidema (2012). 'The 12321 model of Dutch spelling acquisition', *Linguistics in the Netherlands* 29: 111–22.

Neisser, Ulric (1967). *Cognitive Psychology*. Englewood Cliffs, NJ: Prentice-Hall.

Nesset, Tore (2008). *Abstract Phonology in a Concrete Model: Cognitive Linguistics and the Morphology-Phonology Interface*. Berlin: Mouton de Gruyter.

Newbold, Lindsey (2013). 'Variable affix ordering in Kuna', UC Berkeley: Department of Linguistics. Retrieved from https://escholarship.org/uc/item/289583dc

Nikolaeva, Irina, and Andrew Spencer (2012). 'Canonical typology and the possession-modification scale', in Dunstan Brown, Marina Chumakina, and Greville G. Corbett (eds.), *Canonical Morphology and Syntax*. Oxford: Oxford University Press, 207–38.

Nooteboom, Sieb, Fred Weerman, and Frank Wijnen (eds.) (2002). *Storage and Computation in the Language Faculty*. Dordrecht: Kluwer.

Norde, Muriel (2014). 'On parents and peers in constructional networks', Paper presented at *Coglingdays 2014*, Ghent University.

Norris, Dennis, James M. McQueen, and Anne Cutler (2000). 'Merging information in speech recognition: Feedback is never necessary', *Behavioral and Brain Sciences* 23(3): 299–325.

Noyer, Rolf (1994). 'Mobile affixes in Huave: Optimality and morphological wellformedness', in Erin Duncan, Donka Farkas, and Philip Spaelti (eds.), *Proceedings of the Twelfth West Coast Conference on Formal Linguistics*, Stanford, CSLI, 67–82.

Nunberg, Geoffrey, Ivan Sag, and Thomas Wasow (1994). 'Idioms', *Language* 70: 491–538.

O'Donnell, Timothy (2015). *Productivity and Reuse in Language: A Theory of Linguistic Computation and Storage*. Cambridge, MA: MIT Press.

Oehrle, Richard T. (1976). 'The grammar of the English dative alternation', Ph.D. dissertation Cambridge, MA: MIT Department of Linguistics and Philosophy.

Ohala, John J., and Manjari Ohala (1995). 'Speech perception and lexical representation', in Bruce Connell and Amalia Arvaniti (eds.), *Phonology and Phonetic Evidence. Papers in Laboratory Phonology IV*. Cambridge: Cambridge University Press, 41–60.

Oldfield, Richard C., and Arthur Wingfield (1965). 'Response latencies in naming objects', *Quarterly Journal of Experimental Psychology* 17: 273–81.

Ozturk, Ozge, and Anna Papafragou (2008). 'The acquisition of evidentiality and source monitoring', *Proceedings from the 32nd Annual Boston University Conference on Language Development*. Somerville, MA: Cascadilla Press.

Parker, Enid M., and Richard J. Hayward (1985). *An Afar-English-French dictionary: With grammatical notes in English*. London: School of Oriental and African Studies, University of London.

Perlmutter, David (1988). 'The split morphology hypothesis: Evidence from Yiddish', in Michael Hammond and Michael Noonan (eds.), *Theoretical Morphology*. San Diego: Academic Press, 79–100.

Phillips, Colin, and Ellen Lau (2004). 'Foundational issues' (Review article on Jackendoff 2002). *Journal of Linguistics* 40: 1–21.

Pierrehumbert, Janet (1980). 'The Phonology and Phonetics of English Intonation', Ph.D. dissertation, MIT.

Pierrehumbert, Janet (2001). 'Exemplar dynamics: Word frequency, lenition, and contrast', in Joan Bybee and Paul Hopper (eds.), *Frequency Effects and the Emergence of Lexical Structure*. Amsterdam: John Benjamins, 137–57.

Pierrehumbert, Janet, and Mary Beckman (1988). *Japanese Tone Structure*. Cambridge, MA: MIT Press.

Pine, Julian M., and Elena V. M. Lieven (1997). 'Slot and frame patterns and the development of the determiner category', *Applied Psycholinguistics* 18: 123–38.

Pinker, Steven (1989). *Learnability and Cognition: The Acquisition of Argument Structure*. Cambridge, MA: MIT Press.

Pinker, Steven (1999). *Words and Rules*. New York: Basic Books.

Pinker, Steven, and Ray Jackendoff (2005). 'The faculty of language: What's special about it?', *Cognition* 95: 201–36.

Pisoni, David, and Paul A. Luce (1987). 'Acoustic phonetic representations in the mental lexicon', *Cognition* 25: 21–52.

Plag, Ingo (2003). *Word Formation in English*. Cambridge: Cambridge University Press.

Plaster, Keith, and Maria Polinsky (2010). 'Features in categorization, or a new look at an old problem', in Anna Kibort and Greville G. Corbett (eds.), *Features: Perspectives on a Key Notion in Linguistics*. Oxford: Oxford University Press, 106–42.

Poeppel, David, and David Embick (2005). 'Defining the relation between linguistics and neuroscience', in Anne Cutler (ed.), *Twenty-first Century Psycholinguistics: Four Cornerstones*. Hillsdale, NJ: Lawrence Erlbaum, 103–20.

Pollard, Carl, and Ivan Sag (1987). *Information-based Syntax and Semantics*. Stanford: CSLI.

Pollard, Carl, and Ivan Sag (1994). *Head-Driven Phrase Structure Grammar*. Chicago: University of Chicago Press.

Port, Robert and Adam Leary (2005). 'Against formal phonology', *Language* 81: 927–64.

Poser, William (1984). 'The Phonetics and Phonology of Tone and Intonation in Japanese', Ph.D. dissertation, MIT.

Prince, Alan, and Paul Smolensky (2004). *Optimality Theory: Constraint Interaction in Generative Grammar*. Malden, MA: Blackwell.

Pustejovsky, James (1995). *The Generative Lexicon*. Cambridge, MA: MIT Press.

Radden, Günter, and Klaus-Uwe Panther (2004). 'Introduction: Reflections on motivation', in Günter Radden and Klaus-Uwe Panther (eds.), *Studies in Linguistic Motivation*. Berlin: Mouton de Gruyter, 1–46.

Raffelsiefen, Renate (2010). 'Idiosyncrasy, regularity, and synonymy in derivational morphology: Evidence for default word interpretation strategies', in Susan Olsen (ed.), *New Impulses in Word-Formation*. Hamburg: Helmut Buske Verlag, 173–232.

Raphael, Bertram (1969). 'SIR: A computer program for semantic information retrieval', in Marvin Minsky (ed.), *Semantic Information Processing*. Cambridge, MA: MIT Press, 33–145.

Rappaport Hovav, Malka, and Beth Levin (2008). 'The English dative alternation: The case for verb sensitivity', *Journal of Linguistics* 44: 129–67.

Rastle, Kathleen, Matthew Davis, and Boris New (2004). 'The broth in my brother's brothel: Morpho-orthographic segmentation in visual word recognition', *Psychonomic Bulletin and Review* 11: 1090–8.

Reddy, D. Raj, Lee D. Erman, Richard D. Fennell, and Richard B. Neely (1973). 'The Hearsay speech understanding system: An example of the recognition process', *Proceedings of the International Conference on Artificial Intelligence*, 185–94.

Reifegerste, Jana, Antje Meyer, and Pienie Zwitserlood (2017). 'Inflectional complexity and experience affect plural processing in younger and older readers of Dutch and German', *Language, Cognition and Neuroscience* 32, 471–87.

Rooth, Mats (1992). 'A theory of focus interpretation', *Natural Language Semantics* 1: 75–116.

Rosch, Eleanor (1978). 'Principles of categorization', in Eleanor Rosch and Barbara Lloyd (eds.), *Cognition and Categorization*. Hillsdale, NJ: Lawrence Erlbaum, 27–48.

Rosen, Sara (1989). 'Two types of noun incorporation', *Language* 65: 294–317.

Rubino, Carl (2013). 'Reduplication', in Matthew S. Dryer and Martin Haspelmath (eds.), *The World Atlas of Language Structures Online*. Leipzig: Max Planck Institute for Evolutionary Anthropology. http://wals.info/chapter/27

Rumelhart, David (1980). 'Schemata: The building blocks of cognition', in Rand J. Spiro, Bertram C. Bruce, and William F. Brewer (eds.), *Theoretical Issues in Reading Comprehension*. Hillsdale, NJ: Lawrence Erlbaum, 33–58.

Rumelhart, David, and James McClelland (1986). 'On learning the past tenses of English verbs', in James McClelland, David Rumelhart, and the PDP Research Group (eds.), *Parallel Distributed Processing*, (Vol. 2). Cambridge, MA: MIT Press, 216–71.

Ryan, Kevin (2010). 'Variable affix order: Grammar and learning', *Language* 86: 758–91.

Sadock, Jerrold (1980). 'Noun incorporation in Greenlandic: A case of syntactic word formation', *Language* 56: 300–19.

Sadock, Jerrold (1991). *Autolexical Syntax*. Chicago: University of Chicago Press.

Sag, Ivan (1992). 'Taking performance seriously', in Carlos Martin-Vide (ed.), *VII Congreso de Lenguajes Naturales y Lenguajes Formales*. Barcelona: Promociones y Publicaciones Universitarias, PPU, 61–74.

Sag, Ivan (1997). 'English relative clause constructions', *Journal of Linguistics* 33: 431–84.

Sag, Ivan, and Thomas Wasow (2011). 'Performance-compatible competence grammar', in Robert Borsley and Kersti Borjars (eds.), *Non-Transformational Syntax: Formal and Explicit Models of Grammar*. Oxford: Wiley-Blackwell, 359–77.

Sandler, Wendy, Mark Aronoff, Irit Meir, and Carol Padden (2011). 'The gradual emergence of phonological form in a new language', *Natural Language and Linguistic Theory* 29: 503–43.

Sapir, Edward (1921). *Language: An Introduction to the Study of Speech*. New York: Harcourt Brace.

Scalise, Sergio (1984). *Generative Morphology*. Dordrecht: Foris Publications.

Schäfer, Roland (2018). *Einführung in die grammatische Beschreibung des Deutschen: Dritte, überarbeitete und erweiterte Auflage* (Textbooks in Language Sciences 2). Berlin: Language Science Press. http://langsci-press.org/catalog/book/224

Schank, Roger (1973). 'Identification of conceptualizations underlying natural language', in Roger Schank and Kenneth Colby (eds.), *Computer Models of Thought and Language*. San Francisco: W. H. Freeman, 187–248.

Schreuder, Robert, and Harald Baayen (1995). 'Modeling morphological processing', in Laurie B. Feldman (ed.), *Morphological Aspects of Language Processing*. Hillsdale, NJ: Lawrence Erlbaum, 131–54.

Schriefers, Herbert, Pienie Zwitserlood, and Ardi Roelofs (1991). 'The identification of morphologically complex spoken words: Continuous processing or decomposition?', *Journal of Memory and Language* 30: 26–47.

Selkirk, Elizabeth O. (1982). *The Syntax of Words*. Cambridge, MA: MIT Press.

Selkirk, Elizabeth O. (1984). *Phonology and Syntax: The Relation between Sound and Structure*. Cambridge, MA: MIT Press.

Sharwood Smith, Michael, and John Truscott (2014). *The Multilingual Mind: A Modular Processing Perspective*. Cambridge: Cambridge University Press.

Shieber, Stuart (1986). *An Introduction to Unification-based Approaches to Grammar*. Stanford: CSLI.

Shimamura, Reiko (1986). 'Lexicalization of syntactic phrases', *English Linguistics* 3, 20–37.

Siddiqi, Daniel (2019). 'Distributed Morphology', in Jenny Audring and Francesca Masini (eds.), *The Oxford Handbook of Morphological Theory*. Oxford: Oxford University Press, 143–65.

Simon, Ellen, and Torsten Leuschner (2010). 'Laryngeal systems in Dutch, English, and German: A contrastive phonological study on second and third language acquisition', *Journal of Germanic Linguistics* 22: 403–24. doi: 10.1017/S1470542710000127

Sims, Andrea (2015). *Inflectional Defectiveness*. Cambridge: Cambridge University Press.

Smith, Edward, and Douglas Medin (1981). *Categories and Concepts*. Cambridge, MA: Harvard University Press.

Smith, J. David (2014). 'Prototypes, exemplars, and the natural history of categorization', *Psychonomic Bulletin and Review* 21: 312–31.

Smith, Kenny, Andrew Smith, and Richard Blythe (2011). Cross-situational learning: An experimental study of word-learning mechanisms. *Cognitive Science* 35: 480–98.

Smolensky, Paul, and Géraldine Legendre (2006). *The Harmonic Mind*. Cambridge, MA: MIT Press.

Smolka, Eva, Katharine Preller, and Carsten Eulitz (2014). '*Verstehen* ('understand') primes *stehen* ('stand'): Morphological structure overrides semantic compositionality in the lexical representation of German complex verbs. *Journal of Memory and Language* 72: 16–36.

Sowa, John F. (ed.) (1991). *Principles of Semantic Networks: Explorations in the Representation of Knowledge*. San Mateo, CA: Morgan Kaufmann Publishers, Inc.

Spelke, Elizabeth (2000). 'Core Knowledge', *American Psychologist* 55 (11): 1233–43. doi: 10.1037/0003-066X.55.11.1233

Spencer, Andrew (1988). 'Bracketing paradoxes and the English lexicon', *Language* 64: 663–82. doi: 10.2307/414563

Spencer, Andrew (1991). *Morphological Theory*. Oxford: Blackwell.

Spencer, Andrew (2003). 'In defence of morphology', *Lingue e Linguaggio* 2: 231–44.

Spencer, Andrew (2005). 'Word-formation and syntax', in Pavol Štekauer and Rochelle Lieber (eds.), *Handbook of Word-Formation*. Dordrecht: Springer Verlag, 73–97.

Spencer, Andrew (2010). 'Factorizing lexical relatedness', in Susan Olsen (ed.), *New Impulses in Word-formation*. Hamburg: Helmut Buske Verlag, 133–71.

Spencer, Andrew (2013). *Lexical Relatedness: A Paradigm-based Model*. Oxford: Oxford University Press.

Spencer, Andrew (2018). 'On lexical entries and lexical representations', in Olivier Bonami, Gilles Boyé, Georgette Dal, Hélène Giraudo, and Fiammetta Namer (eds.), *The Lexeme in Descriptive and Theoretical Morphology*. Berlin: Language Science Press, 277–301.

Sprenger, Simone (2003). *Fixed Expressions and the Production of Idioms*. Nijmegen: MPI Series in Psycholinguistics.

Stevens, Jon Scott, Lila Gleitman, John Trueswell, and Charles Yang (2017). 'The pursuit of verb meanings', *Cognitive Science* 41 (Suppl. 4), 638–76.

Stokoe, William C. (1960). *Sign Language Structure: An Outline of the Visual Communication Systems of the American Deaf. Studies in Linguistics: Occasional Papers (No. 8)*. Buffalo: Dept. of Anthropology and Linguistics, University of Buffalo.

Stump, Gregory (1998). 'Inflection', in Andrew Spencer and Arnold Zwicky (eds.), *The Handbook of Morphology*. Oxford and Malden, MA: Blackwell, 13–43.

Stump, Gregory (2001). *Inflectional Morphology: A Theory of Paradigm Structure*. Cambridge: Cambridge University Press.

Stump, Gregory (2016). *Inflectional Paradigms: Content and Form at the Syntax-Morphology Interface*. Cambridge: Cambridge University Press.

Stump, Gregory (2019a). 'Theoretical issues in inflection', in Jenny Audring and Francesca Masini (eds.), *The Oxford Handbook of Morphological Theory*. Oxford: Oxford University Press, 56–82.

Stump, Gregory (2019b). 'Paradigm Function Morphology', in Jenny Audring and Francesca Masini (eds.), *The Oxford Handbook of Morphological Theory*. Oxford: Oxford University Press, 285–304.

Swinney, David (1979). 'Lexical access during sentence comprehension: (Re)consideration of context effects', *Journal of Verbal Learning and Verbal Behavior* 18: 645–59.

Swinney, David, and Anne Cutler (1979). 'The access of processing of idiomatic expressions', *Journal of Verbal Learning and Verbal Behavior* 18: 523–34.

Szczepaniak, Renata, and Sebastian Kürschner (eds.) (2013). 'Linking elements: Origin, change, and functionalisation', *Morphology* 23(1) (Special Issue).

Tabossi, Patrizia, Cristina Burani, and Donia Scott (1995). 'Word identification in fluent speech', *Journal of Memory and Language* 34: 440–67.

Taft, Marcus (2004). 'Morphological decomposition and the reverse base frequency effect', *Quarterly Journal of Experimental Psychology* 57A: 745–65.

Taft, Marcus, and Kenneth Forster (1975). 'Lexical storage and retrieval of prefixed words', *Journal of Verbal Learning and Verbal Behavior* 14: 638–47.

Talmy, Leonard (1985). 'Lexicalization patterns: semantic structure in lexical forms', in Timothy Shopen (ed.), *Language Typology and Syntactic Description: Volume 3 Grammatical categories and the lexicon*. Cambridge: Cambridge University Press.

Talmy, Leonard (2000). *Toward a Cognitive Semantics*. Cambridge, MA: MIT Press.

Tanenhaus, Michael, James M. Leiman, and Mark Seidenberg (1979). 'Evidence for multiple stages in the processing of ambiguous words in syntactic contexts', *Journal of Verbal Learning and Verbal Behavior* 18: 427–40.

Tanenhaus, Michael, Michael J. Spivey-Knowlton, Kathleen M. Eberhard, and Julie C. Sedivy (1995). 'Integration of visual and linguistic information in spoken language comprehension', *Science* 268: 1632–4.

Taylor, John R. (2012). *The Mental Corpus: How Language is Represented in the Mind*. Oxford: Oxford University Press.

Thornton, Anna M. (2018). 'Troubles with flexemes', in Olivier Bonami, Gilles Boyé, Georgette Dal, Hélène Giraudo, and Fiammetta Namer (eds.), *The Lexeme in Descriptive and Theoretical Morphology*. Berlin: Language Science Press, 303–21. doi: 10.5281/zenodo.1407011

Tomasello, Michael (2003). *Constructing a Language: A Usage-Based Theory of Language Acquisition*. Cambridge, MA: Harvard University Press.

Touretzky, David (1986). *The Mathematics of Inheritance Systems*. Los Altos, CA: Morgan Kaufmann.

Traugott, Elizabeth Closs (2018). 'Modeling language change with constructional networks', in Salvador Pons Bordería and Óscar Loureda Lamas (eds.), *New Insights into the Grammaticalization of Discourse Markers*. Leiden: Brill, 17–50.

Trips, Carola (2016). 'An analysis of phrasal compounds in the model of Parallel Architecture', in Pius ten Hacken (ed.), *The Semantics of Compounding*. Cambridge: Cambridge University Press, 153–77.

Trueswell, John, Tamara Medina, Alon Hafri, and Lila Gleitman (2013). 'Propose but verify: Fast mapping meets cross-situational word learning', *Cognitive Psychology* 66: 126–56.

Truscott, John (2014). *Consciousness and Second Language Learning*. Bristol: Multilingual Matters.

Tsujimura, Natsuko, and Stuart Davis (2018). 'Japanese word formation in Construction Morphology', in Geert Booij (ed.), *The Construction of Words: Advances in Construction Morphology*. Cham, Switzerland: Springer, 373–98.

Tucker, G. Richard, Wallace Earl Lambert, and André Rigault (1977). *The French Speaker's Skill with Grammatical Gender: An Example of Rule-Governed Behavior*. The Hague: Mouton.

Tversky, Amos (1977). 'Features of similarity', *Psychological Review* 84: 327–50.

Ullman, Michael (2015). 'The declarative/procedural model: A neurobiologically motivated theory of first and second language', in Bill VanPatten and Jessica Williams (eds.), *Theories in Second Language Acquisition: An Introduction* (2nd edition). New York: Routledge, 135–58.

Van de Velde, Freek (2014). 'Degeneracy: The maintenance of constructional networks', in Ronny Boogaart, Timothy Colleman, and Gijsbert Rutten (eds.), *Extending the Scope of Construction Grammar*. Berlin: De Gruyter Mouton, 141–79.

Van der Hulst, Harry (2006). 'On the parallel organization of linguistic components', in Ricardo Bermúdez-Otero and Patrick Honeybone (eds.), *Phonology and syntax – the same or different*. Special issue of the journal *Lingua* 116(5): 657–88.

Van der Hulst, Harry, and Nancy Ritter (2000). 'The SPE-heritage of Optimality Theory', *The Linguistic Review* 17: 259–89.

Van Gestel, Frank (1995). 'En bloc insertion', in Martin Everaert, Erik-Jan van der Linden, André Schenk, and Rob Schreuder (eds.), *Idioms: Structural and Psycholinguistic Perspectives*. Hillsdale NJ: Lawrence Erlbaum, 75–96.

Van Marle, Jaap (1985). *On the Paradigmatic Dimension of Morphological Creativity*. Dordrecht: Foris.

Van Oostendorp, Marc (2008). 'Incomplete devoicing in formal phonology', *Lingua* 118: 1362–74.

Van Valin, Robert, and Randy LaPolla (1997). *Syntax: Structure, Meaning and Function*. Cambridge: Cambridge University Press.

Wasow, Thomas (1977). 'Transformations and the lexicon', in Peter W. Culicover, Thomas Wasow, and Adrian Akmajian (eds.), *Formal Syntax*. New York: Academic Press, 327–60.

Wasow, Thomas (2002). *Postverbal Behavior*. Stanford: CSLI.

Waxman, Sandra, and Raquel Klibanoff (2000). 'The role of comparison in the extension of novel adjectives', *Developmental Psychology* 36: 571–81.

Wegener, Heide (1999). 'Die Pluralbildung im Deutschen - ein Versuch im Rahmen der Optimalitätstheorie', *Linguistik Online* 4(3). https://doi.org/10.13092/lo.4.1032

Weinreich, Uriel (1969). 'Problems in the analysis of idioms', in Jaan Puhvel (ed.), *Substance and Structures of Language*. Berkeley and Los Angeles: University of California Press, 23–81. Reprinted in Weinreich (1980), *On Semantics*. Philadelphia: University of Pennslyvania Press, 208–64.

Werker, Janet, and Richard Tees (1984). 'Cross-language speech perception: Evidence for perceptual reorganization during the first year of life', *Infant Behavior and Development* 7: 49–63.

Weydt, Harald (1972). '"Unendlicher Gebrauch von endlichen Mitteln": Mißverständnisse um ein linguistisches Theorem', *Poetica* 5(3/4): 249–67.

Wiese, Richard (1996a). 'Phonological versus morphological rules: On German Umlaut and Ablaut', *Journal of Linguistics* 32: 113–35.

Wiese, Richard (1996b). 'Phrasal compounds and the theory of word syntax', *Linguistic Inquiry* 27: 183–93.

Williams, Edwin (1981). 'On the notions "lexically related" and "head of a word"', *Linguistic Inquiry* 12: 245–74.

Williams, Edwin (2007). 'Dumping lexicalism', in Gillian Ramchand and Charles Reiss (eds.), *The Oxford Handbook of Linguistic Interfaces*. Oxford: Oxford University Press, 353–81.

Wittenberg, Eva, and Jesse Snedeker (2014). 'It takes two to kiss, but does it take three to give a kiss? Categorization based on thematic roles', *Language, Cognition and Neuroscience* 29: 635–41.

Wittgenstein, Ludwig (1953). *Philosophical Investigations*. Oxford: Blackwell.

Wolf, Maryanne (2007). *Proust and the Squid*. New York: HarperCollins.

Woodbury, Anthony (1996). 'On restricting the role of morphology in Autolexical Syntax', in Eric Schiller, Elisa Steinberg, and Barbara Need (eds.), *Autolexical Theory*. Berlin: de Gruyter, 319–64.

Woodbury, Hanni (1975). 'Noun Incorporation in Onondaga', Ph.D. dissertation, Yale University.

Yang, Charles (2002). *Knowledge and Learning in Natural Language*. Oxford: Oxford University Press.

Yang, Charles (2005). 'On productivity', *Linguistic Variation Yearbook* 5: 265–302.

Yang, Charles (2016). *The Price of Linguistic Productivity: How Children Learn to Break the Rules of Language*. Cambridge, MA: MIT Press.

Yip, Kenneth, and Gerald Sussman (1997). 'Sparse representations for fast, one-shot learning', in *Proceedings of the National Conference on Artificial Intelligence*, 521–7.

Zehentner, Eva (2016), 'On competition and cooperation in Middle English ditransitives', Ph.D. dissertation, University of Vienna.

Zehentner, Eva, and Elizabeth Closs Traugott (in preparation). 'Constructional networks and the development of benefactive ditransitives in English', in Elena Smirnova and Lotte Sommerer (eds.), *Nodes and Networks in Diachronic Construction Grammar* (working title). Amsterdam: John Benjamins.

Zhao, Xu, and Iris Berent (2017). 'The basis of the syllable hierarchy: Articulatory pressures or universal phonological constraints?' *Journal of Psycholinguistic Research*. doi: 10.1007/s10936-017-9510-2

Ziegler, Jayden, Jesse Snedeker, and Eva Wittenberg (2018). 'Event structures drive semantic structural priming, not thematic roles: Evidence from idioms and light verbs', *Cognitive Science* 42: 2918–49.

Zuidema, John, and Anneke Neijt (2017). 'The BasisSpellingBank: A spelling database with knowledge stored as a lexicon of triplets', *Written Language and Literacy* 20: 52–79.

Zwicky, Arnold (1989). 'Idioms and constructions', Proceedings of the Eastern States Conference of Linguistics 1988, 547–58.

Zwicky, Arnold (1996). 'Syntax and phonology', In Keith Brown and Jim Miller (eds.), *Concise Encyclopedia of Syntactic Theories*. Oxford: Elsevier Science, 300–5.

Zwitserlood, Pienie (2004). 'Sublexical and morphological information in speech processing', *Brain and Language* 90: 368–77. doi: 10.1016/S0093-934X(03)00448-6

Zwitserlood, Pienie (2018). 'Processing and representation of morphological complexity in native language comprehension and production', in Geert Booij (ed.), *The Construction of Words: Advances in Construction Morphology*. Cham, Switzerland: Springer, 583–602.

Index of affixes, words, constructions, and schemas

Index of subjects and authors